# THOMAS GREEN
# CLEMSON

# THOMAS GREEN
# CLEMSON

## EDITED BY ALMA BENNETT

I hope you'll enjoy our
biography of the remarkable
Thomas Clemson.

— Alma Bennett

CLEMSON UNIVERSITY
DIGITAL PRESS

Published by Clemson University Digital Press at the Center for Electronic and Digital Publishing, Clemson University, Clemson, South Carolina.

ISBN 978-0-9796066-8-7

## CLEMSON UNIVERSITY
DIGITAL PRESS

Works produced at Clemson University by the Center for Electronic and Digital Publishing include *The South Carolina Review*, its themed series, and monographs such as *Legacy of a Southern Lady, Anna Calhoun Clemson, 1817-1875* (2007), *Women and Clemson University* (2006), and *Integration with Dignity: A Celebration of Harvey Gantt's Admission to Clemson University* (2003). Online editions, previews, and purchase information may be found at our Web site: http://www.clemson.edu/caah/cedp.

Contact the Director, Center for Electronic and Digital Publishing, Strode Tower, Box 340522, Clemson University, Clemson, South Carolina 29634-0522. Tel: 864-656-5399.

Produced with the Adobe Creative Suite CS3 and Microsoft Word. This book is set in Adobe Garamond Pro and was printed by The R. L Bryan Company, Columbia, SC.

Dust jacket design by David W. Dryden, Director, Creative Services
Managing producer: Deborah G. Dunning, Manager of Editorial Services, Creative Services

Interior book design and layout by Charis Chapman, CEDP
CEDP Editorial Assistants: Bridget Jeffs, Jilly Lang, and Jordan McKenzie

# TABLE OF CONTENTS

# List of Illustrations

## Plates

1. *Thomas G. Clemson* by Joseph Bayas Ord
2. *Anna Maria Calhoun Clemson* by Jacobus Joseph Eeckhout
3. *John Calhoun Clemson* by Jacobus Joseph Eeckhout
4. *Floride Elizabeth Clemson* by Jacobus Joseph Eeckhout
5. *John C. Calhoun* by Eugenius F. DeBlock
6. *Floride Colhoun Calhoun* by Eugenius F. DeBlock
7. *Old Man Smoking* by Thomas Green Clemson
8. *Chickens* by Thomas Green Clemson
9. *Virgin and Child* by Cornelis Schut III
10. *Flower Piece* by Daniel Seghers and David Teniers
11. *Adoration* by Frans Francken II
12. "The Philosopher (Supposed to be Rembrandt or Ferdinand Bol)"
13. *Goats and Sheep* by Louis Marie Dominique Robbe
14. *The Castle of Elsinore* by Thomas Fearnley
15. *Tasso in Prison Visited by Montaigne* by Louis Gallait
16. *Girl of Antwerp with Two Dogs* [unknown artist]

## Figures

Thumbnail images of paintings as listed in the 1852 catalogue:

# FOREWORD

## *Allen P. Wood, AIA*
### *Trustee Emeritus*

This biography is written in celebration of Thomas Green Clemson's birth on July 1, 1807. It tells the unique and fascinating history of his life and times. He, for instance, received the best available European education of the times in chemistry, mineralogy, geology, and mining. With his involvement in art, music, and languages, in addition to his activities as a student activist, and, later, as a diplomat, proponent of higher education, education reform, and scientific agriculture, Thomas Clemson possessed very broad and integrated knowledge and varied social and cultural interests. Thus, because of his education and interests and his lifespan (1807–1888), he became the quintessential nineteenth-century Renaissance man.

Nevertheless, throughout his adult life Mr. Clemson constantly worried about money, suffered from chronic depression, and had strained relationships with family, in-laws, friends, and business associates. His symptoms of "subjective feelings of irritability or excessive anger," "poor appetite," and "feelings of hopelessness" are attributed to his depression and unrealized ambitions. Fortunately, his marriage to Anna Maria Calhoun, the daughter of Senator John C. Calhoun, gave him the stability and support he needed. It also gave him the means to fulfill his dream to establish a "people's college." Describing conditions in the South Carolina post-bellum era as "wretched in the extreme," Clemson desired to establish a "high seminary of learning" to deliver a practical, science-based education in the mechanical arts and agriculture.

Before the death of Anna Maria Clemson, Mr. and Mrs. Clemson were true co-partners in their determination to create a college. She actively supported his efforts, and it was her land on which the Clemson Agriculture College of South Carolina eventually would be established. After her death and his many failed attempts to find support for a scientific and agricultural college, Clemson ultimately came to the conclusion that only by his death and a will could their shared dream become a reality.

When his Last Will and Testament became public, immediately following Thomas Clemson's death, there was significant and powerful opposition to the establishment of another publicly supported college in South Carolina. It took legislative and legal action and political and public support for the will to be accepted by the state of South Carolina. And the story of that opposition and support is as interesting as it is complex. Finally, Clemson's will became a reality when the South Carolina House and Senate and the governor accepted and enacted it almost verbatim into law. Having been upheld by the United State Supreme Court, when challenged in a civil suit, Clemson's Last Will and Testament was also validated by the chief justice of the South Carolina State Supreme Court. That validation was the final step in establishing the Clemson Agriculture College of South Carolina, which is now Clemson University.

The Clemson will is unique in the governance of a public university in both the nature and the manner in which those bequests are to be managed. The will is also interesting and unique in other aspects by what it does and does not contain. For example, it gives the Board of Trustees full authority over the institution and the power to regulate all matters pertaining to the institution—duties which can never be taken away or conferred upon any other person or group. This independence has given the Board of Trustees the legal authority to make tough decisions and the flexibility to adapt to changing times and conditions. Unusual for a document written shortly after Reconstruction, Clemson's Last Will and Testament does not disenfranchise anyone or any group. This is further evidence of the forward thinking of Thomas Green Clemson.

The biography is written in a collaged manner so that each chapter focuses on a particular facet of Clemson's life and times. Presented in this manner it offers the opportunity to explore and understand the many facets of this true Renaissance man. While the last chapter takes a more holistic approach, the diversity represented by the biography's twelve authors skillfully reflects the diversity of the collage that was his life and world. You are invited to celebrate with all the many beneficiaries of the Last Will and Testament and the legacy of Thomas Green Clemson.

# INTRODUCTION & ACKNOWLEDGMENTS

## *Alma Bennett, Editor*

In this biography of Thomas Green Clemson, our twelve authors address multiple aspects of his life, a life—1807–1888—which not only frames the nineteenth century and many of its most complex issues, but also reveals Clemson's own complexity, expertise, and vision. In effect, our goal, on Clemson's behalf, has been to answer the kinds of questions raised by the 1897-1898 painting *Where Do We Come From? What Are We? Where Are We Going?* by the French artist Paul Gauguin. Thus, in the first two chapters, Jerome Reel introduces us to Thomas Green Clemson's ancestors and extended and immediate family and then examines the first thirty-one years of his life and education.

With this familial and intellectual context in place, each of the next nine chapters (3 through 11) addresses particular aspects or periods of Clemson's adult life, work, and interests. Together, these chapters create a composite answer to professional and personal questions about what and who the multifaceted Clemson was. In chapter 3, for example, Ann Ratliff Russell, in focusing on the life of Clemson's extraordinary wife, Anna Maria Calhoun Clemson, from their marriage in 1838 until her death in 1875, gives us crucial insights into their marriage, children, and family life; Thomas Clemson's chronic depression; and the pivotal roles Anna played in his life and posthumous legacy.

The fourth chapter, transatlantically co-authored by James Cross and Sabine Godts-Péters, covers Clemson's European years, beginning with his student years in Paris, which included his fighting in the July 1830 Revolution when Parisians overthrew King Charles X's regime. Tracking Clemson's return to Europe in 1844 as the United States chargé d'affaires in Belgium, the authors delineate Clemson's diplomatic contributions during a critical stage of the Industrial Revolution and U.S. international relations. In "The Washington Years" (chapter 5), Alan Grubb explores Thomas Clemson's professional frustrations and, more important, the evolution of his burgeoning agricultural interests, advocacies, and publications from 1851, when the Clemsons returned to the United States from Belgium, until 1861, when, in support of the Confederate cause, he resigned from his long-sought national position as superintendent of agricultural affairs.

Chalmers M. Butler's chapter 6 provides a long-needed evaluation of Clemson's education in Paris, his subsequent publications, and his work as a scientist and engineer. This analysis of Clemson's work as a mining engineer, assayer, metallurgist, and geologist and his related publications leads to Butler's final assessment of Clemson's expertise in the context of fierce competitions for geological survey directorships. In chapter 7, "The Scientist as Farmer," John Kelly follows a different scientific trajectory by focusing on Clemson as an agriculturalist through his various attempts to farm in South Carolina and Maryland—attempts that reveal the challenges of nineteenth-century agriculture, especially in the South. While his farming efforts were not often successful, those experiences intensified Clemson's determination to make science and technology available to American farmers through education.

Abel Bartley's chapter 8 shifts our attention from the sciences to racial issues and the politics of the Reconstruction Era in South Carolina. Within that context, he closely examines the history of education in the state, which, in turn, creates important perspectives into Thomas Clemson's advocacies of and decisions regarding a new college for the state.

In the next two chapters, artistic aspects of Clemson's life and interests are introduced. For instance, William Hiott's chapter 9, a *tour de force* exploration of the Thomas Green Clemson Art Collection, analyzes the collection, which ranges from Old Masters to Clemson's own artwork; traces the paintings from Europe to Long Island to Maryland to Fort Hill and various locations on the Clemson campus; and then addresses the collection as a remarkable nineteenth-century achievement and twenty-first-century legacy. Andrew Levin's chapter 10, on the other hand, explores music—an almost unknown aspect of Clemson's artistic interests. The author first creates nineteenth-century European and New World contexts of classical, popular, and dance music in sites where either Thomas Clemson or Anna Calhoun or the Clemson and Calhoun families lived. After focusing on the importance of music in the Calhoun, Colhoun, and Clemson families, Levin introduces us to a Thomas Clemson who enjoyed all types of music, played popular songs and hymns on his violin, and composed a number of polkas and "a national air," several of which have been performed during and since the bicentennial celebration.

William Hiott's chapter 11 studies the roles that Fort Hill, the home of John C. and Floride Calhoun, played in Thomas and Anna Calhoun Clemson's lives. The site of their 1838 wedding, they lived there with her parents from 1839 to 1842. The Clemsons moved back to Fort Hill in 1872, a year after their two adult children died and three years before Anna's death. A reclusive Clemson lived there until his death in 1888. Still, due to Thomas and Anna Clemson's respective wills and shared vision, Fort Hill formed the nucleus of what would become Clemson College.

Following these pivotal eleven components of Clemson's life and work and his death in 1888, the last two chapters of the biography address questions about his posthumous legacy. The first stage of the answer appears in Chapter 12 in which Clayton Steadman carefully examines the development and unique stipulations of Thomas Green Clemson's Last Will and Testament that culminated, after heated opposition, in its legislative enactment in 1888 and its being signed into law and confirmed in 1889. In the final chapter, Verna Gardner Howell and Jerome Reel create, respectively, the biography's final answer: a full review of Thomas Clemson's life and his remarkable, ongoing legacy that opened its doors in 1893 as the Clemson Agricultural College and continues as Clemson University.

### *About the Biography Project*

The proposal for a new biography of Thomas Green Clemson, the first since 1937, emerged from a conversation between Allen Wood, a member of Clemson University's Board of Trustees, and Alan Grubb, an associate professor of history. As a result, in early 2006, Jerome Reel invited fifteen scholars and specialists to join the biography team, one of the many committees formed to plan the 2007 bicentennial celebration of Clemson's birth. Subsequently, the research for the biography's thirteen chapters carried the authors to archives in Belgium, France, the United Kingdom, Pennsylvania, the District of Columbia, Maryland, Georgia, and around South Carolina, and to countless hours in the Clemson University Libraries and on line. Then the writing, editing, and illustrations work began. This three-year effort has been our labor of love for Thomas Clemson and his "high seminary of learning." Ours, however, are not the only efforts. This biography has required the assistance of a large number of individuals and institutions, and we want to express our gratitude to them.

# ACKNOWLEDGMENTS

Thomas Green Clemson's multifaceted life, work, and interests mandated that we bring together a correspondingly wide range of scholarship and expertise for this biography. It is easy to recognize the expertise the twelve authors bring to their respective chapters. However, embedded in the chapters, the illustrations, and the book itself is a rather invisible host of other individuals and institutions which the authors, the managing producer, and I want to introduce and thank for their important assistance.

Taking an editor's prerogative, I begin the process by expressing my appreciation to the fourteen individuals who joined me on the bicentennial biography team in 2006. Let me start by singling out two invaluable contributors to the book project: Jerome Reel, University historian and professor emeritus of history, and Deborah Dunning, the Department of Creative Service's manager of editorial services. Reel's love for and knowledge of Clemson College/University and the Clemson family have informed every stage of our project, and Dunning's unwavering commitment to the book and her skills are reflected throughout the book. I also am deeply grateful to the chapters' authors—Abel Bartley, Chalmers Butler, James Cross, Sabine Godts-Péters, Alan Grubb, William Hiott, Verna Howell, John Kelly, Andrew Levin, Jerome Reel, Ann Russell, and Clayton Steadman— and to the Foreword's author Allen Wood. It has been an honor to work with these colleagues and to share the evolution of their work.

Now, we fifteen contributors to the biography want to acknowledge many other individuals and institutions. For the book's production, we first want to thank—and praise—Wayne Chapman, a professor of English and the exemplary executive director of the Clemson University Digital Press (CUDP), which is our book's publisher. Next, we thank Charis Chapman for bringing her extraordinary digital publication design skills to our book. We also continue to appreciate the fine work by the staff of our book's printer, the R. L. Bryan Company of Columbia, S.C.; the support and book sales of the Clemson Alumni Association and Randolph N. (Randy) Boatwright, its director of programs and services; and the promotional work of Jacob Barker, public information director of the Department of Marketing Services.

The Department of Creative Services also has proven its remarkable support of the biography through the contributions of its director David W. Dryden, who designed the book's wonderful dust jacket; Deborah Dunning, mentioned earlier; M. Elizabeth Newall, managing editor of *Clemson World* magazine; John L. Mounter, production manager; Cynthia R. Gosey, Patrick D. Wright, and Craig W. Mahaffey, three media resource specialists in photography; and David R. Linteau, information resource consultant.

Thomas Clemson would have been pleased, as we are, that Clemson University students have been involved in the biography's production. These include Clemson University Digital Press editorial assistants—M.A. in English students Jillian Lang (galley setting) and Bridget Jeffs (index) and B.A. in English student intern Jordan McKenzie—and other M.A. in English students: David Foltz (bibliography), Mari Ramler, Jessica Martin, and Jonathan Williams, as well as M.A. in history graduate, Andrew Land (U.S. census material).

## Research Assistance by Clemson-Calhoun Family & Clemson Connections

We begin our research acknowledgments by thanking members of the Clemson and Calhoun families for their valuable contributions to the biography and to the University. These individuals include Creighton Lee Calhoun Jr. and Edith Calhoun, Pittsboro, N.C.; Daniel Clemson, Mechanicsburg, Pa.; Michael and Suzanne Clemson, Kent, England; Eleanor Smith Morris, Edinburgh, Scotland; and Meredith Fuller Coughlan Sonderskov, Philadelphia, Pa. We also appreciate the help of David Russell (Rusty) Simpson, Beaufort, S.C., a descendent of Thomas Clemson's friend and attorney, Richard W. Simpson.

## Research Assistance by Clemson University Faculty & Staff

The acknowledgments lists of the biography's authors habitually begin with the Clemson University Libraries and then move to specific individuals. For example, Special Collections staff members who have been extremely helpful during the past three years include Michael F. Kohl, head of Special Collections; Susan Giaimo Hiott, curator of exhibits; Alan C. Burns, political collections archivist; James E. Cross, manuscript archivist; Dennis S. Taylor, University archivist; as well as Laurie Varenhorst, Shannon Hayes, and Linda Ferry, assistant archivists. While we have appreciated the entire staff of the Robert Muldrow Cooper Library and the Gunnin Library, we want to single out Priscilla Munson, librarian; Edward J. Rock, reference librarian; Kathy S. Edwards, reference librarian; and Rosanne M. Maw, former library specialist.

The Department of Historic Properties has been another pivotal resource for our project, most especially the historical knowledge of William D. Hiott, director of Historic Properties and curator of Fort Hill. Others' helpful work includes that of Kathleen McLellan, administrative assistant; the late Revelie Brannon, former curator of Fort Hill; and Polly Owen, former historic site guide at Fort Hill.

Our authors also have cited a number of emeritus, current, and former Clemson University faculty members for their expertise and/or mentorship. Most frequently mentioned are Ernest McPherson (Whitey) Lander Jr., professor emeritus of history, and Jerome V. Reel, University historian and professor emeritus of history. Others singled out include Charles H. Barron, professor emeritus of chemical engineering; Alma Bennett, professor of humanities and English; Carol Bleser, professor emerita of history; Wayne Chapman, professor of English and executive editor of the Clemson University Digital Press; Patricia Connor-Greene, professor emerita of psychology; Harold Cooledge, professor emeritus of architecture; Alan Grubb, associate professor of history; William D. Hiott, adjunct instructor of history and director of Historic Properties; Robert S. Lambert, professor emeritus of history; Donald M. McKale, professor emeritus of history; Judith M. Melton, professor emerita of German; Ann Ratliff Russell, former instructor of history; the late Alan Schaffer, professor of history; the late Mary Stevenson, librarian; and Lewis Suggs, professor emeritus of history.

Keenly aware of the Clemson University staff members who have given us important assistance, we first must thank Deborah L. Dalhouse, director of Public Service and Agriculture (PSA) Communications, and Peter J. Kent, PSA news writer, for lending us their agricultural and writing expertise. Then we must thank A. Neill Cameron, our University's vice president for advancement; Margaret Pridgen, public information director, Office of Public Affairs; Melissa G. Welborn, research associate, Office of Institutional Research; Barbara S. Rogers and Linda B. Bridges, administrative assistants in the Department of Undergraduate Studies; Gloria F. Walker, administrative coordinator, Office of the Vice Provost for International Affairs; Jeannette Braine-Sperry, administrative coordinator and secretary to the board of trustees; Faith Christner, administrative coordinator, Office of Student Engagement; Rebecca Atkinson, associate director, Office of New Student and Sophomore Programs; Rose Ellen Davis-Gross, associate director, Office of Housing Assignments and Marketing, and Brad Smalling, its undergraduate student intern.

### Research Assistance by Scholars & Experts of Other Institutions

For their help with art and artifacts, we want to recognize Marisa Bourgoin, archivist, Corcoran Gallery of Art, Washington, D.C.; Craig Crawford, painting conservator, American Institute of Conservation (AIC), Columbia, S.C.; John P. Elliott, Marietta, Ga.; Creighton Gilbert, professor emeritus of art, Yale University; Marlene Jutsen, archivist, National Galley of Art, Washington, D.C.; Linda R. McKee, head librarian, The John and Mable Ringling Museum of Art Library, Sarasota, Fla.; Alexander Moore, acquisitions editor, University of South Carolina Press; Frank A. Sarnowski Jr. and the late William S. Belser, fine arts appraisers, Columbia, S.C.; the late Wilhelm (William) Rheinhold Otto Valentiner, director, North Carolina Museum of Art; and Roberta Zonghi, keeper of rare books and manuscripts, Boston Public Library.

For crucial help with the Clemson and Calhoun families and related materials, the biography's authors have relied on the late Julia Wright Sublette's invaluable work on the letters of Anna Maria Calhoun Clemson, as well as the work of other scholars, such as Henry G. Fulmer, manuscript librarian, The South Caroliniana Library, University of South Carolina; Valerie Lutz, librarian, American Philosophical Society, Philadelphia, Pa.; Elizabeth McAllister, reference archivist, Special Collections, University of Maryland; Edmee Reel, former librarian, Clemson, S.C.; Marilyn C. Solvay, director, Sullivan Museum and History Center, Norwich University; Marcia Synnott, professor emerita of history, University of South Carolina; Gail E. Wiese, archives and special collections assistant, Kreitzberg Library, Norwich University; and Clyde Wilson, professor emeritus of history, University of South Carolina. Other important help was provided by the following staffs: the Archives, City of Philadelphia, Pennsylvania; the Historical Society of Pennsylvania, Philadelphia; the Library Company of Philadelphia; and the West Chester Historical Society, Pennsylvania.

We also required and received help from experts in other disciplines, such as Mary L. Butler (Clemson, S.C.), former instructor of French at the University of Mississippi and Texas Southern University; Robin Glass, curator, Dahlonega Gold Museum (Ga.); the Reverend Bob Haden, director of the Haden Institute (Charlotte, N.C.) and diplomate of the American Psychotherapy Association; and the staff of the Music Division, Library of Congress, Washington, D.C.

### A Final Round of Thanks

Having introduced so many institutions and individuals who have helped us with the biography, we fifteen contributors want to conclude by expressing our deep gratitude for the encouragement of our families, friends, colleagues, and administrators. And among the latter, we most particularly appreciate our University's president, James F. Barker, for his interest in and support of the biography project from start to finish.

# Chapter 1

# THE FAMILY OF THOMAS GREEN CLEMSON

*Jerry Reel*

## *Jerome V. Reel*

*Penn's Tree, with the City & Port of Philadelphia on the River Delaware from Kensington,* **William Birch engraving, 1800. Library of Congress, cph 3b27539.**

On September 30, 1800, Thomas Clemson III (1772–1813) was in Lancaster County, Pennsylvania, the county of his birth. The future father of Thomas Green Clemson was there for his wedding to Elizabeth Baker, the daughter of Frederick and Margaretta (Diller) Baker, also of Lancaster County.[1]

After the ceremony and pleasantries, Clemson helped his bride onto his horse, and together they rode off to Philadelphia, where Thomas had lived for some years with his unmarried brother, James. Thomas had built a large home on the southwest corner of Ninth and Filbert Streets, a short city block off High (also called Market) Street, a principal artery of Philadelphia, then the second largest city in the United States with a population of 41,220. The house still stood as late as 1898.[2]

*High Street, with the First Presbyterian Church, Philadelphia*, William Birch engraving, 1799. Historical Society of Pennsylvania.

Thomas Clemson III was descended from James Clemson I, who had been born in Tettenhall, England (b. 1654–d. in Pennsylvania in 1718), to Alexander Clemson (1631–1694) and his wife Elizabeth Green.[3] The Clemson family name occurs in the registers of the parishes between Birmingham, Warwickshire, and Shrewsbury, Shropshire, from 1619 to the present. In the more mobile nineteenth to twenty-first centuries, the family name appears throughout much of Great Britain (some forty-two counties in England, Wales, and Scotland).[4]

James Clemson I, the great-great-grandfather of Thomas Green Clemson, was a blacksmith and a member of the Society of Friends (Quakers). He would marry three times. With his first wife, Katharine Wright of Dudley, he migrated in the 1680s to English America. Probably all seven of his children were with Katharine. Four were daughters: Mary, Hannah, Rebecca, and Sophia; and three were sons: James II, John, and Thomas. By 1699, the family was in West Chester, in the proprietary colony of Pennsylvania, and James Clemson I had purchased two lots in the town of Chichester and an additional four acres in Delaware County.

After the death of Katharine, his first wife, James I married twice more, first to Sarah (birth and last name unknown) and then to Joan Coates, a widow with three sons and one daughter by her first husband. Besides the properties in Chichester Township, James bought 136 acres in Bethel Township in 1702 and 300 acres in Concord Township in 1710, both in Delaware County. By warrant of September 25, 1714, he acquired 500 acres in Philadelphia County, and then on March 18, 1716, another 636 acres in Pequea Valley, Salisbury Township, Lancaster County. Most of this land was sown in wheat, which would become the basis of the family's wealth.[5]

James Clemson I died on July 18, 1718, and his will, dated June 12, 1718, was entered into probate on August 5, 1718.[6] In 1716, Mary, the eldest child, had married Henry Gest, whose parents had arrived in Philadelphia from the Birmingham, England, area on June 11, 1686, aboard the ship *Delaware*. As part of Mary and Henry's nuptial agreement, James I settled the 300 Concord Township acres on Henry Gest in an entailed fee. Mary and Henry would have seven sons and one daughter.[7] Their sixth son, Joseph, married Deborah, the daughter of Joseph and Elizabeth Dickinson of Salisbury Township, Lancaster County, and one of their children, John, would play an important role in the Clemson family during the early 1800s.

After James Clemson I's death, his third wife, Joan, continued to reside in Philadelphia on her own land. Three of his daughters—Mary, Hannah, and Rebecca—each received fifty acres in Lancaster County. The youngest daughter, Sophia, received her father's bonds, held by his widow Joan in *usufruct* probably for her life or until Joan's remarriage. The elder two sons, John and James, each received 200 acres, and Thomas, the youngest, 136 acres, all in Lancaster County.

Young Thomas, known as Thomas I (ca. 1710–1785), and Elizabeth Strode, his wife, would have three sons, John, James III, and Thomas II—a Clemson generation that has been called the fighting Quakers.[8] Thomas II served in the county militia and may have been among the five or six Clemsons who served on the colony's side in the American Revolutionary War.[9] John, the eldest son of Thomas I, was born August 12, 1748, and would die in his home in Salisbury Township on May 17, 1808. On April 24, 1771, he had married Susannah Green, the daughter of Thomas and Mary Green. They produced nine children: Thomas III (1772–1813); James (1774–1813); Joseph (1776–1829); Hannah (1778–1844; married Davis); Elizabeth (1780–1827; married Passmore); Mary (1784–1846; married Joseph Pusey); Sarah (1787–1808); Rachel (1789–1845; married Benjamin Pusey); and Sophia (1792–1861; married Sharpless).

This generation brings us full circle back to the father of Thomas Green Clemson, Thomas III, with whom the chapter began. This eldest son of John and Susannah Clemson, and the future groom of Elizabeth Baker, moved to Philadelphia where he joined his younger brother, James, in the flour business. Other

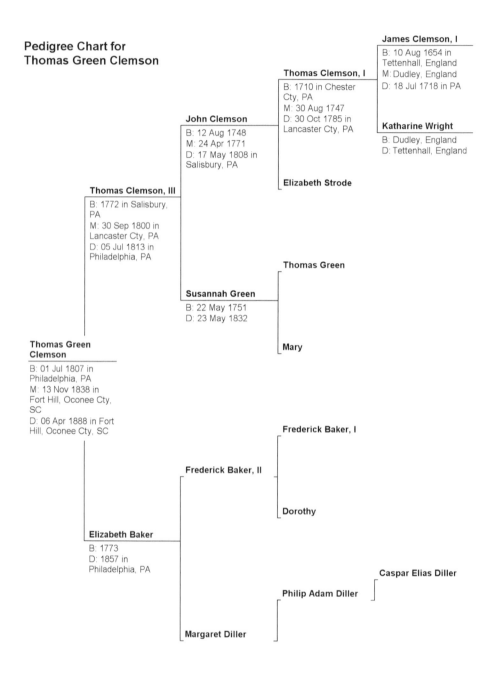

Pedigree Chart for
Thomas Green Clemson

**James Clemson, I**

B: 10 Aug 1654 in
Tettenhall, England
M: Dudley, England
D: 18 Jul 1718 in PA

**Thomas Clemson, I**

B: 1710 in Chester
Cty, PA
M: 30 Aug 1747
D: 30 Oct 1785 in
Lancaster Cty, PA

**Katharine Wright**

B: Dudley, England
D: Tettenhall, England

**John Clemson**

B: 12 Aug 1748
M: 24 Apr 1771
D: 17 May 1808 in
Salisbury, PA

**Elizabeth Strode**

**Thomas Clemson, III**

B: 1772 in Salisbury,
PA
M: 30 Sep 1800 in
Lancaster Cty, PA
D: 05 Jul 1813 in
Philadelphia, PA

**Thomas Green**

**Susannah Green**

B: 22 May 1751
D: 23 May 1832

**Mary**

**Thomas Green
Clemson**

B: 01 Jul 1807 in
Philadelphia, PA
M: 13 Nov 1838 in
Fort Hill, Oconee Cty,
SC
D: 06 Apr 1888 in Fort
Hill, Oconee Cty, SC

**Frederick Baker, I**

**Frederick Baker, II**

**Dorothy**

**Elizabeth Baker**

B: 1773
D: 1857 in
Philadelphia, PA

**Caspar Elias Diller**

**Philip Adam Diller**

**Margaret Diller**

**Prepared by Jerome V. Reel**

members of the large Clemson family are reputed to have profited greatly from the flour trade during the Revolutionary War.[10] Thomas's home was, as previously noted, on Ninth and Filbert, next door to his flour store at Ninth and Market. His brother James eventually opened a second store one block to the west. A younger sister, Mary Clemson Pusey, would be the great-great-great-grandmother of Richard Milhous Nixon.[11]

Elizabeth Baker (1773–1857), Thomas III's bride and the future mother of Thomas Green Clemson, was the daughter of Frederick Baker and Margaretta (Diller) Baker of Lancaster County, Pennsylvania.[12] This American Baker family was descended from an earlier Frederick Baker, who was born in 1732 in Hesse, in the Palatine of the Holy Roman Empire. He and his older brother, John Samuel (b. 1729), left Hesse in 1752, traveled to Rotterdam, and from there to London. From London, they took passage on the *Patience* and landed in Baltimore on July 9, 1752. The two young men had to stay in Baltimore for several months to work off their passage. The brothers migrated to Frederickstown, Maryland, and, because they were Palatine Protestants, they affiliated with the German Reformed Church (Calvinist) there. Having been in their family's flax industry in the Palatine, they ran a linen business, and, by 1761, Frederick married Dorothy (last name unknown).[13]

Their son, Frederick II, migrated to Lancaster County, Pennsylvania, and married Margaretta Diller, either in Fredericksburg or in Lancaster. They had at least two children, Elizabeth and Elias. By this time, the family had affiliated with the Episcopal Church, the surviving remnant

Mrs. Thomas Clemson (née Elizabeth Baker), Thomas Green Clemson's mother. American Philosophical Society.

Elizabeth Baker Clemson's silver mug, engraved with *ECB*. Fort Hill Collection, Clemson University. Gift of Meredith Sonderskov, Philadelphia, Pa.

of the Church of England as it existed in the now independent American colonies. When Elizabeth married Thomas Clemson III on September 30, 1800, the ceremony was conducted by Reverend Muhlenberg, a minister of the Protestant Episcopal Church of the United States of America. This violated the rules of the Quaker meeting, and Thomas Clemson, from an already less than diligent branch of an old Quaker family, was expelled from the Quaker meeting.[14]

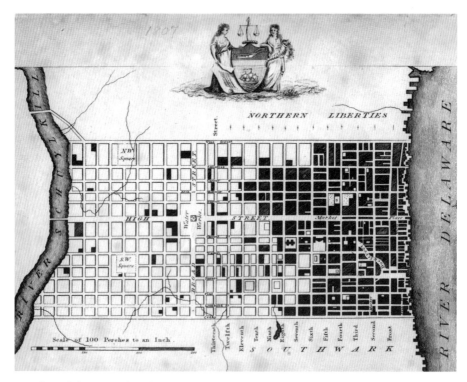

**Plan of the City of Philadelphia (Cedar to Vine Streets and Schuykill River to Delaware River), James Cundee engraving, 1807. Historical Society of Pennsylvania.**

The Philadelphia to which Thomas III brought Elizabeth was the busiest port in the United States. One of its biggest exports was wheat flour, which at the outbreak of the Revolution was being shipped to the Chesapeake area, the Carolinas, and the West Indies. These contacts made the whole Delaware Valley more accepting of the southern "peculiar institution"—slavery—than were the more northeastern colonies and, later, states. This was in spite of the large Quaker presence and the oldest abolition society in North America. The revolutionary struggles helped raise the cost of milled wheat 800 percent. The two armies, local militia, crop destruction, and a decline in the available work force had created a wheat shortage, and the Clemsons—involved in the trade from growing, to milling (in which the Clemsons may have invested), to selling—profited greatly, as did the other fourteen major flour merchants listed in the *Philadelphia Directory* at the end of hostilities.[15] This was the primary cause of the rapid growth of the fortunes of the Clemson family merchants, and it was this prosperity that gave Thomas III the substance to increase his wealth. During his adult years up to his death in 1813, he dealt extensively not only in grain and flour, but also in lumber, in cash loans (with interest), in other forms of commercial loans and credit, and in land speculation, particularly in what was then the undeveloped Broad Street area of Philadelphia.[16]

### *The Thomas Clemson IIIs in Philadelphia*

The Thomas Green Clemson IIIs would have six children (three sons and three daughters) between 1803 and 1814. The first child, named John Baker, was born on August 8, 1803. After his primary education, which may have continued locally in the Manual Labor School, he received a B.A. degree from Princeton College at age nineteen and then advanced his education at the Episcopal Theological Seminary in Alexandria, Virginia. In 1825, he was ordained a deacon in St. Stephen's Church, the church his mother, three sisters, two brothers, and he had attended. Two years later, he was ordained into the priesthood.[17] Shortly thereafter, on September 6, 1827, he would marry Margaretta J. Bull, daughter of the Rev. Mr. Levi Bull, of Chester County, Pennsylvania. Together, they would have four sons and three daughters. Three sons died as children before their mother died on February 25, 1838.[18]

John Baker Clemson would marry three more times. His son, who was named for John Baker's younger brother, Thomas Green Clemson, followed his father into the Episcopalian ministry. The Rev. Mr. Thomas Green Clemson married Sarah Ogden and had several children

The Rev. John Baker Clemson, Thomas Green Clemson's brother. Engraving by John Sartain from portrait by E. W. Mumford. Historical Society of Pennsylvania.

of whom Gertrude Gouverneur Clemson would be the most prominent. She, in turn, married Lewis Smith and bore two sons: Lawrence M. C. Smith, who married Eleanor Houston, and Ludlow Smith, who married Katharine Hepburn. Six children were born to Lawrence M. C. Smith and Eleanor Houston.[19] Another of John Baker and Margaretta Bull Clemson's children, Anne Bull Clemson, married George Lafayette Washington, the son of James Baker's sister, Louisa, and Samuel Walter Washington.[20]

John Baker Clemson and his second wife, Phoebe W. Lewis, had two daughters, Mary and Sallie, who would marry, respectively, William Cloud and Joseph Hartel. John Baker's third marriage, to Martha Smith, and fourth, to Hannah Gibbons, who survived him, were without issue. John Baker spent his later years in West Chester, Pennsylvania. After he died there on February 4, 1891, age eighty-eight, his body was taken back to Philadelphia to be interred with his first wife in Laurel Hill Cemetery, where his mother, Elizabeth Baker Clemson, was also buried.[21]

Thomas III and Elizabeth Baker Clemson also had three daughters and one other son besides John Baker Clemson and Thomas Green Clemson: William Frederick (b. 1811). The eldest of their daughters, Louisa (b. Sept. 4, 1805), later married Samuel Walter Washington, the great nephew of George Washington and the nephew of Dolley Payne Madison. They settled at Harewood, Virginia (now West Virginia). The Clemsons' second daughter, Elizabeth, was born June

Triptych of Thomas Green Clemson's sisters: Louisa Clemson Washington, Elizabeth Clemson Barton, and Catharine Clemson North. Fort Hill Collection, Clemson University. Gift of Meredith Sonderskov, Philadelphia, Pa.

29, 1809. Following her primary and secondary education, she attended Troy Female Seminary from 1824 to 1828.[22] After the seminary, she married the Hon. Mr. George Washington Barton, a descendant of the Rev. Mr. Thomas Barton, a Church of England minister in Lancaster, Pennsylvania.[23]

Thomas Green Clemson, the second son and third child of the Thomas Clemson IIIs, was born on July 1, 1807. His younger brother, William Frederick, was born September 8, 1811, and was not quite two when their father suffered a heart attack and died on July 5, 1813. Intestate when he died at age forty-one, Thomas III left five children, aged almost nine to almost two, and his forty-year-old widow, who was less than two months pregnant with their third daughter.

**Miniature portrait of Thomas G. Clemson as a young man. Feared lost for decades and rediscovered in 2007, the miniature is now in the Fort Hill parlor. On loan to Fort Hill, Clemson University, from the collection of John P. Elliott.**

The Clemsons of Filbert and Ninth in Philadelphia were a prosperous family. Besides the parents and the five children, Thomas III's youngest sister, Sarah, lived with them. Probably, Elizabeth and Sarah helped look after the children and their earliest education. Also in the household were two indentured servants: a German man who did whatever heavy housework was required, was the drayage man for the store, and was the family carriage driver; and an African American woman, who cooked, laundered, cleaned house, and helped look after the children.

Certainly, the Clemsons' life of comfort was affected by Mr. Clemson's death. Because of their close business ties, his unmarried brother James, who may also have lived with them, was named "estate administrator."[24] The initial evaluation of the Clemson estate was $30,000, and household goods were valued at $9,838. Later, this was revised up to $56,000, including the goods (a conservative 2006 estimate is $564,000). The house, store, and Ninth Street Philadelphia lots were not included.

Before the year was out, James Clemson, Thomas III's brother (and Thomas Green Clemson's uncle), died on December 22, 1813, leaving no heirs. His will left his mother an annuity and his brother and six sisters modest remembrances. The will specified that a large portion of his estate would devolve upon his nephews, John Baker, Thomas Green, and William Frederick. In the accounting, which lasted until October 14, 1818, the total, after all but one of the debts were settled, was nearly $40,000. The outstanding debt was to Thomas III's estate, perhaps for the three nephews, for about $25,000. The executors were Joseph Clemson (Thomas III and James's brother) and James L. Martin.[25]

Immediately after Christmas day in 1813, Thomas Clemson's widow, Elizabeth, and Michael Gunkle, a lawyer from East Whiteland, appeared before Sam Bryan, registrar of the Court of Orphans of Philadelphia, and were issued letters of administration. The estate evaluation continued, and the interim inventory of 1814 showed the collection of substantial debts. Some of the collected debts were for rents due on properties, but $1,363 was for salt and $4,294 for whiskey (of which rye represented the largest figure, apple brandy next, and peach brandy least), along with another unspecified $20,068.[26] More documentation was filed October 20, 1817, and the estate was finally closed in 1822. After the young Clemsons' upkeep and education and the daughters' legacies were reserved, the residual for the sons was about $50,000. Mrs. Clemson had her annuity and the use of the house until the last child was married or on his or her own. The store was handled separately.[27] Current rates would place the value of the sons' share at about $800,000.

The next arrangement after Thomas III's death was for the Court of Orphans to appoint a guardian for the children in accordance with Pennsylvania's prevailing laws. And there were now six children to be considered, since Mrs. Clemson had given birth to Catharine Margaret on January 18, 1814.[28] John Gest (May 17, 1783–December 15, 1865), a thirty-year-old Quaker bachelor who had been born in Sadsbury Township, Lancaster County, Pennsylvania, was appointed to serve as the guardian. He was the third son and tenth child of Joseph Gest (ca. 1722–1815), who, in turn, was the sixth son of Henry Gest and Mary, the daughter of James Clemson I and his wife Sarah. John Gest's mother was Deborah, the daughter of Elizabeth Miller and Joseph Dickinson, also Quakers of Lancaster County, Pennsylvania. Thus, John Gest, the appointed guardian, was the second cousin of Thomas III and the second cousin once removed of the six fatherless Clemsons.[29]

**Pedigree Chart for
John Gest**

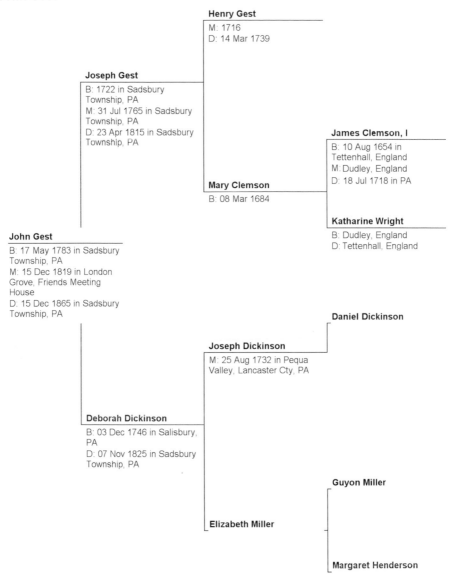

**Henry Gest**

M: 1716
D: 14 Mar 1739

**Joseph Gest**

B: 1722 in Sadsbury
Township, PA
M: 31 Jul 1765 in Sadsbury
Township, PA
D: 23 Apr 1815 in Sadsbury
Township, PA

**James Clemson, I**

B: 10 Aug 1654 in
Tettenhall, England
M: Dudley, England
D: 18 Jul 1718 in PA

**Mary Clemson**

B: 08 Mar 1684

**Katharine Wright**

B: Dudley, England
D: Tettenhall, England

**John Gest**

B: 17 May 1783 in Sadsbury
Township, PA
M: 15 Dec 1819 in London
Grove, Friends Meeting
House
D: 15 Dec 1865 in Sadsbury
Township, PA

**Daniel Dickinson**

**Joseph Dickinson**

M: 25 Aug 1732 in Pequa
Valley, Lancaster Cty, PA

**Deborah Dickinson**

B: 03 Dec 1746 in Salisbury,
PA
D: 07 Nov 1825 in Sadsbury
Township, PA

**Guyon Miller**

**Elizabeth Miller**

**Margaret Henderson**

**Prepared by Jerome V. Reel**

By 1819, John Gest had married Ann Bernard (1792–1883), and they lived at 28 South Tenth Street in Philadelphia. Gest's store was on the northwest corner of High and Tenth Streets, which placed them only one block west of the Thomas Clemsons.[30] This close proximity enhanced Gest's role as legal guardian of the six Clemson siblings; the same is true of his being their cousin. Within the genealogical context of the Clemson, Baker, and Gest families whom this opening chapter has addressed, such proximities make Gest's guardianship a major factor in the next chapter's examination of the life and education of Thomas Green Clemson from 1807 to 1838.

## Notes

1.  Historical Society of Pennsylvania, Philadelphia, PA (hereafter cited as HSP), Elias Baker File, FC Ba; this is a mimeographed description of the Elias Baker mansion in Blair County, PA; a copy of the mimeograph is in the Clemson Papers, Special Collections, Clemson University Libraries, Clemson, SC (hereafter cited as SCCUL).

2.  M. S. (Mattie) Clemson to Sam [last name not given], January 1898, American Philosophical Society, Philadelphia, PA (hereafter cited as APS), MSS Collection 76, Smith Family Papers, Series 31: Clemson Family Papers (hereafter cited as Clemson Papers in Smith Papers, APS). The United States population data used in this chapter are from the U.S. Census Bureau (http://www.census.gov/population/www/documentation/twps.0027.html); these and other census data have been developed by Andrew C. Land, B.S. in History, 2005, and M.A. in History, 2007, Clemson University.

3.  Clemson Papers, MSS 2, SCCUL; there are at least two other Clemson family origin concepts. The first points to Sweden. Jacob Clementson migrated from Trysdale, in Carlstadt parish, Sweden, to New Sweden in North America in 1658. Probably he is the James Clementson or Clemson who died in 1698. His will names a second wife, Bridget, and notes sons and daughters but gives no names, Clementson Papers, 108, HSP; it needs to be remembered that "James" is the Gaelic Celtic and English form of the Latin name "Jacobus," itself a rendering of the Hebrew name "Jacob"; according to the granddaughter of Sophie Clemson Sharpless, a sister of Thomas Clemson III, on page 90 of Acrelius's *History of Sweden*, "a list of all the men, women, and children which are found in New Sweden, now called Pennsylvia [sic], on the Delaware River" contains the name "Jacob Clemsson," as having been born in Sweden. However, the number of his household is listed as "one." Two of the sons of Thomas and Elizabeth Clemson, the Rev. Mr. John Baker and William Frederick, were certain that story of the forebear was correct. However, their aforementioned first cousin twice removed went on to state, "I have not been able from the records to determine that this Jacob Clemsson had any descendants, or find anything to connect him with the family. He left no will on record in New Castle, Philadelphia or West Chester." She visited the Old Swedes Church at Wilmington, Delaware, where Clemsson was said to be a vestryman, but when she examined the vestry minute book, she could not find his name.

    A second possible origin was offered in 1920 by Edward L. Clemson of New Orleans, Louisiana, who wrote to Albert Cook Myers, "I have come to the conclusion that James Clemson was the son of James Clements and Sarah Fields who were friends and settled in Flushing, Long Island, New York, in the year of 1670," New Jersey Archives, 1st series, x, 392; other archives note that Clements was a "son of Gregory Clements of London, executed because he was a member of the High Court of Justice that had condemned King Charles I, for high treason, and his son James (Clemson) had migrated to and settled in New Township in the present state of New Jersey." See *Clemson Family Genealogical Data*, West Chester Historical Society (West Chester, PA: West Chester, Delaware County, 1920), 51.

4.  The information on the British Clemsons has been provided by Michael and Suzanne Clemson of Kent, England, United Kingdom. They have been good friends of Jerome and Edmee Reel since 1988.

5.  Citations to the properties were copied by Alester G. Holmes from the Pennsylvania Archives, *Patent Book*, A, v. 213, and Archives, xix, 2nd series, 602, and are in the A. G. Holmes Papers, MSS 1, SCCUL.

6.  Pennsylvania Archives, *Will Book* D, 98, no. 127.

7.  "Pedigree of the Gest, Geste, Ghest, Geast Family," bound in the *Ancestry of John Gest*, Bausman Collection in HSP.

8.  R. N. Brackett, "Thomas Green Clemson, LL.D., the Chemist, Part I," *Journal of Chemical Education* 5, no. 4 (April 1928): 435.

9.  Raymond M. Bell, Frank Baird, and Margaret Ward, *The Clemson Family of Pennsylvania* (Washington, PA: Washington and Jefferson College, privately printed, 1971), 3; "Troth Papers," *Genealogical Society*, vol. 10 (1920): 293 (hereafter cited as Troth Papers).

10. The typed, unsigned statement of Sophia Clemson Sharpless, sister of Thomas III; Sophia attended school in Philadelphia and lived with Thomas III and his family, Clemson Papers in Smith Papers, APS.

11. Daniel Clemson, Notes accompanying the Clemson genealogy, Clemson Papers, MSS 2, SCCUL.

12. "Baker Mansion"; see also Philadelphia, PA. *Register of Deaths: Cemetery Returns:* Carper to Cuyler, HSP.

13. Raymond Carl Maxwell, *The History and Genealogy of Frederick Baker, Jr., of 1775-1862, together with a brief history of his father, Frederick Baker, Sr., and his uncle, John Samuel Baker, Sr.* (Farmville, VA: Farmville Herald, 1965), 1-4.

14. Bell, Baird, and Ward, *Clemson Family of Pennsylvania*, 3-4; Troth Papers, 10 (1920): 293; Sharpless statement is in Clemson Papers in Smith Papers, APS.

15. Thomas M. Doerflinger, *Merchants and Economic Development in Revolutionary Philadelphia* (Chapel Hill: University of North Carolina Press, for the Institute of Early American History and Culture, Williamsburg, VA, 1986), 86, 125-126.

16. S. F. Hutchkin, *Memoir of the Rev. John Baker Clemson, D.D.* (Philadelphia: George W. Jacobs & Co., 1896), 6.

17. M. S. (Mattie) Clemson to Sam (last name not given), 18 January 1898, Clemson Papers in Smith Papers, APS.

18. (The Rev.) George Boyd, *A Discourse delivered March 4, 1838, in the Church of the Ascension...on the occasion of the death of Mrs. Margaretta Jacobs Clemson* (Philadelphia, PA: William Stavely, 1838), 18.

19. Their second child, Eleanor Smith, holds a Ph.D. in Planning from Harvard and married James Morris, R.S.A., a British architect who practiced in Edinburgh, Scotland, until his death in 2006. They have a daughter, Alexandra, and two sons, Malcolm and Houston. Eleanor Smith Morris sent letters and notes to Jerome Reel from early 2003 to October 2006. In 2003, she was a guest lecturer in Clemson University's School of Architecture and was hosted by Professor James London. Later Eleanor and her husband James attended the Bicentennial of the Fort Hill house in 2003 and visited with Edmee and Jerome Reel for several days. Eleanor and Jim later hosted the Reels at Sugarloaf Orchard, their Philadelphia home, in 2003, when the Reels undertook the first of a number of research visits to Philadelphia.

20. Their great-granddaughter, Meredith Anne Washington Fuller, married Robert E. Coughlan III (deceased). They have one deceased and two surviving sons, Brian and Stephen. After Robert Coughlan's death, Meredith married Robert Sonderskov of New York. Meredith Fuller Coughlan Sonderskov has enriched Clemson University with papers and artifacts of the Clemson family and particularly her ancestor, John Baker Clemson, and his brother, Thomas Green Clemson. These are all now in the Thomas Green Clemson Papers, SCCUL.

21. *Arc American Republican: The Daily Local News* (West Chester, PA), 4 February 1891.

22. Elizabeth Clemson, "Autograph Album," 1824-1828, 2 vols., HSP.

23. Wayne L. Bockelman, "Local Politics in Lancaster County," *Pennsylvania Magazine of History and Biography*, 97 (1973): 97; also see letter from Mrs. Thomas Neilson, Elizabethtown, PA,

to A. G. Holmes, 11 July 1926, A. G. Holmes Papers, MSS 1, SCCUL; she was the daughter of Elizabeth Clemson and G. W. Barton.

24. Philadelphia Archives, *Index of Wills and Administrative Records, 1811-1831*, Book L, file 144, folios 91-92.

25. Philadelphia Archives, *Letters of Wills and Administration of Estates*, Estate of James Clemson, 1817 and 1818.

26  Philadelphia Archives, *Letters of Wills and Administration of Estates*, Estate of Thomas Clemson, 1813, folio 129; the accounting was by Michael Gunkle.

27. Philadelphia Archives, *Administration of the Estate of Thomas Clemson*, Book L, 129, no. 274.

28. The birth dates of the six Clemson children were given by Kali Neilson, a great-grandchild of Thomas Clemson III, based on dates supplied by John Baker Clemson, Memorandum of Kali Neilson, Clemson Papers in Smith Papers, APS.

29. See the Gest genealogical chart cited in note 7.

30. *Wilson's Philadelphia Directory*, 1825.

# Chapter 2

# THE 1807–1838 LIFE AND EDUCATION OF THOMAS GREEN CLEMSON

## *Jerome V. Reel*

Portrait of Thomas G. Clemson as a young man, 1834, by William Kennedy
Barclay (1816–1851). Oil on canvas. Clyde V. Madren Conference Center,
Clemson University. On loan from the estate of T. Ashton Phillips.

Following the death of Thomas Clemson III in 1813 and the subsequent
appointment of his second cousin John Gest as guardian of Thomas and
Elizabeth's six children, their education, of course, was an important issue.
While the paucity of records raises a question about the degree of that importance,
the paucity itself may reflect an aspect of the educational history of Philadelphia.

The Quaker founders of Philadelphia had led the Provincial Council to establish a school within the Meeting in 1683 to teach reading, writing, and arithmetic to boys and girls. Six years later, the Friends Monthly Meeting created a secondary school for males. It offered Bible, mathematics, and natural philosophy. At that stage, formal education ceased, because seventeenth-century Quakers, who had no clergy, had no need for colleges. When Benjamin Franklin proposed the Philadelphia Academy in 1740, it received support from many Quakers, but when, in 1755, it added collegiate instruction, most withdrew their support.[1] By 1800, both secular and religious education at the primary level was conducted by the churches, particularly the Quakers, Episcopalians, Presbyterians, Moravians, Baptists, Roman Catholics, and Lutherans. Most of these schools were open to girls and boys of both congregational and fee-paying families. After 1801, the children of the poor could attend one or another of these schools, and the city paid.[2] By 1813, the Charity School of Philadelphia was open and operating.[3]

Beginning in the winter of 1814, the older Clemson children were enrolled in day school at the Tabernacle Presbyterian Church,[4] then located in Ramstead Place on Fourth Street between Chestnut and Market Streets.[5] That congregation began in 1804 as a break-away congregation of English independents from Second Presbyterian Church.[6] How long the children stayed at Tabernacle Presbyterian School is not known, and there is no solid indication of where each of them went for secondary school. An uncorroborated, late nineteenth-century story suggests that one or more of them may have gone to a school called "Shellpot Hill," and another mentions a "Manual Labor School."[7] The only certainty is that, for Sunday services, Mrs. Clemson owned a pew at Saint Stephen's Episcopal Church on Tenth Street.[8] It is probable that the children went to services with her, because one of her sons, John Baker Clemson, later chose to be ordained as a deacon there in 1825.[9]

## *Norwich Academy, Vermont*

In 1819, Captain Alden Partridge, who had served as the first instructor in civil engineering at the United States Military Academy, opened the American Literary, Scientific, and Military Academy, which came to be known first as Norwich Academy and later, in 1838, having been chartered by the government of Vermont, as Norwich University. Besides the usual courses in the classics, history, and literature, Partridge included such courses as chemistry, astronomy, botany, and mineralogy, along with more "practical instruction" in surveying, mensuration of heights, civil engineering, and agriculture, which were revolutionary in North America. Knowing that the United States had been embroiled in "wars and rumours of wars" almost continuously from 1775 to 1815, Partridge also formed his students into a cadet corps and led them on regular military marches and field trips through the countryside. In 1822 the French language was added to the curriculum.[10]

An early view of the American Literary, Scientific, and Military Academy in its original location in Norwich, Vermont. Classes were held in South Barracks, the central building in the drawing. M. M. Peabody's engraving from drawing by E. F. Johnson. From *Thompson's Gazetteer* (1824): 202. Collection of the Sullivan Museum and History Center of Norwich University, Northfield, Vermont.

Captain Alden Partridge (1795-1854), founder in 1819 of the American Literary, Scientific, and Military Academy in Norwich, Vermont. From *History of Norwich University 1819–1911* by Grenville M. Dodge and William Arba Ellis, vol. 1 (Montpelier, Vermont: Capital City Press, 1911), iv.

Thomas Green Clemson was enrolled in the Norwich Academy for the spring term of 1823. He was fifteen years old. His older brother, John Baker, by then a graduate of Princeton College, sent a letter without a salutation but probably to Partridge with specific instructions for his younger brother's advanced education. Thomas Green, who already had a speaking and reading knowledge of French and a reading knowledge of Latin, and had progressed through Virgil and Horace, was to continue in Latin. He may have continued French either formally or informally. His instruction in Greek (which may have been a new subject) should include all of the *Graeca Minora*, some of the *Graeca Majora*, and into Homer's *Iliad*. Mathematics should progress through seven books of Euclid's propositions through polynomial equations, while the young Clemson should take as much surveying as he could accomplish. In addition, English grammar, geography, history (probably post-Roman), Roman antiquities, Bible, and athletic exercises, particularly fencing, were to be included. John Baker hoped the course could be completed in 1824 or at least by the spring of 1825.[11] He did not mention chemistry, astronomy, agriculture, civil engineering, botany, or mineralogy, but Clemson did study most, if not all, of those subjects.

| age | NAMES. | RESIDENCE. | ROOMS. | Entered |
|---|---|---|---|---|
| 18 | Ira Carpenter, | Keene, N. H. | x No. 44 | May 1823 |
| 14 | George E. Coolidge, | Dorchester, Mass. | 26 | " " |
| 16 | Thomas G. Clemson, | Philadelphia, Pa. | 39 | " " |
| 15 | Thomas T. Craven, Midshipman U. S. Navy. | Portsmouth, N. H. | 16 | June " |

Listing of cadet "Thomas G. Clemson, Philadelphia, Pa." in a *Catalog of the Officers & Cadets of the American Literary, Scientific, and Military Academy* (Windsor, Vermont: Simeon Ide, 1823). Marginalia include Clemson's age and the date he entered the academy. Catalog Collection, Norwich University Archives, Northfield, Vermont.

Thomas Green is listed as a cadet in the catalogs for 1823 through 1824.[12] His name also appears on some class rolls, room inspection reports, and on a receipt for board and laundry. Whether he left at the end of the autumn and winter session in 1825 or in June 1825 is not known.

What is clear is that by 1825 he was home in Philadelphia and was in that region studying mineralogy. Sometime in early 1826 and at eighteen years of age, Thomas Green Clemson read his first professional paper on an analysis of mineral substances to the Geological Society of Pennsylvania. He suggested they would be useful if properly mixed to coat iron for preventing oxidation. Almost at the same time, he conducted an analysis of iron ore, the sample for which was acquired from Franklin County, New York. A third analysis was of hydraulic limestone from Jefferson County, Virginia (now West Virginia). In this work, he noted three different substances including the prevailing blue limestone and also varieties of black and gray. Eight years later, these analyses would be published together in the *Journal of the Franklin Institute.*[13]

## Paris 1826–1831

In the late summer of 1826, Thomas Green took leave of his family and his Philadelphia friends, Ralph Hannoveraly, A. M. Stevenson, and Sam Yorke, as he boarded his ship to sail to France. Stevenson, years later, remembered that Clemson embarked close by the Auction Store in Philadelphia where the young men worked.[14] The date of the sailing, the name of the ship, and the place of landing in France have not been found, but Clemson seems to have proceeded directly to Paris and settled at No. 49 in Rue Mazarin. Whether he remained there until his return to Philadelphia is not known. The first clear picture of Clemson's initial year in Paris is seen in a letter from a fellow American, M. Robinson, who wrote Clemson on November 2, 1884, remembering their meeting fifty-eight years earlier in Paris:

> I recall my first meeting with you there at a reception of General Lafayette soon after his return from the United States in the winter of 1825–1826 when I was struck with your gay nature and an enjoyment of the attractions and novelties of Paris equal to my own.[15]

Obviously, the young Thomas G. Clemson enjoyed public company, particularly the company of luminaries, then and later in his life.

The second and more personal glimpse is a letter from Clemson to his mother, Elizabeth, on August 29, 1828. He does not refer to his scientific study, although other references make it apparent that he was heavily involved in those endeavors. To her, he wrote that "If any person has a restless disposition, I think it is myself. I have a great ambition [and] wish to see and do everything." At this point, Thomas Green had been in Paris "upwards of two years." The mercurial personality (he called it "a restless disposition") had already begun to manifest itself. On the one hand, he found himself "unhappy because I am not at home." A part of his concern was that his financial affairs were not settled, a worry that would follow him through his life. Thus, in this 1828 letter, he instructed:

> if any thing should happen to me whilst absent, I do desire that everything I have in money Bank stock Property etc, may be given to you and to be enjoyed by you whilst living—and after your death that it may be given to those of my sisters who are not married. This is a thing that I should have thought of before I left home for everyman in going to sea is running a risk never to return.

The mention of his estate, without commas, makes it difficult to gather an understanding of the investments or even an estimate of the amount. His disquiet also stemmed from the scarcity of letters his mother had written him. Letters arrived in Paris from Philadelphia via Le Havre every fifteen days, and Thomas Green had received no letters for over a month.

Yet he was happy in Paris, happier that he would have been in Philadelphia. In Paris he felt free:

> There is not that liberty [in the United States] that exists in Paris. People meddling with things that do not regard them. One giving his advice. Another blaming you for this. He plays too much on the flute, on the violin. He does [...]

drink and sleep. If you are seen taking your glass of wine, or play in a game at cards, or at the theatre. O! he drinks! He gambles—He frolics. He is lost.

So he wrote, "I do not think of returning home."[16] Perhaps he has given an insight into his Parisian pleasures and pastimes.

That is not to suggest that he was not busy on scientific matters. One of his letters, later published, was written in Paris, September 18, 1828, to Jacob Green, M.D., professor of chemistry at Jefferson Medical College in Philadelphia. Green and Clemson had met earlier in Paris, and Dr. Green had asked Clemson the name and type of oil burned in France. Clemson investigated and found that the oil was extracted from the grain of a species of cabbage (*Brassica arvensis* or *campestris*) and was called "Huile de Colza." Clemson, however, was not satisfied with the simple answer. He noted that the plant grew throughout France, particularly in the north, with Lille as the center of production, all the way through the Netherlands. Planting, transplanting, cultivating, harvesting, extracting the oil, and preparing it for use were detailed, along with the note that the research was carried out by Louis Jacques Thénard, whose lectures Clemson later would testify in a Philadelphia court he had attended, along with those of Gay-Lussac and Dulong in the Sorbonne (a medieval foundation college of the University of Paris) in 1826.[17] This research might be noted as his first reference to scientific agriculture and, perhaps, demonstrated the broadening of his mind and spheres of interest.

Eight months later, on May 27, 1829, Clemson wrote a letter to Benjamin Silliman, M.D., Yale faculty member and editor of the *American Journal of Science and Arts*, describing Clemson's observation and analysis of a sample of iron ore, which had been found in the Baltimore area and sent to him by a Mr. Warden. Silliman would publish the assay and analysis in a subsequent issue of his journal.[18]

Clemson also broadened his knowledge in practical laboratory chemistry by working in 1826 and the first half of 1827 with the chemist Gaultier de Clowbry. Later, Clemson continued this style of learning with other Parisian chemists, Laugier, Filier, and Robiquet. His acquisition of advanced knowledge grew, and, on November 4, 1828, at the request of the nUnited States consul in Paris, Clemson was admitted to the Royal School of Mines in Paris by the minister of public works as an "irregular student" [*auditeur libre*]. His record indicated he attended, or had permission to be an irregular student, from 1828 to 1832.[19] Clemson spent the remainder of the winter of 1828–1829 and the spring of 1829 at his studies at the Royal School of Mines, but he planned to tour part of the Germanys, especially Saxony, during the summer of 1829. Probably during that visit, he wrote his observations and submitted them to Silliman, who subsequently published them.[20]

In June 1831 Clemson received his certification as an assayer from the Royal Mint of France.[21] After receipt of the certificate, Clemson made plans to return to Philadelphia, but his friends in Paris were not happy with that decision. A Ca-

nadian, Lefte Neal, was upset partially because Clemson would miss the July celebration. That remark is part of a longer letter he sent Clemson from his Parisian
apartment on Rue de la Université. In it, Neal chided Clemson for not delaying
his departure only fifteen days:

> And not one of us can conceive why you do not wish to be present at the celebra-
> tion of the July festival, you, one of the combatants of our three great days; you
> whom I can still see covered with sweat, coming from the firing, and taking, in
> order to return thither, a new strength at a wine shop on the corner of Mazarine
> and Guénégaut Streets at the foot of the barricade. Your leaving before the cel-
> ebration of the anniversary is almost desertion.[22]

The anniversary was of the July Days (28, 29, and 30) of 1830. These days sig-
naled the outbreaks of political and intellectual revolts fifteen years after the Vienna Conference had attempted to re-establish more traditional European governmental and social form at the end of the tumult and wars of 1789 to 1815—the
era of the French Revolution, Reign of Terror, and the Napoleonic empire. In
France, the Vienna Conference had meant the restoration of the royal throne to
be held by Louis XVIII (1755–1824), the brother of the guillotined Louis XVI.
Louis XVIII was as moderate as a Bourbon could be, even tolerating the Bourbon
white banner sandwiched between the Parisian red and blue. His restoration, after Napoleon I's "One Hundred Days" failed return to power, was marked by a
limited franchise and parliamentary government. Upon his death in 1824, he was
succeeded by his younger brother Charles X (1756–1836). Charles was no moderate and adopted a much more repressive form of rule that alienated liberals and
moderates. The growing reactions in 1829 and 1830 led to the uprising of 1830.
Moderates looked to the younger cousin of the direct Bourbons, Louis Philippe
(1773–1850), who would reign from 1830–1848. The son of Louis Philippe Joseph, Duc d'Orleans, who was known during the revolutionary era as Philippe
Egalité, Louis Philippe had been taken by his father, once a supporter of the Third
Estate, to Austria as the revolutionary leadership grew increasingly bloodthirsty.

When in 1830 Charles X abdicated and fled into exile, Louis Philippe was
elected by the parliament as the lieutenant general of France. Liberals or rad-
icals, who wanted a republic, supported the Marquis de Lafayette, an avowed
liberal. Renowned for his support of and participation in the American Revolution, Lafayette had been a member of the opposition during the Restoration and,
upon the accession of Charles X, moved firmly into the radical wing. During the
Revolution of 1830, he served as commander of the National Guard. He was the
liberals' favorite to serve as president of their hoped-for republic. However, the
moderates, in combination with most gentry and ecclesiastical and commercial
houses and authorities, prevailed, and the Orleanist heir became king.

Such a turn of events may shed light on Thomas Green Clemson's decision to leave for hiladelphia fifteen days before the first anniversary celebration in Paris of the July Days of 1830. Certainly it is tempting to imagine a disappointed, republican Clemson, from a family that supported the American Revolution, who harbored loyalty to General Lafayette whom Clemson had seen at least twice and for whose cause and leadership in the July 1830 revolution he had fought.

Whatever the case, one of the coincidences of Clemson's participation in the 1830 French revolution is that the fervor and excitement of those July days would spread into the Belgian provinces and light the separatist feelings there. The Belgians chose Léopold of Saxe-Cobourgh (1790–1864), as King Léopold I (1831–1864), in whose court Thomas Green Clemson later would serve as a diplomat (1844–1851).

## Back to Philadelphia 1831–1832

Thomas Green Clemson arrived back in Philadelphia in the first half of September 1831. No doubt his mother and perhaps some of his brothers and sisters greeted him at home. Then his old friend, A. M. Stevenson, came to see him. Later, Stevenson would recall, "After talking a while you jumped up from your chair and said, 'Come out, let us go to Holahans and get a mug of beer and pretzels,' which you said you had often longed for in Paris—and there we had a long confab."[23] The Philadelphia they walked through had grown to 80,462, although it had slipped in relative size from second behind New York City to third, just edged out by Baltimore.

In February of 1832, Clemson served as one of Pennsylvania's witnesses in the famous trial of Lucretia Chapman (also known as Lucretia Espos Y Mina), along with another woman, probably her sister, for the murder of William Chapman, Esq., of Bucks County, Pennsylvania. Clemson was the twenty-third prosecution witness. He testified that, on September 22, 1831, he had been summoned to aid in the examination of the contents of William Chapman's stomach by Dr. Hopkinson in the laboratory of Dr. Mitchell. Clemson's testimony, which was carefully delivered, indicated that the interior of the stomach was coated with a "brown semi-fluid substance." A tablespoon of the substance, which had a brownish hue, was taken from the stomach for testing. Clemson stated that parts of the stomach were inflamed and the blood vessels were visibly browner than the rest. The substance was subjected to a series of tests, the first two of which revealed nothing, but, when the substance was cleansed of its residue of animal matter, the remains gave off the characteristics of arsenic.

When asked for his *bona fides,* Clemson noted the Parisian chemists, in whose laboratories he had worked, and his diploma from the mint as an assayer. A defense lawyer asked him for his experience as expert; Clemson acknowledged that he had only observed Mr. Robiquet perform such a series of tests for poison but that this was his first direct such examination. However, in it, he assisted Dr. Hopkinson under the continuous witness of Dr. Mitchell. In addition, two other doctors, Hare and Togno, occasionally were present.[24] Clemson's testimony was characterized by a thoroughness and honesty that would mark all of his scientific work.

### Paris 1832

Not yet twenty-five years old, Clemson returned to Paris by April 1832. He started a journal, which began in June 1832 and concluded in February 1837, and which is primarily a series of non-scientific notes, general observations, thoughts, and some expenses. Also included are several letter drafts from 1832 and 1837. On the flyleaf Clemson noted that he still considered the family home on Filbert and Ninth Streets, Philadelphia, as his principal residence.[25]

The journal reveals that Clemson's second stay in Europe would be from April 1832 to late summer of 1834. During that time, he continued his studies in a variety of sciences, worked diligently on his German, and, as an outcome, had an article on iron ore published in the U.S. and then reprinted in the *Journal für Chemie und Physik*.[26] He also analyzed some carbonate of iron and a sample of Harlan "bronzite" for correspondents in the United States. These two analyses were published by Benjamin Silliman in the *American Journal of Science and Arts*.[27]

By October 1834, Clemson had returned to Philadelphia where he stayed perhaps as late as mid-June 1835. With a group of friends, he conducted field work in nearby York County. Subsequently, he read a paper "Observations on the Geology of York County, Pennsylvania" to the Geological Society of Pennsylvania. This non-professional paper was then published as a pamphlet. One passage noted the existence of gold in quartz, and Clemson wrote that these "bear a strong resemblance to those of the gold belt of Georgia, North and South Carolina, and Virginia."[28] These passages may have been prescient of Clemson's later gold-related enterprises.

Again, Clemson returned to Europe. Using Paris as his base, he took a long trip to the United Kingdom, to which he had traveled once before. On his first trip, he had visited parts of England and Scotland. This time he took only day-trips out from London and lodged for a while on Regent Street in London before returning to Philadelphia. Why he went is not known. Perhaps it was a vacation or a search for employment. Whatever the case, by the late spring of 1836, he spent time with Richard C. Taylor in Cuba investigating bituminous coal. In August 1836, Taylor presented their findings to the American Philosophical Society in Philadelphia.[29]

In the late spring 1836, Clemson was back in Paris until early August when he and two of his aunts returned to the United Kingdom. Their travels took them by Lichfield, to Chester, and then to Holywell, Wales, where they stopped and visited St. Winifrid's Well. Clemson's little pocket diary also mentions their passing

Conwy Castle and crossing the Menai River on Telford's remarkable suspension bridge. From Anglesey, they crossed by boat to Dublin. There, Clemson's party was joined by his friend, Huizinga, from the Low Countries, and they traveled north along the Irish Sea. As they passed through small Irish villages, Clemson noted the "mud" and "miserable hovels" in which the Irish peasants lived. The conditions improved markedly when they stopped overnight in Newry and then spent three days in Belfast, the childhood home of one of his aunts. The group went on to Scotland for Clemson's second visit to Edinburgh, where, typical of his disinterest in religion, Clemson dodged morning service at St. Mary's Scottish Episcopal Church in favor of hiking up to Arthur's Seat with his friend Huizinga. Back in Dover, England, Clemson saw Léopold I, King of the Belgians, a glimpse that presaged unexpected connections between the two. After all, three years earlier, the king had received his throne as a result of the revolution in which Clemson participated in 1830, and it would be to Léopold's court that Clemson would be sent as chargé d'affaires in 1844.

### *Auspicious Meetings*

Back in Philadelphia by 1837, Clemson had come to the notice of a group of Missourians: E. F. Pratte, C. C. Cable, and L. C. Linn, who were interested in acquiring a lead mine (LaMotte) in Missouri, but who first wanted an expert opinion. They contacted Clemson and offered him a quarter share for his advice and subsequent supervision. To make the deal final, in the spring of 1838 Clemson went to visit Louis Linn, who was serving as a U.S. senator from Missouri, in Washington, D.C.[30] Linn roomed in the same boarding house as South Carolina Senator John C. Calhoun. In a discussion between the two, Calhoun's purchase of the O'Bar Mine in Georgia came up. As a result, Linn introduced Clemson to Senator Calhoun. It was through this connection that Anna Maria Calhoun, who in 1834 had accompanied her father to Washington as his confidential secretary, met Thomas Green Clemson.[31]

This was a pivotal meeting for the young, single Clemson, whose education ranged from geology, chemistry, docimacy, metallurgy, mining engineering and management, mineralogy, and agriculture to English, French, German, some Latin, a bit of classical Greek, and perhaps some Spanish. Here was a man who enjoyed the companionship of his peers and his elders, as well as dancing, the theatre, and music. Here also was a widely traveled man whose pocket diary remarked on engineering wonders, bridges, gas lighting, rocks, herds, soil, and royalty, as well as the hovels of the European poor; ignored architectural monuments; and paid keen attention to his money. And now, in 1838, just as he turned thirty-one, Thomas Green Clemson was in love.

## Notes

1. Frederick B. Tolles, *Meeting House and Counting House: The Quaker Merchants of Colonial Philadelphia* (Chapel Hill: University of North Carolina Press for the Institute of Early American History and Culture, Williamsburg, VA, 1948), 149–151.

2. Russell R. Weigley, Nicholas B. Wainwright, Edwin Wolf, Mary Maples Dunn, et alia, *Philadelphia: A 300-Year History* (New York: W. W. Norton, 1982), 224–226.

3. *Constitution of the Philadelphia Society for the Establishment and Support of Charity Schools: Incorporated the eighth day of September, 1810* (Philadelphia, PA: Privately published by the Society, 1840), 1–18.

4. Annie B. Roberts, a granddaughter of Thomas III and Elizabeth Clemson, to a Mrs. Hotchkiss, 26 January 1898, Clemson Papers in Smith Papers, American Philosophical Society (hereafter cited as APS), Philadelphia, PA.

5. Willis P. Hazard, *A Continuation of "Watson's Annals"* (1830): 3, 310–311.

6. Deborah Mathias, *Tabernacle Church (Presbyterian and United Church of Christ), A History* (Philadelphia: Privately published, 1974), 1.

7. M. S. (Mattie) Clemson, West Chester, PA, to Sam [last name not given], 26 January 1898, Clemson Papers in Smith Papers, APS.

8. Annie B. Roberts to Mrs. Hotchkiss, 26 January 1898, Ibid.

9. M. S. (Mattie) Clemson, West Chester, PA, to Sam [last name not given], 26 January 1898, Ibid.

10. Jacqueline S. Painter, assistant curator of Special Collections, Henry P. Chaplin Memorial Library, Norwich University, to Robert C. Edwards, president, Clemson University, 12 January 1978, Series 19, 159ff, Special Collections, Clemson University Libraries, Clemson, SC (hereafter cited as SCCUL); William A. Ellis, *Norwich University, 1819–1911; Her History, Her Graduates, Her Roll of Honor* (Montpelier, VT: Capital City Press, 1911), 1–18.

11. See Series 19, 159ff, SCCUL.

12. Ellis, *Norwich University*, 3, 617.

13. These early papers by Thomas Clemson were published in the *Journal of the Franklin Institute* 13 (1834): 78-79, 79-80, and 80, respectively: "Analysis and Observations on Diverse Mineral Substances"; "Assay of an Iron Ore from Franklin County, New York"; "Analysis of Two Varieties of Hydraulic Limestone from Virginia."

14. A. M. Stevenson to TGC, 4 January 1884, Clemson Papers, MSS 2, SCCUL.

15. A. M. Stevenson to TGC, 31 July 1884, Ibid.

16. TGC (Paris) to Elizabeth Baker Clemson (Philadelphia), 29 August 1828. In March 2006, Meredith Sonderskov gave Jerome and Edmee Reel this letter that she had only recently found. Jerome Reel transcribed the letter and gave it, on Ms. Sonderskov's behalf, to be included in the Clemson Papers in the Special Collections, Clemson University Libraries.

17. TGC letter to Jacob Green, 18 September 1828, reprinted in *Journal of the Franklin Institute* 8 (1829): 356; the testimony is extracted from John J. Smith, *Celebrated Trials of all Countries* (Philadelphia, PA: Jesper Harding, 1846).

18. Thomas Green Clemson, "Assay and Analysis of an Iron Ore, (fer titanne), from the environs of Baltimore, (land of Mr. Patterson), received through Mr. Warden," *American Journal of Science and Arts* 17 (January 1830): 42–43.

19. Alester G. Holmes and George R. Sherrill, *Thomas Green Clemson: His Life and Work* (Richmond, VA: Garrett & Massie, 1937), 5n14.

20. Thomas Green Clemson, "The Hartz-Physical Geography, State of Industry, Etc.," *American Journal of Science and Arts* 19 (January 1831): 105–130.

21. The diploma, along with other items, was placed in a metal box in the cornerstone of the main Clemson Agricultural College building (now called Tillman Hall) when it was laid 28 July 1891. See *News Courier* (Charleston, SC), 29 July 1891. The building burned 22 May 1894. When the cornerstone was extracted in 1989 by a team from the Clemson University Facilities and Maintenance Office under the direction of Gary Pringle and opened by the archivists of the Clemson University Libraries' Special Collections, led by Michael Kohl, director, all the contents were found to be irretrievably damaged by heat and water. That fire also destroyed Thomas Green Clemson's library and the law library of his father-in-law, John C. Calhoun.

22. Lefte Neal to TGC, 17 July 1831, Clemson Papers, MSS 2, SCCUL.

23. A. M. Stevenson to TGC, 31 July 1884, Clemson Papers, Ibid.

24. Smith, *Celebrated Trials*. The transcript of this passage from Smith's book was made by Richard Newman Brackett, Ph.D., professor of chemistry at Clemson Agricultural College. The transcript is in Clemson Papers, MSS 2, box 1, 2ff, SCCUL, and the original volume was owned by H. C. Miller, a lawyer from Anderson, SC; Miller's letter to Brackett, offering to let the book be examined, was written on 26 March 1927, and is now in the Holmes Papers, MSS 1, SCCUL. Miller called this trial "one of the most noted known to original jurisprudence."

25. "The Pocket Journal of Thomas G. Clemson," Clemson Papers, MSS 2, SCCUL (hereafter cited as TGC Journal). Some of the transcription work noted in the text is the work of Charles R. Clemson, of Lancaster, PA, which he did in the autumn of 1979. His notes are also in the Clemson Papers, MSS 2, SCCUL. The remainder of the transcription was done by this author. Also included are several letter drafts from 1832 and 1837. The journal covers about 26 months out of those 4 ¾ years. The flyleaf indicates that Clemson still considered the family home on Filbert and Ninth Streets, Philadelphia, as his principal residence. In addition, there are twenty-five pages of receipts and expenses that cover 20 December 1832 to 16 May 1833. Retrospective entries on 27 and 28 July 1833 refer to transactions up to 14 June 1833. The record begins again 20 August 1833 and continues through 31 August 1834. It breaks off again, resuming with one note for 2 February 1835, and resumes from 30 June to winter 1837. Some of the expenses are also noted in the body of the text.

26. Refer to *Journal für Chemie und Physik* [Nuremberg: Schrageschen Buckknadlung] 64 (1834): 63–65.

27. Thomas Green Clemson, "Analysis of American Spathic Iron and Bronzite," *American Journal of Science and Arts* 24 (July 1833): 170–171.

28. Thomas Green Clemson, *Observations on the Geology of York County, Pennsylvania* (Philadelphia: W. P. Gibbons, 1834).

29. Thomas Green Clemson and R. C. Taylor, "Notice of Vein of Bituminous Coal Recently Explored in the Vicinity of Cuba," *Philadelphia Magazine* (1837): 161–167.

30. See Clemson Papers, MSS 2, b1 F 3, July 1837, SCCUL.

31. Ernest McPherson Lander Jr., *The Calhoun Family and Thomas Green Clemson: The Decline of a Southern Patriarchy* (Columbia: University of South Carolina Press, 1983) 2, 3, 30n2, 39–43.

# Chapter 3

# ANNA MARIA CALHOUN CLEMSON:
## "A WIFE WORTHY OF ANY MAN THAT EVER LIVED"

## *Ann Ratliff Russell*

**Belgium-era portrait of Anna Calhoun Clemson in court attire. Attributed to Henri Jean Baptiste Jolly (1812-1853). Oil on canvas. Fort Hill Collection, Clemson University. Gift of Mr. and Mrs. Creighton Lee Calhoun Jr.**

Among the many messages of sympathy Clemson received at the time of his wife Anna's death in 1875, one that must have meant the most to him came from James Rion, a Calhoun family friend and the man who would later become Clemson's own financial advisor and lawyer:

You have lost a wife, who was in every sense of the word a companion for you, not only worthy of affection but of the highest esteem. Her good nature, high spirit, elegance of manners, extensive information and reading, fine intellect, and all the more valuable female accomplishments, fitted her to be a wife worthy of any man that ever lived.

Rion, who had paid a visit to Fort Hill shortly before Anna succumbed to a heart attack, said further: "It is a great, though sad, consolation to me that I saw her so soon" before she died.[1]

The grieving husband's despair was movingly expressed in a letter to his friend Henry Gourdin, as noted in Ernest McPherson Lander Jr.'s work on the Calhoun family and Thomas Clemson: "How disconsolate and wretched I feel," he wrote, "it is impossible for anyone to imagine." There was little comfort for Clemson who buried his wife beside their son in the St. Paul's Pendleton churchyard.[2]

## *Courtship and Marriage*

The marriage of Anna Maria Calhoun at age twenty-one and Thomas Green Clemson, ten years her senior, was undeniably an emotional union based on love rather than a family arrangement that had typified nuptials in the 1700s. Their courtship that began in Washington, D.C., in the spring of 1838 brought together a most unlikely couple. Working for three years with her father in the nation's capital as the copyist of some of his correspondence along with other writings, Anna had expressed a determination never to marry. Usefulness to her father, she felt, was a primary purpose in her life, and the close companionship she shared with Calhoun could well have continued had she not fallen in love with Thomas Clemson, a worldly, well-educated confirmed bachelor from Philadelphia. Although said to have declared there was no woman whom he would ever marry, Clemson was apparently quite smitten by Anna's character and loveliness. Captivated by her large, dark eyes, their extraordinary animation softened by sweetness, he wooed and won the woman who, as a southern lady, obviously identified with class over section in considering marriage to a "Yankee" such as Clemson.[3]

In all likelihood Anna met the man for whom she would consent to leave her father through Senator Louis Linn of Missouri, a colleague of Calhoun as well as a business associate of Clemson and an acquaintance of Anna since her days at Dowson's Capitol Hill boarding house during her first winter in Washington. Whatever the circumstances of the introduction, sometime between Clemson and Anna's meeting in May of 1838 and her departure for South Carolina with her father in mid-July, she had accepted the proposal of Thomas Clemson.[4]

Six weeks after their parting and with no word from Miss Anna Calhoun in response to his letters, Clemson passionately reaffirmed his feelings for her: "My very much beloved dear Anna—I live through you—you are more dear than life—your happiness is my only desire—you are the first and the last—the blessed idol of my life." Although they had apparently reached "an understanding" before she left Washington for her family's Fort Hill plantation, the fact that he had heard nothing from her since then not only added to the ardor of his affections, but bewildered him as well. After almost a dozen epistles and no answer, Clemson, writing on August 19, likened his worry to "a load of excruciating suspense and accumulating anxiety" as to the welfare of one for whom he had declared his love. Fortunately, he heard from Anna the following day and experienced what he described as a most remarkable "revolution of feeling." Happy that her mother and father and sister-in-law Margaret spoke kindly of him, he expressed with certainty his belief that "if love and devoted affection to Anna will veil my numerous and various faults, then I shall be perfect."[5]

While true that Anna was likely closer to her father than anyone else and that her place in his life was never filled by another after she married Clemson, it can be said that in their case the father gained a son rather than lost a daughter. The smart and multi-skilled Clemson had many attributes characteristic of his illustrious father-in-law. According to some observers of Clemson's tall, lean stature and dark hair, he even resembled Calhoun. Nevertheless the ultimate significance of giving away his daughter in marriage, albeit to a man he trusted, was not lost on Calhoun. According to his eldest son Andrew, his father was decidedly more "abstracted" than "affable" at the candlelight wedding ceremony and lavish celebration attended by many guests at Fort Hill on the evening of November 13, 1838.[6]

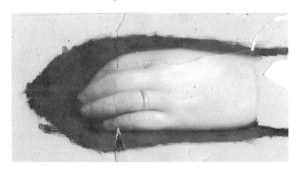

**Study of a woman's delicate hand with the wedding band of Anna Calhoun Clemson, the only extant artist-board portrait study by Thomas Green Clemson. Fort Hill Collection, Clemson University.**

Anna's marriage to Clemson committed her as a wife and eventually as a mother to the traditional duties of domesticity, a virtue of increasing stature in the nineteenth century. Like all married women of her day, she would follow her man's lead and hold their family together, despite the sometimes perilous path of the journey. The road she traveled with her husband was for her by far the most difficult one that she faced. She gave him her love and loyalty above all others as she relinquished "the cherished object" of her life in her father for a choice she thought to be "*the best*" in Clemson. Initially a man resolved in his actions, he was loving and supportive to her. But Anna soon realized that he was tormented in both mind and body by a misunderstood mental illness. Unable to fulfill her own

**Pedigree Chart for
Anna Maria Calhoun**

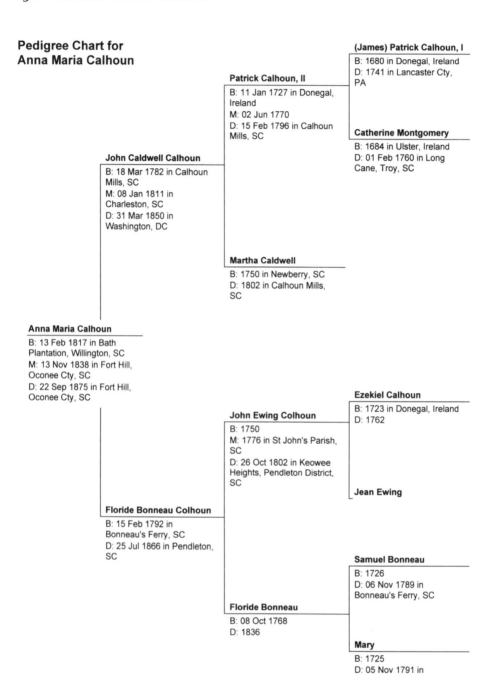

**(James) Patrick Calhoun, I**

B: 1680 in Donegal, Ireland
D: 1741 in Lancaster Cty, PA

**Patrick Calhoun, II**

B: 11 Jan 1727 in Donegal, Ireland
M: 02 Jun 1770
D: 15 Feb 1796 in Calhoun Mills, SC

**Catherine Montgomery**

B: 1684 in Ulster, Ireland
D: 01 Feb 1760 in Long Cane, Troy, SC

**John Caldwell Calhoun**

B: 18 Mar 1782 in Calhoun Mills, SC
M: 08 Jan 1811 in Charleston, SC
D: 31 Mar 1850 in Washington, DC

**Martha Caldwell**

B: 1750 in Newberry, SC
D: 1802 in Calhoun Mills, SC

**Anna Maria Calhoun**

B: 13 Feb 1817 in Bath Plantation, Willington, SC
M: 13 Nov 1838 in Fort Hill, Oconee Cty, SC
D: 22 Sep 1875 in Fort Hill, Oconee Cty, SC

**Ezekiel Calhoun**

B: 1723 in Donegal, Ireland
D: 1762

**John Ewing Colhoun**

B: 1750
M: 1776 in St John's Parish, SC
D: 26 Oct 1802 in Keowee Heights, Pendleton District, SC

**Jean Ewing**

**Floride Bonneau Colhoun**

B: 15 Feb 1792 in Bonneau's Ferry, SC
D: 25 Jul 1866 in Pendleton, SC

**Samuel Bonneau**

B: 1726
D: 06 Nov 1789 in Bonneau's Ferry, SC

**Floride Bonneau**

B: 08 Oct 1768
D: 1836

**Mary**

B: 1725
D: 05 Nov 1791 in Bonneau's Ferry, SC

**Prepared by Jerome V. Reel**

individual identity in her relationship with her husband, she would ultimately find personal happiness in that of her children.[7]

**Mrs. Thomas G. Clemson and her children, Floride Elizabeth and John Calhoun. Tinted photograph, ca. 1848. Fort Hill Collection, Clemson University.**

Following in Clemson's footsteps, Anna traveled in the North; then to Havana, Cuba; to a *"Miner's Hut"* in Georgia; to a dilapidated domicile on the Canebrake plantation in Edgefield District of South Carolina; and finally abroad to Belgium. The separation from her family, especially her father, during the six years of Clemson's diplomatic service at the court of King Léopold I in Brussels, was particularly painful for Anna who dreamed every night of the pleasure of seeing them all again. She felt deeply the distance from her parents and found herself unimpressed with whatever the Europeans valued as treasures. Limited by the responsibility of her two small children and the lack of money from living on her husband's government wages, Anna did not enjoy her experience abroad. She also was concerned for the operation of their Canebrake plantation. However, she supported Clemson's diplomatic endeavors by assuming secretarial duties for the American legation and by accepting social invitations for evening affairs, despite the domestic demands of her days. After a little more than six years spent in Belgium, she gladly returned to the United States with Clemson and their children, Calhoun and Floride, in April of 1851. Following a summer at Fort Hill, she moved about with her family for another two years to various locations in the North before finally settling on a farm near Washington in August of 1853. Unable to obtain a foreign post in the administration of President Millard Fillmore's successor, Franklin Pierce, Clemson had decided to resume farming after having sold his Canebrake property in South Carolina since returning from Europe. However, he still maintained an interest in government service.[8]

### Life with a Troubled Man

Grateful to have her own home place, Anna designated the farm her husband had purchased in Bladensburg, Maryland, as simply "The Home" and proceeded to cope with the demands of managing her household there. During the following years Clemson's increasing irascibility made life difficult for those around him and particularly Anna, who tried to promote family love and harmony in every way. She had earlier revealed much about the nature of her relationship with her husband in a letter of sympathetic advice addressed from abroad to her ailing brother Patrick in 1850. "Don't give way to low spirits," she had written to Pat. She reminded him of her own ill health for four years, from the death of her first-born infant in 1839 to the months following the birth of her daughter Floride at the end of 1842, and attributed her recovery primarily to her attitude in the face of adversity. Furthermore, she continued, "we all know the state of the mind influences greatly the body, & nothing is more injurious, even to those who are in good health, than habitual despondency," her own husband, "Mr. C.," being "a case in point of *that*." Although he was, she told Pat, liable to the "*blues*" and "dyspeptic & *ailing*," at the time of their marriage, "he is now as hearty a man as you will meet in a summer's day." She always believed that his ill health arose mainly from his mental state and confided "*entre nous*": "I commenced by never worrying him myself, & trying to prevent his having any real cause to fret, & then, when he got low spirited, I amused him, & joked with him, & tho' *I took him too old*, & can never make him a gay or amiable man it is really wonderful how much he has improved." In telling comments to her brother about her husband's behavior, Anna admitted that Clemson, though sometimes "*cross*" in spells of gloom, was much easier to humor and cheer up again. "The fits," she said, "are far apart & yield easily to my efforts."[9]

Anna's belief that her husband's mental state was much improved toward the end of their stay in Belgium was short-lived as his disposition back at home became increasingly moody. The condition of dysthymia from which Clemson apparently suffered caused a chronically depressed mood that negatively affected his actions, especially with regard to such medical symptoms as "subjective feelings of irritability or excessive anger," "poor appetite," and "feelings of hopelessness." It is not surprising that without pharmacological therapy, now recognized as effective treatment of a depressive personality, Anna's attempts to cheer her husband out of what she called the "*blues*" only succeeded in the short term. Today, with appropriate therapy, including not only drugs but also counseling and psychotherapy, an estimated 80 percent of clinically depressed people can improve quickly. Life-long relief from this widespread psychological illness is, by all accounts, realistic. Unfortunately, however, in Clemson's case, without the care that is now available, the seriousness of his misunderstood condition worsened and caused personal distress and disability within his family, despite all that Anna could do to keep the familial peace she prized dearly.[10]

Anna wrote to her daughter Floride away at her Aunt Elizabeth Barton's boarding school in Philadelphia in September of 1856 that her father ate little but complained much, knowing that the thirteen-year-old would be glad to hear that he was still very kind and amiable. She admonished Floride not to mention this in her response that Clemson would probably read, because she did not wish him to think mother and daughter spoke of such matters. Aunt Barton, who was Clemson's younger sister, could be trusted to keep the subject of her brother's depression confidential. As he seemed to miss both Floride and her brother Calhoun, who at age fifteen was being treated for a spinal condition in Northampton, Massachusetts, Clemson was more devoted than ever to his little one-year-old daughter Cornelia (Nina) born in the fall of 1855. Anna, who knew Floride would know how lost she was without her and Calhoun, confided to her daughter that "If it were not for baby, I could not stand it." Despite being far from well, Clemson remained pleasant and amiable though as usual convinced, according to Anna, that he would "die in a poor house."[11] Anna obviously tried to spare her daughter from worry by softening verbally the realities of daily life she faced with her husband.

A typical example of expenses that worried Clemson was the calisthenics training that Anna thought necessary for Floride's educational curriculum. As Anna did not like to oppose Clemson's wishes, she regretted that his sister, rather than speaking to him about Floride's taking the course, had not simply billed him for the cost to which he typically objected beforehand. Distressed also at his refusal to give money for a cloak that his sister said Floride needed, Anna herself promised to send $20 in March to pay for the item. She also sent her daughter $5 bank notes that she had received from her widowed mother, Floride Calhoun, in South Carolina.[12]

With young Calhoun Clemson's return home from the North in November of 1856, Anna, along with Clemson, concluded that the young teenager's health must take precedence in their lives for the next few years. Unable to do any reading or writing because of headaches, Calhoun, like his parents, worried about his backwardness that Anna instructed Floride not to mention to him. Not only did Clemson try by conversation to interest his son in science, but according to Anna, he also continued to keep up with the water cure treatment that Calhoun had undergone in Massachusetts. Rousing the household at five o'clock in the morning with his preparations, Clemson proceeded to pack the unwilling boy for one hour in a wet sheet, covered by five blankets. He then rubbed his son with a wet and then a dry sheet and later in the day supervised a sitz bath with Calhoun wrapped in a blanket in a tub of water for thirty minutes. A wet bandage worn around his waist and a diet of the simplest food completed the hated regimen that Calhoun called the "water tortures." "I really feel for him," Anna wrote to Floride, and added, "it is enough to run one crazy, to see the state of the two rooms, which I must right up."[13]

Calhoun's condition did improve by Christmas and New Year's, and by the spring of 1857, Anna also had good news to report to Floride about her father's having been approached by the Belgian minister, M. Bosch, in regard to the possibility of his being sent back to Europe. Upon instructions from the minister of foreign affairs and King Léopold I, Bosch had requested that the new U.S. president, James Buchanan, and his secretary of state, Lewis Cass, give the Belgian mission to Clemson, who felt highly complimented. As the matter appeared certain, Clemson made plans to sell The Home if possible and have Anna live with Floride in a house in Philadelphia near his youngest sister, Catharine North. Calling the mission a godsend for her husband, Anna thought it the best thing that could happen, as she told Floride that her father's worrying and dissatisfaction made himself and everyone around him miserable. In particular, she said, "it is a good thing Calhoun should be separated from him for a while," and, although she disliked greatly both the idea of leaving The Home and the trouble of moving, the pleasure of being with her daughter again reconciled her to the situation.[14]

However, after six weeks with no commitment by the administration to Clemson's appointment to the Belgian post, the possibility of his resuming diplomatic service became much less certain. President Buchanan later said that great political pressure prevented him from acceding to Belgium's request on behalf of Clemson. Whatever the case, since, according to Anna, he had been "so buoyed up" by the hope of getting "so essential" an office, she dreaded the effect this disappointment would have on him. Thus instead of preparing to move in June of 1857, she, along with the whole household, anxiously awaited Floride's homecoming from school.[15]

Apparently the fourteen-year-old's summer stay at The Home turned out to be a stressful one, ending in a family quarrel on the day she departed for Philadelphia in September. Described by Anna as "that thunder storm," the unexplained dispute followed three months of friction and seemingly "left no material for further explosives." Since her daughter's departure "Quiet, if not peace, has reigned," she wrote to Floride. Clemson's failure to receive the diplomatic appointment to Belgium could well have resulted in a depressive spiral characterized by a dysphoric state of anxiety with an irritability that contributed to hostility between father and daughter.[16]

Even though Clemson would not improve much, Anna nevertheless wanted Floride back at school to let her mind be at ease. Calhoun, she said, was unusually affectionate and attentive to her at home, and they got on very well. In fact the arrival of Anna's brother Pat, "a favourite" with her husband, meant "no change or storm," since, as she reminded Floride, Clemson was always more pleasant in her uncle's presence.[17]

Carrara marble bust of Cornelia (Nina) Clemson. Sculpted ca. 1858 by Hiram Powers (1805–1873). Fort Hill Collection, Clemson University.

Clemson's decision, despite Anna's disapproval, to send Calhoun to study with his uncle, The Reverend Baker Clemson, in Claymont, Delaware, led to a hard stint of loneliness for her. With Floride already away at her Aunt Barton's academy in Philadelphia, Anna wrote to her daughter, "If it were not for Nina, I do not think I could bear it." The little girl, at a year-and-a-half and "one of the smartest children," in her mother's eyes, would sit at length on her father's lap and call herself "papa's Nina."

Some months following both Calhoun and Floride's return to The Home, it was their little sister's unexpected death from scarlet fever on December 20, 1858, that provoked such despondency in Clemson that Anna's mother in South Carolina urged her daughter to do all in her power to prevent her husband from committing suicide. In a letter that she had received from him almost eight months after Nina's passing, Mrs. Calhoun found her son-in-law to be "still dwelling on going to his child," because "life is a burden to him." Fearing that he would put an end to himself, she admonished Anna that he would lose his mind or something worse if he did not lay aside those awful feelings. Apparently the severe emotional stress caused by his daughter's death had brought about a clinical condition of double depression with a major depressive episode superimposed on the distraught Clemson's dysthymic disorder.[18]

Shortly after Mrs. Calhoun's warning, Anna learned from Laura Leupp, the daughter of Clemson's close friend and financial advisor, Charles Leupp, that her own father had committed suicide. Leupp, a wealthy New York City leather merchant, had shot himself, partly the result of his involvement with financial schemer Jay Gould. This news deepened the despondency that Clemson had suffered since Nina's death. He sounded "so depressed in spirits" in a letter to his uncle Elias Baker, who expressed his astonishment at such language of despair from one whom he thought should be a happy and contented man. "You must not *always* look at the 'Black Side' of things," had been his uncle's response to

Clemson's grumbly complaints, as he advised him to look instead on the bright side. Although sympathetic to the pain of Clemson's loss of both his little daughter and friend Charles Leupp, Elias reminded his nephew that he had a wonderful wife and two fine children, a competence in money matters, and the enjoyment of a lovely home. "Why should you," he wrote, "grumble, complain, and make yourself miserable?" If all was well with Anna, then Clemson, his Uncle Elias maintained, should not complain about anything.[19]

Anna may well not have shared fully with Clemson her personal feelings of sadness in the aftermath of Nina's death. In her personal album, however, she had written poignantly of her sorrow. Questioning where her "angel" Nina was, why she was taken, and what the nature of their relationship would be "in another world," Anna grieved at the thought that mother and child would never meet again. A child's devotion and sweet dependence, so special to a mother, would, she wrote, be lost forever, and any meeting of the spirit hereafter a disappointment to her heart. Recalling other loved ones as well in a reverie of the past when she was young and happy, she felt her heart close and life become once more sad and gloomy with the approach of a footstep (perhaps that of her husband).[20]

Evident here in her album's private expression of sentiments is the effect, in part, of Clemson's desolation and despair on his wife, his "very much beloved dear Anna." Understanding what psychiatric scholar Kay Redfield Jamison describes as the "compelling, contagious, and profoundly interpersonal" nature of moods, one can see how Clemson's depressive disorder altered not only his own perceptions and behaviors, but Anna's as well.[21]

While Floride went south in the fall of 1859 to spend some time with her grandmother, Anna remained with Clemson and Calhoun at The Home. Apparently she must have indicated some apprehension about her daughter's not being there to her sister-in-law Sue, the wife of Clemson's younger brother William. Her sister-in-law, who hoped that she would have a pleasanter winter than anticipated, wondered why she had not kept Floride with her and sent Calhoun away as she had thought of doing. "Sister Sue" also urged Anna to confide openly about her son's condition. William Clemson, in a letter to his niece Floride, made his own caustic comments about her "*poor sick brother*," but expressed real concern that her "poor mother" would be "cooped up" during the winter with her husband and eighteen-year-old son. "I am afraid it will be more than she can bear," he wrote, trusting that God would "protect her." Irritated about Calhoun's not going to school and instead being allowed to hunt and ride and generally do as he pleased in order "to restore his *weak* and *shattered* frame and *strengthen* his delicate *constitution*," his uncle exclaimed, "Poor boy! what will he turn out to be?"[22]

Calhoun in fact soon left The Home for a hunting and fishing expedition to Florida in the company of his English friend, G. H. Dunscomb. Anna, "cooped up with only her husband," wrote to Floride that her "father is uncommonly ami-

Thomas Green Clemson from a carte de visite, ca. 1860. Printed on the reverse: "Alex Gardner Photographer to the Army of the Potomac/Galleries/511 Seventh Street and 332 Pennsylvania Av/ Published by Philip & Solomons, Washington DC." Littlejohn Photographs, Special Collections, Clemson University Libraries.

able, as he always is when we are alone, both because he is dependent on me & when you children are not here, many reasons why I must interfere with him do not exist, & I can let him do as he chooses." Nevertheless she admonished her daughter to guard her comments in correspondence, as her father always asked to read her letters and seemed to be much interested in them.[23]

When in January of 1860 Clemson accepted the offer of Secretary of the Interior Jacob Thompson to head the Patent Office's agricultural department, Anna felt that the occupation would be a great thing for him, and he in turn was much pleased by the opportunity. Finding her husband to be in excellent health and spirits at the time he assumed the duties of his position in February, she thought the government work would be rejuvenating for him, even though the $2,000 salary was much less than he had anticipated.[24]

Anna informed Floride that her father got on famously in his new office. And describing their preparation for spring planting on the farm, she wrote, "you know I am overseer," with Clemson giving the orders and she herself having them executed. Anna was also pleased to note her husband's inclination to improve the place and hoped that he would continue in that spirit.

She made no direct mention of the fact that she was pregnant with her fifth child, although she indicated needing household help for the summer. In early March 1860, at age forty-three, she suffered a miscarriage. "I cannot imagine what *caused the accident*," she told Floride and Mrs. Calhoun. Since she had felt badly for three months, she supposed "it was to be." Even though still somewhat weak and confined to bed by the doctor, she was, she said, wonderfully well. "Your father," she assured Floride, "is as kind as he knows how. He was terribly frightened & stranger still very much *disappointed*." Perhaps Anna's considering Clemson's disappointment as strange could signify a greater sense of relief rather than grief on her part in the matter.[25]

While recuperating after her miscarriage, she had a vision of her father John C. Calhoun, who had been dead for ten years; Anna subsequently recorded in her album his appearance to her in the dream:

> I lay in bed, but not it seemed to me asleep, though my eyes were shut, when suddenly, but with an evident intention to avoid alarming or surprising me, my father stood beside me.—I come, my daughter, said he, to speak with you, & I do so now, that your mind is more independent of your body, than when you are awake, that I may spare you the shock, always felt, when matter comes in contact with disembodied spirit. You are right, my daughter, not to give way to the delusions of spiritualism—I do not say there are devils, *for evil is not created*, but from want of knowledge, comes error.—I cannot explain to you many things—human language has no words, for what the human mind cannot conceive, of the great mysteries *on this side*. Continue to strive to know & do the right, & to elevate by every measure your soul, & when you come on this side all will be clear.

Anna seemed to hear from her father the words she wished to speak but did not dare say to her husband:

> Tell Mr Clemson he must do this also, or those he loves will be as invisible to him on this side, as they are now—for the universe is vast, & *like dwells with like*—Tell him he has not fulfilled the trust I had in him when I gave him my daughter. And now I go my daughter, but before I leave you, it is permitted you should see all those you love on this side.—Then I saw them all, each with the most familiar & loved expression—Their eyes were more *living* than in life, & as I encountered the glances of each, they seemed to emit as it were, an unspoken language. Soul spoke to soul. Tho' perfectly *life like*, they seemed less *flesh like*. The soul seemed to pierce its outward covering—it seemed to me there was less of form than countenance—
> March 1860[26]

We will have to surmise the actual meaning of this encounter with her father for Anna, but there are various levels of interpretation given by The Reverend Bob Haden, an authority in dream analysis for therapists, clergy, and individuals. Haden suggests that, from the spiritual perspective, the dream primarily reflects communication with a world beyond this one and therefore is reassuring of its existence. In a secular sense, it shows the strong bond that Anna shared with Calhoun. Representing the "wise old man" with a message for Anna and Clemson, her father is a positive, "primary animus" (animating or actuating spirit) figure, advising each "to strive to know & do the right, & elevate by every measure your soul." In that phrase, Anna could well have thought she heard an echo of Calhoun's often expressed motto, "The duties of life are greater than life itself." Clemson, the "other primary animus figure," represents a certain negative aspect of Anna's "critical nature within" that somehow restricts the development of her character to its possible potential. The dream in part is about her need as a wife to work with Clemson in order to fulfill her own individual identity, and it seems to be calling for her to "receive the wisdom" from Calhoun and convey its message to Clemson. Her alienation from the man she had once thought to be *the best* is evident, since the vision of Calhoun directs Anna to tell him, first, that he must heed his advice "or those he loves will be as invisible to him on this side as they are now," and, second, that "he has not fulfilled the trust" with which Calhoun gave him his daughter. Although Anna recorded the dream soon after its occurrence, she did not show it to anyone until she gave a copy to close family friend, James Rion, fifteen years later in 1875, fully aware that he would later show it to Clemson.[27]

During her recuperation after the miscarriage, Anna received understanding and affectionate letters from Floride. She basked in her daughter's love since she got "so little of that kind of thing." Despite the fact that Clemson's disposition had improved dramatically since his suicidal sentiments had so concerned Mrs. Calhoun and his uncle Elias Baker, he apparently could not communicate with his wife. The "feelings of hopelessness" symptomatic of Clemson's condition of dysthymia caused "clinically significant distress or impairment" in his relations with others and could well have prevented the expression of emotions Anna longed to hear.[28]

Soon after the return of both Floride and Calhoun to The Home in the spring of 1860, Clemson went to Europe on official government business that summer.

*Left:* **Photograph of John Calhoun Clemson, age 20, lieutenant in the Confederate Army, in Civil War uniform, ca. 1861. Fort Hill Collection, Clemson University.** *Right:* **Daguerreotype of Floride Elizabeth Clemson, age 15, ca. 1858. Fort Hill Collection, Clemson University.**

Back home from abroad at the end of October, he was, according to Anna, in a *"wonderfully good humour,"* although "how much longer it may last," she said to Floride, "there is no knowing." With Calhoun off to South Carolina to spend time in the company of his grandmother and great-uncle James and Floride in New York City visiting her friend Laura Leupp, Anna was getting anxious to have her daughter at home again. Floride's cooperation, she felt, would be necessary if the household was to live tranquilly as Clemson seemed most desirous to do. "Let it not be our fault," she continued, "if he again breaks out" in anger. Begging her daughter for both of their sakes to act patiently with her father upon her return home, she asked of Floride no more than she demanded of herself. "I make no reference to past events, & strive to avoid all subjects of discussion," Anna wrote.[29]

Glad that Calhoun, now in fine spirits, was going to do all in his power to please his Uncle James in South Carolina and hopeful that all might turn out well for her son in the year ahead, Anna still worried what action would result from the recent election of antislavery Republican President Abraham Lincoln. Sympathetic to southern sentiments that felt Lincoln's election pushed to extremity the reasons to secede, she acknowledged that South Carolina and all the South "could not perhaps draw back from their solemnly expressed determination without dishonour." Anarchy and confusion seemed inevitable since Anna had no faith in disunion as a *"remedy."* Nevertheless she gloried to think that her state preferred "death to dishonour" and trusted that all might turn out better than she could imagine possible. She did not want to be blamed if the Office of Superintendent of Agricultural Affairs that was *"all important"* to her husband was terminated. She said little about what Clemson should do, leaving him, she said to Floride, "free to act as he pleases."[30]

### The Civil War Years and Its Aftermath

Clemson resigned his government position on March 9, 1861, following the formation of the Confederate States of America in February. South Carolina had led the way by seceding in December under the political leadership of Anna's cousin, Governor Francis Pickens. The promise for the future that Anna had felt when her husband received his government appointment in January of 1860 was now overshadowed with peril as war erupted in April of 1861, dividing the country for four years and separating families, such as the Clemsons. Clemson and Calhoun left Maryland in June and ultimately joined the Confederate forces, although Anna and Floride did not go south until near the end of the fighting.[31]

Mother and daughter moved temporarily in June of 1864 to a comfortable five-room place outside of Beltsville, near Baltimore and on the railroad. Having rented out The Home and its land, they had the troublesome task of packing up personal possessions that they could not carry with them. Anna must have been particularly concerned about her husband's collection of paintings acquired during his diplomatic tenure in Brussels. Along with his own amateur works in oil, some of them copied from King Léopold's acquisitions in the Royal Art Galleries, were pieces attributed to such notables as Rubens, Hals, Robbe, and Bossuet. Anna carefully packed and sent them to relatives in Altoona, Pennsylvania, where they safely survived the war.[32]

Six months after their harrowing journey south in the summer of 1865, Anna and Floride were reunited first with Calhoun and then Clemson at Mrs. Calhoun's "Mi Casa" home in Pendleton. Mrs. Calhoun had sold Fort Hill to her son Andrew back in 1854, and his death shortly before the war's end in the spring of 1865 left Anna as the survivor of all of her siblings and Andrew's debt for the purchase of Fort Hill still owed to his mother. To Floride, her brother Calhoun who came back from the Civil War on foot looked "very handsome & well, considering his privations" in a Yankee prison on Johnson's Island in Lake Erie for twenty-one months. Her father, she thought, also looked "pretty well for a man well on to 60." Clemson, who was discharged from the Army of the Trans-Mississippi Department, had signed his Parole in very shaky script in Shreveport, Louisiana, on June 9. He arrived in Pendleton on July 1, riding unceremoniously in an open wagon on the morning of his fifty-eighth birthday. A little over two weeks after their reunion at Mi Casa, Floride found her father to be nicer and more pleasant than she had ever seen him. She described him as really affectionate and amiable and "a dear old fellow."[33]

The Clemsons during the war had experienced hardship and adversity, but although the crisis of conflict was now over, perhaps the most difficult days were yet to come. The war had staggered South Carolina's economy; the post-bellum result was widespread suffering throughout the state. The once prosperous Pendleton was now a place of misery and need, and those who had lived the good life there were reduced to varying stages of abject poverty. The white citizens of Pendleton and throughout South Carolina continued to fight for the right to control their community's affairs and restore its order and harmony. Both Anna and Thomas Clemson had a strong social sense that was sympathetic to the distress of those around them. She especially participated in every good endeavor and distinguished herself among her neighbors. In the role of community leader that she undertook alongside her husband, her service was a true credit to the memory of her father whose maxim (mentioned earlier), "The duties of life are greater than life itself," she had often imparted to her son as a young boy. Not surprisingly then, amid the community's prevailing poverty, the Clemsons contacted some of their wealthy northern friends and asked for money to provide relief for the pitiful plight of their neighbors. The friendships of the elite that had transcended the sectionalism between the North and South both before and during the war continued in its aftermath as well.

Acknowledging the receipt of $500 in April of 1866 from Washington banker William Wilson Corcoran, Anna not only thanked him for his noble gift, but also for the pleasure it gave her to bring comfort to so many. Clemson also appealed to Corcoran for financial aid in rebuilding the shattered economic life of South Carolina and was hopeful that the state would still live with help from many such supporters as he.[34]

Anna encouraged her husband's interest in the promotion of scientific education in the South by making their home a focus of life in Pendleton and providing hospitality to those who shared his vision of an animated system of agriculture as the main remedy to the distress which the region was suffering. However, her primary concern in the summer of 1866 was the constant care required by her mother, whose yearlong ordeal with cancer mercifully came to an end on July 25. According to the terms of Mrs. Calhoun's will, inclusive of codicil, read on August 6, Anna was her mother's principal heir. She was the first recipient of three-fourths of the bond and mortgage claim on Fort Hill owed to her mother by her brother Andrew's estate, along with most of the extant personal property and furniture, silver, and jewels. Given the right to dispose of the Fort Hill inheritance in "a last will and testament duly executed by her," Anna could do with the Calhoun home place as she saw fit. Floride, who acknowledged her grandmother's generous part on her own behalf, received outright a fourth part of the Fort Hill property title and was the designated successor to her mother's separate estate that would go to her brother Calhoun only if Floride died without either a will or an heir.[35]

Some four months before her death, Mrs. Calhoun had filed suit against her son Andrew's family for his estate's unpaid, almost $40,000 debt for Fort Hill. A few weeks before her death in July of 1866, the court decision for foreclosure against her daughter-in-law Margaret and grandchildren was issued. Andrew's heirs immediately appealed the verdict against them and began a legal battle for reversal that would last until early in 1872. Since Anna had inherited from her mother three-fourths of the securities in dispute, the case in question was of special significance for the Clemsons.[36]

### *A Shared Project in the Midst of Tragedies*

Despite the fact that Clemson was a plaintiff in the problematic litigation over the ownership of Fort Hill, he continued to make the case for scientific education in the South his priority. Well qualified for leadership in the Pendleton Farmers' Society with his expertise in agricultural affairs, he was elected in 1866 and again in 1868 as its president, a position formerly held by John C. Calhoun. As part of a committee he appealed by "Circular" for the founding of "an institution for educating our people in the sciences to the end that our agriculture be improved, our worn impoverished lands be recuperated, and the great natural resources of the South developed." Concluding that the location of such an institution would appear best adapted to upper South Carolina, "not excelled, if equalled" for health and climate by any other part of the continent, the "Circular" claimed the picturesque mountain region comparable to Switzerland. Unfortunately the distribution of this printed directive did not generate the widespread support needed for such an enterprise. Clemson became utterly discouraged by the seeming lack of interest in scientific education in the South and withdrew from the Pendleton Farmers' Society in 1870. He would later renew his efforts for a school with his wife's support.[37]

Anna was sympathetic to her husband's goal and understood the discouragement he felt at his inability to promote an interest in the scientific study of agriculture. At the same time she was pleased that Floride, who in 1869 had married Gideon Lee Jr. of New York, was happy in her new life at their "Leeside" home in Carmel. The birth of a baby girl, Floride Isabella, on May 15, 1870, not only brought much joy to the family, but also made more meaningful than ever the relationship Anna shared with her daughter. Writing from Leeside early in 1871, Floride assured her mother that the baby, who had been ill and weak and without any liveliness, was trying to play, calling her father, sitting up feebly, and even giving faint smiles. In a telling reference to Clemson's apparent antagonism toward his daughter, Floride wrote, "As to father's anger with me, it is probably not real....I am sorry for it, but know nothing I could do would help it. I know if the chance comes you'll make the best of it." Very likely Clemson's frustration at the failure to interest others in the scientific study of agriculture not only aroused his ire toward the South, but affected his attitude toward Floride as well. The effect of this important issue on Clemson also must have had an impact on Anna.[38]

Unfortunately, the untimely death of twenty-eight-year-old Floride Clemson Lee (probably from tuberculosis peritonitis) on July 23, 1871, left a grief-stricken family who mourned her loss and a child who would never know her mother. Stunned by the demise of their daughter, the Clemsons were even further devastated by the sudden death of their thirty-year-old son Calhoun, who was killed instantly in a train wreck only seventeen days later on August 10. Referring to the tragic accident in a note of sympathy, friend Henry Gourdin said simply, "Humanity cannot comprehend the justice of such terrible calamities."[39]

Anna, now alone beside her husband, faced a man grown old and bitter. Disheartened by his earlier failed efforts to establish an agricultural school for South Carolina and now despondent at the death of his children, Clemson depended upon his wife to sustain his sagging spirits. His discouragement about the school he had envisioned was overshadowed by the unnatural tragedy they had endured. However, his dream of an agricultural and mechanical college for South Carolina now became increasingly important to Anna who began to think of it as a merited monument to her father and their son. Despite the legal controversy that prevailed with her brother Andrew's family over her inheritance of the property from her mother's estate, she knew that the land needed for such an institution would be hers when the matter was settled and she took possession of Fort Hill. Making her last will and testament within two months after her son's death, Anna left ownership of all present and future property in her own estate, as well as the right to give away said inheritance, to her "beloved husband." Should she survive him or should he as the survivor die intestate, her "granddaughter, Isabella Lee," would become her heir.[40]

Litigation involving Anna and Clemson, acting as her trustee, in connection with her brother Andrew's family over the estate of Floride Calhoun, was settled by an auction of the Fort Hill property in nearby Walhalla on January 21, 1872. Mrs. Calhoun's executor, lawyer Edward Noble, secured Fort Hill for Anna by his bid on the property with the mortgage willed to her as its principal recipient. Her deceased daughter Floride's fourth part of the Fort Hill deed had passed to her own child, Anna's granddaughter. Except for insignificant court costs, no money was involved as Anna inherited her three-fourths share of the estate and Floride Isabella Lee, her mother's one-fourth. The following year Anna and Gideon Lee, as his daughter's guardian, officially apportioned the property with Anna receiving 814 acres, including the Fort Hill home where she and her husband were already living, and young Floride 288 acres. With Clemson as the heir to Anna's real property and estate, the opportunity for him to establish the agricultural college that he had long desired was thus made possible by the bequest of his wife, signed and sealed on September 29, 1871.[41]

The long spell of cold and disagreeable weather that followed the settlement of Mrs. Calhoun's estate in January of 1872 was, as Anna reported to her Uncle James at his Millwood plantation, "very hard on Mr Clemson's health & spirits—confining him to the house, & preventing persons coming in to distract his mind." Despite Clemson's continuing very indifferent disposition and her own discomfort with neuralgia, she was looking forward to a visit from her son-in-law who planned to escort her and her husband back to his home in New York. In the midst of preparations to move from Mi Casa to Fort Hill, the stay at Leeside was a happy interlude after a wearisome, four-day journey by land from Pendleton to Carmel. Clemson's health was better and his spirits somewhat improved at first. However, he seemed to Anna "gradually falling back into the old hopeless state," and she greatly feared he would never be better. Their "dear little grandchild," she found "very bright & interesting," "very affectionate," and "wonderfully little spoilt, *considering*."[42]

### Finally to Fort Hill

The Clemsons returned to Mi Casa after more than two weeks in the North and were able to move to Fort Hill at the end of June 1872. They found the farm in much disorder after several years of tenant occupancy, with the exception of the main house. In Anna's view, the "utter neglect, & wanton mutilation of the place" by her brother Andrew's family was a disgrace. Clemson's rift with Anna's brother Andrew over money had ultimately ruined her relationship with him and his family over the years. Loyalty to her husband superseded all else for this essentially good sister who had always taken her sibling role seriously. Once again a planter, Clemson, like others in the South during the post-bellum period, was forced to enter into contractual relationships with free black laborers in an attempt to find replacements for their former slaves. However, his central concern, like Anna's, was the promotion of interest in the school they both wanted to establish.[43]

On August 9, 1874, Anna personally selected a committee to issue a "Circular" calling for statewide support of a plan to build on land at Fort Hill a scientific agricultural institution whose existence would commemorate the career of her father. Prepared by William Henry Trescot, one of the leading scholars of the state, the "Circular," as cited in the 1937 Clemson biography by Alester G. Holmes and George R. Sherrill, was entitled "Scientific Education" and noted the Calhoun legacy at Fort Hill and the statesman's role in South Carolina history. "No nobler monument could be raised to the great Carolinian," asserted the Circular, "than such an institution on the spot where the tradition of his great and beautiful life would be most strongly felt." Four years later in a letter to his Washington friend, W. W. Corcoran, Clemson himself would ask for help with the school project that he and Anna, lacking funds, had been unsuccessfully promoting.[44]

Anna complained little about her health problems. She was much overweight and suffered from neuralgia and heart trouble that could take her life suddenly, as it had that of her brother Andrew. On September 22, 1875, while Clemson was away from home, he received word from a messenger that his wife was quite sick. Hurrying home in his buggy, he met a servant just outside the inner gate of the yard who told him respectfully, in answer to his inquiry about her condition, that she was dead. Horrified at the news, he rose up and gave his horse a tremendous cut. As the animal dashed through the gate, the wheels of the buggy hit the gate post so that Clemson was pitched some distance from the vehicle, causing some to think for a time that he, too, was dead.[45]

At age fifty-eight Anna had succumbed to a heart attack as she had predicted she would. Family and acquaintances of the Clemsons were formally invited to attend afternoon funeral services for her at St. Paul's Church in Pendleton on September 24, the same day that the *News and Courier* in Charleston carried the announcement of her death, under the heading *Death of Mrs. Clemson*:

> Mrs. Clemson, the last surviving child of the Hon. John C. Calhoun, died at Fort Hill, Pendleton on Wednesday evening at 5 o'clock. The tidings of her death, which will be universally regretted, carry the people of South Carolina back, in thought, to the time when her illustrious father guided the destinies of

the State, and remind them how often, in the trying days since the war, we have vainly longed for a single hour of that 'dead Dundee.'[46]

Apparently the month before Anna's death, close family friend James Rion had visited Fort Hill, and it was then that Anna gave him a copy of the dream, recorded in her album, in which a vision of her father had appeared to her fifteen years earlier. Presumably she expected Rion to share with Clemson her father's message to her and her husband, which Rion later did. Thinking that the end could possibly be near for her, as it proved to be, and aware of what difficult days would lie ahead for Clemson, she obviously wanted him, in the words of her father, "to continue to strive to know & do the right." With concern for his welfare in light of all that they had lost and perhaps fearful of what he might do when left alone, she left out from Rion's copy of the dream the direction from her father to tell Clemson that he had "not fulfilled the trust" with which he had given him his daughter. Thomas Clemson would never know how much he had failed his "very much beloved dear Anna." Cursed with chronic depression throughout their marriage, he could neither control his belligerent behavior nor convey convincingly the "love and devoted affection" he had professed for her on the eve of their marriage.[47]

Three months after Anna's death, Clemson sent a copy of his wife's vision of her father to spiritualist Dr. John J. F. Gray for an explanation of its meaning. The two men had met a few years earlier when Clemson, while visiting at his son-in-law's in Carmel, had attended séances in New York City. Evidently interested in spiritualism, he had, according to Anna, enjoyed "wonderful experiences" communicating with the spirit world. Glad to hear from Clemson personally and to possess a copy of the vision, Dr. Gray replied with absolute certainty that "Mr. Calhoun appeared to & spoke with his daughter, as related by her." The powerful phenomenon of Calhoun's presence was apparently more meaningful to Dr. Gray and presumably to Clemson as well than the dutiful message of Calhoun's spirit to "continue to strive to know & do the right."[48] However, Thomas Clemson's later founding of the school Anna wanted to commemorate the illustrious career of her father, John C. Calhoun, witnessed her husband's commitment to the words she had hoped he would hear.

### Notes

1.  Jas. H. Rion to Thos. G. Clemson, 25 September 1875, in Clemson Papers, Special Collections, Clemson University Libraries, Clemson, SC (hereafter cited as SCCUL).
2.  Ernest McPherson Lander Jr., *The Calhoun Family and Thomas Green Clemson: The Decline of a Southern Patriarchy* (Columbia: University of South Carolina Press, 1983), 242.
3.  Glenna Matthews, *"Just A Housewife": The Rise and Fall of Domesticity in America* (New York: Oxford University Press, 1987), 9–10. Anna to Maria Simkins, 2 August 1838, in Julia Wright

Sublette, "The Letters of Anna Calhoun Clemson, 1833–1873," vol. 1 (Ph.D. dissertation, Florida State University, 1993), 188 (hereafter cited as Sublette); Lander, *Calhoun Family and Thomas Green Clemson*, 3. TGC to Anna Calhoun, 5 August 1838, in Clemson Papers, SCCUL.

4.  Lander, *Calhoun Family and Thomas Green Clemson*, 3. "Anna Maria Calhoun's Album," 1 October 1838, in Clemson Papers, SCCUL. Anna Calhoun to Maria Simkins, 21 May 1838; Anna Calhoun to Patrick Calhoun, 21 May 1838; Anna Calhoun to Patrick Calhoun, 30 May 1838; Anna Calhoun to Maria Simkins, 22 July 1838, in Sublette, vol. 1, 166–168, 171–172, 175n1, 181, 181n1–182, 182n2.

5.  TGC to Anna Calhoun, 5 August 1838; TGC to Anna Calhoun, 19 August 1838; TGC to Anna Calhoun, 20 August 1838, in Clemson Papers, SCCUL. [Signature faded] to Maria Simkins, 22 July 1838, in Sublette, vol. 1, 182n2.

6.  Clyde N. Wilson, ed., *The Papers of John C. Calhoun*, vol. 14 (Columbia: University of South Carolina Press, 1981), xv–xvi. Mary Bates (wedding guest) to Anna C. Clemson, 19 April 1850, in Calhoun Papers, SCCUL. Richard W. Simpson, *History of Old Pendleton District* (Anderson, SC: Oulla Printing & Binding Company, 1913), 18. Compiled by Edwin H. Vedder, *Records of St. Paul's Episcopal Church of Pendleton, South Carolina* (Greenville, SC: A Press, Inc., 1982), 36. *The Pendleton Messenger,* 16 November 1838.

7.  Matthews, *"Just A Housewife": The Rise and Fall of Domesticity in America*, 9–10. Catherine Clinton, *The Plantation Mistress: Woman's World in the Old South* (New York: Pantheon Books, 1982), 37, 40. Anna Clemson to Maria Simkins, 2 August 1838, in Sublette, vol.1, 188.

8.  Anna Clemson to John C. Calhoun, 1 June 1844; Anna Clemson to John C. Calhoun, 24 January 1846; Anna Clemson to John C. Calhoun, 20 April 1846; Anna Clemson to John C. Calhoun, 27 September 1846, in Sublette, vol. 1, 410–411, 415. Lander, *Calhoun Family and Thomas Green Clemson*, 138–139, 141–142.

9.  Anna C. Clemson to Patrick Calhoun, 1 February 1850, in Sublette, vols. 1–2, 464–465, 476, 476n1.

10. Patti Connor-Greene, Alumni Professor of Psychology, Clemson University, telephone conversation, 21 May 2003; *Diagnostic and Statistical Manual of Mental Disorders,* Fourth Edition (Washington, DC: American Psychiatric Association, 2000), 376–379; John M. Davis, M.D., Ph.D., and James W. Maas, M.D., eds, *The Affective Disorders* (Washington, DC: American Psychiatric Press, Inc., 1983), 236, 238, 406; Public Document, National Institutes of Health, *Depression: Effective Treatments Are Available* (Rockville, MD: NIH Publication No. 96–3590, U.S. Department of Health & Human Services, 1996); Rich Wemhoff, Ph.D., ed., *Anxiety & Depression: The Best Resources To Help You Cope* (Seattle, WA: Resource Pathways, 1999), 2, 30. Depression is often "misunderstood" by both those sufferers and "their loved ones who share the pain."

11. Anna C. Clemson to Floride Clemson, 14 September 1856; Anna C. Clemson to Floride Clemson, 21 September 1856, in Sublette, vol. 2, 494, 497, 500.

12. Anna C. Clemson to Floride Clemson, 16 November 1856; Anna C. Clemson to Floride Clemson, 20 September 1857, in Ibid., 531, 601.

13. Anna C. Clemson to Floride Clemson, 9 November 1856; Anna C. Clemson to Floride Clemson, 21 December 1856; Anna C. Clemson to Floride Clemson, 28 December 1856, in Ibid., 524–525, 537, 542.

14. Anna C. Clemson to Floride Clemson, 4 January 1857; Anna C. Clemson to Floride Clemson, 5 April 1857, in Ibid., 545, 576, 576n1–578.

15. Anna C. Clemson to Floride Clemson, 17 May 1857; Anna C. Clemson to Floride Clemson, 14 June 1857, in Ibid., 586, 596.

16. Anna C. Clemson to Floride Clemson, 12 September 1857; Anna C. Clemson to Floride Clemson, 20 September 1857, in Ibid., 598, 600. Davis and Maas, eds., *The Affective Disorders*, 236.

17. Anna C. Clemson to Floride Clemson, 20 September 1857; Anna C. Clemson to Floride Clemson, 27 September 1857, in Sublette, vol. 2, 600, 604, 606.

18. Anna C. Clemson to Floride Clemson, 31 May 1857; Anna C. Clemson to Floride Clemson, 19 October 1857; Anna C. Clemson to Floride Clemson, 1 November 1857, in Ibid., 592, 617, 621–622. Lander, *Calhoun Family and Thomas Green Clemson*, 179. Floride Calhoun

to Anna Clemson, 12 August 1859, in Clemson Papers, SCCUL. *Diagnostic and Statistical Manual of Mental Disorders*, 373, 377.

19. Laura Leupp to Anna C. Clemson, 6 October 1859; Elias Baker to TGC, 24 October 1859, in Clemson Papers, SCCUL. Lander, *Calhoun Family and Thomas Green Clemson*, 183.

20. "Anna Maria Calhoun (Clemson's) Album," in Clemson Papers, SCCUL.

21. TGC to Miss Anna Calhoun, 19 August 1838, in Ibid. Kay Redfield Jamison, *Touched With Fire: Manic-Depressive Illness and the Artistic Temperament* (New York: Simon & Schuster, 1993), 18, 25.

22. Sister Sue to Anna Clemson, 24 October 1859; Wm. F. Clemson to Floride Clemson, 13 November 1859, in Clemson Papers, SCCUL.

23. Lander, *Calhoun Family and Thomas Green Clemson*, 184. Anna C. Clemson to Floride Clemson, 13 November 1859; Anna C. Clemson to Floride Clemson, 11 December 1859, in Sublette, vol. 2, 730, 743.

24. Anna C. Clemson to Floride Clemson, 8 January 1860; Anna C. Clemson to Floride Clemson, 12 February 1860, in Ibid., 754, 766.

25. Anna C. Clemson to Floride Clemson, 26 February 1860; Anna C. Clemson to Floride Clemson, 8 March 1860, in Ibid., 769–772, 772nn2–3.

26. "Anna Maria Calhoun (Clemson's) Album," in Clemson Papers, SCCUL.

27. The Reverend Bob Haden, Individual Analysis of "Anna C. Clemson's Vision Of Her Father, John C. Calhoun, Ten Years After His Death." Bob Haden, director of the Haden Institute in Charlotte, NC, is a Jungian pastoral counselor, Episcopal priest, and diplomate of the American Psychotherapy Association. His master's thesis was entitled *The Use of Dreams in Spiritual Direction*, and he studied at the C. G. Jung Institute in Switzerland. Ann Russell, "Her Father's Daughter, Anna Calhoun Clemson," *Carologue* (Charleston, SC: South Carolina Historical Society, Autumn, 1996), 14, 23. Anna to Maria Simkins, 2 August 1838, in Sublette, vol. 1, 188. James Rion's August 1875 copy of Anna C. Clemson's "Vision," March 1860, Calhoun Papers, The South Caroliniana Library, University of South Carolina.

28. Anna C. Clemson to Floride Clemson, 18 March 1860, in Sublette, vol. 2, 774. *Diagnostic and Statistical Manual of Mental Disorders*, 380–381.

29. Lander, *Calhoun Family and Thomas Green Clemson*, 196, 198. Anna C. Clemson to Floride Clemson, 4 November 1860; Anna C. Clemson to Floride Clemson, 11 November 1860, in Sublette, vol. 2, 794–795, 798–799.

30. Anna C. Clemson to Floride Clemson, 11 November 1860, in Ibid., 799–800.

31. Ann Russell, "'Holding Court' at a Yankee Prison: Anna Calhoun Clemson Behind Enemy Lines," *Carologue* (Charleston, SC: South Carolina Historical Society, Spring 1990), 4.

32. Compiled by Mrs. P. H. Mell, "The Clemson Collection of Paintings Donated To Clemson Agricultural College," Clemson Papers, SCCUL. Labels of identification that Anna wrote and pasted on the back of each picture, along with a manuscript inventory of personal property made after returning to the United States from abroad, would later form the basis of a catalog for "The Clemson Collection of Paintings Donated To Clemson Agricultural College." Alester G. Holmes and George R. Sherrill, *Thomas Green Clemson: His Life and Work* (Richmond, VA: Garrett & Massie, 1937), 35.

33. Russell, "Anna Calhoun Clemson and the Origins of Clemson University," *The United Daughters Of The Confederacy Magazine* (Richmond, VA: United Daughters of the Confederacy, June 1990), 13. Charles M. McGee Jr. and Ernest McPherson Lander Jr., eds., *A Rebel Came Home: The Diary and Letters of Floride Clemson 1863–1866*, Revised Edition (Columbia, SC: University of South Carolina Press, 1989), 88–89, 89n41, 90–91. Parole of Thomas G. Clemson issued by United States government, 9 June 1865, in Clemson Papers, SCCUL.

34. Russell, "Anna Calhoun Clemson and the Origins of Clemson University," *The United Daughters Of The Confederacy Magazine*, 13–14. Walter Edgar, *South Carolina: A History* (Columbia, SC: University of South Carolina Press, 1998), 377, 396. Holmes and Sherrill, *Thomas Green Clemson*, 27–29, 145. Anna C. Clemson to William Wilson Corcoran, 28 April 1866, in Sublette, vol. 2, 865, 865n2.

35. Holmes and Sherrill, *Thomas Green Clemson*, 28, 143, 145. D. W. Lee to TGC, 29 January 1867, in Clemson Papers, SCCUL. Anna C. Clemson to William Wilson Corcoran, 28 April 1866, in Sublette, vol. 2, 865–866. McGee and Lander, eds., *A Rebel Came Home*, 109.

"Digest of Court Opinions," in *The Clemson Agricultural College Bulletin*, vol. 21, no.1 (Post Office, Clemson College, SC: The Clemson Agricultural College of South Carolina, January 1925), 22–25.

36. Lander, *Calhoun Family and Thomas Green Clemson*, 142–143, 233, 239. In 1854 Mrs. Calhoun and her daughter Cornelia had agreed to the sale of Fort Hill to Andrew for the sum of $49,000, inclusive of fifty slaves and supplies along with the house and land with living quarters in the home reserved for both mother and daughter. Unfortunately for Andrew's finances, the contract that he had negotiated for the sale of his plantation in Alabama was rescinded by the prospective buyer after he had already approached his mother about selling her home. The resulting settlement between the two men left Andrew with the ownership of his Alabama property at the same time that he had entered into the agreement with his mother and Cornelia to buy Fort Hill. Despite a large debt and the management of two plantations, he moved his family back to South Carolina and left an overseer in charge of his land in Alabama.

37. In March of 1866 Clemson as administrator for his late sister-in-law Cornelia had joined with his mother-in-law Mrs. Calhoun to bring suit against her son Andrew's family for the money owed on the Fort Hill debt. With Mrs. Calhoun's death in July, Clemson was the plaintiff in the matter along with Edward Noble as Mrs. Calhoun's executor. Lander, *Calhoun Family and Thomas Green Clemson*, 233. Holmes and Sherrill, *Thomas Green Clemson*, 145. The first president of the Pendleton Farmers' Society founded in 1815 was Col. Thomas Pinckney, son of former Governor Thomas Pinckney and grandson of Eliza Lucas Pinckney, "who had long ago introduced indigo culture into South Carolina." Compiled by Mary Stevenson, *The Diary of Clarissa Adger Bowen, Ashtabula Plantation, 1865, and...The Pendleton-Clemson Area, South Carolina, 1776-1889* (Pendleton, SC: Research and Publication Committee Foundation, 1973), 105. "Circular," Pendleton Farmers' Society, 24 November 1866; Minutes of the Pendleton Farmers' Society, 8 October 1868, in Clemson Papers, SCCUL. Ernest McPherson Lander Jr., "The Founder, Thomas Green Clemson, 1807–1888," in *Tradition: A History of the Presidency of Clemson University*, Second Edition, Donald M. McKale and Jerome V. Reel Jr., eds. (Macon, GA: Mercer University Press, 1998), 14–15. Russell, "Anna Calhoun Clemson and the Origins of Clemson University," *The United Daughters Of The Confederacy Magazine*, 14.

38. Book of Common Prayer and the Calhoun Family Bible, at the Fort Hill historic house museum at Clemson University. Anna C. Clemson to James Edward Calhoun, 3 October 1869, in Sublette, vol. 2, 881. Lander, *Calhoun Family and Thomas Green Clemson*, 237. Floride C. Lee to Anna C. Clemson, 4 February 1871, in Clemson Papers, SCCUL. Lander, "The Founder, Thomas Green Clemson, 1807–1888," in *Tradition*, eds., McKale and Reel, 14–15.

39. Ernest McPherson Lander Jr., *The Life And Times Of Ella Lorton, A Pendleton SC Confederate* (Clemson, SC: Clemson Printers, 1996), 111. Russell, "Anna Calhoun Clemson and the Origins of Clemson University," *The United Daughters Of The Confederacy Magazine*, 15. H. Gourdin to TGC, 12 August 1871, in Clemson Papers, SCCUL. Lander, *Calhoun Family and Thomas Green Clemson*, 152.

40. Russell, "Anna Calhoun Clemson and the Origins of Clemson University," *The United Daughters Of The Confederacy Magazine*, 15. *United States Circuit Court District of South Carolina, Isabella Lee vs. Richard W. Simpson*, 11, in Richard W. Simpson Papers, Special Collections, Clemson University. The State of South Carolina, "Will of Anna C. Clemson," 29 September 1871, Probate Court Records of Oconee County, Walhalla, South Carolina.

41. Lander, *Calhoun Family and Thomas Green Clemson*, 239. "Will of Anna C. Clemson." "Digest of Court Opinions," in *The Clemson Agricultural College Bulletin*, vol. 21, no.1, 14.

42. Anna C. Clemson to James Edward Calhoun, 8 February 1872; Anna C. Clemson to James Edward Calhoun, 24 March 1872; Anna C. Clemson to James Edward Calhoun, 26 May 1872; Anna C. Clemson to James Edward Calhoun, 23 June 1872, in Sublette, vol. 2, 882, 884–886, 888. Lander, *Calhoun Family and Thomas Green Clemson*, 241. Russell, "Anna Calhoun Clemson and the Origins of Clemson University," *The United Daughters Of The Confederacy Magazine*, 15.

43. Lander, *Calhoun Family and Thomas Green Clemson*, 240. Anna C. Clemson to James Edward Calhoun, 24 February 1867, in Sublette, vol. 2, 868. At the time of Clemson's marriage to Anna, he had entered into a fateful business venture with her father and his future brother-

in-law Andrew. Clemson thought that he was ultimately cheated by Andrew, and Anna felt keenly his resentment of her brother. James L. Roark, *Masters Without Slaves: Southern Planters in the Civil War and Reconstruction* (New York: W. W. Norton, 1977), 163. Labor Agreement, Jan.1874–75, State of South Carolina, County of Oconee, "Articles of Agreement between Thos. G. Clemson Trustee on the one part and the undersigned freedman, and women on the other part," Clemson Papers, SCCUL. Holmes and Sherrill, *Thomas Green Clemson*, 150.

44. Ibid., 150–153. Russell, "Anna Calhoun Clemson and the Origins of Clemson University," *The United Daughters Of The Confederacy Magazine*, 15.

45. Lander, *Calhoun Family and Thomas Green Clemson*, 241–242. R. W. Simpson to W. M. Riggs, 5 November 1911, in Riggs Papers, Special Collections, Clemson University.

46. Russell, "Anna Calhoun Clemson and the Origins of Clemson University," *The United Daughters Of The Confederacy Magazine*, 15. Handwritten invitation: "The friends and acquaintances of Mr. and Mrs. Thomas G. Clemson are invited to attend the funeral services of the latter at St. Paul's Church today at 3 o'clock P. M. Sept 24th 1875," Clemson Papers, SCCUL. *News and Courier*, 24 September 1875.

47. TGC to Anna Calhoun, 19 August 1838; TGC to Anna Calhoun, 20 August 1838; "Anna Maria Calhoun (Clemson's) Album"; Jas. H. Rion to TGC, 25 September 1875, in Clemson Papers, SCCUL. James Rion's August 1875 copy of Anna C. Clemson's "Vision," March 1860, Calhoun Papers, University of South Carolina.

48. Ibid. Anna C. Clemson to James Edward Calhoun, 23 June 1872, in Sublette, vol. 2, 889. Dr. John J. F. Gray to TGC, 28 December 1875, in Clemson Papers, SCCUL.

# Chapter 4

# THE EUROPEAN YEARS:
## THOMAS GREEN CLEMSON AS STUDENT, ACTIVIST, AND DIPLOMAT

## *James P. Cross and Sabine Godts-Péters*

**Portrait of Thomas Green Clemson painted in Belgium. Family tradition attributes the work to Eugene DeBlock, although its style more closely resembles that of Joseph Eeckhout. Oil on canvas. Fort Hill Collection, Clemson University. Gift of Mr. and Mrs. Creighton Lee Calhoun Jr.**

A man of eclectic interests with an active intellect, Thomas Green Clemson was a Renaissance man in his own right. In 1826, pushed by his interest in chemistry and the desire for better scientific training than the United States could offer at the time, Thomas Clemson went to Europe. His experiences over the next six years had a transforming influence on his life. He established residence in Paris on the Left Bank and became active in student life. He attended classes offered by professors at the University of Paris [*La Sorbonne*] and the Royal College of France [*Le Collège royal de France*], worked in chemical laboratories, and audited a four-year course of study at the School of Mines [*L'Ecole des mines*]—one of the world's leading schools for mining engineers and managers at the time. Subsequently, he passed a public examination for certification as a qualified assayer by the Royal Mint of Paris [*La Monnaie royale de Paris*]—the French equivalent of the U.S. Mint located in Philadelphia. Moreover, Clemson was connected in Paris to liberal, intellectual, and social circles and actively participated in the Paris revolt in July 1830 that led to the overthrow of King Charles X.

Although disillusioned with the aftermath of the 1830 revolt, Thomas Clemson clearly enjoyed his time in Europe and wanted to return. In 1844, with the help of his father-in-law, John C. Calhoun, who was the newly appointed secretary of state, Clemson was able to return as the highest ranking U.S. diplomat to the Kingdom of Belgium where he stayed for an unprecedented six years. Throughout this period, he was held in high regard by King Léopold I and the Belgians. Clemson's best-known diplomatic achievement was his role in the negotiation of the first treaty of commerce and navigation between Belgium and the United States—a treaty which opened the door to the dramatic expansion of trade between Belgium and the United States and, more broadly, between continental Europe and the United States. Clemson also played a role in other issues. These included settling the indemnities issues for the U.S. property loss in Antwerp during the 1830 bombing of the port by the Dutch; negotiating for an extradition and postal treaty; and urging an upgrade of the senior U.S. diplomatic rank in Belgium from chargé d'affaires to minister. After returning to the United States in 1851, he kept alive his Belgian links. In 1860 Clemson was awarded the Order of Léopold medal by King Léopold I in appreciation for his service to Belgium.

## *A Student in Paris*

As discussed in Chapter 2, Thomas Clemson, at the age of nineteen, arrived in Europe sometime during the summer of 1826. By his own account he attended lectures at the Sorbonne[1] and the Royal College of France[2] by the renowned chemists and physicists Louis Jacques Thénard,[3] Joseph Louis Gay-Lussac,[4] and Pierre-Louis Dulong.[5] These early contacts with leading scientists appeared to be extremely important in guiding young Clemson. For example, Gay-Lussac was the chair of physics at the Sorbonne. In 1829 he was named the chief assayer of the Office of Quality Control at the Royal Mint of Paris.[6] A French Canadian classmate confirmed how fortunate he and Clemson were to be exposed to and enjoy the friendship of many of those in the Paris scientific inner circle, including Jean-Baptiste Elie de Beaumont,[7] Pierre-Jean Robiquet,[8] André Guenyveau,[9] Ours

Dufrénoy,[10] Pierre Berthier,[11] Joseph Louis Gay-Lussac, Louis Jacques Thénard,[12] and others. Most of these eminent geologists, engineers, chemists, and physicists had common links to the Polytechnic School [*L'Ecole polytechnique*][13] that trained engineers; the School of Mines that trained mining engineers and managers; the Sorbonne that trained scientists; and the Royal Mint of Paris.

The lectures at the Sorbonne, along with his work in the chemical laboratories of Gaultier de Clowbry and André Laugier,[14] led to Clemson's acceptance in 1828 to the School of Mines as an auditor—a special status for foreign students. It was indeed a requirement for acceptance to the school for students to have an adequate background, specifically in chemistry and physics.[15]

The School of Mines had been officially created by the Council of State of King Louis XVI in 1783. It was the first mining school in France and the eighth in Europe after Sverdlosk, Joachimsthal, Clausthal, Berlin, Freiberg, Chemnitz, and Madrid.[16] Mining in France had largely been neglected throughout the Middle Ages, but the dawning of the Industrial Revolution in Europe and the growing need for minerals, coal, and iron brought new attention to the industry. In 1744 a law was passed requiring state authorization to exploit resources underground, and beginning in 1766 mining concessions were taxed in an effort to raise funds for a future school of mines. Until the creation of the School of Mines, France had to rely on mining engineers and managers primarily from central Europe. Led by the chemist and mineralogist Balthasard-Georges Sage, it was argued that, in order to stimulate the mining industry and transform mining from an art to a science in France, a mining school had to be created, specifically to train mining engineers, scientists, and managers.

Because of the dependence of the French Mint on minerals and mining, it was decided to locate the School of Mines at the Mint in L'Hôtel de la Monnaie under the direction of Sage.[17] By the time Clemson attended the school, it had moved to the Hôtel Vendôme, located on rue d'Enfer, and had grown from a small three-year program for a handful of students to a prestigious four-year program attracting both French and foreign students. A reform of the school in 1816 allowed qualified foreign students with authorization from their embassies to attend classes as auditors.[18]

According to records of the School of Mines, Thomas Green Clemson was enrolled as an auditor from 1828 to 1832.[19] The school records for auditors do not list the courses he took, but based on a letter from his classmate Lefte Neal and Clemson's successful examination at the Mint, it seems that he was a serious student. In addition it should be noted that Pierre Berthier was chair of docimacy at the School of Mines and Elie de Beaumont was a joint chair for geology.[20] According to Neal it was Berthier who also gave Clemson a certificate and held him in very high regard.

At the School of Mines, Clemson would have attended classes from November 15 to April 15. Classes were held daily during the week from 8:00 a.m. to 4:00 p.m., and exams took place during the last half of April. The course of study, which was designed to develop theoretical and practical knowledge, included mineralogy, geology, docimacy, mining, mining industry and factory management, metallurgy, design, German, and English.[21] It seems that Clemson was especially interested in chemistry, docimacy, and geology and excelled in those areas. This would also explain his desire to receive formal certification as an assayer from the Royal Mint in 1831.[22]

There is little formal record of his day-to-day life in Paris, but, by piecing together references in letters, we can conclude that, in addition to his formal studies, Clemson was active in Parisian social circles, attending formal receptions such as that for General (Marquis de) Lafayette and other dignitaries.[23] Clemson most likely had good contacts at the U.S. Embassy since they authorized his attendance at the School of Mines. Fluent in French and outgoing, he seemed to be very popular.

### A Political Activist in the Glorious Three Days of July 1830

Thomas Clemson was a student in Paris at an important time in European history. The French Revolution had sparked a desire for liberal reform and independence from despotic rule. Despite the restoration of the crown in France in 1815 after Napoleon's defeat, the French became discontent with the increasingly authoritarian rule of the Bourbon monarchy of Charles X. In July 1830, Charles's attempt to revoke the constitutional limitations on his power and that of his ministers met with revolt. For three days, beginning on July 28, 1830, Parisians—led by the students of the Polytechnic School [L'Ecole Polytechnique], veterans of the Napoleonic wars, and the National Guard—attacked City Hall [L'Hôtel de Ville] to reclaim the Republic. King Charles's forces could not stop the 10,000 insurgents, and the regime was overthrown. In August 1830, revolts followed in Brussels, leading to Belgian independence in 1831, thirteen years before Clemson would arrive at the Belgium capital as a U.S. diplomat.

Thomas Clemson was an active participant in the "Glorious Three Days" of July 1830 in Paris. Lefte Neal, in his letter to Clemson pleading with him to attend the first anniversary celebration of their victory, recalled, "you, one of the combatants of our three great days; you whom I can still see covered with sweat, returning from the firing line and taking, in order to return there, new strength at the wine shop on the corner of Mazarine and Guénégaut [sic][24] streets at the foot of the barricade."[25] At the time of the revolt Clemson lived very close to the fighting on 93 Mazarine Street on the Left Bank. Clemson and his classmates at the School of Mines, the majority of whom were graduates of the Polytechnic School, must have joined their younger colleagues from the Polytechnic in the revolt. We can imagine the scene as depicted in paintings such as Eugene Delacroix's *Liberty Leading the People* [*La liberté guidant le peuple 28 juillet 1830*] and Hippolyte Lecompte's *The Battle of the Rue de Rohan on July 29, 1830* [*Combat de la rue de Rohan le 29 juillet 1830*]. As both paintings suggest, Clemson, an imposing figure at 6'6" and affectionately nicknamed "the giraffe" by his friends, would have been a welcomed addition to the fight.

***Liberty Leading the People, July 28, 1830* by Eugene Delacroix. Oil on canvas. Original in the Louvre, Paris. Réunion des Musées Nationaux/Art Resource, N.Y.**

The students of the Polytechnic School were in strong opposition to the regime, and fifty of them joined the insurgents to lead the attack. One of the students, Vaneau, was shot and died in the fight.[26] It is clear that the students, including Clemson, were adamantly in favor of a regime change. Nevertheless, although King Charles X was overthrown, a constitutional monarchy was preserved under the Duke of Orleans who became King Louis Philippe I. In his graduate thesis, Nickels R. Beacham reported that Clemson received the French Legion of Honor for participating in the revolt. There is no record of this in the archives of the French Legion, but some of them burned in 1870.[27]

Reflecting on the events of 1830 in a dispatch to Washington, D.C., in 1848, Clemson remained clearly disappointed by the regime of Louis Philippe, noting that during the fighting of July 1830 the Duke of Orleans had remained hidden, only to emerge at the end of the battle to be "imposed upon France [as King Louis Philippe I] by a few people." Clemson described the king as separating himself from his people and embarking on a course of conduct that would ultimately lead to his exile in 1848.[28] This may explain Clemson's refusal to participate in the one-year anniversary celebration in July 1831 and why there is no reference in his papers to the French Legion of Honor, which only Beacham mentioned without giving his sources. Whatever the case, this stimulating political and scientific environment in Paris had an enormous influence on the formation of young Clemson and laid the foundation for his future activity in science and diplomacy.

### Interim Years 1833–1844

Clemson went back to the United States for the summer of 1831 and then returned to Paris to complete his studies later that fall. During this period, there are also indications that he worked on a mine surveying project in Germany[29] and that, as Jerome Reel discusses in Chapter Two, he also made several European tours with family members and friends. Although there is no record of the exact date of his return to the United States, by mid-1833 he was back in Philadelphia working as a mining engineer. Clemson put his education to work and became active in the Geological Society of Pennsylvania, coal exploration in Cuba, and gold mining in Georgia; he even invested in mining activities in Missouri and South America.[30] Clemson's activities brought him to Washington, D.C., where, in June 1838, he met and fell in love with Anna Maria Calhoun, the daughter of John C. Calhoun. Six months later, they married at the Calhouns' home in South Carolina. In 1840 the Clemsons moved from Philadelphia to South Carolina. Anna was in poor health, and John C. Calhoun invited Clemson to manage the declining Fort Hill plantation. Here Clemson's activity shifted from mining to agriculture. He successfully turned the plantation around and in 1843 purchased one of his own for $24,000.[31] In the meantime, Anna had regained her health at Fort Hill, and the Clemsons had two children there in 1841 and 1842.

### The Appointment as Chargé d'affaires

Back in the United States Clemson dedicated himself to mining and agriculture, but Europe stayed on his mind. After John C. Calhoun's appointment as secretary of state in early 1844 under President John Tyler, Clemson became openly interested in the diplomatic corps and expressed a desire to return to Europe. In a letter to Andrew Pickens in 1844, Calhoun wrote about Clemson: "I found he was so anxious to visit Europe and to spend a few years there, that I thought it was better to gratify him."[32] It seems likely that Clemson always had the desire to return to Europe even though he dedicated himself to activities in the United States. Anna, however, was not as favorably disposed and needed convincing.[33] In a letter to Calhoun after his appointment, Clemson suggested that "a year" in Brussels should give great pleasure to Anna. In a letter to Anna announcing Clemson's appointment, Calhoun put the financial benefits of the appointment in the first paragraph.[34] It is not clear how much convincing Anna needed to move with her young children to Brussels, but subsequent correspondence from Anna in Brussels to her father indicated that she was not particularly happy there.[35]

Although Clemson was held in high regard in scientific circles, there is little indication that he had high level political connections in Washington, D.C., aside from John C. Calhoun. The two had a warm relationship, and their correspondences indicated affection and mutual respect. Calhoun, however, was not fond of the spoils system in which he would have to use his political influence to find Clemson a diplomatic assignment. As a result, Calhoun looked for European posts that were open or would be opening within the next year. In a letter to his daughter on May 5, Calhoun indicated that the position of chargé d'affaires was open in Brussels and that on the previous day President Tyler had agreed to assign the post to Clemson pending Senate approval. Calhoun did not mention any other post that was immediately available but indicated that he thought Clemson would like Brussels because of its proximity to Paris and prefer it to a post in Naples which would not open until the following year.[36]

One month later, the thirty-six-year-old Thomas Green Clemson was unanimously confirmed by the Senate as the United States chargé d'affaires in Belgium.[37] His appointment officially began on June 17, 1844, and he arrived in Belgium on October 4, 1844, after a stop in Paris. Clemson's uncontested and unanimous approval by the Senate to the position speaks highly of his qualifications. He was fluent in French and, because of his educational background and experience in Europe, was most likely among the best qualified young men of his day to represent the United States in Belgium.

Thomas Green Clemson's nameplate as U.S. chargé d'affaires in Belgium. Fort Hill Collection, Clemson University.

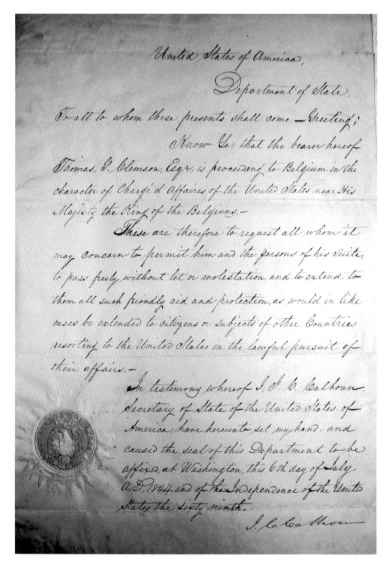

**Document, signed by Secretary of State John C. Calhoun, authorizing Thomas Green Clemson's envoy as U.S. chargé d'affaires to Belgium. Fort Hill Collection, Clemson University.**

Clemson arrived in Europe at a critical time in the continent's transformation during the Industrial Revolution. The European nations' struggles included trade liberalization versus protectionism, Protestants versus Catholics, powers of church versus state, capitalists versus workers rights, and absolutism versus democracy. The newly created country of Belgium was no exception.

### Belgium: A New State in Europe

Following the defeat of Napoleon and his exile to Elba in 1814, the great European powers of the day—France, Prussia, England, Austria, and Russia—met in Vienna to determine the future map of Europe, including the fate of Belgium (then referred to as Southern or Austrian Netherlands) and the seven northern United Provinces (Northern Netherlands). There was support for the creation of a state strong enough to prevent French expansion northward. King William I of the Netherlands wanted to unite the two regions into one centralized state. In 1815, with the blessing of the Great Powers, he proclaimed himself King of the United Kingdom of the Netherlands, and later that year his son fought in the Battle of Waterloo near Brussels that resulted in Napoleon's final defeat.

William had difficulty unifying his kingdom because of the underlying historical differences between Belgium and the Netherlands, most notably Belgium's annexation by France in 1794. The southern region (Belgium) was dominated by Catholics and a French-speaking political and social class. It was undergoing early industrialization in the provinces of Liege, Hainaut, and Flanders and was protective of its new industry against British competition. The northern region (the Netherlands) was Dutch-speaking, predominantly Protestant, and had a more commercially based liberal economy.

Beginning in the 1820s, King William's attempts to unify the two regions ran into opposition, primarily because of underrepresentation of the South in the parliament and discriminatory economic, language, and education policies that favored the Dutch-speaking North over the French-speaking South. In the South the dominant Catholics and minority Liberals joined forces and in 1828 forged an organized opposition movement. In August 1830, one month after the July riots in Paris, riots broke out in Brussels. In an effort to quell the uprisings, William deployed the army. This prompted the opposition to proclaim Belgian independence on October 4. Following the October proclamation, a group of 200 representatives of the Belgian upper and middle classes ratified a new constitution which guaranteed basic, liberal political principles, such as the balance of powers, the central role of an elected parliament, the restriction of royal power and ministerial responsibility, and the freedoms of opinion, assembly, press, religion, education, and language.[38] With a new constitution in place, the search began for a monarch. In the meantime the Great Powers met in London in November 1830 to determine the fate of Belgium and the Netherlands. In January 1831 they agreed to support an independent Belgium.

The German Prince Léopold of Saxe-Cobourgh Gotha was eventually selected; he accepted the Belgium crown on July 21, 1831. The Duke of Nemours, French King Louis Philippe's son, had been considered, but he ran into British opposition.[39] Léopold turned out to be an excellent choice. He had good military and diplomatic training and was well connected with the ruling elites in Russia,

England, and France. He had fought with the Russians against Napoleon in 1814, married the British Crown Princess Charlotte in 1816, served as a matchmaker for his family (arranging for his sister to marry the brother of the British king), and later served as advisor to their daughter, Queen Victoria. Léopold's wife died unexpectedly in 1817. After becoming King of the Belgians in 1831, Léopold looked for

a good political match and married the daughter of King Louis Philippe of France. His connections to the English crown and new links to France ensured the independence of the new Belgian State against continued Dutch attacks.[40] Still, sporadic fighting would continue until 1839, when King William finally ended the war.

Although Léopold privately criticized his restricted powers, he publicly behaved as an exemplary constitutional monarch throughout his reign. Clemson in fact praised Léopold for his liberal policies and diplomacy during the political unrest and revolts that swept much of Europe in 1848 and resulted in the overthrow of King Louis Philippe in France.[41] Léopold had modern ideas on economics and helped support Belgian industrialization. Clemson reported after his first meeting with Léopold in 1844 that he found the monarch to be "very well informed." Clemson was

**Franz Xaver Winterhalter's portrait of the Duke of Saxe-Cobourgh Gotha, Léopold I, King of Belgium, shown in the uniform of colonel of the cuirassiers. 1831. Oil on canvas. Réunion des Musées Nationaux/Art Resource, N.Y.**

impressed with his knowledge of Belgium's mineral wealth and his being well versed in scientific, economic, and trade issues.[42]

While the relationship between Léopold and Louis Philippe may have put Clemson in an uneasy position, he seemed to handle it very well during his stay in Europe. Only after Louis Philippe's exile in 1848 did Clemson severely criticize the French monarch for his conduct beginning in 1830.[43] This is the first time that Clemson publicly expressed his disappointment and disillusionment with the 1830 regime change in France in which he had participated as an idealistic young student. Despite this clear hostility, Clemson had been received by King Louis Philippe in Paris on his way to Brussels and commented on the meeting, "I considered this a proper mark of respect as well to the able statesman and King as the father-in-law of his Majesty Léopold to whose court I have the honor to be accredited."[44]

Industrialization moved quickly under King Léopold. Less than five years after proclaiming independence, Belgium started construction of the first rail network on the European continent, a project that fueled industrial growth. Belgian coal and mineral wealth lay in the French-speaking southern areas around Liege and Hainaut, sparking the industrial boom there. Brussels became the financial center with the leadership of the Société Générale and the Banque de Bruxelles. New limited companies also were founded in the capital. As a result, Belgium quickly became the second most industrialized state in the world after England.[45]

Industrialization, however, created two worlds in Belgium: the increasingly urban, progressive, and secular industrial centers—mostly in the south (Wallonia)—and the stagnant, agrarian countryside—mostly in the north (Flanders), with the exception of the textile industry in Ghent. Clemson arrived with his family in the midst of these developing divisions in the country. A number of crop failures from 1844 to 1846—the first two years the Clemsons were in Brussels—led to famine and migrations from rural Flanders to Wallonia. The worsening conditions of the working class prompted Clemson to compare the condition of slaves in the American South to European workers:

> The misery of the working class [in Europe] is due to the conflict between capital and labor. Capital is omnipotent and the system in Europe is worse than Negro slavery. With us in the United States with the relation of master and slave the slave is not worried over a short crop. Masters must provide. Negroes are better fed, work less and are in every respect in a more elevated condition than the laboring class of Europe.

He added, "Slaves are vastly more easily governed and crime among them infinitely less."[46]

The conditions in Belgium were also observed by Karl Marx, Friedrich Engels, and other communist followers. Marx arrived in Brussels the same year as Clemson and resided there with Engels from 1844 to early 1848, before returning to Paris to participate in the revolts. While in Brussels, Marx wrote the *Communist Manifesto*, which was published in February 1848.[47] During these same four years, rapid industrialization and the desire to expand trade prompted Belgian leaders to seek favorable trade agreements with other countries. Within this context a new interest in a bilateral trade agreement between Belgium and the United States emerged.

## The U.S. Political and Economic Context

Politically, by the mid-1800s, the United States was influenced by at least three major national sentiments that were molding the young nation. The first was isolationism and the principle of "no entangling alliances" advocated by President George Washington in his 1796 Farewell Address to the nation. The second was nationalism, enshrined by President Monroe in the Monroe Doctrine, which was presented in 1823 at his seventh State of the Union address. The doctrine proclaimed the U.S. opinion that European powers should no longer colonize the Americas or interfere in the affairs of sovereign nations there. The United States would view such action as hostile toward itself. The third U.S. tenet involved a sense of providence reflected in the political philosophy of Manifest Destiny—the belief, common among nineteenth-century statesmen and business leaders, that the United States was destined and deserved to govern the North American continent from the Atlantic to the Pacific Oceans. Thus, Clemson entered into the diplomatic corps at a delicate moment in U.S. relations with European powers, particularly over the future of Texas.

The economic context was also a factor in United States foreign policy and had an influence on Clemson's role in Brussels. In the 1840s the U.S. economy was largely divided between the industrial and shipping interests of the North, characterized by rapid population growth and urbanization, and the agrarian interests of the South, dominated by cotton, dependent on slavery, and largely rural with little industrialization. The South was dependent on exporting raw materials to Europe, while the North was interested in expanding its industrial exports while protecting its new industries and growing merchant fleet against European competition.

## Clemson's Roles in the Bilateral Relations between the United States and Belgium

During the fifteen years following the independence of Belgium, the bilateral relations between the United States and Belgium were often strained. The three main sources of tension between the two countries involved questions about the indemnification for American property lost during the bombing of Antwerp by Dutch forces in 1830; the future of Texas (annexation to the United States or an independent state with European support); and the failure to ratify a treaty of commerce and navigation. The first two points were partially solved before Clemson's arrival in Brussels. In 1842, Virgil Maxcy, the U.S. chargé d'affaires in Brussels, had succeeded in obtaining from the Belgian government a commitment for indemnity for the destruction of American goods in the port of Antwerp bombed

by Dutch troops. However, the actual payments and the full resolution of the issue were due to Clemson's diplomatic pressure in October 1845.[48] The Texas issue
was resolved when the United States annexed it as a state in 1845 and treaties were
signed with the major European powers. This gave Clemson the opportunity to
concentrate on the commercial issues.

During the first contact between Clemson and General Goblet d'Alviella, the
Belgian minister of foreign affairs, Goblet discussed the opportunity of negotiating a treaty of commerce and navigation with the United States.[49] The negotiations took place in the general context of a dispute between advocates of free trade
and advocates of protectionism, as well as during the first phase of liberalization
of trade under the pressure of Great Britain.[50] As was previously mentioned, the
United States was generally pro-trade, but it applied relatively high tariffs on industrial goods. A tariff compromise in 1842 set the tariff on such goods at 32
percent.

It is helpful to remember that during the period after 1815, when Belgium
was under Dutch authority, Dutch commercial policy had caused extreme tension
between the Dutch North and Belgian South. In 1821, the Dutch parliament
adopted a low tariff system by which tariffs could not exceed 6 percent of the
value for manufactured goods. By comparison, at that time, the tariffs were 35–45
percent of the value in the relatively liberal United States and 45–55 percent
in Great Britain.[51] The Belgians, strongly opposed to this liberal policy, argued
that it favored Dutch commercial activities in the North but disadvantaged the
new southern manufacturing industries. Discussions in parliament revealed the
tensions between the South and North that can be seen as one of the economic
reasons for the 1830 revolution.[52]

Despite continued opposition to the liberal custom system after independence
in 1830, the young Belgian government did not adopt global reforms. However,
protectionist measures were taken for the textile and metallurgical industries and
for agriculture.[53] In July 1844, with the adoption of a new tariff law [*droits dif-
férentiels*], Belgium adopted a more protectionist system but one that was adapt-
able to different situations. The law specifically provided for lower tariffs for the
importation of goods from the producing country shipped directly to Belgium
on Belgium ships. The aims of the law were threefold: to promote the creation
of a mercantile marine; to find overseas markets for Belgian manufactured goods
through reciprocal arrangements; and to facilitate the negotiation of new commercial agreements.[54]

Prior to Clemson's arrival in Brussels two commercial agreements—one in
1833, the other in 1840—had been negotiated and adopted by the U.S. Senate but had been rejected by the Belgian Parliament. The first agreement was
concluded in January 1833 on the pattern of the treaties usually signed by the
Americans. The Belgian government ultimately rejected the treaty because it was

considered too liberal for Belgian industry and the statute of neutral ships, in case of war, caused concern for Britain.

On the first point the Belgians considered that the treaty was not advantageous for them, since the value of U.S. exports to Belgium was much greater than Belgian exports to the United States. It was feared that a more liberal trade agreement would only exacerbate the imbalance, particularly at the expense of the Belgian manufacturing industry.[55] Second, the agreement provided advantages for neutral ships in case of war. This was a point of contention between the United States and Britain. The British were especially concerned that, in case of conflict with the United States, a neutral Belgium might side with the United States. At the time, diplomatic pouches between Belgium and the United States traveled on British ships. This allowed the British to monitor negotiations and pressure the Belgian government to reject the treaty.[56]

A second agreement had been passed by the U.S. Senate in March 1840. However, this agreement also received a similarly embarrassing rejection by the Belgian parliament, because it was viewed as being too liberal and because there were discussions underway to revise Belgium's commercial policy and make it more protectionist.[57]

In the days following the arrival of Clemson in Brussels, diplomatic overtures were made to him by both Jean-Baptiste Nothomb, the Belgian prime minister and minister of the interior, and by Count Goblet d'Alviella, the minister of foreign affairs. Clemson's arrival obviously came at a time when, in light of the two previous agreement failures, the Belgians were motivated to conclude a trade agreement with the United States.

A number of factors contributed to a more positive environment in Belgium for concluding an agreement. First, the parliament had successfully adopted a new trade policy [*droits differentials*] that opened the way for new negotiations. Second, as industrialization expanded, there was a growing need to find new markets for manufactured goods while still protecting industry at home.[58] Third, there was interest in establishing a direct steamship line from Antwerp to New York. This was a key priority for Belgium after completing the railway connections with the Zollverein (the new German customs union) in 1844 and with France in 1846. It was hoped that Antwerp would become the port through which goods traveled between the United States and other overseas countries and the future Germany.[59] Thus the primary objectives for the Belgians were to develop new markets for their manufactured goods and ensure a return on their heavy investment in transportation infrastructure.

Despite the fact that Clemson initially was not given any authority to negotiate a treaty, he appeared to be prepared to enter fully into discussions.[60] Before his departure, Secretary of State Calhoun, in private instructions, told him that the United States would be delighted to review any commercial treaty Belgium would offer.[61] Prime Minister Nothomb and Foreign Minister Goblet worked for three months in consultation with Clemson on a treaty proposal based on the treaty of 1840 and provided Clemson with a draft treaty in March 1845. Soon thereafter Clemson dispatched the draft to the new U.S. Secretary of State James Buchanan for review and comment. The draft was received favorably by both Buchanan and the newly elected President James Polk. Buchanan responded, informing Clemson that he had been granted "full power to negotiate and conclude a Convention accordingly."[62] Buchanan cautioned, however, that there must be guarantees in place to ensure that a third attempt at a treaty did not fail, and he insisted that the treaty must first be adopted by the Belgian government and then submitted for ratification to the U.S. Senate.[63] On the Belgian side, Foreign Minister Goblet instructed Charles Serruys, the Belgian chargé d'affaires in Washington, not to intervene in the negotiations as they were being conducted directly between Clemson and Belgian authorities.[64] A change in government in Belgium in July 1845 caused some minor delays, but the new Foreign Minister Adolphe Deschamps and the government were supportive of the treaty. Clemson successfully concluded the negotiations, and in November 1845 the treaty was presented to the Belgian Parliament for approval. The treaty was approved in December 1845, despite the perception that it favored the United States. According to Clemson the reason the treaty was finally approved by the Belgian government was that a third rejection of a treaty would have been too embarrassing (especially since this one had been drafted by the Belgians); moreover, a rejection of the treaty would have diminished the chances of Antwerp's becoming the port of choice for U.S. trade and eventually that of other nations.[65] The United States Senate subsequently ratified the treaty on March 29, 1846, and the treaties were exchanged the following day.

This treaty of commerce and navigation between the United States and Belgium was a twenty-page document that would last for ten years. It was one of the most progressive trade treaties of the day and contained a number of interesting elements. Key points included "most favored nation" trade privileges; mutual recognition of ships, with American ships being treated as Belgian ships in Belgian ports and Belgian ships being treated as American ships in American ports; the reimbursement to American ship owners by the Belgian government of any fees or duties levied by the Dutch government on American ships passing on the Scheld River through the Netherlands to get to the port of Antwerp; and a tariff exemption on all goods to and from the United States passing through Belgium, provided the Belgian rail system was used for land transportation.[66] These elements of the treaty provided incentives to open a steamship line between New York and Antwerp, rather than between New York and Bremen or Hamburg, and to use the Belgian transportation infrastructure.

The treaty was very well received in the United States. Calhoun, who was now in the Senate, wrote to Clemson:

I now write simply to inform you that the treaty (of commerce with Belgium) has been ratified by the Senate in a manner highly honorable to you. There was but one vote against it, and that only on general ground, opposed to all reciprocal treaties in reference to Navigation. It seems to be generally admitted, not only that the treaty was highly advantageous, but that it was the best treaty of the kind we had ever made.[67]

After the ratification of the treaty Clemson continued to support the idea of establishing a direct steamship line between Antwerp, Ostende, and a U.S. port because of Belgium's central location and rail network. To his disappointment, however, in 1849 the United States decided to establish a line between New York, Southhampton, and Bremen without passing through either Ostende or Antwerp.[68]

Despite the failure of the New York-Antwerp steamship line initiative, the treaty clearly had a positive impact on trade and shipping between Belgium and the United States. During the period from 1846 to 1856, U.S. exports to Belgium increased by 115 percent while Belgian exports to the United States increased by 500 percent. From 1845 to 1850, U.S. shipping to Belgium increased by 30 percent while Belgian shipping to the United States increased by 187 percent.[69]

In addition to the 1846 treaty of commerce and navigation, Clemson's best known diplomatic achievement in Brussels, he was involved in discussions for a treaty of extradition, and he offered thoughtful reflections on the state of United States foreign policy and on the political, economic, and social conditions in Europe. The treaty of extradition proved impossible at the time because of incompatibilities with the two countries' judicial systems.[70] On the question of U.S. foreign policy, Clemson was very critical of the appointment of chargé d'affaires, in terms of both prestige as well as salary, to carry out the functions of a senior diplomat.[71] He argued in favor of raising the post to at least the minister level as was the case for most of the equivalent senior diplomats in Brussels and in Europe. He pointed out that in the Netherlands, for instance, the U.S. chargé d'affaires was not even invited to formal dinners at the court.

Clemson also was critical of the management of foreign policy under Secretary of State Buchanan. In a letter to Calhoun he wrote: "Our foreign relations whilst you were at the helm were exceedingly active, and were all working with effect which has told well, but really we are fast falling into perfect inactivity for want of direction." In a subsequent letter, Clemson commented: "No attention appears necessary to us from the Department. My impression is that there is great need for reformation here."[72] In addition, he was a strong and early advocate of selecting and assigning diplomats with appropriate language skills.[73]

Clemson certainly was interested in the condition of workers during this period of industrialization. As noted earlier, he was in Brussels during the years when Marx and Engels lived there (1844–1848). Clemson considered the condition of slaves in the United States to be superior to that of the working class in Europe. In 1847

**Chair given to Thomas Green Clemson by King Léopold I. Fort Hill Collection, Clemson University.**

he wrote: "The labouring classes of Europe so far as I have had the opportunity of seeing and judging, are infinitely more miserable than the slaves of the United States." He went on to insist that the establishment of slavery in Europe "would be the greatest blessing that could be bestowed on the peasantry of Europe."[74] At the same time, Clemson saw opportunities for U.S. cotton to replace the declining linen industry in Flanders.[75]

Clemson would have to return home from October 1848 to April 1849 for family reasons. His mother was very ill, and he had financial concerns with a new plantation he had purchased prior to his departure for Brussels. He was back in Belgium in 1850 when both Calhoun and President Zachary Taylor died. Taylor was replaced by Millard Fillmore, and Daniel Webster became the new secretary of state. In 1851 Webster replaced Clemson with Henri Bayard.[76]

When Clemson returned to the United States with his family, he was held in high esteem by King Léopold and the Belgian authorities. In a letter dated March 1, 1851, the Belgian Foreign Minister Constant d'Hoffschmidt stated:

> Due to his forward and enlightened thinking, Mr. Clemson was given, during his stay in Brussels, the best wishes and esteem of the government, which does not see without regret the end of our relations, already well established and that have been so enjoyable and useful for the consolidation of friendly relations between our two countries.[77]

This 1851 endorsement of Clemson's attributes and contributions represents a certain culmination of much that he had learned since he first went to Europe in 1826 as a young student; participated in progressive intellectual circles in Paris; and discussed the future of European politics, monarchy, constitutional monarchy, and republicanism with some of the best minds in Paris. Moreover, he, alongside classmates, General Lafayette, and other veterans of the Napoleonic wars, had actively participated in the revolt of 1830 to overthrow King Charles X, but Clemson was soon disappointed by the outcome and the rule of King Louis Philippe. After Clemson's return to the United States in 1833, he focused on mining and agriculture. Still, he remained attracted to Europe, and when the possibility presented itself with John Calhoun's appointment as secretary of state in 1844, Clemson eagerly returned. However, Clemson seemed to have learned from his 1830 experiences to distinguish between real politics and idealism— a fundamental difference between both European and American domestic and foreign policies at the time, and perhaps still today. Evidence of that awareness can be seen in his letters from Belgium, which were pointedly guarded when referring to public personalities in Europe. For example, he was received by King Louis Philippe in Paris in 1844 on his way to Brussels, but made no disparaging remarks in his correspondence following the meeting. It was not until 1848, after Louis Philippe was exiled, that Clemson criticized his rule at length, detailing sentiments he had harbored since 1830. Yet in the same letter he praised Louis Philippe's son-in-law, King Léopold I of Belgium. Clemson sincerely respected Léopold from their first encounter in October 1844 and remained in good relations with him throughout and after his posting in Brussels. In 1860, eight years after Clemson's return to the United States, King Léopold I awarded him the Order of Léopold, one of the highest honors given to a foreigner.

*Left*, original Order of Léopold I medal, given to Thomas Green Clemson in 1860. On loan to Fort Hill, Clemson University, from the collection of John P. Elliott. *Right*, recast medal, presented in 2004 to Clemson University Provost Doris Helms by Prince Phillip of Belgium. Fort Hill Collection, Clemson University.

## A Legacy with a Life of Its Own

Even though the original medal was thought, for decades, to be lost, Clemson's efforts and achievements in Europe, first as a young scholar and then as a diplomat, have taken on a life of their own. For instance, over 150 years after Clemson negotiated the first United States-Belgium treaty of commerce and trade, Belgium remains an important trading partner with the United States and, in particular, with South Carolina. In fact, Belgium is among the state's top ten trading partners, purchasing over $300 million of South Carolina's exports, and some fifteen Belgian companies employ over 2,600 South Carolinians within the state. Other current exchanges and partnerships are more surprising. On December 7, 2004, Clemson University inaugurated the Thomas Green Clemson University Brussels Center (CUBC) in collaboration with the ICHEC Brussels Management School.

Prince Phillip of Belgium's presentation of recast 1860 Order of Léopold I medal to Doris R. Helms, Clemson University Provost, December 7, 2004. *Left to right:* Prince Phillip; Christian Ost, Rector of ICHEC Brussels Management School; Elizabeth Belenchia, President of Carroll Properties Corp.; James P. Cross, Clemson University Vice Provost of International Affairs; and Doris Helms.

*Left to right:* ICHEC Brussels Management School Rector Christian Ost, Clemson University President James Barker, and UCL Rector Bernard Coulie cut the ribbon at the dedication of the Thomas Green Clemson University Brussels Center building in Brussels, Belgium, June 7, 2007.

The ceremony included Prince Phillip of Belgium's presenting a recast copy of the 1860 Order of Léopold medal to Clemson University Provost Doris Helms.

Two and a half years later on June 7, 2007, and in collaboration with ICHEC and the Catholic University of Louvain, a Clemson delegation led by President James Barker celebrated the opening of the Thomas Green Clemson University Brussels Center building at No. 5 Avenue de Broqueville. Between 2004 and 2006, over 250 European and American students, faculty, staff, and members of the business community participated in educational, research, service, and economic development activities through the Brussels Center. In these and future collaborative initiatives, the effects of Thomas Clemson's European years will continue to evolve as a vibrant work in progress on both sides of the Atlantic.

### Notes

1. "La Sorbonne" is the usual name given to the University of Paris, a theological faculty founded in the thirteenth century. The Sorbonne was closed during the period of the French Revolution. Its buildings were given to the University of Paris by Napoleon in 1808 and, since 1821, have been used for the Faculty of Literature and Sciences, some of whose lectures Thomas Clemson attended.
2. Le Collège Royal de France, now named Le Collège de France, was founded in the sixteenth century. This institution, unique in Europe, organizes free lectures on major scientific topics by prestigious scientists.
3. Louis Jacques Thénard (1777–1857), a French chemist, taught at the College Royal de France; at the Sorbonne, where he was dean of the Faculty of Sciences from 1821 to 1841; and at the Ecole Polytechnique [Polytechnic School].
4. Joseph Louis Gay-Lussac (1778–1850), a French chemist, began teaching at the Ecole Polytechnique in 1818. In 1829, he became chief assayer at the Royal Mint of Paris. He was close to the revolutionary movement, and in 1831, after the July Revolution, he was elected to the French Parliament.
5. Pierre-Louis Dulong (1785–1838), a French physician and chemist, taught at the Ecole Polytechnique where he was the academic dean [*directeur des études*].
6. Email from Jean-Marie Darnis, Monnaie de Paris, to Sabine Godts-Péters, 13 June 2006. See also www.polytechnique.fr/bcx/associations/gaylussac/pages/assofrGL.html.
7. Jean-Baptiste Elie de Beaumont (1798–1874) was a famous French geologist who, in 1840, co-authored with Ours Dufrénoy the first geological map of France. Elie de Beaumont was a professor at the College de France and, from 1827 to his death, a professor at the Ecole des Mines.
8. Pierre-Jean Robiquet (1780–1840), a French chemist, was a lecturer at the Ecole Polytechnique as well as a professor at the Ecole de Pharmacie [School of Pharmacy].
9. André Guenyveau (1762–1861) was a professor of metallurgy at the Ecole des Mines from 1822 to 1840.
10. Ours-Pierre-Armand Petit-Dufrénoy (1792–1857), a geologist, was co-author with Elie de Beaumont of the first geological map of France. Dufrénoy became a professor of mineralogy at the Ecole des Mines in 1845; three years later, he became its director. After research and observation in England, he contributed to the introduction in France of modern processes for metallurgical production.
11. Pierre Berthier (1782–1861) was a professor of docimacy at the Ecole des Mines from 1816 to 1848. His geological research helped to modernize agriculture.
12. Lefte Neal to Thomas Clemson, 17 July 1831, Clemson Papers, Special Collections, Clemson University Libraries, Clemson, SC (hereafter cited as SCCUL).

13. L'Ecole Polytechnique was founded in 1794 by intellectuals of the Revolution for the purpose of giving students a foundation in mathematics, physics, and chemistry required for entrance into specialized schools, such as the Ecole des Mines.

14. André Laugier (1770–1832) was a chemist and mineralogist.

15. See www.annales.org/archives/s/c6.html, 6.

16. See www.euromin.w3sites.net/nouveau_site/musees/ensmp/HISTf.html, 3.

17. See www.annales.org/archives/x/ecole.html, 6.

18. Ibid., 26.

19. Email from Marie-Noelle Maisonneuve to Sabine Godts-Péters, 30 January 2006. Maisonneuve is responsible for alumni records at the Library of the Ecole des Mines in Paris.

20. See www.annales.org/archives/x/c6.html, 7. Docimacy is the art or practice of applying tests to ascertain the nature and quality of objects, such as metals or ores.

21. Ibid., 23.

22. An assayer is one who examines metallic ores or compounds for the purpose of determining the amount of any particular metal in the same, especially of gold or silver.

23. Alester G. Holmes and George R. Sherrill, *Thomas Green Clemson: His Life and Work* (Richmond, VA: Garrett and Massie, 1937), 9.

24. Today, the street is Rue Guénégaud.

25. Lefte Neal to TGC, 17 July 1831, Clemson Papers, SCCUL.

26. See www.polytechnique.fr/institution/historique, 4.

27. See Nickels R. Beacham, *Thomas Green Clemson, a Minor Diplomat of the Old South* (Unpublished master's thesis, Graduate School of Arts and Sciences, Duke University, 1933), 121.

28. See dispatch number 52, 6 March 1848, quoted in Holmes and Sherrill, *Thomas Green Clemson*, 83–85.

29. Holmes and Sherrill, *Thomas Green Clemson*, 7.

30. Ibid., 11. See also John W. Rooney, *A Study in American Foreign Policy in Mid-Nineteenth Century: Belgian-American Diplomatic and Consular Relations, 1830–1850* (Louvain, Belgium: l'Université de Louvain, Recueil des Travaux d'histoire et de philology, 1969), 18.

31. Ibid.

32. Clyde N. Wilson and Shirley Bright Cook, eds. *The Papers of John C. Calhoun*, vol. 18 (Columbia: University of South Carolina Press, 1988), 174.

33. Ernest McPherson Lander Jr., *The Calhoun Family and Thomas Green Clemson: The Decline of a Southern Patriarchy* (Columbia: University of South Carolina Press, 1983). 79. See also Anna Calhoun Clemson to John Calhoun, 1 June 1844, *Papers of John C. Calhoun*, vol. 18: 693.

34. John C. Calhoun to TGC, 4 June 1844, *Papers of John C. Calhoun*, vol. 18: 709.

35. More on Anna Calhoun Clemson's feelings about Brussels can be found in her correspondence edited by Jane W. Sublette, *The Letters of Anna Maria Calhoun Clemson, 1833–1873*, 2 vols. (Ph.D. Diss., Florida State University, 1993).

36. See Holmes and Sherrill, *Thomas Green Clemson*, 70, who cite the *American Historical Association Report*, 1899, 2: 115. See also *Papers of John C. Calhoun*, vol. 18: 470. The letter is dated 10 May, not 5 May, as indicated by Holmes and Sherrill, 11.

37. John C. Calhoun to TGC, 12 July 1844, *Papers of John C. Calhoun*, vol. 19: 317.

38. Petra Gunst and Maarten Van Ginderachter, *Belgium: A Historical View* (Brussels, Belgium: Belvue Museum, 2004), 4.

39. Els Witte, Eliane Gubin, Jean-Pierre Nandrin, and Gita Deneckere, *Nouvelle Histoire de Belgique* (Brussels, Belgium: Editions Complexe, 2005), 76.

40. Gunst and Ginderachter, *Historical View*, 74.

41. Holmes and Sherrill, *Thomas Green Clemson*, 84–85.

42. Ibid., 74.

43. Ibid., 83–84.

44. Ibid., 72.

45. Witte, Gubin, Nandrin, and Deneckere, *Nouvelle Histoire de Belgique*, 125–141.

46. For text of Clemson's dispatch number 37 (27 February 1847), see Holmes and Sherrill, *Thomas Green Clemson*, 82.

47. See http://www.historyguide.org/intellect/marx.html, 2.

48. Rooney, *Study in American Foreign Policy*, 212–214.

49. TGC to John C. Calhoun, 17 October 1844, as cited in Holmes and Sherrill, *Thomas Green Clemson*, 71–74, and as summarized in the *Papers of John C. Calhoun*, vol. 20: 95.

50. Paul Bairoch, *Victoires et Déboires, Histoire économique et sociale du monde du 16ᵉ siècle a nos jours* (Mesnil-sur-l'Estrée: Gallimard, Folio Histoire, 2002), 2: 294. For detailed accounts of the negotiations, see the following sources: Nickels R. Beacham, *Thomas Green Clemson, a Minor Diplomat of the Old South* (Master's thesis, Duke University, 1933); John W. Rooney, *A Study in American Foreign Policy in Mid-Nineteenth Century: Belgian American Diplomatic and Consular Relations 1830–1850* (Louvain, Belgium: Universite de Louvain, 1969); and Pierre-Henri Laurent, *Conflict and Accommodation in Belgian Diplomatic and Commercial Relations, 1830–1846* (Ph.D. Diss., Boston University, 1964).

51. Bairoch, *Histoire economique et sociale*, 294.

52. Max Suetens, *Histoire de la politique commerciale de la Belgique depuis 1830 jusqu'a nos jours* (Brussels: Editions de la Libraire encyclopédique, 1955), 7–8. See also Witte, Gubin, Nandrin, and Deneckere, *Nouvelle histoire de Belgique*, 20–21.

53. Suetens, *Histoire de la politique commerciale de la Belgique*, 8–10.

54. Ibid., 45.

55. See *Negociations entre le Belgique et les Etats-Unis*, n.d., Archives of the Ministry of Foreign Affairs of Belgium, Dossier 2062.

56. Suetens, *Histoire de la politique commerciale de la Belgique*, 17.

57. Ibid., 18. See also *Negociations entre le Belgique et les Etats-Unis*, n.d., Archives of the Ministry of Foreign Affairs of Belgium, Dossier 2062.

58. Laurent, *Conflict and Accommodation in Belgian Diplomatic and Commercial Relations*, 226. See also letter from Count de Briey, minister of foreign affairs, to King Léopold I, January 1842, Archives of the Ministry of Foreign Affairs of Belgium, Dossier 2062.

59. See Belgian government report, *Extrait du rapport decenal sur la situation administrative del la Belgique—1841–1850, commerce*, 3–4.

60. TGC to John C. Calhoun, 17 October 1844, Clemson Papers, SCCUL.

61. Rooney, *Study in American Foreign Policy*, 195.

62. James Buchanan, U.S. secretary of state, to TGC, 17 March 1845. There is disagreement about the date of this letter. Holmes and Sherrill indicate March 17 (*Thomas Green Clemson*, 78); Rooney gives September 10 (*Study in American Foreign Policy*, 204); and Laurent gives September 17 (*Conflict and Accommodation*, 211).

63. Rooney, *Study in American Foreign Policy*, 205.

64. Count Albert Goblet d'Alviella to Charles Serruys, 5 April 1845, Archives of the Ministry of Foreign Affairs of Belgium, Dossier 2062.

65. Rooney, *Study in American Foreign Policy*, 211. Also see *Annales parlementaires du Royaume de Belgique, Rapport de la commission chargée d'examiner le projet de loi relative au Traité de Commerce et de Navigation conclu entre le Belgique et les Etats-Unis d'Amérique le 10 novembre 1845.*

66. Rooney, *Study in American Foreign Policy*, 215–216.

67. John C. Calhoun to TGC, 29 March 1846, *Papers of John C. Calhoun*, vol. 22: 783.

68. Rooney, *Study in American Foreign Policy*, 215–216.

69. See *Commerce of the United States with European countries, 1790–1896* (Washington, DC: U.S. Government Printing Office, 1897).

70. Rooney, *Study in American Foreign Policy*, 214–215.

71. Ibid., 217–218. See also Lander, *Calhoun Family and Thomas Green Clemson*, 97.

72. TGC to John C. Calhoun, 10 July 1845, *Papers of John C. Calhoun*, vol. 22: 17; and TGC to John C. Calhoun, 27 March 1846, *Papers of John C. Calhoun*, vol. 22: 766.

73. Lander, *Calhoun Family and Thomas Green Clemson*, 95–96.

74. TGC to James Buchanan, 27 February 1847, as cited by Rooney, *Study in American Foreign Policy*, 219–220, and also by Holmes and Sherrill in *Thomas Green Clemson*, 83.

75. TGC to John C. Calhoun, 12 August 1845, *Papers of John C. Calhoun*, vol. 22: 69–73.

76. Rooney, *Study in American Foreign Policy*, 223.

77. Constant d'Hoffschmidt, Belgian minister of foreign affairs, to Bosch Spencer, Belgian chargé d'affaires in Washington, DC, March 1851, Archives of the Ministry of Foreign Affairs of Belgium, Dossier 10377.

# Chapter 5

*Alan Grubb* (signature)

# THE WASHINGTON YEARS

## *Alan Grubb*

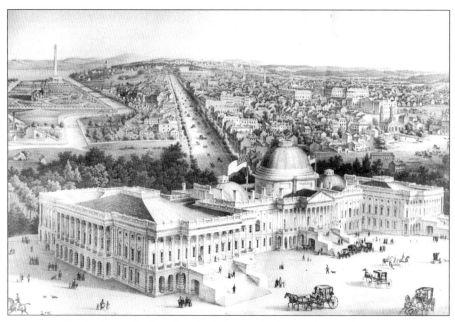

*Capitol—Bird's Eye View* by Edward Sachse. Lithograph, 1859.
**Kiplinger Washington Collection.**

When Thomas Green Clemson returned from Belgium in 1851, his life and career were at a crossroad, and the next decade was to be taken up with trying to find a focus or outlet for his many talents and ambition. Thus in the Washington area, Clemson began a complex search to find what he termed "honorable" employment, a search in which he was repeatedly disappointed by the vicissitudes of Washington politics, exacerbated even more in the decade by growing sectional conflicts and the slavery issue.

In one of his many writings about Clemson, the historian Ernest Lander refers to Clemson's "mercurial" temperament, despondent moods, indifferent health, and frequent tactlessness in personal relations.[1] This, too, complicated his ambition; the frustration of Clemson's ambition, in turn, contributed to his irritability. Anna Clemson's letters of the period reveal a sorely tried woman, a woman who worked hard to keep family peace and soothe and reassure the worrying Clemson. But without Calhoun and Calhoun's prominence and connections, Clemson was left to find his way in the difficult corridors of Washington politics and to find an effective outlet for his ambition. Shortly after his return to the United States, he wrote R. K. Cralle, Calhoun's former secretary, that

> Under the present circumstances it would suit me better to go abroad than to stay here without occupation and to lead an inert fruitless life. I could educate my children in Europe more efficiently than it would be in my power to do here. Had I a comfortable, healthy home with sufficient fortune to live, office would not tempt me; as it is, I shall make no undignified move so long as I wish to keep company with my conscience.[2]

But Clemson did not think he was of sufficient means to do so, and in any case he was still hoping for a diplomatic post. In late January he expressed to Cralle his frustration at not knowing where he stood with the new administration[3]; a few weeks later he again complained of the party politics involved in doling out diplomatic posts, commenting with a bitterness that did not hide his personal disappointment, "If the party to which I belong can stand to see me sacrificed, so be it."[4] Clearly, without Calhoun's support, Clemson's prospects were not good, as he indicated to Cralle in March: "I have nothing new to impart upon the subject of my prospects."[5]

## *Starting Again in Maryland*

In May he announced that he and his family were preparing to settle in Maryland, in Prince George's County, just outside Washington, on a farm the Clemsons were to call "The Home." He wrote Cralle, explaining his decision but also expressing his dissatisfaction with his situation:

> I have not written you since my return from New York, which was soon after you left, because I had nothing particular to impart, nor have I much that is reassuring at this time. You doubtless saw an account of John's [John C. Calhoun Jr., Anna's brother] appointment as Secretary of the Legation to Paris. I knew nothing of it until I saw it in the papers. He never expressed to me a desire to go abroad or that he was in Washington for that purpose. When he was appointed he wrote his sister that his friends had secured the place for him & there was a card placed by the administration to pay me and other interests by the smallest possible office. The game was clear the harder my friends urged my appointment the more sure his, as soon as it was known he would accept. I feel deeply mortified for my friends & wounded that my brother-in-law bearing his father's name should at his early age have acted so treacherously. He knew from our own lips over & again what was being done in my behalf & yet he was silent to us about his own movements & that too when I was interesting myself in his affairs. It is said that John Van Buren

will go to Paris; if so, what a union of names John Van Buren as chief of Legation & John C. Calhoun as secretary. The papers contain a list of appointments settled yesterday, among them Mr. Sibley of Alabama to Brussels, Broom of N Jersey to Berlin & Auguste Belmont, another foreigner, to the Hague. You know he has been agent of the Rothschilds. All the appointments made appear to have political causes entirely, some of them I know, and most of them are completely & entirely unfit. So much for the man that was elevated to the Presidency being above cliques.... Where in the name of Heaven are we going to?

No doubt sorely disappointed, he concluded despairingly, "I am now at a loss to know what to do, or which way to direct my face. Can you not point out something that will give me a useful, honourable & satisfactory occupation?"[6] Clemson was to return to this theme often during the decade, as he did also to the idea of returning to Europe. "I feel disposed to cross the Atlantic," he wrote his uncle Elias Baker in August 1852, "for I find it so difficult to get pleasantly fixed here on small means in a situation promising health that I may be drawn back to Europe in self-defense."[7]

**Watercolor presumably of The Home, Bladensburg, Maryland.
Fort Hill Collection, Clemson University.**

In the end Clemson decided to take up permanent residence in Bladensburg, Maryland. Why did Clemson pick this location? Anna's letters indicate that this was his, not her, choice, though she was anxious to have her family settled. Holmes and Sherrill, in their 1937 biography of Clemson, indicate that his reasons for settling in Bladensburg are not entirely clear. "Unfortunately," they write, "he gave no intimation of his motive, so any reasons are purely speculative." Yet they speculate that "perhaps" the place was offered at an attractive price, or "perhaps" he had further political ambition, or "better still, he may have returned from his Belgian and European observations and experiences with the fixed purpose of devoting himself to the improvement of agriculture in the United States."[8] Indeed, on June 8, 1853, Clemson and his wife purchased 100 ¾ acres about a mile from Bladensburg, Prince George's County, Maryland, for $6,725. Clemson's own letters, however—the one cited above and another to Cralle on July 10, 1853—suggest pretty clearly that he hoped his residence near Washington would enable him to obtain at some point government employment suited to his talents. Of his purchase of property just outside Washington he wrote Cralle:

> Since I wrote you I made the purchase of a hundred acres of land near Bladensburgh [sic], Maryland, about a mile & a half from this latter place & about four miles from the Capitol. The position is fine, the land good, the lookout extensive, the health undoubted & the improvements, small & will require additions if we continue there. The house is surrounded by a fine grove of trees, & there is considerable fruit....I attended the sale & purchased it for about $7000, two years since it was sold for $10,000. This said, I made a cheap purchase. I am at least within reach of the conveniences of population, a short walk to the Baltimore & Washington railroad. Have mills & other necessities at hand. We shall go there & try it & will be in possession & perhaps on the spot about the first day of August....It is a short ride of half an hour from Washington & in sight of Rives's House on the railroad.[9]

Thus, if frustrated in any hoped-for appointment, for the moment he seemed satisfied—as satisfied as the restless, tormented Clemson ever could be—and settled down as a gentleman farmer to plant and make improvements on the farm, to conduct agricultural experiments, and to supplement his income by importing Belgian furniture, guns, tapestries, and other articles for friends and relatives.[10]

Having chosen Bladensburg to live in, this decision did not keep Clemson from often complaining and, on occasion, threatening to pull up stakes and move back to Europe. He was to write Baker frequently in the decade, mostly about business but almost always with complaints about his lack of success as a farmer. In this area Clemson had serious doubts about his aptitude. "I find I am better suited," he wrote Baker in January 1854, "for other occupations than farming but I suppose in time I shall acquire experience if it does not cost me too dear."[11] He continued to complain about the farm throughout the decade, however. In July he wrote Baker, indicating not only his frustrations with farming but his problems with his laborers and his attitude—even animus—toward blacks:

> My farming operations have gotten along badly—on account of the difficulty I have with workmen. They are difficult to be had at any wages and worthless (for the most part when procured). I have thought that it would be impossible for me to farm here as I have been doing & must make some arrangements that will

be more satisfactory. Negroes I think will be the resort that I shall be compelled to—they are hazardous & give much trouble & require constant watching, besides [being] so near the frontier they may leave you and once in the hands of the abolitionists, adieu. I shall persevere as long as I can hold out & when I can do it no longer I will place you in possession of the place.[12]

The next year, in December, he was still complaining that "My farming operations commence badly," and in October 1855 that "My farm goes on slowly. I find it slow work, hard to get hands & they are not worth much when you get them."[13] In November 1855 he was even more despairing:

I have almost concluded to break up here & clear out somewhere to parts unknown. The proximity to Washington makes labour scarce & dear. I can not compete with the government either in letting labourers idle their time or giving them wages equal to what they can get there for doing little to nothing. I have neither the temperament nor the health to be continually worried & perplexed with this kind of farming which has proved to be expensive & for that reason out of the question. The next question is where to go to. My inclination is for Europe where one can live quiet & on his means, at which my family all rebel— and can live much cheaper there than here, indeed get more for nothing than money will buy here.[14]

Eventually, if only for a time, he found someone to manage his farm in whom he had confidence—"My man Neides continues to work," he wrote Baker in June 1856, "and he appears to understand how to farm"—and though Clemson's outlook did not much improve, he turned to other interests, particularly agricultural science and experimentation, for which he had far greater aptitude.[15]

Clemson was always a difficult personality. Certainly, he was well-read, highly intellectual, adept in the arts, and well-versed in the scientific literature of the day. However, this man of many talents, as Lander has noted, never could quite seem to find a satisfactory niche for his talents and ambition, a dilemma that was not resolved during the Washington years. Then there were Clemson's many money-making projects which nearly always turned out badly. These included his brief stint at managing Fort Hill for his father-in-law; his efforts as a gentleman farmer at Canebrake and later in Maryland; his imprudent loans to family members that almost inevitably involved him in family discord; and his investments in silver mining and in the iron business with his uncle, Elias Baker, in Altoona, Pennsylvania. Each turned out badly or at least not as successfully as he would have liked, while his sights were really on public employment, the failure of which left him despondent, ever more depressive and difficult to deal with.[16]

All his life Clemson was subject to chronic depression, made worse now by his personal frustrations. Ann Russell, in her previous chapter on Anna Calhoun Clemson, draws a detailed, often painful picture of Clemson's mental state and chronic depression, and the consequences it had for family peace. Clemson suffered from the condition of dysthymia, which caused his depression. Anna tried to humor him when he fell into his cross or gloomy periods, or what she had described, earlier in their marriage, as "his blues." However, as her letters to her daughter, Floride, during the period indicate, these moods of depression, exacerbated by his personal frustrations, made him a difficult companion and father. "Unfortunately, however, in Clemson's case," Ann Russell writes, "without the care that is now available, the seriousness of his condition worsened and caused personal distress and disability with his family, despite all that Anna could do to keep the peace she prized dearly."[17]

The property purchased by Clemson after their return from Belgium has an interesting history. The farm, which they called "The Home," was originally part of a larger tract purchased by William Diggs, who called his estate "Chillum Castle Manor." The estate home stood north of what is today Bunker Hill Road between 31st and 32nd Streets. The 100 acres on which the manor stood later became known as Clemson Place, after Thomas Green Clemson. By 1891 the 100 acres of Clemson Place had been subdivided by George A. and J. Estcourt Sawyer, Army officers from Seattle, and they named the subdivision Mt. Rainier after the famous mountain peak in their home state. The area developed later into a suburb of Washington, with Mt. Rainier's incorporation in 1910. Nothing of the rural character of the area remains, except the Riversdale Plantation house of

Detail, *Bladensburgh District No. 2, Prince George's County, Maryland* (G. Hopkins, Philadelphia, 1878). Clemson home is in lower left; Charles Calvert's property is at top. Special Collections, University of Maryland Libraries.

Clemson's friend and fellow agricultural pioneer, Charles Benedict Calvert.[18]

In Clemson's day, Prince George's County was overwhelmingly agricultural. The great wealth in the county came "from the land, tobacco, and from slaves." It was, then, an area much like Clemson was familiar with in South Carolina; indeed, as one local history notes, "More slaves worked here than in any other county in the state, and the gentry, the old families who led our social and public life, lived in a style befitting the legends that linger about them."[19] Moreover, the plantation economy of Prince George's County was at its height. By 1860 the county was producing more than thirteen million pounds of tobacco annually. In addition to tobacco, the area produced more than 300,000 bushels of wheat and about 700,000 bushels of corn, and local farmers owned 5,000 horses, 4,000 milk cows, 9,000 sheep, and 25,000 swine. Much of the farm work was done by slaves; among the 2,000 white families in the county, there were 850 slaveholders holding 12,500 slaves.[20]

The gentlemen planters of the area were active in local agricultural societies; many, in fact, were in the forefront of the agricultural reform movement of the day. Dr. John H. Bayne, a local physician, gained a national reputation as "the prince of horticulturalists," while W. W. W. Bowie, a tobacco planter near Collington and later governor, wrote extensively for agricultural journals and government publications. Politically, too, Clemson would have found the area congenial. A local history notes,

> The politics of this county were markedly conservative in the antebellum period, and the voters usually elected Whigs to local office. There was virtually no sympathy at all—among the whites—for the radical tenets of abolitionism, and the leaders of Prince George's were firm in their defense of the slave system. Thomas J. Turner was publisher of the *Planters' Advocate*, an Upper Marlboro newspaper begun in 1851. In the inaugural issue he wrote, 'We believe domestic slavery, as it exists among us, to be a truly conservative and beneficial institution—right in view of God and man, and as such, we will ever maintain it.'[21]

Foremost among these wealthy, aristocratic planters was Charles Benedict Calvert, whose plantation, Riversdale, was near The Home and with whom Clemson formed a close friendship and shared a similar interest in agricultural reform. Calvert was the scion of a prominent Maryland family whose mother's family, the Stiers, came originally from Belgium—one more thing they had in common—and on the Calvert side, he was related to Charles Calvert, the fifth Lord Baltimore and, by marriage, to George Washington's stepson, John Parke Custis. Calvert's parents had inherited Riversdale when his wife's parents had returned to Belgium; following her death, Charles's father turned to farming and business ventures, and by 1828 he had become the richest man and largest landowner in Prince George's County. Charles Benedict inherited Riversdale in 1838 and soon became known as a progressive planter who was active in agriculture reform.

George Callcott gives a portrait of Calvert that indicates perfectly why Clemson would see in him a natural ally:

> Descended from the Lords Baltimore, the son of a wealthy planter and an aristocratic Belgian mother, handsome, debonair and charismatic, Calvert was a patrician in the finest Jeffersonian tradition. Graduating from the University of Virginia at 19, he returned to Riverdale [town] in Prince George's County to take over his father's estate. The plantation mansion, which still stands about a mile from the institution he founded, then looked out upon marble terraces, fountains, arbors, lakes, pagodas and immense greenhouses. His 2,200-acre hay and dairy farm became nationally famous for its use of scientific experimentation. Typically, within a year he might donate a score of prize bulls to neighboring farmers who agreed to breed and care for them according to his instructions.[22]

**Charles Benedict Calvert.**
**Library of Congress, LC-USZ6-245.**

The Calvert and Clemson families socialized during the years the Clemsons lived in Maryland, but, for Clemson, Calvert was most important because of their similar interest in agricultural issues, particularly agricultural education. Calvert served as a member of the Maryland House of Delegates in 1839, 1843, and 1844, and later, though a defender of slavery and particularly opposed to abolitionist activity, he was elected as a Unionist to Congress. He also served as president of Prince George's County Agricultural Society and the Maryland State Agricultural Society and in the late 1850s was vice president of the United States Agricultural Society, which held annual meetings in Washington. Moreover, he is considered the man most responsible for the founding of Maryland Agricultural College, the establishment of which Clemson enthusiastically supported.[23]

Clemson too would have found Washington a sympathetic environment, for it was very much a southern city, both in its sensibilities and sympathies. He was familiar with its party politics and partisanship which, if they now worked against him, he still hoped to turn his way. He also would have been drawn there—

*Above: Washington, D.C., with Projected Improvements* by Benjamin Franklin
Smith Jr. (Smith and Jenkins, N.Y., 1852). Library of Congress, cph 3b06655.
*Below: City of Washington from beyond the Navy Yard* by George Cooke. William
J. Bennett engraving (Lewis P. Clover, 180 Fulton Street, N.Y., 1834).
Library of Congress, cph 3b51990.

certainly in preference to South Carolina where he no longer had property—as a place with superior facilities for study and research, and for opportunities for contacts with congenial agricultural leaders and to hear and deliver papers on scientific questions. It was easy, as countless foreign (and American) visitors did, to make fun of Washington as a capital city. Mrs. Mortimer, a British travel writer (who, unlike the many others before and after her, had never herself visited the city), observed in 1854 that "Washington is one of the most desolate cities in the world; not because she is in ruins, but for the opposite reason—because she is unfinished. There are places marked where houses ought to be, but where no houses seem ever likely to be."[24] Washington had a reputation for delay or abandonment of public improvements and was still—apart from its politics—a sleepy, and alternately dusty or damp, southern town. But it was improving during the decade. As a journalist wrote in 1859 for *Harper's*, "During the last five years Washington has made amazing strides toward permanent grandeur; and already the 'City of Magnificent Distances' has become more remarkable for its magnificence than for its distances. No longer are our legislators compelled to wade through a morass in order to pass from the Capitol to the White House."[25]

***Smithsonian Institution from the North East.*** **Designed and drawn by James Renwick. Lithograph (Sarony and Major, 117 Fulton Street, N.Y., 1849).**

Of particular interest to Clemson would have been the completion of the Smithsonian Building in 1855, for it was there that he attended and presented scientific papers and lectures which filled his time as he waited, hopefully, for public employment.

## *Joining the Circle of Agricultural Reformers*

In their biography of Clemson, Holmes and Sherrill entitle the chapters devoted to Clemson's Washington years as "Interest in Scientific Agriculture" and "Advocacy of Agricultural Education," and they see his role in both agricultural experimentation and the promotion of agricultural education as "prominent." "One is surprised at the wide variety of his interests, and the breadth and depth of his knowledge of agriculture and its related fields," they write, and add, "he made contacts with the leaders, he wrote the journals, and made valuable contributions to scientific agriculture in the United States."[26] In particular they note that Clemson in 1856 was asked by the editors of the *American Farmer* to write an article on the *Year Book of Agricultural Progress and Discovery for 1855 and 1856*; his article on "The Sources of Ammonia" appeared in the *American Farmer* for May 1856. In 1858 the *American Farmer* carried another article by Clemson in which he gave a method of examining marl. The following year, by special request, he prepared an article on "Fertilizers" for the *Patent Office Report of 1859,* along with other articles during the period for agricultural journals with titles like "Lime," "Action on Lime," "Ammoniacal Manures," "Sources of Ammonia," "Price of Labor and Land," "Scientific Discovery and Progress," "An Act to Establish and Endow an Agricultural College in the State of Maryland," "The Importance and Advantage of Scientific Instruction for the Advancement of Agriculture," "Preparation of Seed," "Microscopic Organisms," "Organic Matter," "Agricultural Requirements of the South," and "The Principles of Agriculture."

These articles indicate Clemson's deep involvement in the debate on soil composition and nutrients and the application generally of chemistry to agriculture. To both involvements, he applied his background in chemistry and mineralogy and his considerable knowledge of Europe's extensive scientific literature and its far more advanced scientific and technical education and agricultural experimentation. He wrote too about the results of his own experimentation at The Home. Regarding the latter, in a postscript to an article on "The Sources of Ammonia" which appeared in the *American Farmer* (May 1856), in which Clemson responded to an earlier article by Dr. Pendleton, in the spirited and somewhat combative tone that was typical of such scientific exchanges, he enclosed statements or "certificates" from neighboring farmers. These testified to the results of his 1854 experiment in planting crops with and without Peruvian guano which demonstrated the use of the popular fertilizer made no difference and, indeed, had "failed signally."[27]

Such debates preoccupied Clemson during these years, and they reveal his intense interest in practical agriculture. Clemson himself indicated this at a meeting of the U.S. Agricultural Society in Washington in 1857, during which a lengthy conversation arose between himself and Dr. Antisell of the Smithsonian Institution and two gentlemen from New York, named Waring and Olcott, as to the exhausting effect of sorgho upon soils. In the course of this conversation, which the society subsequently voted to have printed, Clemson remarked, "The subject is one of immense importance, and I never approach it without becoming humility, and the proper sense of my own inadequacy to comprehend the beginning of such a gigantic subject."[28] On the basis of these articles and his other activities, Holmes and Sherrill argue, quite persuasively, that Clemson achieved considerable prominence as an agricultural scientist even if, as they acknowledge, like other early leaders in the field at the time, he was right in some of his theories and wrong in others. "Since he was a careful observer, a profound thinker, and a gifted writer," they conclude, "Clemson was a pioneer, and his work helped to lay the foundations for further investigation, experimentation, and research."[29] This judgment would seem to be borne out by the October 1857 article in the *American Farmer* in which, after discussing agricultural experimentation at Riversdale, Calvert's plantation, Clemson was identified as "formerly chargé to Belgium, and so well known here as a chemist and writer in scientific subjects."[30]

It is not the intention of this chapter to examine these works or Clemson's reputation as a scientist—that will be left to others in this volume with training in such matters—but rather to put Clemson's work as an advocate of scientific agriculture and agricultural education into the larger context of the national agricultural movement of the period. There he may not have been the most prominent advocate of scientific agriculture, but he was indeed important, and through his involvement in the movement, he learned and contributed much that helped shape his vision of the agricultural college that would be his legacy.

What Clemson and others like him were advocating in the way of technical education was what European scientists like Liebig at Giessen or Johnston at Edinburgh were already doing. Alfred True's *A History of Agricultural Experimentation and Research in the United States, 1607–1925*; Paul Gates's *The Farmer's Age, 1815-1860*; and Earle Ross's *Democracy's College: The Land-Grant Movement in the Formative Stage* are three authoritative books that discuss in great detail, if in different ways, the efforts of agricultural advocates to respond to the needs of farmers.[31] These advocacies were threefold: agricultural experimentation or scientific agriculture; the establishment of technical schools and colleges (sometimes in the literature of the period termed "industrial education") which would eventually culminate in the Morrill Act in 1862 and the establishment of land-grant institutions; and federal support of agriculture and of a separate, cabinet-level department of agriculture. None of these things was achieved until later, and their eventual success was, as these authors emphasize, a collective endeavor, the result of many groups working together at the local, state, and national levels. Thus, as Alfred True observes of the passage of the Morrill Act, the creation of the Department of Agriculture, and later the Hatch Act, these enactments "represented the combined efforts of different individuals and institutions. Agricultural science grew chiefly as the result of numerous small additions to knowledge, credit for which it was increasingly difficult to give to individuals."[32] And the movement's eventual success was due to the persistence of these individuals, not public opinion, for as Earle Ross notes of the establishment of land-grant colleges, "As usual, the enthusiasts could readily secure endorsement for their plan from legislatures and organizations, but there was no indication of spontaneous public interest."[33] Clemson figured prominently in all three aspects of the agricultural movement: in scientific agriculture and experimentation; in agricultural education; and in the establishment of a national agricultural agency.

Pressure for agricultural reform came particularly from the activity of local, state, and national agricultural associations and the publicity of agricultural journals. The establishment of the United States Agricultural Society in 1852, with its local and state branches and annual meetings in Washington, was particularly important as it served to focus attention on these issues and bring pressure to bear on state legislatures and Congress. One of the most colorful and effective of the many spokesmen on agricultural education was Jonathan Baldwin Turner, a native of Massachusetts and graduate of Yale. Turner's "plan" was to be the subject of much debate. While the plan eventually bore the name of Justin Morrill, the Vermont congressman who introduced the legislation in Congress, the impetus and outline of the unique land-grant plan came from Turner, who has been justly called "the John the Baptist" of the creation of land-grant colleges. Like many or most of these men involved in the agricultural reform movement, including Clemson, Turner had varied interests. In Turner's case these included abolitionism, anti-Mormonism, psychiatry, Mesmerism, spiritualism, Biblical criticism, monetary reform, inland waterways, anti-monopoly, national capital removal, and mechanical invention, as well as agricultural experimentation and educational extension and reorganization. The latter, however, was his particular passion, and he made of it a crusade—his plan was widely printed and distributed, and he spoke in its behalf tirelessly. Illinois was the first state to adopt it, but Turner's crusade became truly national in focus. Other states put forth similar proposals, some by recommendations, others by petition asking Congress to establish (a) a separate Agricultural Bureau and (b) a national institution for the teaching of agriculture. Turner's plan was presented to the U.S. Agricultural Association and published in the U.S. Patent Office Report, which gave it even wider publicity. Turner was dogged in his efforts but was told that it was not politically prudent to push the matter in Congress. In 1857 Representative Morrill introduced a resolution in the House substantially incorporating Turner's plan, but it was reported back unfavorably by the Committee on Public Lands. Introduced again, it passed both the House and Senate but was vetoed by President Buchanan. Thereafter it was overwhelmed by the secession crisis, and only in 1862, when Morrill introduced it again and many of its earlier critics and opponents (many of them from the South) had disappeared from Congress, did it finally pass.[34]

Another early and influential advocate of agricultural education was the famous newspaper editor, Horace Greeley, who, along with Harrison Howard, an idealistic cabinetmaker, sponsored a People's College Association which called for the establishment of colleges of agricultural and mechanical training. Like Turner, Greeley was a colorful individual with a multitude of interests, which he publicized in his highly influential newspaper. Greeley's *New York Tribune* was very much a personal vehicle, and there he publicized the various schemes and causes he supported: the communitarian ideas of Fourier; free land to settlers; federally sponsored internal improvements like roads, canals, and railroads; alleviation of the conditions of the working classes; the curtailment of the accumulation of wealth in the hands of a few; temperance; women's rights; and opposition to slavery and its extension. Greeley also enthusiastically embraced the cause of technical education. In explaining the need to establish what he called a People's College, he wrote:

> Our present financial collapse results directly from the public want of such training as this College is destined to supply. We have only professional men in abundance, but civil and military engineers in sufficiency; yet the captains of industry, who are to double our grain crops and teach us how to exterminate the devastating insects that rob the farmer of his anticipated harvests, are yet to be furnished. We need an education which will win the attention and aspirations of our enterprising youth from filibustering in Central America and plotting paper cities on the Yellow Stone to the fertilizing and beautifying the green hills and rural valleys that surround their childhoods' homes; we want, in short, a People's College.[35]

In the end the People's College failed, the funding promised by Charles Cook not being forthcoming, and the importance of the project for the land-grant movement, at least in the minds of agricultural reformers, was that such education would require government, not private, aid.

The agricultural reformers also focused on another possible vehicle of agricultural education and the promotion of scientific experiment and public support: the Smithson Bequest. James Smithson, a British scientist, had left his fortune to his nephew, but stipulated that if his nephew died without children his fortune should go to the United States—which he had never visited—to found at Washington an establishment to promote "the increase and diffusion of knowledge among men." In 1835 Smithson's nephew died without heirs, and Smithson's bequest was accepted by the United States Congress. However it was not until 1846, after much debate, that Congress finally determined how the bequest would be filled. Many agricultural reformers hoped to utilize it for their cause. The U.S. Ag-

ricultural Society, which was the chief center of agricultural effort and the advocacy for a federal department and agricultural colleges, proposed that the Smithson
Bequest be used to set up a national agricultural school, library, and experimental
garden. In 1854 the Maryland Agricultural Society presented a proposal for an
agricultural school with an experimental farm at Mount Vernon. Four years earlier, Dr. Lee, in his Patent Office report of 1850, had proposed that Congress
establish a scientific program at West Point, and there were other proposals for a
national establishment in this area, including the one from then Representative
Morrill in 1856 for "establishing one or more national agricultural schools upon
the basis of the naval and military schools" and to be supported at public expense.
In the end Congress decided otherwise on how the Smithson Bequest should be
spent. Still, the Smithsonian's establishment as an institution to promote science
pleased advocates of scientific agriculture like Clemson and his associates in the
Maryland and U.S. agricultural societies. The United States Agricultural Society,
which had its headquarters at the Smithsonian, thus made use of it in discussing
and presenting its proposals to supporters in Congress. The importance of these
proposals was, as Earle Ross indicates, the argument for national or federal support.[36] Similar appeals were made by other groups, but these, like Turner's efforts
and those of the U.S. Agricultural Society and Morrill, encountered opposition,
both in the Committee on Agriculture and Congress itself.

   Agricultural reformers had more success at the state level, at least in some
states like Maryland, where, largely thanks to the efforts of Clemson's friend,
Charles Benedict Calvert, the state of Maryland in 1856 passed an act "to establish and endow an agricultural college in the State of Maryland," its support to
be provided by stock subscriptions (that is, private subscription) supplemented
by a $6,000 annual appropriation from the state.[37] The experimental farm, which
most agricultural reformers considered a vital part of agricultural education, was
secured by the purchase, at an extremely generous price, of part of Calvert's Riversdale estate. The college was organized in 1858, and instruction began the following year. The establishment of the Maryland Agricultural College followed
successful state action elsewhere—with Pennsylvania chartering in 1854 the first
such agricultural college (subsequently Pennsylvania State University) and Michi-
gan following in the next year.

   Clemson's exact part in the founding of Maryland Agricultural College is un-
clear, and unfortunately most of the records regarding the institution's founding
were destroyed. Holmes and Sherrill argue the probability of a strong connection
in the institution's founding, as they do also of his playing a prominent role in the
movement for agricultural education that culminated in the Morrill Bill in 1862,
of which the founding of Maryland Agricultural College was a part. They write:

   To any person familiar with Clemson and his attitude toward scientific education, it is inconceivable that he should have lived in a suburb of Washington,

attended the meetings of the Maryland and United States Agricultural Societies, and not have been connected with this movement. It is not known whether or not he had any official connection with the undertaking, as the records of the societies of the day are rather meager, but his own statement shows that he was interested in and worked for the bill [they are referring here to the bill that eventually became the Morrill Act of 1862]. In a letter to W. W. Corcoran in 1878, Clemson said, 'The efforts which we made at the Smithsonian Institution before the war to found such institutions in each State was passed in 1862, donating to each State land scrip for the purpose.'[38]

Indeed it *is* inconceivable that Clemson did not have some part in these activities, particularly the founding of Maryland Agricultural College.

The exact part is still somewhat difficult to determine. However, there is abundant evidence of his strong advocacy of Calvert's efforts even if he was not among the institution's original trustees, which was hardly to be expected since those Calvert assembled as shareholders or trustees of the institution were, for obvious reasons, mostly wealthy planters like himself and men who boasted proud old Maryland names.[39] Clemson himself was more modest in describing his role. In a letter to Corcoran thanking him for reading to the president of the Agricultural Society of Maryland a letter which Clemson had published on the subject of the need of a scientific institution in the December 1856 issue of the *American Farmer*, he stated, "I am myself but a private individual and not connected officially with the matter, but it has my warmest sympathy and cooperation and I shall take pleasure in announcing your intended liberality."[40] He had also published in its September 1856 issue a letter to Robert Bowie, another colleague from the Maryland Agricultural Society, in which Clemson publicly stated his support of the venture.[41] Further, in a letter to Corcoran, responding to Corcoran's request of a contribution to the funding of the institution, after indicating his enthusiasm for the project, Clemson declared: "I hope that you and other friends of this institution will have a success in your efforts in this good cause. The establishment of such a school will not only benefit the Md. state, but be of incalculable authority to the agricultural interests of the whole country. I will cheerfully contribute the sum named in your note."[42] That Clemson, always a chronic worrier, particularly about money, gave so willingly is testimony to his enthusiasm for the project and the larger effort at agricultural reform of which the college was an important part.

This Clemson made clear in a letter—really an article in the form of a letter— that he wrote, dated February 1859, to the *American Farmer*. Besides being a plea for scientific education, the letter constituted a review of his and others' various activities through the Maryland Agricultural Society and U.S. Agricultural Society, the meetings at the Smithsonian, and particularly the recent meeting of the Advisory Board of Agriculture at the Patent Office at which, as he put it, "gentlemen, connected with agriculture, from the different parts of the United States" were "requested to give their opinion, as to the best mode of promoting or benefiting agriculture." In relating the tenor of this meeting, Clemson also indicated his own views and those of his colleagues. This letter expresses those views so well that it needs to be quoted here in full:

> So far as I could judge, there was unanimity in favour of Scientific Education and I remarked with much satisfaction, that all those I heard speak, expressed not only their individual opinion, but the wants of the community in which they lived. Some thought that an independent agricultural bureau, having at its head a Secretary, equal in rank, etc., with the other Departments, was essential, not only for fostering and protecting agriculture, but particularly necessary to aid the treaty making power. Whilst all, as far as I could learn, were in favor of donations of lands, from the public domain to the States, on certain conditions, for the establishment of Agricultural Colleges.
>
> The establishment of Scientific Universities in the different States, not special to agriculture alone, but including that art, (for it is based upon the Sciences,) would I think better fill the objects in view.
>
> Some were of opinion that there should be established within the District of Columbia, an experimental farm, attached to the Department. The establishment of a Department, and a Farm, at the seat of Government, does not appear practicable in the present state of political feeling, throughout the country. Those who look upon the Federal Government as one of delegated, and constitutional powers, would undoubtedly oppose any such measure, whilst they would, I think, cheerfully advocate the donation of public lands for a purpose so essential to the advancement of all the arts, including agriculture, as scientific education, through the individual States. Indeed, if the question of donations of land, to the several States, for such a purpose, was properly presented it would, I think, pass both Houses of Congress, without a dissenting voice.

Further, and with great eloquence and an eye to their critics, Clemson argued the benefits of agricultural education for the future of the country, seeing in agricultural science and experimentation the only recourse for an agricultural society in which, as previous history had amply demonstrated, the land would eventually be exhausted. Thus, with great perception, he observed:

> I have long been of opinion that the time would surely come, when in this country, more than in any other, the demand for scientific instruction, and that in its highest grade, would be imperative. I have seen the subject rolling on and gathering daily strength, with the diffusion of general information. It appears to me that it must be a consequence of information and reflection. No one more than myself appreciates the blessings of our civilization, which are greatly due to the influence of the classics, and I believe that they will continue to have a most happy effect for all time, in their sphere—but at the same time it appears no less

clear, that the sciences are destined to increase the amount of knowledge in the world, far beyond what imagination conceives. The want of adequate scientific instruction is everywhere felt more and more, and as population increases, and our once fertile lands are exhausted, it will become a necessity. When nature's bank refuses to honour the drafts of population for meat and bread the resources of science be appealed to, and it will then be discovered that there is no hope out of it; nay, it is a fact already known to many, that science is the only foundation upon which we can depend for the increase of facts or for the recuperation of exhausted lands, or sustaining the fertility of those that are tilled.

The day is not far distant when the fertile lands in the West will all be taken up. 'The unbounded West,' as it has been called, is found to have limits, and much of it is known to be too sterile to support population. In the mean time population will continue to increase in an unprecedented manner, and much of the land that was once considered inexhaustible, has been worked improvidently, worn out, and thus denuded of vegetable covering, and in many instances soil abandoned, unprotected, to the devastating ravages of the atmospheric agents. The melancholy result of improvident husbandry is not limited to a few acres, but extends over entire regions. The economical gatherings of time have disappeared, but a small part has been harvested, whilst the most has been washed into gullies, thence into streams, and finally to the ocean—nature's great reservoir, where she gathers together her life resources, for the wants of future creations, perhaps of an entirely different order from those that have peopled the earth heretofore.

Those who believe that I indulge in fancy sketches, can refer to the statistics of production in our country, and they will find, that what I have figured, is already upon us, not in one instance, or to a limited extent, but on the contrary in every state, and wherever sufficient time has elapsed to show the impoverishing effects of the course pursued, throughout the entire country. It is not surprising. These consequences are mathematically true, and as certain as the return of the seasons, or that the sun will rise and set to-morrow.

The solution, or solutions, Clemson envisioned was science and a new kind of education. His comments are particularly striking in the way he anticipates, if from the different perspective of soil exhaustion, Frederick Jackson Turner's famous "frontier thesis," as well as Clemson's emphasis on fertilizer which eventually became a revenue earner for the college his bequest created. Clemson wrote:

The object of education is to make us, whilst we live, useful to ourselves and to mankind, with as little harm to others as possible. The fact of our coming into existence imposes upon us duties, which are greater than life itself; and if we so live, that when inevitable death comes, we can say that we have used our intelligence, through life, to guide us, to the best of our knowledge, we may calmly and confidently anticipate whatever may be our future. Science would appear to be the most elevating of occupations for the mind. If we are not permitted to comprehend the Almighty, his works and the laws that govern the universe, are at least partially within our comprehension, and their contemplation must exalt the understanding and purify the mind.

The utility of such institutions, as we have been speaking of, would greatly depend on the manner they are projected and carried on. Men of the highest character, ability and acquirements, should be selected, and with such advantages, great consequences might be confidently anticipated. Each in its own State would form a centre, around which other institutions would come into activity. Preparatory schools of various kinds and usefulness, would spring up, and their benign influence would extend and be felt to every part of the earth where a printed sheet would circulate.

Such institutions would naturally be charged with all questions of scientific interest. Investigations connected with the natural history of geology, mineralogy, and agricultural fitness of soil and the peculiar adaptations to which the resources of different States are best suited, would there be elaborated and kept to be referred to and used as required. The learned faculty, each in his line, would engage in original and important research, by which knowledge would be increased, whilst the immediate objects of the institutions would be the diffusion of facts on all scientific subjects. It would be vain to attempt to fix a limit to the benefits that would thus be conferred upon mankind and their effects upon society.

And Clemson concluded by urging adoption by Congress of what was then being advocated by fellow reformers and presented by Justin Morrill, an action which he said would be "scarcely less significant than the Declaration of Independence."[43]

Such a statement expresses well the thinking of Clemson and his friends. Calvert expressed similar views in a letter he wrote to a Baltimore businessman, J. C. Nicholson, explaining the purpose of the newly founded Maryland Agricultural College—a description that fits equally well the kind of education Clemson envisioned at the institution his own bequest established. Calvert wrote:

We expect to teach everything that is taught in the best universities and in addition to those branches we shall require every student to learn scientific and practical agriculture and mechanics which of course will require him to engage at certain hours in all the outdoor operations of the farm and workshops. They will also be required to study agricultural chemistry, botany, mineralogy, geology, entomology, animal and vegetable physiology, mathematics in general and particularly as applied to agriculture such as surveying, leveling, drawing and in truth everything that will make the student a practical and scientific man. The means to have an institution superior to any other, and we shall have such a one if the farmers are only true to themselves and give us the sufficient means to erect the buildings and fairly start the institution.[44]

**Half-plate daguerreotype of U.S. Patent Office, Washington, D.C. Photograph by John Plumbe Jr., ca. 1846. Library of Congress, cph 3g03596.**

Their thinking reflected the wealthy planters or gentleman farmers they nearly all were, but also the emphasis on scientific research and experimentation that both Clemson and Calvert deemed essential. Clemson's promotion of these ideas, both in the founding of Maryland Agricultural College and the discussions and presentations that eventually led to the land-grant act, was therefore significant.

Soon, in fact, Clemson was to have a short-lived opportunity to realize these ideas. In January 1860, the *Quarterly Journal of Agriculture* announced that Secretary of Interior Jacob Thompson had invited Clemson to organize an Agricultural Bureau which was to supersede the operations previously under the Patent Office. Thompson's offer could not have come at a more propitious time both in Clemson's personal life and his long-frustrated search for public employment. Always subject to severe depression, he was particularly dispirited at this point, so much so that his Uncle Elias Baker, responding to his frequent complaints, counseled him, "You must not always look at the 'Black Side' of things, give the 'Bright Side' equal and the same thought and see if you have reason to complain and grumble as you do."[45] This was good advice but difficult for Clemson to follow. He had a difficult relationship with his daughter, Floride, who was high-spirited and a constant source of friction. Anna tried to smooth things between them, as she also tried to pull him through his melancholic, bitter moments, but he was often despondent. For instance, in the spring of 1855 he fretted over his drought-stricken farm, and when, in the early spring of 1857 he could not find a tenant to replace Neides, he talked of selling out. Then his mood changed momentarily when he learned that King Léopold of Belgium had requested the incoming Buchanan administration to return Clemson to his diplomatic post, but his hopes were soon dashed when Secretary of State Lewis Cass, who had earlier given his approval, put him off and the position was given to someone else. Then, on December 20, 1858, his youngest child, Cornelia (Nina), upon whom he doted, died suddenly of scarlet fever. Her death left him distraught. He grew even more despondent when, in October 1859, his friend and financial advisor Charles Leupp committed suicide. Clemson wrote his uncle Elias that he thought it "the most fortunate thing that could occur to me if the Grave would close over me and relieve me from a life that is becoming a heavy burden to carry."[46]

### *Finally, a New Position*

At this point Clemson's fortune changed. He was offered a public position of the kind he had long sought and the opportunity—or so it seemed—to promote some of the ideas he and others had been championing. This came with the offer of the position as superintendent of agricultural affairs within the Patent Office. Clemson served there in a long list of surprisingly capable, if underfunded, experts serving agricultural needs. Specifically, those in charge of the Agricultural Bureau collected data concerning crops and methods of plowing, planting, cultivating, and feeding; they published an Annual Report that helped publicize farmers' experiences and experiments; and they began free distribution of seeds. Henry L. Ellsworth, appointed commissioner of patents in 1836, had done particularly well by the job, John Quincy Adams remarking of his work in 1845 that "Ellsworth has turned the Patent Office from a mere gim-crack shop to a great and highly useful public establishment." But his successors fared less well and were often criticized for the political character of the Patent Office, while the inadequate funding allotted the Patent Office for its agricultural functions greatly irked agricultural leaders.[47] The criticisms of agricultural leaders were not always consistent. For example, many agricultural publications, as well as local, state, and national agricultural societies, complained of the insufficient funds allotted by the Patent Office for its work and, like the United States Agricultural Society, called for a separate agricultural department dedicated to the needs of agriculture, an idea that went back to George Washington in his last presidential address to Congress in 1796. However, others, even agricultural advocates like Horace Greeley but particularly seedsmen, seeing in some of its activities like the free distribution of seeds unwonted competition, complained of the Patent Office's "wastefulness."

Daniel J. Brown, as editor and compiler of the annual agricultural volumes published by the Patent Office from 1854 to 1859 and head of the agency during the period, was especially attacked, so much so that he finally became politically untenable and was dropped from the Patent Office. This made Clemson's appointment possible, and in January 1860 he was informed by Secretary of the Interior Jacob Thompson that the Buchanan administration planned to enlarge the Agricultural Bureau of the Patent Office and make it a separate division within the department. Since Thompson desired a scientific person to be in charge, and no doubt impressed by the articles that Clemson had published and his reputation as a scientist, Thompson offered him the position as superintendent of agricultural affairs. Though disappointed by the salary offered, Clemson readily accepted. The new position, as Ernest Lander notes, was "an exhilarating challenge," and Clemson's health and spirits immediately improved.[48] "My time," he wrote his uncle

Elias Baker, explaining why he could not give much thought to business, "is absorbed to the extent of having but little to give to other than public duties."[49]

Clemson threw himself enthusiastically into his position. But he soon encountered difficulties—both within the Patent Office and the political establishment—in implementing some of the ideas that he and his friends advocated. For although his appointment was generally well received, there was opposition to reorganization within the Patent Office. In particular Philip F. Thomas, the new commissioner of patents, did not share his predecessor's views about the proposed separation of the Agricultural Office and refused to allow a change in the existing organization.[50] Eventually Secretary Thompson overruled Thomas and made the proposed separation, and Clemson, upon taking up his position and pending consummation of the transfer and management of his office, was placed as superintendent of agriculture under the secretary of interior. Clemson's position remained ambiguous, however, as the difference of opinion between Thompson and Thomas over a separate agricultural bureau was also reflected in Congress and, in the end, blocked. "The Government brought me here to organize the Agricultural Bureau," he complained to his uncle Elias, "but I fear that I shall do but little because they will not let me, and Congress will most probably fail to give us the appropriation necessary to do what the country expects."[51] He was right. An article entitled "What the Government is Doing for Agriculture," which appeared in the *Quarterly Journal of Agriculture* a short time later, explains well the confused situation and the frustration Clemson experienced:

> Congress voted an appropriation of $60,000 for the collection of agricultural statistics and the distribution of seeds, nor was there any desire manifested to have it expended in any different manner than heretofore. Even those Representatives who had professed to be in favor of an 'Agricultural Bureau' held their peace when the appropriation was voted, and it passed without calling the 'ayes and noes.' Consequently the Secretary of the Interior did not feel disposed to carry out his views expressed during the meeting of the United States Agricultural Society last winter, and the Commissioner of Patents has absolute control of the expenditures of the 'agricultural appropriation.' It is understood that Mr. Clemson submitted a plan for organizing a separate Agricultural Bureau to the Secretary of the Interior, but it has neither been adopted nor published.[52]

In the end, like the establishment of land-grant agricultural schools, a separate agricultural department, such as he and others had argued for, had to wait until another day. Blocked in his efforts to reorganize the agricultural bureau, Clemson was sent to Europe by Commissioner Thomas to purchase seeds and cuttings. How long he was gone is not known, but according to Holmes and Sherrill, "the rift between the North and South which led to the Civil War was growing very rapidly and Clemson, being thoroughly in sympathy with the Confederacy, found himself out of harmony with the administration." On March 9, 1861, he sent his resignation to C. B. Smith, the new secretary of the interior, explaining that he had tendered his resignation earlier to Jacob Thompson, but at Thompson's urging remained to complete the annual report for 1860. With that done, Clemson continued, "I have determined to defer my purpose no longer, and beg leave hereby to resign the commission I hold."[53]

That report is indeed the best record of his activities as superintendent of agriculture, as it is also an eloquent summation of the ideas and conviction that had occupied him for a decade. It was, in the words of John V. Donnelly, "perhaps the most visionary in its recommendations and the most outspoken in its language."[54] Clemson began by asserting the urgency and necessity of an agency devoted solely and independently to the needs of agriculture:

The requirements of the present age, and the importance of the permanent importance of the subjects embraced in its operations, demand that the power of this agency of the Government should be enlarged. This opinion was expressed in the views I had the honor to submit to the Secretary of the Interior at the period of my being called by that functionary to the position of Superintendent of Agricultural Affairs.

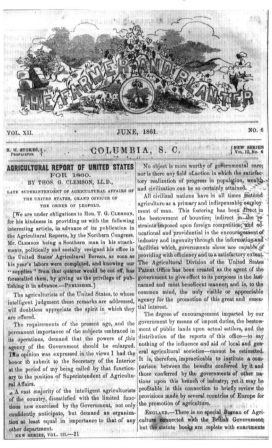

Title page of T. G. Clemson's Superintendent of Agriculture report for 1860. *The Farmer and Planter* (Columbia, S.C.), June 1861.

This recommendation, he said, was supported by "a vast majority of the intelligent agriculturalists of the country, dissatisfied with the limited functions now exercised by the Government"; they, he asserted, "not only confidently anticipate, but demand an organization at least equal in importance as any other department." "I should be wanting in fidelity to the trust reposed in me," he declared by way of support of his proposal, "were I not earnestly to urge a more efficient encouragement to this great basis of all prosperity. The enlarged organization I have proposed is indispensable to the prosperity of our country; and the consummation of such a creation is an achievement in which man may be proud to engage."

Clemson conceded that in the early stages of the country's existence, during the Revolution and its early years, there had been more pressing needs. But the country's needs, and the needs particularly of agriculture, had changed and, notwithstanding the obstacles of party politics and suspicion of government power, a national agricultural policy was imperative:

> That the great interest of agriculture should be without suitable representation in the Government appears as an anomaly, and indicates a want of appreciation of the true state of our civilization. The present embryotic organization owes its existence to ideas of expediency expressed in the form of an annual grant to collect and distribute seeds and cuttings and information on their culture. That it should prove inefficient for the accomplishment of great and far-seeing enterprises is necessarily incident to its limited foundations and unstable tenure. The remedy is with the American people and their legislators; and it is confidently believed that, as the members of the great producing family become imbued with these truths, they will manifest their opinions by firm and vigorous action. An adequate organization and corresponding appropriations will be greeted throughout the land with the approving response of millions. A Department established under such auspices for the benefit of the paramount agricultural interest of the country, should be separate and apart from all influences other than those prompted by the highest regard for the public good, unobtrusive in its conduct as in nature, and having truth for its object. It should endure untrammelled, and free from all partisan considerations. It should know no section, no latitude, no longitude. It should be subservient to no party other than the great party of production.

While Clemson praised the current agency and its commitment to scientific discovery, the nation's welfare, he argued, was tied to agriculture's success and its advancement, and this could only occur if Congress became more actively involved in the preservation and promotion of the agricultural industry and the proper exploitation of its resources:

> There are questions of serious import connected with the management of these lands which may not longer be postponed without sinister and momentous detriment to the future welfare of the country. As is elsewhere intimated in these remarks, the mineral wealth of the nation, so intimately connected with agricultural prosperity demands the highest and most intelligent offices of the Government, guided by the lights of science. These great national resources cannot be neglected with impunity; they demand more than any other portion of the nation's dependencies, other cares than they have received; and this interest

could not be placed in better keeping than under a Department of Agriculture of ample capacity and power.

He then listed the duties to be performed by such an agency. They included (1) the promotion and coordination of agricultural societies in the country and collection and dissemination of "correct statistical information which could be collected in any other manner, and which would be of untold interest and advantage to our country and the world"; (2) the publication of an annual Report on Agriculture; (3) "the study of indigenous plants for familiar cultivation in our country"; (4) "entomological investigations into the nature and history of predatory insects which have proved so injurious to our crops of cereals, fruits, &c., and also to timber"; (5) experimentation in irrigation and "methods of renovating lands, of keeping them in a constant state of fertility, and of producing crops which cannot be obtained in any other way without further outlay than by use of water" and thereby transforming land "now waste and entirely unproductive" into profitable cultivation; (6) the stocking of rivers with fish, which, he declared, was "a matter of great interest, and can only be carried out by the Government." Such activities, he noted, "has not only attracted the attention of European governments, but it has been repeatedly carried into successful operation there," but regrettably only "upon a limited scale," and "in a section of this country."

And, finally, Clemson returned to his notion that such work could not be done within the existing Patent Office, which ill-served the needs of both patent interests and those of agriculture. The government therefore should restructure the agencies so that the responsibilities for agriculture should fall upon the shoulders of someone familiar with the relevant sciences and accountable for that task alone. In short, a national agricultural policy and agency were absolutely essential, and this was the sensible—the necessary—way to proceed.[55]

In this declaration, Clemson anticipated the functions of the Department of Agriculture and other enactments later. These ideas were not original with him, of course; rather he assembled and embodied—in an eloquent and often impassioned manner, replete at times with literary and historical allusions—the principal ideas and themes of the agricultural movement. The influence of Clemson's report can be debated, for events pushed aside deliberation on his recommendations as they also brought to a close his Washington years. In fact his report was published only after his resignation from office. But stillborn though it might have been, his report indicates the prominent part he played in the agriculture reform movement and that if his name is not associated in the public memory, as is Morrill's, with these enactments, he was nonetheless, as Holmes and Sherrill maintain, "one of the leaders of this movement, and he deserves honorable mention."[56]

## Casting His Lot with the South

Lincoln's election in November 1860 put the Clemsons in a great state of excitement about the secession crisis and, naturally, under a cloud of suspicion. Having resigned his position in March, he, accompanied by Anna, made a brief business trip back to South Carolina. Writing his uncle Elias from Montgomery, Alabama, he indicated his view of the situation: "We are preparing for war, and if the North wants it & the black republicans force it upon us, they will surely have it & they will find out that war will not take place in this ground, it will be carried home to them until they cry peace."[57] It was there that he received news that war was imminent, and on April 11, the eve of the firing on Fort Sumter, he and his wife decided to return to their son and daughter in Maryland. Despite the war and an uncertain future, once back in Maryland, he made an effort to plant crops and fruit trees on his farm, though he also prudently made arrangements to transfer the farm to his wife's name.[58] He was, however, under suspicion for his southern sympathies and restricted in his movements. "In answer to your kind letter of this past 21st," he wrote his uncle on May 24, "I have to say that it is most prudent for me to stay at home or rather not to show myself in Washington." He went on to say, "As for myself as I have said before, it becomes me not to show my face often where there are so many persons interested in supporting a Union that to all intents & purposes is defunct. There appears to be no liberty of thought allowed & if they have dubbed me a traitor in the New York papers, I do not know what dictator Lincoln might take it in his head to visit upon mine." And he concluded: "Thank you for your kind information, but at the present juncture of affairs I can not leave home for I do not know how soon I may be driven hence. If I came to leave my family, I fear that my name, however little known anywhere, might be sufficiently so to call down harsh treatment of sentences."[59] In June, having settled his legal affairs, he left for the South with his son, both subsequently to volunteer in the Confederate Army, leaving his wife in Maryland to defend the property. The Washington years were ended.

Clemson's career does not follow the trajectory biographers might prefer, with each step of the way being a step toward some greater triumph. His career was repeatedly disrupted by events—by setbacks in Calhoun's ambitions, by Calhoun's death and the loss of a powerful patron, by the nature of partisan politics, by the Civil War, by family tragedy and conflict, and doubtless also by his own temperament and mental state. These factors bring to mind George Orwell's famous statement that "viewed from the inside," that is from one's own perspective, every man's life seems a failure. Clemson, viewing his life from the perspective of his Washington years, might have drawn the same conclusion: once more his life ambition, his mission, his opportunities had eluded him. But viewed from other perspectives this was not the case. The ideas Clemson embodied, argued for, and debated were, in fact, eventually realized through others' creation of the Department of Agriculture and enactment of the Morrill Act establishing land-grant colleges. And Clemson's continuing efforts led directly to the institution that bears his name and embodies so many of his ideas. The Washington years were a critical part of that legacy.

## Notes

1.  Ernest McPherson Lander Jr., *The Calhoun Family and Thomas Green Clemson: The Decline of a Southern Patriarchy* (Columbia: University of South Carolina Press, 1983), viii.
2.  Thomas Green Clemson to Richard Kenner Cralle, 13 January 1853, Calhoun Papers, MSS 200, folder 409, Special Collections, Clemson University Libraries, Clemson, South Carolina (hereafter cited as SCCUL). Cralle had been Calhoun's personal secretary. Clemson worked closely with Cralle in preparation of the publication of Calhoun's papers. These were published as *The Works of John C. Calhoun*, 6 vols. (New York: D. Appleton, 1851-1856).
3.  TGC to Cralle, 30 January 1853, Calhoun Papers, MSS 200, folder 409, SCCUL.
4.  Ibid., 27 February 1853.
5.  Ibid., 8 March 1853.
6.  Ibid., 25 May 1853.
7.  TGC to Elias Baker, 6 August 1852, Clemson Papers, MSS 2, Box 8, folder 2, SCCUL.
8.  Alester G. Holmes and George R. Sherrill, *Thomas Green Clemson: His Life and Work* (Richmond, VA: Garrett and Massie, 1937), 96-97.
9.  TGC to Cralle, 10 July 1853, Calhoun Papers, MSS 200, folder 410, SCCUL. Clemson's decision may also have reflected his wife Anna's influence, for although she was not enthusiastic about the socializing that might be required to further Clemson's ambition, she was anxious to settle down, and clearly this could not be done in South Carolina, Clemson having sold the Canebrake estate and given the family situation at Fort Hill. Moreover, ever the dutiful wife, she wanted to do nothing to indispose the irritable Clemson, subject to bouts of serious depression, all the more in the circumstances of his career frustrations. See Lander, *Calhoun Family and Thomas Green Clemson*; and Ann Russell, *Legacy of a Southern Lady: Anna Calhoun Clemson, 1817-1875* (Clemson, SC: Clemson University Digital Press, 2007).
10. Clemson's business activities are detailed in his letters to Elias Baker and Charles Leupp, his financial advisor and business agent, of which there are a considerable number in the Clemson papers. The most valuable of these letters, or at least those in which Clemson most reveals himself, are those to Baker. Clemson's letters to and from Elias Baker can be found in Clemson Papers, MSS 2, Box 8, SCCUL; for Charles Leupp, see Clemson Papers, MSS, Boxes 1-2, SCCUL.
11. Ibid., 15 January 1854.
12. Ibid., 19 July 1854.
13. Ibid., 26 December 1854, and 6 October 1855.
14. Ibid., 3 November 1855.
15. Ibid., 24 June 1856.
16. Lander, Preface, *Calhoun Family and Thomas Green Clemson*, viii.
17. Russell, *Legacy of a Southern Lady*, 263-264.
18. George Denny, *Proud Past, Promising Future: Cities and Towns in Prince George's County* (Brentwood, MD: Dilden Company, n.d.). See also *Atlas of Prince George's County, Maryland, 1861* (Baltimore, MD: Simon J. Martenet, C.E., 1861); and *Atlas of Fifteen Miles around Washington including the County of Prince George's County, Maryland* (Philadelphia: G. Hopkins, 1878). Denny indicates in *Proud Past, Promising Future* that Calhoun lived in the home prior to his death, but this is a mistake since the Clemsons were out of the country at the time of Calhoun's death and, as indicated, did not purchase the property until 1853.
19. "Prince George's County: Over 300 Years of History," Prince George's County Tricentennial (1996), http://www.pghistory.org/PG/PG300/antebel.html.
20. Ibid.

21. Ibid.; Clemson's own views on slavery are somewhat ambivalent, even if his allegiance to the South was not. Lander notes in his book: "It is of interest to note Clemson's attitude toward slavery. Born in Pennsylvania, he nonetheless became a strong supporter of the institution. When he offered to sell his plantation [Canebrake], at first he wished to retain his Negroes, he said, because 'they are the most valuable property in the South, being the basis of the whole Southern fabric.' But he was not blind to the economic limitations of slavery. He went on to say: 'My experience tells me that the Institution of slavery is at all times good for the negro (no labourers in the world are so well off), at times good for the master, but very bad for the State.'" Lander, *Calhoun Family and Thomas Green Clemson*, 92; Clemson was to have similarly ambiguous views on secession, but once done, his loyalty was clear. His wife's views, on the other hand, were more outspokenly supportive of slavery. She wrote her father from Belgium (24 January 1846) that she told Europeans, after seeing the plight of the poor there, "Make your working classes in Europe as happy as the slaves & then come back to me, & we will talk about the abolition of slavery"; Russell, *Legacy of a Southern Lady*, 214; Lander has a similar citation of Anna C. Clemson's argument that "wage slavery in Europe was worse than chattel slavery in the South." Lander, *Calhoun Family and Thomas Green Clemson*, 92.

22. George H. Callcott, *A History of the University of Maryland* (Baltimore, MD: Historical Society, 1966), 136. While the Calvert estate was named Riversdale, the nearby town later changed its name to Riverdale.

23. There are excellent accounts of Calvert in Callcott's *History of the University of Maryland*, 131-152, and, more briefly, in his recent *The University of Maryland at College Park, A History* (Baltimore, MD: Noble House, 2005). For the Calvert family and their importance to the region, see the following: "Riverdale Mansion, A Maryland Treasure for 200 Years," http://www.lessor.net/riverdale/Riverdale.html; Christina A. Davis, *The Riverdale Story: Mansion to Municipality* (Riverdale, MD: Town of Riverdale Park, 1996); "Prince George's County: Over 300 Years of History," http://www.pghistory.org/ PG/PG300; "Julia Calvert Stuart, Cleydael's History: Calverts and Stiers," http://www.cleydael.org/calverts.shtml; and "Town History, 1800-1899," http://ci.riverdale-park.md.us/History/Nineteenth.html.

24. Mrs. [Favell Lee] Mortimer, *Far Off, Part II: Africa and America Described 1854*, in *The Clumsiest People in Europe, or: Mrs. Mortimer's Bad Tempered Guide to the Victorian World*, ed. by Todd Pruzan (New York: Bloomsbury Publishing, 2005), 165. Mrs. Mortimer was but one of a long list of visitors, particularly British, from Fanny Trollope to Charles Dickens to Mrs. Trollope's son Anthony, who had little good to say about the city; American visitors were equally critical. See John W. Reps, *Washington on View: The Nation's Capital since 1790* (Chapel Hill: University of North Carolina Press, 1991); Howard B. Furer, *Washington, A Chronological and Documentary History* (Dobbs Ferry, NY: Oceana Publications, 1991); and Bob Arnebeck, *The Seat of Empire: A History of Washington, D.C. 1790-1861*, Chap. 4, "Insecurity and Grandeur: 1841 to 1861," http://geocities.com/bobarnebeck/finalfour.htm.

25. Reps, *Washington on View*, 132.

26. Holmes and Sherrill, *Thomas Green Clemson*, 121-122.

27. Ibid., 109-110. Holmes and Sherrill reproduce the full text of these affidavits detailing Clemson's experiments.

28. Ibid., 115.

29. Ibid., 121-122.

30. *American Farmer* 12, no. 4 (October 1857): 120.

31. Earle Ross, *Democracy's College: The Land-Grant Movement in the Formative Stage* (Ames: Iowa State College Press, 1942), 16. Ross notes the multitude and variety of agricultural remedies offered, but observes that many came from people of doubtful competence and often little scientific knowledge. He writes, "New agricultural practices became the hobby of medical leisure; theologians and sentimental journalists made a fashionable fad of horticulture and landscaping; and self-trained practicing civil engineers rendered their services without the restraints and checks of the higher mathematics."

32. Alfred Charles True, *A History of Agricultural Experimentation and Research in the United States, 1607-1925* (Washington, DC: United States Department of Agriculture, 1937), 111.

33. Ross, *Democracy's College*, 65-66.

34. See Ross for a discussion of the often halting steps, replete with setbacks, to adoption of the Morrill Bill and the dispute of authorship, regarding whether Turner or Morrill should be called the "father" of the land-grant act. Like True, Ross considers it an achievement of the agricultural movement of the period. Of Turner's part he writes: "He, like all the other 'fathers,' whether inspirational agitator or constructive organizer, contributed in greater or less degree to an organic act which in basic principles epitomized a quarter century of observation and discussion." Ross, *Democracy's College*, 54.
35. Ibid., 24.
36. Ibid., 40-41.
37. Ibid., 30-32. For a fuller account of the founding of Maryland Agriculture College, see Callcott's *History of the University of Maryland*, 131-152. There were similar efforts in others states; indeed, as Ross notes, "Apparently every state from Massachusetts to California that had a projected institution or even a vaguely planned scheme of industrial education was represented by one or more of these petitions." Ross, *Democracy's College*, 42-44. One of the more interesting of these proposals—and unusually detailed—was that of the distinguished planter and later Civil War general Philip St. George Cocke, president of the Virginia State Agricultural Society. Cocke's "ingenious, comprehensive plan of state agricultural education" resembled in many of its features those in other states, like Turner's in Illinois, and, as elsewhere, encountered sectional, sectarian, and class interests and, in the end, was blocked by the Civil War. Ross notes that southerners were also hampered by their need to defend slavery. Ibid., 33.
38. Holmes and Sherrill, *Thomas Green Clemson*, 128.
39. Callcott, *History of the University of Maryland*, 133-139. Callcott identifies them as from the Eastern Shore: James T. Earle, William T. Goldsborough, John C. Groome, and Samuel Hambleton; from the southern counties: John S. Skinner, Nicholas B. Worthington, Robert Bowie, John H. Sothoron, Allen Bowie Davis, and William N. Mercier; from near Baltimore: Ramsay McHenry, Charles Carroll, John Merryman, and Thomas Swann; and from the western counties: John O. Wharton, Thomas Perry, J. Dixon Roman, and George R. Dennis. In the Calvert papers at the University of Maryland, there are numerous letters to and from many of these men regarding the college's founding and of discussions and actions of the Maryland Agricultural Society; there are no letters to Clemson on these matters which may reflect that, being neighbors and himself attending some of the sessions of the Maryland Agricultural Society where founding the college were discussed, he and Calvert did not need to correspond on these matters or that not being a Marylander they saw his value more as a scientist and at the national level. Certainly Clemson's March 1859 letter to the *American Farmer*, cited below in note 43, suggests that he was very much involved in these efforts.
40. TGC to W. W. Corcoran, 3 January 1857, Clemson Papers, MSS 2, Box 3, folder 14, SCCUL.
41. *American Farmer* 12, no. 3 (September 1856): 69.
42. TCG to Corcoran, 5 January 1857, Corcoran Papers, Library of Congress, 39: 55 ½.
43. Thomas Green Clemson, "The Necessity and Value of Scientific Instruction," *American Farmer* 14, no. 1 (March 1859): 275-277. The letter to the editors is dated February 1859.
44. Charles Benedict Calvert to J. C. Nicholson, 29 September 1858, Calvert Papers, University of Maryland, MDMS 5473.
45. Elias Baker to TGC, 24 October 1859, Clemson Papers, MSS 2, Box 8, folder 2, SCCUL.
46. Lander, *Calhoun Family and Thomas Green Clemson*, 180-183. For this period of Clemson's life, see also Russell, *Legacy of a Southern Lady*.
47. Paul W. Gates, *The Farmer's Age* (New York: Holt, Rinehart, and Winston, 1960), 331.
48. Lander, *Calhoun Family and Thomas Green Clemson*, 183; True, *History of Agricultural Experimentation and Research*, 33-34; Holmes and Sherrill, *Thomas Green Clemson*, 130.
49. TCG to Elias Baker, 12 April 1860, Clemson Papers, MSS 2, Box 8, folder 2, SCCUL.
50. Philip Thomas, in a letter to Jacob Thompson, secretary of the interior, dated 12 May 1860, explained his opposition to the proposed change: "Sir, In the course of several conversations which I had with you since I entered upon the duties of Commissioner of Patents, touching the contemplated change in the relations which have heretofore subsisted between the Agricultural Office and the Patent Office, I took occasion to remark that I differed from my predecessor, Mr. Bishop, as to the policy and necessity of the proposed separation. Subsequent reflection has served to strengthen the opinion heretofore expressed by me on that subject. In

Mr. Bishop's letter to the Department, of the date of the 11ᵗʰ of January 1860, the principal reason assigned by him for advising the separation, besides the want of congruity between the two offices, is, that the entire time of the Commission is required in attending to the legitimate business of his office. It is true that the duties of the Commissioner of Patents are arduous and require the devotion of much of his time to their performance. Notwithstanding this, I think that sufficient leisure may be found to enable him to control and manage the Agricultural Office. At all events, unless it is your purpose to erect the office into a separate bureau, I am willing to undertake the labor and responsibility of its management, and I flatter myself that with the valuable aid of Mr. Clemson, and your own council [sic] and assistance, the office may be made more efficient and more acceptable to the Agricultural community than before." Clemson Papers, MSS 2, Box 3, folder 18, SCCUL. This is the letter Holmes and Sherrill refer to as being in the archives of the Secretary of the Interior.

51. TCG to Elias Baker, 12 April 1860, Clemson Papers, MSS 2, Box 8, folder 2, SCCUL.
52. *Quarterly Journal of Agriculture*, cited in Holmes and Sherrill, *Thomas Green Clemson*, 133-134.
53. Ibid., 134.
54. John V. Donnelly, "Genesis: The Birth of the FDA in the Patent Office," 20, leda.law.harvard.edu/leda/data/341/Donnelly.pdf.
55. *Report of the Commissioner of Patents for the Year 1860* (Washington, DC: Government Printing Office, 1861). H. R. Exec. Doc., No. 48, 36ᵗʰ Congress, 2nd Session, 5 (1861).
56. Holmes and Sherrill, *Thomas Green Clemson*, 140.
57. TCG to Elias Baker, 4 April 1861, Clemson Papers, MSS 2, Box 8, folder 2, SCCUL.
58. Power of attorney over property in Prince George's County, signed by Clemson, 5 April 1861. Clemson Papers, MSS 2, Box 4, folder 2, SCCUL.
59. TCG to Elias Baker, 24 May 1861, Clemson Papers, MSS 2, Box 8, folder 2, SCCUL.

# Chapter 6

# THOMAS GREEN CLEMSON:
## SCIENTIST AND ENGINEER

## *Chalmers M. Butler*

Page from Thomas Green Clemson's letter to John C. Calhoun, August 5, 1842, describing Clemson's engineering work at Calhoun's O'Bar gold mine in Dahlonega, Georgia. Thomas Green Clemson Papers, Special Collections, Clemson University Libraries.

Thomas Green Clemson was a chemist of impeccable credentials and outstanding background for the mid-nineteenth century, and he possessed a deep understanding and working knowledge of mineralogy and geology. He also was a highly competent mining engineer with particular strength in metallurgy, derived from his foundation in chemistry. Judging from the papers and letters that he left, one sees in Clemson a propensity for applications of chemistry, but no evidence has been found that he contributed to the pool of fundamental knowledge in this basic science. Evidently, he focused his energies on the applications of these disciplines to accomplish practical results in commerce, industry, and agriculture, especially in fertilizer. Clemson was a man of wide interests, extending beyond chemistry and engineering to art, music, farming, hunting, politics, and, in particular, to education.

The importance of education to young Clemson manifests itself in his choice to travel to Paris in 1826 at age nineteen to study chemistry through 1831 or, perhaps, 1832, at the University of Paris [*La Sorbonne*] and the Royal College of France [*Le Collège royal de France*], and mining engineering at the School of Mines [*L'Ecole des mines*], under, by most counts, the finest nineteenth-century chemistry and mining engineering faculties in the world. Moreover, as Clemson later stated in court testimony, he was examined at the Royal Mint [*La Monnaie royale de Paris*] and certified as an assayer in June 1831.

Clemson was a skilled practitioner with a deep understanding of the science underlying chemistry, a man who held knowledge in high regard. From 1830 to 1836 he authored numerous journal papers and co-authored another with R. C. Taylor in 1839. After his service as chargé d'affaires to Belgium from October 4, 1844, to January 8, 1852, he published seven additional papers in the period from 1856 to 1859. From inspection of his published papers, one gleans facts about the man as an applied scientist. Chemist R. N. Brackett, who studied fifteen of Clemson's papers published before 1850, notes that twelve pertained directly to chemistry and include assays and analyses of iron ores, minerals, hydraulic limestone, copper ore, and coals, plus one on methods for manufacturing Nordhausen sulfuric acid in Germany. The other three, he explains, include a geological examination of a region of Virginia, an investigation of the physical geography of the Hartz region of Germany, and an assessment of the iron ore of Yates County, New York. The 1839 paper by Clemson and Taylor reports the findings of their analysis of bituminous coal outcroppings near Havana, Cuba. His last seven papers pertain to agriculture and further reveal his expertise in chemistry, mineralogy, and geology.

Upon his return to the United States from France in 1832 with his education in chemistry, mining engineering, and allied sciences, Clemson sought to establish himself as a professional consultant. During these early professional years, when prestigious jobs for qualified scientists were few in number, he applied for the position of state geologist in both New Jersey (1835) and Pennsylvania (1836), but, though well qualified for such a post, Clemson ultimately received neither appointment.

During late 1842 and early 1843, Clemson was in charge of John C. Calhoun's O'Bar gold mine near Dahlonega, Georgia, in an area where, in the sixteenth century, gold may have been mined by laborers of Ferdinand De Soto. The summer and part of the fall of 1842 are a short chronological span in the life of Clemson, but the prodigious, extant correspondence between Calhoun and him is a rich record of his mining engineering at an actual mine, from which one has the opportunity to examine his engineering prowess.

The above paragraphs provide a sketch of selected facets of T. G. Clemson's education and professional career as a chemist and mining engineer. Each is elaborated upon in the following pages, and the details are carefully documented in order to place in plain view some of Clemson's accomplishments and experiences.

## Clemson's Paris Education

Knowledge and understanding of the principles underlying a discipline and skill in analyzing the interactions among these principles are the marks of a chemical or physical scientist. To these, add skill in selectively synthesizing the consequences of these principles within a constraining environment for the purpose of creating a desired result, and one has the marks of an engineer. Knowledge and understanding of principles are acquired through investigation and study. Skill comes from practice and experimentation, not only physical but also mental, within the framework of these principles. Many strategies lead to the acquisition of knowledge and understanding, but all effective methods, when stripped of their trappings, reduce to personal observation of fundamental phenomena and study of the writings and recordings of experts. Of course, in numerous ways the deepening of intellect, acquisition of knowledge, and development of skills can be significantly enhanced and rendered more efficient through the guidance of experienced teachers. Thomas Green Clemson wisely elected to seek further education in Paris under the direction of the world's acknowledged experts in chemistry and allied sciences, as well as in mining engineering, rather than to rely solely on unaided self-education or on guidance by less esteemed science and engineering mentors in the United States.

Clemson traveled to Paris in 1826 at the age of nineteen, and there he studied chemistry, geology, and mining engineering through 1831 or, perhaps, 1832.[1] A brief outline of the stature and accomplishments of scientists and engineers under whom he studied in Paris reveals, in part, the quality of the education to which Clemson was exposed, and, in addition, it sheds light on the background that he likely acquired. His professors and mentors are identified in two sources: one is a July 17, 1831, letter[2] to Clemson from Lefte Neal, a friend and fellow Paris student from Canada, written just days prior to Clemson's impending departure from Paris, and the other is an excerpt[3] from the record of a Bucks County, Pennsylvania, murder trial (December 1831 and February 1832) at which Clemson testified as an expert witness in chemistry.

During his Paris years, Clemson attended lectures by or worked under the guidance of Arcet, Jean-Baptiste Elie de Beaumont, Pierre Berthier, Ours Dufrénoy, Joseph Louis Gay-Lussac, and André Guenyveau, among others. These professors are named in the farewell letter (in French) of July 17, 1831, to Clemson from Lefte Neal, who is effusive in his description of Clemson's standing with his professors, suggesting that he was a good student, who enjoyed the respect of his teachers and mentors:

> ...M. Berthier, whom I saw on the 12th regrets to see you leave. It was indeed wittingly that this scholar, the first [greatest] analyst of the century, gave to you the certificate that you bear. For the way in which he spoke to me of his great pupil is worth even more than the certificate. I congratulate you with all my heart for all the keen interest that you have inspired in all your teachers. You should feel a noble pride in thinking that you are honored by the friendship of an Elie de Beaumont, whose beautiful system of geology has just received the confirmation of the new discoveries made in India and in many other parts of the globe; of a Robiquet, whose numerous works and whose learned and numerous analyses reveal to us a successor to Vanquelin, of a Thénard, of a Gay-Lussac, of an Arcet, all on the summits of science, and of their learned collaborators, the learned engineer-in-chief Guenyveau, the engineer Dufrénoy, celebrated teacher in the most celebrated school in France. Few French, my dear Clemson, are as happy [fortunate] as we.
>
> In your country you are going to apply the knowledge acquired in our first [best] schools of Paris; and, thank God, it will not be knowledge that will be lacking in the geologist, the chemist, or the physicist....[4]

Clemson was engaged by the Bucks County Court authorities to participate—as an expert witness for the prosecution—in the analysis of the contents of a murder victim's stomach to determine if poisons were present. No doubt Clemson was selected for this undertaking on the basis of his acknowledged expertise in chemistry, even at the young age of twenty-four years. In order to apprise the court of his qualifications and background as an expert in chemistry, Clemson, under oath, offered the following testimony:

> ...before 1826, I engaged in acquisition of chemical information in the United States. In 1826 I went to Europe, and in the fall of that year entered the practical laboratory of Mr. Gaultier de Clowbry; at the same time I attended the lectures of Thénard, Gay-Lussac, and Dulong, as delivered at the Sorbonne, Royal College of France. In 1827 I entered the practical laboratory of Langier and Fiber and afterwards the private laboratory of Robiquet; after which I gained admittance to the Royal School of Mines. I was then examined at the mint, and received my diploma as Assayer. It is dated June 1831. I then came to the United States, where I arrived in the fore part of September, 1831.[5]

Title page of the published proceedings of the murder trial of Lucretia Chapman (Dec. 1831 and Feb. 1832), in which Thomas Green Clemson testified as an expert witness for the prosecution (Philadelphia: G. W. Mentz, 1832).

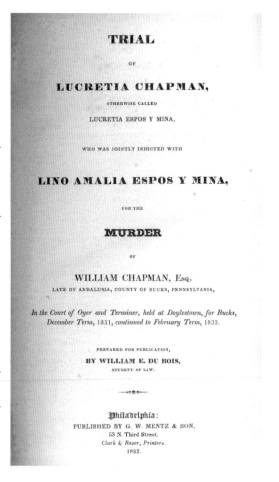

TRIAL

OF

LUCRETIA CHAPMAN,

OTHERWISE CALLED

LUCRETIA ESPOS Y MINA,

WHO WAS JOINTLY INDICTED WITH

LINO AMALIA ESPOS Y MINA,

FOR THE

MURDER

OF

WILLIAM CHAPMAN, Esq.

LATE OF ANDALUSIA, COUNTY OF BUCKS, PENNSYLVANIA,

In the Court of Oyer and Terminer, held at Doylestown, for Bucks, December Term, 1831, continued to February Term, 1832.

PREPARED FOR PUBLICATION,

BY WILLIAM E. DU BOIS,

STUDENT OF LAW.

Philadelphia:

PUBLISHED BY G. W. MENTZ & SON,

53 N. Third Street.

Clark & Raser, Printers.

1832.

From the above segment of testimony, one has a partial list of the names of Clemson's professors and mentors, learns that he attended the Royal School of Mines, and finds that the Royal Mint certified him as an assayer. For many years no independent evidence surfaced confirming that Clemson actually attended the school until his enrollment as an auditor during 1828 to 1832 was claimed in a letter of July 1, 1926, from M. Chesneau, director of the School of Mines in Paris, to Robert Skinner, council general of the United States in Paris.[6] About his search of the school's records, Director Chesneau writes,

I have been unable to find any record of a student by the name of Clemson either in the minutes or the directory of former students of the school. However, I entertained some doubts on the matter as a note under date of Nov. 4, 1828, indicated that a young American by the name of Clauson was authorized to attend classes at the school of mines [sic]. A further search of our archives revealed the fact that the Clauson of 1828 was none other than Thomas Clemson.[7]

Chesneau explains the details of his search and then says further, "a blue slip has just been discovered in the name of Clemson (Thomas), 1828–1832, which means that Thomas Clemson attended the classes at our school as 'auditeur libre,' from 1828 to 1832; therefore, the Clauson of November 4, 1828, can be no other person but Thomas Clemson."[8] Actually, evidence that Clemson attended the School of Mines has been available since the early 1830s: four journal papers published by Clemson bear the school's name as the author's affiliation.[9]

In his farewell letter, Neal is explicit about the rapport Clemson enjoyed with his eminent teachers and mentors and underscores their admiration for their American pupil. From Neal's observations, one infers that Clemson was looked upon as a serious and good student by the faculty. The letter also lists faculty to whom Clemson was exposed, in addition to those named by him in his Lucretia Chapman trial testimony.[10]

Who were these professors, teachers, and mentors? Among them one finds pre-eminent nineteenth-century scientists. For instance, Joseph Louis Gay-Lussac, who held professorships in both physics and chemistry and is claimed by both communities, discovered two fundamental gas laws, one of which bears his name and pertains to the temperature-volume behavior of gases. The other speaks to the way in which two gases combine and is known as *the law of combining volumes.* His careful experimentation enabled Gay-Lussac to demonstrate that inert gases, subject to a specified rise in temperature, undergo the same volumetric expansion. His discovery of the laws of chemical combination in gases aided in the establishment of the all-important atomic theory and led the way to *Avogadro's law.* The scientific world was amazed at some of Gay-Lussac's experimental findings in the combining of gases. For instance, Bernard Jaffe[11] describes the paradoxical outcome of one such experiment: "one volume of hydrogen chloride gas when brought in contact with one volume of ammonia gas yielded a white powder, and no residue of either gas left." Gay-Lussac also contributed to the development of analytical chemistry, especially titration, and introduced the name *pipette*, still used today.[12]

**Joseph Louis Gay-Lussac, preeminent nineteenth-century scientist under whom Thomas Green Clemson studied in Paris. The Edgar Fahs Smith Memorial Collection, Department of Special Collections, University of Pennsylvania Library.**

Louis Jacques Thénard was also a chemist of wide interests, who discovered hydrogen peroxide and developed cobalt compounds from which he created a practical pigment for French porcelain known as *Thénard's blue.* Thénard and Gay-Lussac together were the first to isolate the element boron (1808), and they pioneered photochemistry. A baron who was knighted, Thénard served as dean of the Paris Faculty of Sciences in 1822, and, ultimately, became (1845–1852) the chancellor of the University of Paris, the highest position in the French university system. He authored an expansive, prestigious, and widely adopted, four-volume chemistry textbook, *Traité de chimie élémetaire, théorique et pratique,* which underwent six editions during 1813–1836 and was translated into German, Italian, and Spanish, with parts into English.[13] Pierre-Louis Dulong was trained as a physician but became interested in botany, then chemistry and mathematics, and finally made his mark in physical chemistry and physics. He held professorships in chemistry in the Faculty of Science, Paris, and in physics at the Polytechnic School [*Ecole Polytechnique*], and he served as the director of the Polytechnic for eight years. He made many important contributions to both physics and chemistry, the most celebrated of which is the Dulong and Petit *law of constant atomic heat capacity,* developed in collaboration with the mathematical physicist Alexis Therese Petit, who died in 1820 before Clemson's arrival in Paris in 1826. This relationship between atomic weights of elements and their specific heats had a profound effect on the development of the system of atomic weights, upon which so much of modern physical science is founded. They also demonstrated that Newton's *law of cooling* is valid only for small temperature differences. *Dulong's hypothesis,* arrived at empirically, provides the means for a practitioner to compute the approximate heating value of a fuel from knowledge of its chemical composition.[14]

Pierre-Jean Robiquet, a professor of chemistry at the Polytechnic School, who today would be labeled a pharmaceutical chemist, is credited with the discovery of caffeine, among other compounds, and of codeine in opium.[15] Pierre Berthier discovered bauxite and was professor of assaying and head of the laboratory at the School of Mines. He was an expert in mineralogy and mining engineering and is credited with important contributions to techniques for locating and analyzing mineral deposits, especially those of phosphates, for use in agriculture. In his well-known and widely used *Traité des essais par la voie sèche,* Berthier prescribes accurate and practical field procedures for mineralogists and mining engineers.[16] Jean-Baptiste Elie de Beaumont served for fourteen years as engineer-in-chief of mines of France and was professor of geology at the School of Mines in Paris. He and Ours Pierre Dufrénoy, also an engineer and geologist, prepared the great geological map of France, a sixteen-year undertaking.[17]

These gifted scientists at the School of Mines offered courses in which were covered subterranean topography, mining techniques, ore processing, analytic mineral chemistry, mineralogy, geology, hydraulic and steam engines, and drafting, plus laboratory practice. After the second year, students undertook field study trips to mining or metallurgical regions. Study of a subject was complete when a prescribed level of attainment was reached, typically realized only after another year at the School of Mines. Then more field study trips were required for a student to complete the course of study.[18]

The noted American science historian, Bernard Jaffe, explains, "Previous to 1840, American students of chemistry went to Paris to study under Dumas, Gay-Lussac, and Thénard."[19] Much earlier, the famous Swedish chemist, Jons Jacob Berzelius, widely referred to as "the organizer of scientific chemistry," had reminisced in the winter of 1823–24 to a young colleague, who, in turn, recorded Berzelius's mentioning "Gay-Lussac, Thénard, Dulong, Wollaston, H. Davy, and other distinguished men of science of that period, upon whose shoulders we of a later generation now stand….Chief in his esteem and veneration were Gay-Lussac and Humphry Davy."[20] Of the five international chemists Berzelius revered, three were Clemson's teachers mentioned in Neal's letter, and Berzelius chose Gay-Lussac as one of the two for whom he reserved worldwide preeminence. Robert D. Purrington, American physicist and noted science historian, writes,

> During the forty years before 1830, France was peerless among the scientific nations of the world. The names LaPlace, Poisson, Berthollet, Ampere, Fourier, Carnot, Fresnel, Biot, Cauchy, Gay-Lussac, Lavoisier, de Morveau, Fourcroy, Dulong, and Petit do not exhaust the roll of scientific luminaries working in France during this period. Despite the inclinations of scientists such as Fresnel and Fourier to eschew untestable hypotheses, French discoveries proved crucial in propagating the atomic theory. Notable among them was the work of Pierre Louis Dulong (1785–1838) and Alexis Therese Petit (1791–1820).[21]

Clemson's professors Gay-Lussac and Dulong are among the most esteemed in Purrington's view, with Dulong and Petit the paragons of the early nineteenth century.

## *The Chemist*

The high quality of the education in chemistry and mining engineering to which Clemson was exposed in Paris and the rapport he enjoyed with his world-famous professors, e.g., Gay-Lussac, Thénard, and Dulong, as claimed in classmate Lefte Neal's letter,[22] suggest that Clemson's advanced education in chemistry must have been extraordinary, especially in the early nineteenth century. Moreover, the subsequent selection of Clemson as an expert witness by the Bucks County Court, Pennsylvania, to aid in the analysis of the stomach content of a murder victim underscores the confidence the authorities held in Clemson and his knowledge of chemistry.[23]

Dr. R. N. Brackett,[24] who in 1891 joined the faculty of Clemson College, Clemson, South Carolina, and who served for many years as head of the Chemistry Department, published a two-part paper in the April and May, 1928, issues of the *Journal of Chemical Education* entitled, "Thomas Green Clemson, LL.D., the Chemist, Parts I[25] and II."[26] Part I provides a sketch of Clemson's life, especially as a scientist, and a description of analyses of papers authored by Clemson. In Part II Brackett discusses Clemson's interest in and contributions to scientific education:

> During the period 1830 to 1836, part of which time he was a student at the School of Mines, and at the Royal Mint, and the remainder still living in Paris, fifteen papers were published under Clemson's name and one jointly with R. C. Taylor. Of these fifteen papers, twelve are distinctly chemical[:] assays and analyses of iron ores, minerals, hydraulic limestone, copper ore, and coals; one on piperin; and one on the method of manufacture of Nordhausen sulfuric acid in Germany. The other three papers by Clemson were on the physical geography, etc., of the Hartz; [a] geological examination of the country between Fredericksburg and Winchester, Va; [and] native iron of Yates County, New York. The joint paper of Clemson and Taylor was on a vein of bituminous coal in the vicinity of Havana, Cuba.[27]

Brackett's invaluable list[28] of these papers, with which he concludes Part II, reflects the following publishers and titles:

### Transactions of the Geological Society of Pennsylvania
1. "Analysis of the Copper Ore of Hunterdon County, New Jersey." 1 (1835): 167.
2. "Examination and Analysis of Several Coals and Iron Ores Accompanying Mr. R. C. Taylor's Account of the Coal-field of Blossburg." 1 (1835): 220–223.
3. "Analysis of the Minerals Accompanying Mr. E. Miller's Donation." 1 (1835): 271–274.
4. "Analysis of Some of the Coal from the Richmond Mines." 1 (1835): 295–297.
5. "Notice of a Geological Examination of the Country between Fredericksburg and Winchester, in Virginia, Including the Gold Region." 1 (1835): 298–313.
6. "Notice of Native Iron from Pen Yan, Yates County, New York." 1 (1835): 358–359.

### Journal of the Franklin Institute
7. "Analysis and Observations on Diverse Mineral Substances." 13 (1834): 78–79.
8. "Assay of an Iron Ore from Franklin County, New York." 13 (1834): 79–80.
9. "Analysis of Two Varieties of Hydraulic Limestone from Virginia." 13 (1834): 80.

### Silliman's Journal (aka American Journal of Science and Arts; since 1880, American Journal of Science)
10. "Assay and Analysis of an Iron Ore (fer titanne) from the Environs of Baltimore." 17 (1830): 42–43.
11. "Notice of Piperin." 17 (1830): 325–356.
12. "The Hartz—Its Physical Geography, Etc." 19 (1831): 105–130.
13. "Notice of the Method of Manufacturing the Smoking Sulphuric Acid, as Practiced at Nordhausen, Braunlage, and Tanne in Germany." 20 (1831): 347–350.
14. "Analysis of American Spathic Iron and Bronzite." 24 (1833): 170–171.

**American Farmer**
15. "Sources of Ammonia." 11 (1856): 339.
16. "The Importance and Advantage of a Scientific Institution for the Advancement of Agriculture." (Letter to J. T. Earl, Esq., president of Maryland State Agricultural Society, October 4, 1856) 12 (1857): 161.
17. "Microscopic Organisms, etc." 12 (1857): 114.
18. "The Marl Formations: Their Composition and Value." 13 (1858): 5.
19. "Infusorial Organisms." 13 (1858): 5.
20. "The Necessity and Value of Scientific Instruction." 14 (1859): 275–277.

**Others**
21. [with R. C. Taylor, co-author], "Notice of a Vein of Bituminous Coal, Recently Explored in the Vicinity of Havana, in the Island of Cuba" (1836). *American Philosophical Society Transactions* 6 (1839): 191–196.
22. "Description et analyse de la Seybertite, nouvelle espèce minérale." *Annal. des Mines* 2 (1832): 493–495.

To the above list could be added an 1844 paper[29] by Clemson in the journal, *The Orion*. This interesting paper is on gold, including extraction from the earth, metallurgy, mineralogy, assaying, and its history; its pages are replete with descriptive terms of chemistry-based techniques, such as *departing* and *sweating a guinea*, both of which are, of course, applications of chemistry but which Clemson would classify as assaying and metallurgy. For this reason, the content of this twenty-third paper is addressed later in terms of mining engineering.

From his study of Clemson's papers on chemistry and from his perspective as a chemist who had benefited from almost a century of subsequent enhancements in the science, Professor Brackett characterizes chemist Clemson as a highly skilled practitioner in fundamental chemistry: "It has not been found that Dr. Clemson made any contribution to the development of chemistry as a science, but that he had an exceptional grasp and clear understanding of chemical facts and principles, was a competent analyst, and that he had a keen appreciation of the dependence of agriculture and industry on chemistry."[30] Edgar F. Smith, Blanchard Professor of Chemistry at the University of Pennsylvania, partially confirms Brackett's observation: "It is said that Thomas G. Clemson (1807–1888), educated in Chemistry at the School of Mines in Paris, was the first to announce the discovery of the diamond in the itacolumite of North Carolina. Other minerals were announced by him at various times, but his contributions to pure chemistry do not seem to be well known."[31] In applications in agriculture, Brackett again characterizes Clemson as an accomplished chemist with a practical bent:

> Clemson's interest in agricultural chemistry is shown by the numerous papers on this subject which were published in the *American Farmer*, but more especially by his two papers on 'Fertilizers,' published in the Patent Office Reports,

Agricultural Division, for 1859 and 1860. Together these two papers constitute a scholarly, and for the time very complete treatise on agricultural chemistry, and show a thorough knowledge of the status of chemistry, both as a science and in its applications, especially to agriculture, but to industry as well. His familiarity with the literature of chemistry and its applications, past and current, is abundantly shown by numerous quotations and citations. These papers contain a number of original suggestions and interpretations, and several references to his laboratory and work, which prove that Dr. Clemson was a practical chemist of ability.[32]

Clemson is credited by some scientists with the discovery of phosphoric acid in atmospheric air about which he spoke and wrote, but others award credit for this important finding to a French chemist M. Barral, a disparity which drew the ire of American physician and professor, Dr. Thomas Antisell,[33] who reported his dissatisfaction in a letter to the editor of the *American Farmer* in which the discovery was first published:

In the number of your excellent journal for May, 1856, Mr. Clemson states, from his own inquiries and experiments, that phosphoric acid exists in the air and in the snow and rain water percolating through the atmosphere. This deduction is quite original on his part, and he deserves much credit for the clearness of the enunciation and the continuousness of the exposition of the means by which this acid is found as a normal constituent of the atmosphere: I mean the infusoria and animalculae which exist everywhere....(*American Farmer,* May, 1856, Vol. XI, page 330.) In a letter addressed to the President of the Maryland State Agricultural Society, in October, 1856 (*ibidem,* Vol. XII, page 162), he [Clemson] repeats the statement and declares the presence of infusoria and the decomposition of animal matter to be abundant sources of ammonia and phosphoric acid in the air. In the paper on microscopic organisms, published in the *American Farmer* for October, 1857, the fact of the presence of phosphoric acid in the air...is distinctly pointed out; and this whole matter was strongly set forth before the United States Agricultural Society at the meeting for 1857. The novelty of the fact stated then struck the writer of this with considerable surprise at the time, but...we may look upon it as an acknowledged fact that this acid—the phosphoric—must be looked upon as a normal constituent of the atmospheric air.

I have been led to make the foregoing general observations upon the atmospheric constituents, and the new fact with regard to it with which Mr. Clemson has enriched science, because I perceive that in the *Presse Scientifique de deux monds* [sic; *mondes*] for 1ˢᵗ December, 1860, a statement that M. Barral, a French chemist of considerable eminence, has communicated to the Academy of Sciences a similar discovery; which he asserts he made lately, but which he had suspected seven years ago, namely, the presence of phosphoric acid in the air....It is not often discoveries are made by men of science in this country in anticipation of European chemistry, as has happened in this instance, and when made, as they have been so lately in Europe, the effect will be that the credit of this discovery will be given to M. Barral and not to the present Superintendent of the Agricultural Department of the United States [Clemson] to whom it justly belongs. As the original memoirs and communications of this discovery have been made to your journal, I take the opportunity of publishing, through your columns, the facts of the case, which show that this discovery, now claimed by France, was made before, and published in this country in the columns of the *American Farmer* in 1856.[34]

Though born and educated in Ireland, Dr. Antisell resolutely asserts his fellow American's privilege to claim to be the first to identify phosphoric acid in air.

Clemson's contributions to scientific agriculture are elaborated elsewhere in this book, so information provided here on this subject is limited to support of his eminence as a chemist. In this regard, Alester Holmes and George Sherrill report that "in his article on 'Fertilizers' outlined elsewhere, he assembled the experiments, theories, and knowledge from all parts of the world and pointed out practical means of applying them to agriculture in the United States. In this article alone he refers to…[forty-two eminent scientists are listed by name, including his Paris professors Gay-Lussac and Berthier], and many other noted scientists."[35] Other evidence of Clemson's ability as an applied chemist can be found in Brackett[36] and in Holmes and Sherrill.[37]

### Mining Engineer

Mining in the Southern Appalachians dates back many years with copper mining dating to prehistoric times. Gold was found near Dahlonega, Georgia, in the late 1820s and lured treasure hunters to area towns, swelling them by thousands in the years immediately following the discovery, but, when gold was discovered in California in 1848, most of the miners "rushed" west, effectively emptying Dahlonega and surrounding towns.[38] Notwithstanding this exodus, gold mining near Dahlonega survived with modest success into the twentieth century and provided a rather continuous supply of income for mine owners and skilled miners. John C. Calhoun became interested in ownership of a gold mine, probably in hopes of bolstering his always-precarious income from an enterprise that did not require his regular, physical presence on site. According to Sherry L. Boatright, who searched the pertinent deeds and litigation records thoroughly, Calhoun purchased what became known as the Calhoun Mine or the O'Bar Mine and owned it, perhaps initially with his son Andrew Pickens Calhoun, from June 28, 1833, until his death on March 31, 1850.[39] The mine is located in present-day Lumpkin County, Georgia, about four miles south of Dahlonega on a hillside overlooking the banks of the Chestatee River.[40] Calhoun leased or rented the mine for a share of the take from 1833 until June of 1842, when Clemson took over direction of its operation.[41]

As early as 1830 members of the United States House of Representatives from gold-producing states urged the establishment of federal assaying offices in order to standardize the valuation of mined gold, but, after no progress in creating legislation, the effort evolved into demands by a few senators that the United States Mint be branched. Led by John C. Calhoun and supported by a handful of senators from gold-producing states, the effort met with success on March 3, 1835, when President Andrew Jackson signed into law a bill creating branch mints in Charlotte, Dahlonega, and New Orleans.[42]

By the early part of the nineteenth century when Clemson returned home from Paris to embark upon a career, mining of various metals had been practiced for more than 6,000 years,[43] and there is evidence that gold, which often was found on the surface of the earth in several forms, had been used for ornamental purposes prior to any human record.[44] Methods of mining and releasing gold from its *in situ* environment, primarily by washing or panning, were known by the Egyptians prior to 3800 BCE.[45] Although gold is often found in the form of nuggets on the surface of the earth and in stream beds, most must be extracted from within the earth and subsequently parted from the material in which it is embedded. It is usually found as minute particles, as a fine powder, or in very, very thin layers within sand, gravel, shale, slate, or rock of varying hardness, and it often is concentrated in veins within these materials. Through the years, numerous techniques have been developed for removing gold from its host material, with the method of choice dependent on the material and its form as well as on the configuration of the gold. If the gold is embedded in rock, shale, or slate, the composite is crushed by pounding and then is ground into a powder, after which the unwanted lighter-than-gold material is washed away, leaving the gold as a residue. If the host material is softer than rock or slate, the crushing step may not be needed. And the gold recovered from the washing process often can be further refined by smelting. These methods have been perfected over many, many years, and the details of the steps may vary depending on the nature of the gold and its host material encountered by the miner.[46]

Crushing is accomplished by laborers pounding with hammers or by stamps, the latter a simple device comprising a very hard stone or iron base on which the hard ore is placed and a stone or iron head for pounding the ore. Once the ore has been crushed into small particles, it is often reduced further in size to a fine powder by means of a mortar and pestle or is ground by a mill fashioned from abrasive wheels much like those of a gristmill used to produce meal or flour from grain. Often a sieve is used in an intermediate step to separate large particles to be stamped again.[47] Washing could be as simple as water poured over the pulverized gold and host material on a flat board, it could be done in a pan with water,

**Water-driven stamp mill (ca. 1830-1840), similar to the one constructed under Thomas Green Clemson's supervision at the O'Bar Mine in Dahlonega, Georgia. The Dahlonega Gold Museum.**

or it could be accomplished by means of water passing through a sluice bearing the pulverized material.[48] If ore conditions are suitable, the sieving and washing can be accomplished in a single step by a *rocker* designed to sieve and wash simultaneously.[49]

As they are described and illustrated in line drawings in *De Re Metallica* (1556), ganged stamps, or *stamp mills,* which obviously were invented prior to 1556, reduced manual labor and increased the rate of crushing ore. These mills are based on the principle of the hand-operated stamp but are driven by humans, draft animals, or the weight of water. In the case of a stamp mill powered by a water wheel, the angular displacement of the turning water wheel is transformed via linkages and cams into periodic translational motion which serves to lift and subsequently drop the heads of an array of individual stamps ganged together.[50] *De Re Metallica* includes eleven illustrations of stamp mills having different numbers and sizes of ganged, individual stamps.[51] Grinding mills and rockers also can be arrayed and driven by water or other sources of power.

While in Washington in the spring of 1842, John C. Calhoun learned[52] that a new gold strike had occurred at his O'Bar mine and, because he worried that his property—now apparently much more valuable[53]—might be compromised, he asked a trusted friend John R. Mathewes of nearby Clarkesville, Georgia, to visit the mine and report what he found. In the same letter Calhoun informs Mathewes, "I shall write to my son-in-law, Mr. Clemson, and request him to make a visit for me, as soon as he arrives home from Cuba."[54] Calhoun did write to Clemson at Fort Hill, not a great distance from Dahlonega, and asked that he go to the mine to investigate and to protect Calhoun's interests. Calhoun follows with another letter expressing hope that Clemson will find it "convenient" to comply with the request and states further that, even though he has no reason to distrust his two lessees, his agent is not present at the mine and he fears that he may lose heavily if gold continues to be extracted in abundance.[55] From a letter to Clemson from Calhoun,[56] one infers that Clemson and his family arrived in Charleston from Cuba on or before May 27, 1842, so he should have reached Calhoun's mine by very early June.

A few days later on June 10, Calhoun left Washington,[57] for the first time ever during a session of Congress,[58] and reached Dahlonega sometime before June 14[59] where he met Clemson, who had hastened to the mine, departing Fort Hill very soon after receiving Calhoun's request. Initially Clemson lived in a tent on the mine property but apparently decided, soon after arrival, that he could serve Calhoun's interest most effectively by a stay of some length. And so, he and his hands began construction of a cabin at the mine site.[60] In his words, "I have had McDaniel [sic; Matthew McDonald?] and Daniel employed in putting up a stable & lumber house for bacon, meal, tools &c. All they require now is covering so that by the time Mrs. Calhoun & Anna arrive I shall have every thing very comfortable—as they I am sure will find."[61]

Lander gives an account of the gold taken from the O'Bar mine by Clemson and his workers and provides interesting descriptions of the Spartan life endured by Clemson and his wife and, occasionally, other family members, in the rugged North-Georgia hills of the O'Bar mine site.[62] As entertaining as Lander's narrative of life at the mine site is, the focus here is upon Clemson's mining activities as his prowess as a mining engineer is uncovered. Though not highly erudite from a modern-day engineer's point of view, letters from Clemson to Calhoun are rich in many of the details of the mining techniques employed by Clemson during his operation of the O'Bar mine, roughly from early June through the first week of October in 1842, with a short stint in early January of 1843.[63]

Clemson first arrived at O'Bar in early June of 1842 and immediately conducted a survey of the mine and its ongoing activities in order to acquire an appreciation of the mine activities upon which to base a preliminary plan for the operation. Aside from providing shelter for himself and others in his party, he faced several concurrent problems. It was mandatory that he keep the hands working and producing gold albeit initially using methods employed prior to Clemson's arrival; otherwise, Calhoun's venture would collapse due to failure to offset operating costs by revenue from gold.[64] Clemson surveyed the site in search of new veins of gold in order to acquire the data needed to place bounds on the size that the mining operation should ultimately reach, and he assayed the gold found in order to estimate the yield that might be realized.[65]

In a letter of June 28, Clemson conveys encouraging information to Calhoun and in doing so reveals confidence in his own mining experience: "so you perceive thus far our plan of operations works admirably. Some of the pans gave, not including the rock specimens, I think may safely say from forty to fifty penyweights [sic] of loose gold. I have seen a good deal in the way of mining but this specimen of the capability of the mine passes every thing I have heard of—& if it continues as I think it will for reasons I shall assign, you may really say that money is no object."[66] In fact, Clemson's words, "I have seen a good deal in the way of mining," characterize a person who judges his mining experience above the ordinary. Clemson also reveals familiarity with mining engineering methods when he writes:

> I think after they have finished the buildings in progress I shall set about putting up a dam & small mill below the junction of the two branches. To beat the ore by hand will be too expensive (not expensive for the ore will warrant that) but it will give occupation to too many hands which must be avoided for the accumulation of persons will decrease the yield, few resist the temptation of gold. If we conclude to work before the mill is constructed it will require extra hands for the rocker & hands to wheel the ore to the rocker. Whether the rocker is started or not I think an additional number of hands can be kept at work with advantage. If the construction of the mill (which will be cheap) meets with your aprobation [sic], they will be required about the dam race &c. I think that a road cut down taking advantage of the slope not making it too rapid & hauling it from the mouth of the mine in a cart drawn by oxen will be for some time the best mode of operating—it will be the most economical at first if not always. Beating by hand is a long & tedious operation[;] a mill with three or four stamps will do all the work we want & will require little attendance. McDaniel has constructed several here abouts & he says he thinks the water will be sufficient to drive that number of stamps.[67]

Here Clemson writes of "stamps" used in mining to crush and pulverize materials, in this case gold-bearing rock, and rockers used to separate gold from the crushed aggregate. Moreover, he suggests knowledge of how to construct a water wheel to drive the stamp mill, and it is apparent that he, with help from McDaniel, will construct the dam, wheel, and stamp mill.

In mid-July, Clemson, in part, occupied himself with additional analyses—assaying—of the gold being produced so he could determine what future extraction techniques might be most efficient and lead to optimum use of available labor. All the while he contemplated plans to improve the operation by implementing mining techniques not used before at the O'Bar. However, at this time he seems less certain than in late June that construction of a water wheel and mill is wise, as can be inferred from the use of the word *if* in a parenthetical expression about McDaniel made by Clemson: "He is honest & useful & *if* [author's emphasis] we build a mill will be necessary."[68] About the continuing search for ore, Clemson reports to Calhoun,

I put two hands to experimenting on the side of the hill due north, where [    ] made the discovery. We have found some specimens & those rocks which do not contain visible gold yield amazingly well when beaten up—& what is surprising gave coarse heavy gold. It is not continuous to the bottom of the hill nor have I been able to find it on this side—I cannot say if the present ore will continue. But if it does it will be the next richest vein, to that already discovered, that has been found in the country. The ore is very hard and white. When the gold is visible it occurs in solid roundish pieces often continuing from one end of the specimen to the other....My present impression is that it is entirely a distinct vein from the one we are working & which is so rich. Now that I have gotten regularly to work it will not take a very long time for me to possess myself of [a] pretty good idea of the extent of the gold bearing rock.[69]

As Clemson and the workers collected ore from the mine and concentrated the gold itself by methods in place when Clemson arrived at the O'Bar, he spent at least some of his time and energy devising techniques to improve yield without increasing labor and incurring the associated costs. All of these plans were tempered day by day as the miners pursued a vein and Clemson evaluated its yield. On July 31, he informs Calhoun of the installation of a railroad for hauling ore, "The rail road is down & working well."[70] And he continues, "On the morning I left I hired a hand to test on the other side of the ravine to the North, & I am pleased to say that at 10 foot in the vein is large (2 or 3 inches) & rich in gold."[71] After weighing the data, projecting potential production, and reconsidering more than once his decision to automate the mine and take advantage of water power, Clemson convinces himself in the positive and writes to Calhoun on July 31, "As soon as I can spare McDaniel to go at other work I will commence the building for a mill as I am now confident (as far as confidence can go without a perfect knowledge) that we shall have enough to do for some time for a mill. But I would much rather you were here before we progress far as I am in hopes you will be."[72]

In mine tunnels, water encroachment is an ever-present problem and can be dangerous to a miner, not to mention an interference to those who follow a vein that eventually becomes submerged. The statement below relates how Clemson, the engineer, addresses such a difficulty and uses his knowledge and skill to project a reasonable course of action:

The rock is very hard and increasing in that particular & the vein poorer than I have seen it—this is at the extreme end of the tunnel. & the water which comes in is becoming very embarrassing. This made necessary that I should set about investigating the ground with a view to running an adit level upon the vein, without which it will be difficult to work it in the direction of the inclination. I find the tunnel & consequently the auriferous dips at angle of 21° & its direction is 60° E[ast] of North. We have penetrated from the mouth of the tunnel just 80 feet and at that spot I find by calculation that the greatest depth below the surface is 26 feet—in the plan the line AB is just 26 feet. It is not extraordinary that at that slight depth there should be water. I find that a prolonging of the line DA to C will carry it to 160 feet at which distance, if the inclination continues to be 21° from A to C, a level 52 feet below a spot on the surface perpendicular to C, will strike it [,] drain it &c [;] the length of the level will be about 168 feet & I judge that it will be more advantageous to run it from the South side than the North—for many considerations. But if the prospect should not be better when I return I shall not commence that work—until after your arrival. I had anticipated a change at water level but am very much disapointment [sic] at finding water on such a ridge which cannot be less than 200 feet above the river chestatee. I have already stated to you that my opinion was (from what [I] have seen at the mine) that the vein was auriferous within certain limits and if I am correct in that statement and the main line be already terminated there remains little more gold to extract.[73]

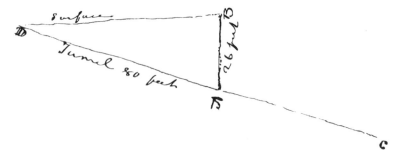

**Thomas Green Clemson's sketch of a tunnel axis, included in his August 5, 1842, letter to John C. Calhoun. (See excerpt of this letter above and the chapter's opening illustration.) Thomas Green Clemson Papers, Special Collections, Clemson University Libraries.**

The calculation upon which Clemson based the prediction that the vertical depth from surface to tunnel end is 52 feet for a 160-foot-long tunnel, declined 21° from the horizontal, is very interesting and would not be within the capacity of a person devoid of knowledge of trigonometry, geometry, or what today is called engineering graphics. He probably measured the 80-foot tunnel length and estimated or roughly measured the 21° tunnel declination with a protractor, allowing him to find the 26-foot intermediate depth. Once the intermediate depth is determined, finding the tunnel depth of 52 feet for a 160-foot-long tunnel is very easy. With modern engineering background and a handy electronic calculator, the author finds that the 26-foot intermediate depth should be 28.7 feet provided the 21° declination is correct. Measurement of tunnel declination angle in the hilly terrain of the O'Bar mine would be inaccurate even with today's instruments, so, in view of what he had at his disposal, Clemson's calculations are impressive and adequate for the application he intended. With knowledge of the depth of the end point C of the extended (imagined) tunnel, Clemson could tunnel toward C from a point on the side of the hill at an elevation below that of C, hopefully strike the gold vein near C, and follow the vein back toward the original tunnel. The new tunnel, because of its designed slope, would provide self-drainage as the miners followed the vein.

At times the gold yield did not justify the added expense of modernizing the operation and, as always, Clemson did not want to incur additional cost of improvement without concurrence from Calhoun. By September 6 Clemson was again pessimistic and so informs Calhoun:

> There is nothing transpiring here that is wrong but the misfortune of our getting but little gold, whilst the expenses of the establishment are going on, notwith-standing the economical scale upon which we are mounted; still the expenses will destroy the profits without an income beyond what we are getting at present....I have done a good deal of work since your absence & with your presence we may be able to make some changes & come to results without disapointment [sic].[74]

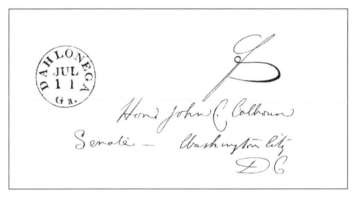

**Thomas Green Clemson letter from Dahlonega, Georgia, to U.S. Senator John C. Calhoun, July 11, 1842. Thomas Green Clemson Papers, Special Collections, Clemson University Libraries.**

The descriptions above of the exchanges between Clemson and Calhoun are representative of what one finds in their numerous other letters during mid-1842 and very early 1843 and provide abundant evidence of Clemson's knowledge of gold mining methods. The mill was ultimately constructed and completed some-time between November 8 and December 9, as is ascertained in two letters, one by Matthew McDonald on November 8 to Calhoun stating, "I have not got my mill underway as yet"[75] and another[76] in which Clemson informs Calhoun of a letter of December 9 from McDonald who states that the mill is running. In the same letter,[77] Clemson tells Calhoun that McDonald has received the jar of mercury that Clemson had asked Calhoun to order on July 25—"You had bet-ter bring with you from the North an Iron jar of Mercury. You are aware that it comes in jars of Iron & when the mill is built it will require a good deal of that metal which you can procure much cheaper North."[78] In the age-old amalgamation technique, which no doubt Clemson studied as a student at the School of Mines, mercury or quicksilver is mixed in a slurry with powdered gold and its host material, allowing the mercury to form an amalgam with the pure gold, leaving the host material behind. The mercury is removed by forcing it through a skin or cloth strainer enabling the miner to capture the contained gold.[79]

Ever hopeful of finding a technique for improving the yield of his mine, Calhoun passes on to Clemson a letter containing information about a method for treating ore reputed to be used in Russia, and, in doing so, remarks, "It will, however, I suppose, contain nothing that is not familiar to you."[80] Clemson replies with confidence derived from his scientific background:

The information contained in the printed extract is not new to me. I have often stated to you that the only means by which all the gold could be extracted, from the ores here found, is by smelting; but there are many difficulties which prevent the practice of that mode. If the ore be simply heated to the point of fusion of the gold it would I think advance nothing—because the ore by itself is not fusible & the fine gold disseminated through so great a proportion of ~~gold~~ *rock* would prevent the small particles of that metal from uniting & forming by their reunion pieces or buttons sufficiently large to be separated without loss by ulterior washing. Nor is there sufficient Iron in the majority of ore to form any thing like a treatment founded upon the reduction of the oxide of Iron, nor am I convinced that the reduction of the oxide of Iron would facilitate the collection of the contained gold. Indeed I have great doubts as to the alloying of Gold & Iron (& place no confidence in that statement, if which is somewhat doubtfully expressed, is there meant that the gold & Iron alloy.) If there was an abundance of lead to be procured cheap, there would be a great probability of a treatment being formed through the medium of that metal, by which greater quantities of gold could be saved at remunerating prices. A smelting process would be far more expensive than the present crude modes of collecting. They are however very efficient so far as the clean coarse gold is considered but entirely inefficient for the fine gold or that which is covered with a thin coating of the oxide of Iron. I have thought upon the subject a good deal & the conclusions at which I have arrived are, that no process can be instituted at once without a good deal of *preliminary* research to be made upon the ores of the countrey [sic] in a laboratory, & in the countrey and as I have stated to you, the officers of the mint should be men of scientific capability entirely adequate to the investigation of such a subject—without which little advancement in the process can be expected—& no place is so fit as the mint which should have supplies of such substances as are necessary for chemichal [sic] research. As to the miserable mode in which the mint is at present supplied, if capability were present & those enquiries part of the duties of the officers they would be prevented for the want of the necessary conveniences, as it is the supplies are scarce adequate to more than the ordinary routine of assaying &c. But Sir granting all the conveniences at hand I know not where the capacity would be found—for that kind of capacity is not intuitive.[81]

Clemson thus tells Calhoun that there is nothing new to him in the abstract from Russia and that smelting is very expensive and, for reasons given based on alloying of gold with iron or lead, might not offer improved extraction. No procedure without research conducted on the local ore holds hope of improved efficiency, and such research can be supported only by a laboratory with competent chemists and instrumentation, stocked with an adequate supply of chemicals. Analyses of the type needed do not yield to intuition, Clemson declares, and the laboratory and its personnel at the U.S. Branch Mint in Dahlonega fall far short of meeting this need. Clemson's education and his practical work experience in the leading chemistry laboratories of his time in Paris qualify him well to specify what is needed to support analyses and to render judgment of the U.S. Mint laboratories.

After some absence from the mine, Clemson returns and submits a report to Calhoun on the water wheel and mill:

> The wheel at the mill is pretty well constructed & very efficient. One of less diameter would not have answered. It runs all day & the water of the branch alone will turn it & keep the stamps in motion, but the amount of water in the branch without the dam (or when the latter is low) does not move it with as much rapidity as desirable. McDaniel thinks it can pound 150 bushels a day, which I think is above the quantity of work it is capable of performing without a flush stream. There are some little changes to be made which will make the whole work better.[82]

Clemson continues, "The arrangement of the whole affair works well & notwithstanding the small number of hands there is no mine in the country doing the same amount of profitable business."[83] He again writes to his father-in-law and then expresses satisfaction over the long term, "The beauty of the whole is the small number of hands & the compactness of the whole arrangement which can go on with out any difficulty but merely requ[i]ring common attention."[84] Apparently, Clemson feels that he has realized his goal of leaving in the hands of Calhoun an efficient, automated, and productive mine requiring minimum labor. And after returning home to Fort Hill from the O'Bar for the last time, Clemson writes to Calhoun, "The Mine and everything is going on as well as you can expect with a man of Mr. McDaniels [sic; Matthew McDonald's] roughness. But the main point is he is honest which is not a thing daily to be met with any where [and in] the gold region out of the question. I gave him some directions to follow about some little improvements in the mill &c & I now think that it will produce handsomely and regularly."[85]

In all likelihood, no mining methods or technologies employed at the O'Bar mine, or at any of the other mines in the Georgia gold region, were new to Clemson, given his education at the School of Mines in Paris and his subsequent experience. As a student he learned about applications of steam engines in mining, but surely procurement of such an engine would have escalated operating costs well beyond the affordable investment in the water wheel fabricated from on-site hewn lumber and blacksmith iron.[86]

### Assayer, Metallurgist, and Geologist

In an 1844 invited paper entitled "Gold and the Gold Region,"[87] Clemson sketches the history of gold and some of its uses and attractions, lists a number of areas of the world in which gold is found, and mentions some of their common geological features. He explains that gold occurs in a large variety of physical shapes and degrees of purity, nearly pure in some instances but often in combination with a host material. Gold ore may contain other metals or, at the other extreme, gold may appear as a trace in the ore of another metal.[88] Interestingly, Clemson writes that

> in the sixteenth century, Ferdinand de Soto and his followers, explored the country between Florida and the Ohio, in search of gold....In Washington County, Georgia, the remains of an old furnace were discovered some time since, and specimens of various kinds, from near that locality, were submitted to me for my judgment....But what goes far to prove that the Spaniards visited the country around Mount Yonah, in Habersham [County], are discoveries of ancient habitations and works for gold mining, laid bare by the recent gold operations. Among other articles that have fallen under my notice, is a small pair of silver cigar tongs, which were disinterred from several feet below the surface of the ground, and which are precisely similar to those now used by the Spaniards for holding their 'cigaritos,' or paper cigars.[89]

Clemson also mentions a cup dug from a pit and fabricated from very hard quartz, thought by many to be an incantation cup of the aborigines, but he judges it to be of European "fabric" and for use as a mortar for "purposes connected with the extraction of gold."[90] In this paper, Clemson displays a superb knowledge of gold, its history, and its various discovery sites. Notwithstanding the extent of discussion reserved for gold, he also gives the reader a synopsis of the metallurgy and mining of iron ore, especially in the United States. He goes on to write about determining the purity of gold. For an approximate analysis for finding the purity of a gold sample, Clemson says the "touch-stone" is commonly used due to the method's speed and simplicity, but, if greater precision is needed and the quantity of the sample is not small, the assay is always the resort, and he proceeds to explain *depart*, a metallurgical operation involving several chemicals, especially nitric acid.[91] Probably both to entertain and educate the reader, Clemson writes:

> Gold is soluble in nitro-muriatic acid, or Eau Regale and a knowledge of this fact gives rise to the fraud, called in England, 'sweating a guinea.' The piece or pieces to be robbed are submitted to the action of the above named mixture, and if not permitted to remain too long under its influence, a portion of gold is removed equally from all parts of the surface without sensibly defacing the impression or form of the coin. When a sufficient number of pieces have been passed through the solution, the gold is precipitated and fused, and, by this means, in time, a considerable quantity is often obtained to the detriment, of course, of the currency.[92]

Such comments convey but a sampling of the information in Clemson's 1844 paper.

He was keenly sensitive to the value of science to business and commerce and was concerned that the United States' lack of scientific sophistication not only impeded national progress but also was costly in hard cash. In a letter to James T. Earle in 1856, published in the *American Farmer,* Clemson writes[93] concerning the U.S. currency minted in the early and mid-nineteenth century and comments that he knew as a student in France of the flow of our currency to Europe and of the extraction of traces of gold present in our silver coinage. Always the advocate of more science literacy and education, he contrasts the skill of European scientists, who understood the technology for separating gold and silver from ore bearing both, to that of our mint employees who seem unable to address the problem of allowing significant gold to remain in the silver and leave the country at the price of silver. He recalls in Belgium years later, when he was chargé d'affaires, having seen large quantities of our uncirculated silver coin fresh from the U.S. Mint undergoing gold extraction. And he adds that, when he was recalled from Belgium in 1851 after his tenure of service as chargé d'affaires, he was offered the agency for purchasing and collecting U.S. coins for shipment to Belgium.[94]

While a student in the School of Mines, Clemson served as a consultant to interests here in the United States. He conducted an analysis of an iron ore found in New York State which, subjected to techniques then current in the United States, did not lend itself to the production of iron. This ore was analyzed by Clemson and found to be that of "natural steel," and a procedure was prescribed for the production of a steel suitable for manufacture of high-quality tools and implements. Ultimately, an enterprise on the brink of financial ruin became successful.[95] Similarly, an ore found in abundance near Baltimore defied all attempts at successful smelting, and another capital-intensive business appeared to be heading toward failure. A half-ton of ore was shipped to Clemson in Paris for analysis, and, after conducting an assay, he formulated a method for efficient production of high-quality iron from this ore. Clemson was proud to report that the process had been put into practice, "greatly to the pecuniary advantage of the proprietors."[96]

For a period of time from 1837 to 1839, Clemson was affiliated with Mine LaMotte in Missouri and wrote a paper on the subject. Other than a record of his claim at a public gathering at the mine site that mining techniques used in the past were primitive and would be improved, little or no technical information is found in this paper. It reminds one of a prospectus more than of a scientific paper.[97] He apparently owned[98] a one-fourth interest in Mine LaMotte at one time, but affiliated financial matters created an extended source of worry for Clemson.[99] An 1839 paper by Clemson and Taylor reports their findings of an analysis of bituminous coal outcroppings near Havana, Cuba.[100] The owners must have been pleased with the work, for they offered Clemson the directorship of the mine as he informs Calhoun in a letter of January 10, 1841: "Since I wrote you last I have received an offer to take the direction of a mine in the environs of Havana. I have accepted the appointment so far as to make a preliminary visit provided they agree to my terms....The terms are high but considering the duty, distance &[c.] not exorbitant."[101]

### Geological Survey Directorships

Land, raw materials, minerals, fuel, and water and water power were among the principal physical needs in the lives of the early citizens of the United States. Many of these life-supporting requisites were right before the eyes of the nineteenth-century Americans, but others were uncovered only through systematic exploration. Knowledge of location, accessibility, and quantities of these resources was very important, as was classification and documentation for future reference. North Carolina and South Carolina were the first two states to address this dearth of information by authorizing or initiating geological surveys in 1823 and 1824, respectively, followed by surveys in Massachusetts in 1830; Tennessee and Maryland in 1831; New Jersey, Connecticut, and Virginia in 1835; and Maine, New York, Ohio, and Pennsylvania in 1836.[102] The importance of and benefits to be accrued from state geological surveys were appreciated by leaders in science and commerce, and a number of influential politicians in the various states saw the surveys as keys to economic development. Not surprisingly, geologic data were viewed as pertinent in the knowledge base compiled to support the defense of the young nation, as evidenced by a directive by the Secretary of War John C. Calhoun to Major Stephen H. Long that he lead an expedition in 1819–1820 from Pittsburgh to Denver at the eastern reaches of the Rocky Mountains for the purpose of collecting information about the sparsely explored region. Major Long was accompanied by an entomologist and a botanist-geologist who surveyed and recorded geological features along the expedition route and its environs.[103]

Upon his return to the United States from France in 1832[104] with his education in chemistry and mining engineering, augmented with substantial background in geology and mineralogy, Clemson sought to establish himself as a chemist and a consultant[105] in mining engineering. Geological surveys in the United States were in their infancies in the first third of the nineteenth century and were among the few technological enterprises that offered employment opportunities to scientists of Clemson's educational background. New Jersey authorized its survey on February 19, 1835,[106] and Pennsylvania did so on March 29, 1836,[107] and Clemson applied, or, perhaps, friends applied in his behalf, for the position of state geologist[108] of both states. But he was appointed to neither of these choice posts.

Clemson's pursuit of the appointment to head the New Jersey geological survey is inferred from an April 11, 1835, letter written by Henry Darwin Rogers, himself a candidate anxious to secure the position, to his well-known friend Joseph Henry, in which Rogers asks Henry to influence New Jersey Governor Vroom and members of his staff in favor of Rogers's appointment. At this time Joseph Henry lived in Princeton, New Jersey, where he was a professor at New Jersey College, later to be renamed Princeton University, and was an acquaintance of the governor. Excerpts from the letter include:

> …In a former interview with the Governor at Somerville I had a good deal of conversation from the *general tenor* of which I was induced to be sanguine of my success. I find that afterwards some other names were brought before his notice and backed I presume with a good amount of weight in their favour.…It has occurred to me that an interview on your part[,] if I can ask you to attempt so unpleasant a task, with the Governor…would be perhaps the most useful thing remaining to be done.…I wish you in conversation on the subject to dwell with stress on the necessity there is that the executor of the survey be a *Chemist*, for the analysis of the *soils* & many mineral products is to be one half of the useful portion of the plan. Now most of my competitors are not chemists.
>
> The Geologist again ought to be a To[po]grapher which I do not think one of them is. I mean he ought to be familiar from practice with field research of a scientific kind such as I have witnessed with De la Beche in Eng. so that when necessary he can *amend* or *resurvey* his *map*.
>
> Clemson is neither Geol[ogist], topographer nor naturalist, knowing nothing of *fossils* so essential to all accuracy in the science. Mr. Pierce of Conn, was spoken of by the Governor as an ardent cultivator of the subject. True he did some years ago…, but this does not make him the fitter man for the survey.… Tho Clemson understands a little mineralogy & chemistry, [of] geology he is grossly ignorant in all its improvements as you may readily see by reading his pamphlet on York County, Pa. Come to Phila & you will learn the true position here of this very specious intriguer.
>
> The circumstance that my brother Wm. has received the appointment to the survey in Va. which will be something superior is certainly a reason why I

could perform that of Jersey better [than] any other person. For all discoveries made in the *same formations* I could have knowledge of long before they could reach anyone else in print & thus I should work with greatly improved light. If a chance occurs dwell on these points & pray let me hear from you as soon as you have anything to communicate.[109]

Aware from a recent audience with the governor that other candidates to head the New Jersey survey are under serious consideration for the position, Rogers writes to Henry to request that he speak to the governor in the writer's behalf. After presumptuously relating to Henry the attributes and background a qualified candidate must possess, Rogers disparages Clemson by name. From Rogers's letter in which he (1) asks an influential friend to support his candidacy for a state position by speaking to the governor, (2) defines the background and qualifications candidates must possess, and (3) declares the lack of these defined attributes in two persons named explicitly in the letter, one can only infer that the persons named are themselves candidates for the position. The editors of the Joseph Henry papers share the inference that Clemson was a candidate for the position of New Jersey state geologist.[110]

Rogers submitted to both legislative bodies unsolicited, detailed plans for organizing and performing surveys, even though at the time neither state had done more than contemplate the benefits of geologic data.[111] If Rogers's rather intrusive strategy to ensure appointment, including his specifications of qualifications of candidate directors, should be adopted, other candidates for the directorship would be at a decided disadvantage, as noted by a Rogers biographer as well as by the editors of the Henry papers.[112] Moreover, Rogers points out to Henry that benefits would accrue to the New Jersey survey should he become the director, owing to the assured scientific collaboration of his brother, William Barton Rogers, the state geologist of Virginia, especially insofar as the common geology of the contiguous regions of the two states is concerned. He, thereby, draws the criticism, "scientific nepotism," from the editors of the Henry papers: "Pierce and Clemson could, no doubt, counter the previous arguments [inadequate qualifications for the position]; this [nepotism] was unanswerable."[113]

On March 9, 1835, a mere eleven days after the New Jersey Legislature passed a bill authorizing a geological survey on February 26, Joseph Henry wrote to Rogers, "I know you must be very anxious to learn something relative to the Geological survey and I am sorry that I can give you no definite information with regard to the final result."[114] A period of eleven days seems a very short time for Rogers to become anxious, given that he must receive the announcement of the position, prepare and submit an application, and inform Henry that he had not received notice of an offer, unless, of course, Rogers had been apprised of the circumstances of the position and offer well prior to February 26, before which the job would not have been created, at least not officially.

Clemson was also a candidate for the head of the Pennsylvania survey, as one learns from Calhoun-Clemson scholar, E. M. Lander Jr., who says[115] that the Pennsylvania position was offered *tentatively* to Clemson. Interestingly, however, an April 3, 1839, letter from Calhoun to Clemson suggests not only was a firm offer tendered by Governor Porter, but also it was definitely accepted by Clemson: "You have, in my opinion, done right in accepting the offer [of the position of state geologist] made to you from the Governor of Pennsyl[vani]a [David R. Porter]. It is in line with your profession."[116] Calhoun also writes to his daughter Anna Calhoun Clemson[117] and to his brother-in-law James Edward Calhoun,[118] informing them of the offer and of his approval of Clemson's acceptance. A letter of May 4, 1839, from Calhoun to Anna C. Clemson reveals that Clemson was not appointed Pennsylvania state geologist, but no hint of what spoiled the deal is offered.[119]

Thus, Clemson was not the director of either survey, for Henry Darwin Rogers was appointed director of the New Jersey survey in 1835 and of the Pennsylvania survey in 1836, and he served in the former position until 1842 and in the latter at least through 1858.[120]

### Criticisms by Henry Darwin Rogers

In seeking support to promote his candidacy for the directorship of the New Jersey Geological Survey, Henry Darwin Rogers asked Joseph Henry to approach New Jersey Governor Peter D. Vroom in his behalf, and, in his letter, Rogers writes, "Clemson is neither Geol[ogist], topographer nor naturalist, knowing nothing of *fossils…*" and "Tho Clemson understands a little mineralogy & chemistry, [of] geology he is grossly ignorant in all its improvements as you may readily see by reading his pamphlet on York County, Pa. Come to Phila & you will learn the true position here of this very specious intriguer."[121] Given the criticism[122] of Clemson by Rogers, one is led to ask who this man was.

Henry Darwin Rogers was born in Philadelphia in 1808, but spent most of his early years in Baltimore. He was one of four brothers who became well-known scientists, all of whom were educated principally by their father, Dr. Patrick K. Rogers, a physician and later professor of natural philosophy at William and Mary College.[123] In 1829, before his twenty-second birthday, Henry Rogers was elected professor of chemistry and natural philosophy, Dickerson College. Soon, however, he clashed[124] with the authorities, and his tenure lasted only through March 1831, when his service was terminated by the Dickerson trustees due to disagreements over academic discipline, adherence to the classics,[125] and lack of courses available to students in practicable subjects.[126] After leaving Dickerson College, Rogers worked for a railroad company, lectured to laymen on subjects in the sciences, and pursued his interests in scientific writing until May 19, 1832, when he sailed for London to pursue further study[127] as well as to lecture in the sciences to the working class.[128] Though educated in mathematics and chemistry and though he refused to teach geology at Dickerson, it was shortly after arriving in London that Rogers began to turn much of his attention to the subject of geology.[129] As opposed to a formal curriculum at a university, his studies in England appear to have comprised writing and publishing, inspecting and analyzing specimens in London museums, and attending public lectures by, and mingling with, many of the principal British scientists of the day.[130] After only a year in England, Rogers returned to Philadelphia in the summer of 1833 and began a study of U.S. geology, particularly that of the Appalachian Mountains.[131] On January 2, 1835, Rogers was elected a member of the American Philosophical Society, and on January 6 he was elected professor of geology and mineralogy at the University of Pennsylvania.[132] He was appointed state geologist of New Jersey in 1835 and of Pennsylvania in 1836,[133] two positions pursued by Clemson.[134] In 1840 Rogers and Edward Hitchcock organized the American Association of Geologists, which in 1848 evolved into the American Association for the Advancement of Science,[135] and in 1863 Rogers became a charter member of the U.S. National Academy of Sciences.[136] George P. Merrill, head curator of geology (1917–1929) at the United States National Museum, wrote, "he [H. D. Rogers] was unquestionably the leading structural geologist of his time and was designated by the English geologist, J. W. Judd, foremost in the school of American orographic geology."[137]

Rogers and his brother, William Barton Rogers, professor of geology and natural philosophy at the University of Virginia (1835–1853), were the prime movers in the establishment of the Massachusetts Institute of Technology; William served as the first president of MIT (1862–1870) and served again during 1878–1881.[138] In 1857, having failed in his efforts to secure appointment to the Rumford professorship at Harvard,[139] Henry Rogers was elected to the Regius professorship of natural history at the University of Glasgow, which position he held until his death in 1866.[140] While in Scotland, Rogers was elected to membership in the prestigious Royal Society of London.[141]

Controversy and personal attacks and counterattacks were not foreign to Rogers in 1835 and throughout most of the remainder of his career in the United States. They range from near defection of young geologists employed by him in the New Jersey and Pennsylvania surveys, involving such scientists as J. Peter Leslie[142] (subsequently, professor of mining, University of Pennsylvania, dean of the Towne Scientific School, and director of the second geological survey of Pennsylvania), to acrimonious encounters with those who sought to ensure that he not be appointed to the Rumford professorship at Harvard. In ten pages of her biography of Rogers, Patsy Gerstner tells the story of the Rumford professorship controversy and describes the pro and con stances taken by prominent Bostonians.

Given his ultimate stature as a scientist and his support from leaders of Joseph Henry's reputation,[143] one can hardly discount Rogers's criticism of Clemson. Perhaps Clemson was not as well qualified to lead the Pennsylvania and New Jersey surveys as was Rogers or, perhaps, Rogers's strong desire to secure these appointments and thereby to realize steady income prompted him to become overzealous, or even reckless, in denigrating other candidates. And he may have suspected that Clemson sided with part-time geologists in the Philadelphia area who feared diminished employment opportunities resulting from competition for jobs from Rogers, the first full-time professional geologist in the Philadelphia area. This perceived unfair playing field did not endear Rogers to his predecessors in the Philadelphia community of geologists, almost all of whom were acquaintances through membership in the recently organized Geological Society of Pennsylvania, which Clemson served as recording secretary.[144]

Whatever the case, Rogers's criticism of Clemson's competence and expertise in chemistry, geology, and mineralogy is unfounded in view of Clemson's premier Paris education and his published contributions to the scientific literature by 1835. In fact, it is not unthinkable that, at the time Rogers wrote to Henry, Clemson's knowledge and understanding of chemistry exceeded what Rogers had acquired under his father and through self study.[145]

### A Final Overview

Thomas Green Clemson was educated in Paris under the finest chemistry and mining engineering faculty the world had to offer in the early part of the nineteenth century, and, upon returning to the United States, he established himself as a consultant in chemistry and mining engineering, which profession he pursued actively for a number of years. He applied for the position of state geologist in both New Jersey and Pennsylvania but, in both cases, was unsuccessful. Even while a student in Paris, Clemson began writing papers for publication in scientific journals, and, though his interests changed over time and his productivity abated during some periods, he continued to write for much of his life. His papers are a rich source of information upon which one can base an evaluation of Clemson as a scientist and engineer, but no source is richer than the extensive collection of letters exchanged with John C. Calhoun on the latter's O'Bar mine in Georgia. These letters afford a reader the opportunity to follow Clemson step by step as he fashions and implements a mining strategy peculiar to what he faced at the O'Bar and commensurate with Calhoun's objectives, and they reveal Clemson's engineering acuity and his knowledge of gold and gold mining. Later in life, he maintained his interest in science but devoted more and more of his time and energy to politics and to bringing technology to bear on problems in agriculture. Thomas Green Clemson was a man of wide interests, extending well beyond chemistry and engineering, whose last years were occupied with his lifelong passion: furtherance of science education.

## Notes

1. Clemson's early education is outlined by Jerome V. Reel in Chapter 2. Reel also traces Clemson's travels in Europe and between the United States and Europe.

2. Lefte Neal to Thomas Green Clemson (hereafter, TGC), 17 July 1831, Clemson Papers, Special Collections, Clemson University Libraries, Clemson, SC (hereafter SCCUL).

3. Sworn testimony, 21 February 1832, of Thomas G. Clemson as the twenty-third witness for the prosecution in the trial of Lucretia Chapman for the murder of William Chapman of Andalusia, Bucks County, Pennsylvania, in the court of Oyer and Terminer, held at Doylestoun, for Bucks County, February term, 1832. It is recorded in J. Jay Smith, *Celebrated Trials of all Countries and Remarkable Cases of Criminal Jurisprudence* (Philadelphia, PA: Harding, 1835); Alester G. Holmes and George R. Sherrill, *Thomas Green Clemson, His Life and Work* (Richmond, VA: Garrett and Massie, 1937), 4–5.

4. See Lefte Neal to TGC, 17 July 1831, SCCUL.

5. See TGC testimony, 21 February 1832, in the Lucretia Chapman murder trial.

6. R. N. Brackett, "Thomas Green Clemson, LL.D., the Chemist, Part I," *Journal of Chemical Education* 5, no. 4 (April 1928): 433–444; Holmes and Sherrill, *Thomas Green Clemson*, 4–5.

7. Ibid.

8. Ibid.

9. Thomas G. Clemson, "Assay and Analysis of an Iron Ore (fer titanne) from the Environs of Baltimore," *Silliman's Journal* [also known as *American Journal of Science*] 17 (1830): 42–43; Thomas G. Clemson, "Notice of Piperin," *Silliman's Journal* 17 (1830): 325–356; Thomas G. Clemson, "The Hartz—Its Physical Geography, Etc.," *Silliman's Journal* 19 (1831): 105–130; Thomas G. Clemson, "Description et analyse de la seybertite, nouvelle espèce minèrale," *Annal. des Mines* 2 (1832): 493–495.

10. See TGC testimony, 21 February 1832, in Lucretia Chapman murder trial.

11. Bernard Jaffe, *Crucibles: The Story of Chemistry*, 4th ed., revised (New York: Dover Publications, 1976), 123.

12. Charles Coulston Gillispie, ed., *Dictionary of Scientific Biography*, vol. 5 (New York: Scribner, 1972), 317–327; Forrist Jewett Moore, *A History of Chemistry*, 3rd ed., revised by William T. Hall (New York: McGraw-Hill, 1939), 122–125; Robert D. Purrington, *Physics in the Nineteenth Century* (New Brunswick, NJ: Rutgers University Press, 1997), 77, 133; William Francis Magie, *A Source Book of Physics* (New York: McGraw-Hill, 1935), 165–173; Jaffe, *Crucibles: The Story of Chemistry*, 87, 98, 123–124, 127, 134–135.

13. Gillispie, ed., *Dictionary of Scientific Biography*, vol. 13 (New York: Scribner, 1976), 309–314; Moore, *History of Chemistry*, 122–125; Jaffe, *Crucibles: The Story of Chemistry*, 98.

14. Gillispie, ed., *Dictionary of Scientific Biography*, vol. 4. (New York: Scribner, 1971), 238–242; Moore, *History of Chemistry*, 161–167; Purrington, *Physics in the Nineteenth Century*, 133; Ernst Von Meyer, *A History of Chemistry*, trans. from German (London: Macmillan, 1891), 207–208; Magie, *Source Book of Physics*, 178–181.

15. Gillispie, ed., *Dictionary of Scientific Biography*, vol. 11 (New York: Scribner, 1975), 494–495 (hereafter cited as Gillispie, *DSB*).

16. Gillispie, *DSB*, vol. 2 (1970), 72.

17. Gillispie, *DSB*, vol. 4 (1971), 347–350.

18. Ibid.

19. Bernard Jaffe, *Men of Science in America,* revised ed. (New York: Simon and Schuster, 1958), 320–321.

20. Moore, *History of Chemistry*, 173–174.

21. Purrington, *Physics in the Nineteenth Century*, 125–126.

22. Lefte Neal to TGC, 17 July 1831, SCCUL. Farewell letter in French, written upon Clemson's departure from Paris.

23. The trial of Lucretia Chapman for the murder of William Chapman of Andalusia, Bucks County, is recorded in J. Jay Smith, *Celebrated Trials of all Countries and Remarkable Cases of Criminal Jurisprudence* (Philadelphia, PA: Harding, 1835). Clemson examined the content of the victim's stomach on 22 September 1831 and testified under oath on 21 February 1832.

24. Wright Bryan, *Clemson, An Informal History of the University 1889–1979* (Columbia, SC: R. L. Bryan Company, 1979), 39.

25. R. N. Brackett, "Thomas Green Clemson, LL.D., the Chemist, Part I," *Journal of Chemical Education* 5, no. 4 (April 1928): 433–444.

26. Brackett, "Thomas Green Clemson, LL.D., the Chemist, Part II," *Journal of Chemical Education* 5, no. 5 (May 1928): 576–585.

27. Ibid., Part II: 438–439.

28. Ibid., Part II: 584–585.

29. T. G. Clemson, "Gold and the Gold Region," *The Orion* 4, no. 2 (April 1844): 57–66.

30. Brackett, Part I: 438–439.

31. Edgar F. Smith, *Chemistry in America: Chapters from the History of the Science in the United States* (New York: D. Appleton, 1914), 219–220.

32. Brackett, Part I: 443–444.

33. James A. Steed, associate archivist, Smithsonian Institution Archives, Washington, DC, in private communication to author, 17 January 2007. Steed writes, "Dr. Antisell was a Washington doctor, trained in medicine and chemistry.…However, he was not a member of the Smithsonian staff." From a Georgetown University Library website (provided by Steed), one learns that Antisell also was a professor of chemistry at Georgetown University and the University of Maryland.

34. Brackett, Part I: 440–441.

35. Holmes and Sherrill, *Thomas Green Clemson*, 122.

36. Brackett, Part I: 433–444.

37. Holmes and Sherrill, *Thomas Green Clemson*, 47–69, 92–122.

38. Susan L. Yarnell, *The Southern Appalachians: A History of the Landscape*, Report SRS-18 (Asheville, NC: Southern Research Station/USDA, 1998), 13.

39. Sherry L. Boatright, *The John C. Calhoun Gold Mine: An Introductory Report on its Historical Significance*, Report to State of Georgia, Department of Natural Resources, Historic Preservation Section, 17–19. See 15 June 1974 photocopy in SCCUL. Boatright traces deeds and reviews litigation and thereby confirms Calhoun's ownership. She mentions other spellings of *O'Bar*, which derive from short-term ownership of the mine by Robert Obarr: *Obarr, O'barr, O'bar*.

40. Clair M. Birdsall, *The United States Branch Mint at Dahlonega, Georgia: Its History and Coinage* (Easley, SC: Southern Historical Press, 1984), 25.

41. Ernest M. Lander Jr., *The Calhoun Family and Thomas Green Clemson: The Decline of a Southern Patriarchy* (Columbia: University of South Carolina Press, 1983), 46.

42. Birdsall, *United States Branch Mint at Dahlonega, Georgia*, 1–2.

43. William Barclay Parsons, *Engineers and Engineering in the Renaissance* (Baltimore, MD: Williams and Wilkins, 1939), 177.

44. Georgius Agricola, *De Re Metallica*, Trans. from 1st Latin Ed. of 1556 by Herbert B. Hoover and Lou H. Hoover (1912; repr., New York: Dover Publications, 1950), unnumbered footnote, "Historical Note on Gold," 399.

45. Ibid.

46. Ibid., 267–351.

47. Ibid., "Historical Note 8," 279–283.

48. Ibid., 267–351.

49. Robert S. Lewis, *Elements of Mining* (New York: John Wiley and Sons, 1945), 226.

50. Agricola, *De Re Metallica*, 279–287.

51. Ibid., 284–287, 299, 313–314, 320–321, 373, 501.

52. John C. Calhoun to John R. Mathewes, 22 May 1842, in Clyde N. Wilson, ed., *The Papers of John C. Calhoun*, vol. 16 (Columbia: University of South Carolina Press, 1984), 254–255 (hereafter cited as Wilson, ed., *Papers of JCC*).

53. The press got word of a strike at the mine of the famous Calhoun and published the news widely. See Wilson, ed., *Papers of JCC*, vol. 16, unnumbered footnote, 255.

54. Ibid.

55. John C. Calhoun to TGC, 28 May 1842, in Wilson, ed., *Papers of JCC*, vol. 16, 259–260.

56. Ibid. In his letter to Clemson, Calhoun writes, "Mr. Clapp delivered me your letter yesterday, which gave me the agreeable intelligence that you, Anna & John had arrived safely in Charleston." Calhoun's letter is dated 28 May, so the Clemsons arrived on or before 27 May 1842.
57. Dixon H. Lewis to Richard K. Cralle, 10 June 1842, in Wilson, ed., *Papers of JCC*, vol. 16, 274. Dixon writes to Cralle that Calhoun "left here this morning for Dahlonega."
58. Ibid., xxvii.
59. Anna Calhoun Clemson to Maria E. Simkins, 14 June 1842, in Wilson, ed., *Papers of JCC*, vol. 16, 278. Anna writes in this letter that Calhoun "is now in Dahlonega."
60. TGC to JCC, 23 June 1842, in Ibid., 282–283.
61. Ibid. In the TGC to JCC letter of 23 June 1842, in Wilson, ed., *Papers of JCC*, vol. 16, 282–283, the phrase "I have had McDaniel [sic; Matthew McDonald?]" appears. This uncertainty about Matthew McDonald and McDaniel, both of whom worked at the O'Bar mine, is, in fact, founded on a number of similar confusions in Clemson and Calhoun's letters about the O'Bar operations.
62. Lander, *Calhoun Family and Thomas Green Clemson*, 46–67.
63. Clemson arrived before 14 June 1842 (see Anna Calhoun Clemson to Maria E. Simkins, 14 June 1842, in Wilson, ed., *Papers of JCC*, vol. 16, 278). He departed Dahlonega during the first week of October, 1842 (see Lander, *Calhoun Family and Thomas Green Clemson*, 53).
64. TGC to JCC, 28 June 1842, in Wilson, ed., *Papers of JCC*, vol. 16, 288–291.
65. Ibid.
66. Ibid.
67. Ibid.
68. TGC to JCC, 15 July 1842, in Ibid., 311–314.
69. Ibid.
70. TGC to JCC, 31 July 1842, in Ibid., 346–347.
71. Ibid.
72. Ibid.
73. TGC to JCC, 5 August 1842, in Ibid., 349–351.
74. TGC to JCC, 6 September 1842, in Ibid., 444–445.
75. Matthew McDonald to JCC, 8 November 1842, in Ibid., 533–534.
76. TGC to JCC, 13 December 1842, in Ibid., 569–570.
77. Ibid.
78. TGC to JCC, 25 July 1842, in Ibid., 331–333.
79. Agricola, *De Re Metallica*, 295–298.
80. JCC to TGC, 3 August 1842, in Wilson, ed., *Papers of JCC*, vol. 16, 347–348.
81. TGC to JCC, 14 August 1842, in Ibid., 387–390.
82. TGC to JCC, 23 January 1843, in Ibid., 624–626.
83. Ibid.
84. Ibid.
85. TGC to JCC, 29 January 1843, in Ibid., 635–637.
86. For the reader interested in a thumbnail sketch of the O'Bar mine and Clemson's activities there, the letter from TGC to Captain Patrick Calhoun, 12 October 1856, SCCUL, is recommended; see also Holmes and Sherrill, *Thomas Green Clemson*, 66–68.
87. Thomas G. Clemson, "Gold and the Gold Region," *The Orion* 4, no. 2 (April 1844): 57–66.
88. Ibid.
89. Ibid.
90. Ibid.
91. Ibid.
92. Ibid.
93. Thomas G. Clemson, "Letter to Jas. T. Earle," *American Farmer* 12, no. 6 (Dec. 1856): 161–163.
94. Ibid.
95. Ibid.
96. Ibid.
97. Thomas G. Clemson, *Observations of the La Motte Mines and Domain in the State of Missouri* (Washington, DC: Blair and Rives, 1839), 1–16.

98. Holmes and Sherrill, *Thomas Green Clemson*, 64–66.

99. Ibid.

100. Richard C. Taylor and Thomas G. Clemson, "Notice of a Vein of Bituminous Coal, Recently Explored in the Vicinity of Havana in the Islands of Cuba," *American Philosophical Society Transactions* 6 (1839): 191–196.

101. TGC to JCC, 10 January 1841, in Wilson, ed., *Papers of JCC*, vol. 15, 420–422.

102. George P. Merrill, *The First One Hundred Years of American Geology* (New Haven, CT: Yale University Press, 1924), 94, 101, 127.

103. Ibid., 69.

104. Clemson traveled from Europe to the United States and back several times after completing his formal education in Paris, which is traced by Jerome V. Reel in Chapter 2 of the present volume.

105. Henry Darwin Rogers to Joseph Henry, 11 April 1835, in Nathan Reingold, ed., *The Papers of Joseph Henry*, vol. 2 (Washington, DC: Smithsonian Institution Press, 1975), 374n5.

106. Patsy Gerstner, *Henry Darwin Rogers, 1808–1866, American Geologist* (Tuscaloosa: University of Alabama Press, 1994), 45.

107. Ibid., 52.

108. "State geologist" and "director or head of state geological survey" are used synonymously.

109. Henry Darwin Rogers to Joseph Henry, 11 April 1835, in Reingold, ed., *The Papers of Joseph Henry*, vol. 2, 373–375.

110. Ibid., 375n8.

111. Gerstner, *Henry Darwin Rogers, 1808–1866*, 45–46.

112. Henry Darwin Rogers to Joseph Henry, 11 April 1835, in Reingold, ed., *Papers of Joseph Henry*, vol. 2, 375n8; Gerstner, *Henry Darwin Rogers, 1808–1866*, 45–46.

113. Ibid., 375n8.

114. Joseph Henry to Henry Darwin Rogers, 9 March 1835, in Ibid., 364.

115. Lander, *Calhoun Family and Thomas Green Clemson*, 18.

116. Wilson, ed., *Papers of JCC*, vol. 14, 598–599.

117. Ibid., 600–601.

118. Ibid., 602–603. James Edward Calhoun had changed his name from James Edward Colhoun.

119. Ibid., 612–613.

120. The following sources confirm that Henry Darwin Rogers, not Clemson, was appointed state geologist in both New Jersey and Pennsylvania: George P. Merrill, *First One Hundred Years of American Geology*, 167; Marc Rothenberg, ed., *The History of Science in the United States: An Encyclopedia* (New York: Garland, 2001), 478–479; Clark A. Elliott, ed., *Biographical Dictionary of American Science: The Seventeenth through the Nineteenth Centuries* (Westport, CT: Greenwood Press, 1979), 218–219. The 1836 date of Rogers's appointment to the Pennsylvania position might prompt one to question why Calhoun would correspond with family members in April and May of 1839 on the matter of Clemson's potential appointment.

121. Reingold, ed., *Papers of Joseph Henry*, vol. 2, 373–375.

122. Ibid.

123. Emma Rogers, ed., *Life and Letters of William Barton Rogers*, vol. 1 (New York: Houghton, Mifflin, 1896), 10–11; Rothenberg, ed., *History of Science in the United States*, 478–479; Elliott, ed., *Biographical Dictionary of American Science*, 218–219; Merrill, *First One Hundred Years of American Geology*, 167–168; Gillispie, ed., *DSB*, vol. 11 (New York: Scribner, 1975), 504–506.

124. Henry Darwin Rogers to William Barton Rogers, 2 February 1830, in Emma Rogers, ed., *Life and Letters of William Barton Rogers*, vol. 1 (New York: Houghton, Mifflin, 1896), 83–84.

125. Gerstner, *Henry Darwin Rogers, 1808–1866*, 19. The trustees actually made the decision on 10 February 1831 to terminate him, but allowed Rogers to finish the term.

126. Ibid., 18.

127. Rogers, ed., *Life and Letters of William Barton Rogers*, vol. 1, 92; Rothenberg, ed., *History of Science in the United States*, 478–479; Merrill, *First One Hundred Years of American Geology*, 167–168.

128. Gillispie, ed., *DSB*, vol. 11 (New York: Scribner, 1975), 504–506.

129. Rothenberg, ed., *History of Science in the United States*, 478–479; Gillispie, ed., *DSB*, vol. 11, 504–506.

130. Henry Darwin Rogers to William Barton Rogers, 6 March, 30 March, and 22 May 1833, in Rogers, ed., *Life and Letters of William Barton Rogers*, vol. 1, 104–108.

131. Ibid., 115; Rothenberg, ed., *History of Science in the United States*, 478–479; Merrill, *First One Hundred Years of American Geology*, 167–168.

132. Rogers, ed., *Life and Letters of William Barton Rogers*, vol. 1, 115; Merrill, *First One Hundred Years of American Geology*, 167–168.

133. Rogers, ed., *Life and Letters of William Barton Rogers*, vol. 1, 119; Merrill, *First One Hundred Years of American Geology*, 167–168; Rothenberg, ed., *History of Science in the United States*, 478–479.

134. See *Geological Survey Directorships* section of this chapter.

135. Rothenberg, ed., *History of Science in the United States*, 478–479; Gillispie, ed., *DSB*, vol. 11, 504–506.

136. Gillispie, ed., Ibid.

137. Merrill, *First One Hundred Years of American Geology*, 167–168.

138. Gillispie, ed., *DSB*, vol. 11, 504–506.

139. Gerstner, *Henry Darwin Rogers, 1808–1866*, 150.

140. Regius professor: "a holder of a professorship founded by royal subsidy at a British university." See Frederick C. Mish, ed., *Webster's Ninth New Collegiate Dictionary* (Springfield, MA: Merriam Webster, 1983), 992.

141. Gerstner, *Henry Darwin Rogers, 1808–1866*, 208.

142. Gillispie, ed., *DSB*, vol. 8 (New York: Scribner, 1973), 260–261; Rothenberg, ed., *History of Science in the United States*, 313–314; Merrill, *First One Hundred Years of American Geology*, 498–499.

143. Bernard Jaffe writes of Joseph Henry, "Henry was the most distinguished man of science in America at this time. He enjoyed an international reputation." In Jaffe, *Men of Science in America*, 200. And Leonard Carmichael, secretary of the Smithsonian Institution during 1953–1964, says, Henry "was probably the greatest scientist born in America between the days of Franklin and the Civil War." In Carmichael, *Joseph Henry (1797–1878) and his Smithsonian Institution* (New York: The Newcomen Society in North America, 1956), 9. The international unit of magnetic induction is the *henry* in honor of Joseph Henry. See also Robert Sullivan, "Castle in disrepair," *The Washington Post*, Sunday Regional Edition (Washington DC: The Washington Post Company, April 1, 2007), B01. It is of interest that Joseph Henry was invited by Clemson to be a trustee of the educational institution envisaged by Clemson—ultimately founded as the Clemson Agricultural College (TGC to J. Henry, 24 August 1874, Smithsonian Institution Archives Records Unit 26, Office of the Secretary, Incoming Correspondence), but Henry declined, saying, "My engagements in connection with the Light House Board, in addition to those relative to the Smithsonian, are occupying all my time." Henry closed the letter with, "I am, however, willing to indorse [sic] your proposal as fully as you may desire." In J. Henry to TGC, 10 September 1874, Thomas Green Clemson Papers, SCCUL.

144. Merrill, *First One Hundred Years of American Geology*, 139.

145. Moreover, instruction and practice in mineralogy and geology were integral parts of the curriculum at the School of Mines during Clemson's attendance (Gillispie, *DSB*, vol. 4 (1971), 347); and Clemson's certification as assayer from the Royal Mint suggests further mastery of knowledge of importance to one who leads or conducts a geological survey.

# Chapter 7

## THE SCIENTIST AS FARMER

### *John W. Kelly*

As superintendent of agricultural affairs, Thomas Green Clemson received this medal as a United States delegate to an 1860 international agricultural exposition and conference in France. Fort Hill Collection, Clemson University.

Thomas Green Clemson was not born into farming—he married into it. And like any marriage, Clemson's relationship with agriculture had its ups and downs. Marrying Anna Maria Calhoun, daughter of South Carolina scion and U.S. Senator John C. Calhoun, wedded Clemson in 1838 to the southern plantation culture.

John C. Calhoun was an elite member of South Carolina's planter class. The Fort Hill plantation exemplified the upland plantation in the later half of the nineteenth century. A progressive agriculturist, Calhoun pursued making his holdings self-sufficient and profitable by growing short-staple cotton, the dominant cash crop of the South. The life of a planter was not entirely pastoral. Calhoun fretted over cotton prices, available credit, slave labor issues, weather, soil fertility, land values, and a host of family concerns brought on by the interaction of people and problems.

Living in this world required Clemson to use his curiosity, intellect, engineering expertise, and scientific preparation. It would be a life of practical application of the skills he learned in the lecture hall and laboratory, as well as in the field.

That Clemson began his serious education at Norwich Academy was both a benefit and a harbinger. Founded in 1819 by Alden Partridge, Norwich Academy in Vermont was a school that mixed classical studies and the applied sciences of the times with a military culture. It was here—four years later—that Clemson was attracted to science, particularly chemistry.

It is interesting to note that Alden Partridge, president of Norwich Academy which became Norwich University, is credited with being the first to ask Congress to create land-grant colleges. On January 21, 1841, Partridge urged Congress to share the revenue from public land sales among the states proportionately to finance institutions that would teach science, agriculture, engineering, manufacturing, and commerce. It was the first recorded proposal to Congress for such institutions.[1]

Sixteen years later, U.S. Representative Justin S. Morrill of Vermont sponsored legislation for giving federal public land to the states for agricultural and mechanical colleges. The bill was first introduced to the House on December 14, 1857. The Morrill Land Grant Act passed Congress in 1859, but was vetoed by President James B. Buchanan in February of 1860. The bill was reintroduced in 1861 and signed by President Abraham Lincoln in July of 1862.

After the Norwich Academy, in 1826 Clemson continued his education in France. In Paris, Clemson attended laboratories conducted by leading French researchers in the physical sciences. Home to the "founder of modern chemistry," Antoine Laurent Lavoisier (1743-1794), France was a center of learning and experimentation.[2] Leading scientists there, as in Germany and England, looked to unlock the properties of the air we breathe. Lavoisier termed the two basic gases *oxygene*—oxygen—and *azote*, which scientist Jean Antoine Claude Chaptal (1756-1832) later named *nitrogene*—nitrogen.[3]

By the time Clemson studied in Paris, chemists had shown the link between nitrogen and the vital role it played in growing crops. Four scientists—Boussingault, Liebig, Lawes, and Gilbert—made many of the notable contributions to the new science of agronomy. Jean-Baptiste Boussingault (1802-1887), a French chemist and professor of agriculture and analytical chemistry at the Paris Conservatoire des Arts et Métiers, is credited for creating the practice of agricultural field experiments. His contemporary, Justus von Liebig (1803-1873), was a German chemist whose laboratory made the University of Giessen the most influential chemical school in the world; many of the most accomplished chemists of the nineteenth century attended it for their early training. John Bennet Lawes (1814-1900) was a British agricultural chemist who started the Rothamsted Experimental Station, the first agricultural research station in the world, while Joseph Henry Gilbert (1817-1901) was a British chemist who held the directorship of the chemical laboratory at Rothamsted and the Sibthorpian chair of rural economy at Oxford.[4] Boussingault, a leader in the research on nitrogen-fixing legumes, had an oddly coincidental connection to Clemson. While there is no account of the two having met, both men began their careers as mining experts, were avid agronomic scientists, and, at various times in their lives, ran their fathers-in-law's farms.[5]

In previous studies of Clemson's life, available sources created some confusion about the length of his stay and studies in France. For example, in court testimony on February 21, 1832, in Bucks County, Pennsylvania, Clemson stated that he went to France in 1826 and returned in 1831. Other records report that he was a non-degree student from 1828 to 1832.[6] While such sources have tracked various aspects of Clemson's transatlantic life between 1831 and 1837, the research of Jerome Reel, as seen in Chapter 2, reflects the most thorough summary of its complexity and Clemson's student years between 1826 and the spring of 1837, when he returned to Philadelphia.[7]

## Marrying into Southern Agriculture

Returning to the United States, Clemson began work as a consulting engineer. Based in Philadelphia, he traveled often to Washington, D.C., where a friend introduced him to Anna Maria Calhoun, with whom he fell in love and to whom he proposed marriage. The couple married in South Carolina on November 13, 1838, at Fort Hill. In the time-honored tradition of not losing a daughter but gaining a son, John C. Calhoun embraced a son-in-law who shared common interests in science and progress. Like his father-in-law, Clemson believed in the power of science to improve civilization.[8]

Calhoun saw himself as a progressive farmer, seeking to improve agricultural and animal husbandry practices at Fort Hill.[9] As did many plantation owners, Calhoun and Clemson traveled widely and read agricultural literature.[10] From the 1830s until the start of the Civil War (1861), more than eighty southern agricultural journals were published. In addition to the journals, a number of daily and weekly newspapers devoted space to agricultural issues. In 1853 *The Journal of the United States Agricultural Society* identified forty-three newspapers nationwide, ten of which were in the South. While many publications appeared, their mortality rate was high; the majority of them lasted fewer than three years.[11]

Clemson would turn to Calhoun for advice about becoming a planter.[12] Through conversations and correspondence that lasted until Calhoun's death in 1850, Clemson received both an avuncular education and more than a few rude awakenings about planter class culture and managing an upland plantation.

The typical plantation in western South Carolina and northern Georgia raised cotton as a cash crop and grew other crops to supplement income and provide for its own needs. For example, in addition to short-staple cotton, Calhoun grew corn, oats, rye, wheat, and vegetables. He also kept an orchard and vineyard. Cattle and hogs browsed in his pastures, while poultry populated his barnyard. Additionally, many planters either kept beehives or knew the location of honey trees.[13] During the winter, slaves were assigned to clearing land, splitting rails, mending fences, digging ditches, repairing buildings and dams, butchering hogs, shelling corn, packing cotton, and other tasks that competed with tending crops.

As any farmer—rich and poor alike—will say, the idyllic picture of farming belies a harsh landscape of problems and worries. For Clemson and his fellow upland planters, the most pernicious problem was cotton production. It was a deal with the devil: cotton provided the planter with his wealth, but it robbed the land of its fertility. Cotton—along with corn that served both as a cash and sustenance crop—took a heavy toll on the soil. For both, planters resorted to clean cultivation, requiring hoes and plows to remove the leavings and furrow new rows.[14]

**Map of Pickens, Anderson, Abbeville, and Greenville Districts. From *A Rebel Came Home: The Diary and Letters of Floride Clemson, 1863–1866*, Charles M. McGee Jr. and Ernest M. Lander Jr., eds., revised ed. (Columbia: University of South Carolina Press, 1989).**

Backcountry farmers practiced "infield-outfield cultivation," clearing forestland and using it for corn, small grains, hemp, flax, and short-staple cotton until the land was depleted. The worn land was then turned into cattle pasture, and new cropland was cleared.[15] The economic fact of life was that land was cheap and labor costly. Uncleared public lands sold for as little as $1.25 an acre while a slave laborer could cost $865. Here was the crux of the South's economic Achilles' heel. Slave labor was not free labor. Figuring in the purchase of slaves drove up the costs of farming. To recoup labor costs, slaves had to be in the field, growing cotton.[16]

Tilling practices not only depleted the soil, but also left the land vulnerable to erosion, leaving it barren, rocky, and rutted. As scholar John S. Otto points out, "Uplands planted in cotton lost as much as 195 pounds of soil per acre annually. In typical upstate topography the life of a cotton or corn field was short, fertile for only a few years before it was abandoned to briars and broom sedge. There was always new land to clear at the edge of the woods."[17]

Such poor treatment of the soil must have disheartened Clemson. His training in France and his readings in agricultural journals exposed him to the value of manuring and planting legumes. Manuring meant more than using animal droppings; it applied to any soil amendment, such as marl (calcium carbonate rich clay) and guano. Legumes, such as clover and peas, were known to be nitrogen-fixers, restoring the fertility to the soil, while also serving as cover crops to prevent erosion.

Clemson was convinced of the need to manure old fields if they were to produce adequate yields. His desire, however, ran into the economic realities of southern agricultural practices. A few years later, writing to Calhoun from Belgium, Clemson, after describing the positive aspects of Canebrake, his plantation in Edgefield County, South Carolina, went on to discuss the need to manure Canebrake's land and the costs that prevented him from doing so:

> It is truly a place possessing a rare combination of advantages, and if it were stocked as it should be, it would be unrivalled. There is a very extensive range in the neighborhood, which would sustain a large stock of cattle, etc., which would so manure those beautiful fields, as to carry their production as high as any land in the United States....I have not been able to carry into execution what I had anticipated doing when I purchased the place. My force and my stock are in no wise sufficient to cope with the difficulties, and as it is there is too much dead capital in the land for me to carry.[18]

Fertilizing fields required time and much labor to remove manure from stalls and sties, transfer it to storage areas for composting, and then to spread it on fields. Massive amounts were needed if the recycled material were to meet the crops' nitrogen needs.[19] Since land was cheap and abundant, it encouraged planters to clear more land rather than care for existing acreage. New land would be cut and cleared.[20] And there was always new land available further west from Alabama to Texas, a situation that would ultimately cause competition between regional planters. Western planters would vie for commodities and credit. Their lands were more fertile and closer to river transportation, providing them with lower growing costs and raising their profit margin.[21]

Already, the stress of Western expansion had touched Clemson directly. He had hardly settled in to his marriage when John C. Calhoun and his eldest son, Andrew Pickens Calhoun, invited the new in-law to invest in a plantation in Alabama. Named "Cane Brake" in Marengo County, the arrangement was for Andrew to operate the place, with his father supplying the slaves and equipment and Clemson providing the money to buy the land. "Thus," as Ernest McPherson Lander points out, "within a few weeks of joining the Calhoun family Clemson had made his father-in-law and brother-in-law deeply indebted to him, a mistake he would rue for the rest of his life."[22] The Alabama Clemson-Calhoun investment would never bring a profit. Weather, bad timing, lack of labor, drought, mounting debt, and low cotton prices would plague the plantation.

Throughout his life Clemson worried about his finances. In financing Cane Brake in Alabama, he had expected repayment from Andrew. It was not forthcoming. Clemson repeatedly and heatedly sought his money, asking his father-in-law to act as negotiator. Delay continued, and it embittered Clemson, who was not used to living on credit. The Calhouns, as did much of the planter class, saw credit not so much as debt but as a way of life. Their land holdings, slaves, homes, and farm tools were their wealth. It was a society that was land-rich and cash-poor. To Clemson, a meticulous and prudent man, the idea of being in debt and the delay of a repayment must have been infuriating.[23]

Nevertheless, Clemson longed to run a plantation. In 1839 he agreed to run Midway, owned by James Edward Calhoun, Anna's uncle. The plantation was on the Savannah River in the Abbeville District of South Carolina.[24] Clemson had much to learn, and Calhoun advised him to seek advice from George McDuffie, a local planter. "You will, of course, be a good deal at a loss this year from the want of experience," Calhoun wrote. The senator added the admonition that his son-in-law should curb his enthusiasm for scientific agriculture: "It is hazardous to depart from the established practice without much caution and experience."[25]

Despite Anna's praise for her husband, telling a friend that he had become "quite the planter," Clemson was unhappy at Midway. Part of the reason was that the land was worn out, but Anna writes in a letter of another reason—the one Calhoun had admonished Clemson about: "Mr. Clemson found Uncle James so utterly impractical in everything relating to planting, and so determined not to change any of his peculiar notions that he could neither do himself nor Uncle James justice and father advised him…to remain no longer but to get off as civilly as possible."[26]

The Clemsons escaped from Midway to Fort Hill in the fall of 1840. Clemson managed the place for Calhoun while the senator was in Washington, D.C. Applying his skills and energies, Clemson excelled. He kept the senator informed via a constant flow of correspondence. A December 1840 sampling of Clemson's letters to Calhoun creates a vivid picture of the daily chores, repairs, and improvements which Clemson was methodically addressing at Fort Hill:

> Yesterday (Monday) and today the wagons have been hauling ice, the cart and wagons yesterday, the cart and one wagon today, the other wagon has been going to prepare the homestead with wood for Christmas week. The ice was about an inch thick and very easily collected from the pond and brought on shore, where it was piled up and whence hauled to the ice house over the new road which has thus far appeared indespensible [sic].... The gin was put in operation yesterday and runs well requiring but little water in comparison with the mill. The clearing is progressing, and the ditch through which Sawney's branch is to run into the dam nearly terminated.
>
> We are driving on as fast as we can, but if we do not do as much as you anticipated, it is partly owing to the innumerable things to be done, which are daily coming to light and which it is impossible to foresee, for it really appears as if everything has been neglected and everything to be renovated. Mr. Fredericks [new overseer Clemson hired] seems to be desirous of doing [well] and if he continues will I think give satisfaction. His services at the smith shop will of themselves economize a great deal.
>
> ...The place is in very much in want of a suitable house for keeping tools and working in on rainy days. I find it impossible to get along without it and therefore have determined to remove the old bathing house (which stands near the old poultry yard) up near the smith shop. It can be done in a short time and will answer a good purpose. The negro cabins of which you spoke to Mr. Fredericks will take a good many boards to cover them. The four ditchers will necessarily have to quit their present work and go to riving, and making rails for the lower part of the plantation. [27]

Pleased with conditions at Fort Hill, Calhoun wrote to Clemson: "You have kept me so fully informed on all points connected with the plantation operations that I seem myself to understand what is going on almost as well, as if I was at home. It is a great relief to me."[28]

In the December 1840 letters, it is significant that Clemson mentioned Fredericks's talents in blacksmithing. Tool-making was an essential activity. Plantation blacksmiths or local craftsmen made most of the tools and implements. Standardization of parts and sizes was virtually unknown, and quality was hit or miss, depending on the skills and pride of the smith. The lack of store-bought equipment—due to the reluctance to spend hard-to-come-by cash and the desire for self-sufficiency—slowed the introduction of improved designs, materials, and

Deed of Conveyance of the Canebrake plantation from Arthur Simkins to
Thomas Green Clemson, October 9, 1843. Thomas Green Clemson Papers,
Special Collections, Clemson University Libraries.

skills in the South. Educated planters, such as Clemson and Calhoun, kept up with improvements through journals and newspapers, encouraging their blacksmiths to innovate, sometimes leading to patents. In 1859, the U.S. Patent Office recorded about 100 farm implements and mechanical inventions by Southerners.[29]

## A Plantation of Their Own

In November 1843, the Clemsons bought Canebrake plantation in Edgefield County, South Carolina. It was purchased from Arthur Simkins, brother-in-law of James Edward Calhoun, with Clemson agreeing to pay $24,000 for the plantation and twenty slaves. About two miles from Saluda, Canebrake encompassed 1,050 acres and got its name from the dense cover of cane that grew along the banks of the Little Saluda River.[30]

Among the plantation's attractions was its proximity to the railroad. Anna wrote in a letter that the terrible roads between Aiken and Fort Hill had concerned Clemson. With roads rutted and muddy, railroads were an important link from farm to market. They also provided a comfortable way of personal travel and delivered goods to backcountry planters. South Carolina had a network of rail lines connecting Columbia, Camden, Greenville, Spartanburg, Abbeville, and Charleston. Later a branch line was constructed from Anderson to Greenville, which filled out a rail route from Charleston to Knoxville. Another line that ran from Columbia to Charlotte provided access to the rich valleys of the Catawba and Yadkin rivers and gave Charleston a link to railroads to the North.[31]

The Clemsons finally had a home of their own, but the family would not stay there long. Before his first harvest, Clemson had been appointed chargé d'affaires to Belgium, thanks to Calhoun's becoming secretary of state in the Tyler administration. Clemson and his family arrived in Brussels in October 1844. Being abroad presented Clemson with the problem that absentee owners had to contend with—finding an overseer or farm manager who could run the plantation.

At first, the situation looked promising. Calhoun wrote to his son-in-law in Brussels that he had stopped at Canebrake in the spring of 1845. Calhoun found the place to be well managed, in large part due to the hiring of Mr. Bland, the new overseer. Bland's predecessor apparently had left without notice and failed to pick up the pay he was due.[32]

Despite the glowing reports, Canebrake did not flourish, and, as early as September 1845, Clemson had decided to sell it:

> When the next installment on the place shall have been paid, I will have expended near about $24,000, including negroes, and everything as it stands, and to put it into a condition to be agreeable or profitable, it would require every cent I have in the world, and more besides. As it is I should be governed by my plantation, instead of my governing it, and this is the rock upon which hundreds of thousands have been wrecked in the United States, and as many more will be

swamped from a like cause, which I am desirous to avoid if possible. From what you say, there appears to be a probability of my being able to sell the plantation without loss; it cannot go satisfactorily without my presence, which under the circumstances I cannot give....I have therefore concluded to sell the plantation, stock, and implements, and if I can, retain the negroes, at least for some time. They are good, were selected out of many....If the negroes can be retained, I do not wish them to leave the State, or to be hired where they would be badly treated or their lives jeopardized in an unhealthy position. The gang consists of thirty-seven in all. Of these twenty-four are working and thirteen children."[33]

Four years later, writing to Calhoun on August 1, 1849, from Brussels, Clemson summarized his feelings about the Canebrake investment:

But as I could not live there, and had no one to attend to my interests, it may be fortunate for me to have sold it at any price. It is a lesson that has cost me dear. I hope to [be] done with Southern property, and shall feel greatly relieved, and thankful when what I have is safely invested in a country where it will yield me an interest of which I have been deprived for years.[34]

CANE BRAKE

1050-ACRE PLANTATION BELONGING TO
THOMAS GREEN CLEMSON, 1842-1851. CLEMSON
CHARGÉ D'AFFAIRES TO BELGIUM, 1844-1851,
AND FOUNDER OF CLEMSON UNIVERSITY, LIVED
AT CANE BRAKE FROM JANUARY TO JULY 1844.
IN HIS ABSENCE COL. FRANCIS PICKENS AND
SEN. JOHN C. CALHOUN OFTEN VISITED CANE
BRAKE AND ATTENDED TO ITS BUSINESS.

The lesson Clemson was learning was the relentless peril of plantation cash flow. Canebrake wasn't bringing in income—it had not provided $1,000 in five years—and his continuing feud with Andrew over repayment of the Alabama investment left Clemson pinched. His $4,500 annual diplomatic salary—and more—was needed to cover his living expenses in Belgium. More pressing, he owed Simkins for Canebrake: a $5,000 payment was due in January 1846. He wrote Calhoun to prod Andrew for the

**Historic marker, on Highway 387, east of Saluda, S.C., at the site of the Canebrake plantation of Thomas Green Clemson. Saluda County Historical Society.**

money owed. Calhoun wrote back saying he would seek a loan for Clemson from the Bank of the State of South Carolina.[35]

Thus, rather than bring up the uncomfortable subject of money with his son, Calhoun offered Clemson the planters' solution—adding to his debt. Calhoun did get a $14,000 loan from the bank in time to satisfy Simkins. But Calhoun's friend and cousin Francis Pickens fretted over Calhoun's position between Clemson and Andrew: "I fear his Alabama obligations have embarrassed him," Pickens related to James Edward, Calhoun's brother, "…and the Bank will entangle him."[36] It would not be until December 1850 that Clemson would sell Canebrake, for which he received $38,000.

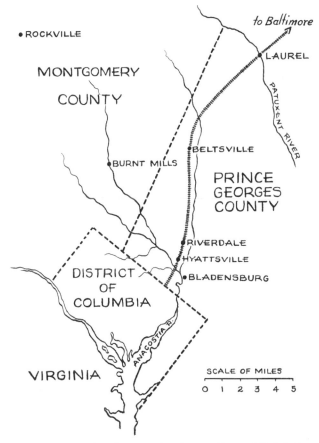

**Map of the Bladensburg-Beltsville, Maryland, area. From *A Rebel Came Home: The Diary and Letters of Floride Clemson, 1863-1866*, Charles M. McGee Jr. and Ernest M. Lander Jr., eds., revised ed. (Columbia: University of South Carolina Press, 1989).**

The years 1850 and 1851 were tumultuous ones for Clemson. In March 1850, John C. Calhoun died, leaving his estate unresolved. In April of 1851 Clemson and his family left Brussels for the last time and docked in Philadelphia in May. After a short time, Anna and the children traveled to Fort Hill while Clemson finalized the sale of Canebrake. The Clemsons then headed back north. There, Clemson found a farm in Bladensburg, Maryland, which he bought in June 1853 for $6,725. Since the farm had gone for $10,000 in 1851, Clemson considered it a bargain.[37]

The Clemsons took up residence in August 1853. The 100-acre farm was known as Chillum Castle Manor, but Clemson changed its name to "The Home." The house was in the middle of a grove of trees, with a sizable fruit tree orchard on the farm. The Home was located ideally for Clemson. It was a little more than a mile from Bladensburg and within sight of a railroad, on which he traveled to Washington, D.C.[38] Despite Clemson's intent to return to farming, his yearning was for another federal government position. His wait would be a long one. It would be 1860 before he was again appointed to a federal post.

Meanwhile, the Clemsons settled into domestic life. At the time the family moved in to The Home, Clemson's son, Calhoun, was twelve years old and his daughter, Floride, was nearly eleven. During 1854 and 1855, Clemson took on a tenant farmer, who left a year later. The farm endured a drought in 1855, and Clemson turned to other activities. He became an importer, bringing in Belgian furniture, firearms, and other articles.[39] In addition, he kept tabs on an ironworks in Clarkesville, Georgia, in which he had invested.

Clemson also kept up with his pursuits in scientific agriculture. In 1854, he conducted a series of field trials to judge the effectiveness of guano—South American bird droppings that were a powerful fertilizer.[40] Maryland was an ideal location for Clemson's experiments. Virginia and Maryland farmers were among the first to raise the issue of soil fertility. Farmers there began rotating soil-exhausting corn and wheat with cover crops that restored soil nutrients. They also used marl, lime, guano, and bone meal to add nutrients.[41]

In addition to publishing a large number of articles on these nutrients, Clemson performed two field trials with guano. He reported his results, saying he did not find the fertilizer to be especially valuable. After those negative findings, he further experimented with planting crops without guano, while simultaneously experimenting with seed preparation. The results of two of these experiments were certified by his neighbors and subsequently published as attachments to one of Clemson's articles in the *American Farmer*. For example, on September 4, 1856, S. C. Crawford's certificate testified:

> I the undersigned, am resident of Prince Georges County, Md. and live on the farm adjoining that of Thomas G. Clemson. I am, and have been for three years perfectly acquainted with all the agricultural operations of Mr. Clemson; and have observe[d] the result of his experiments in cultivating land without manure, and by means of seed prepared in a peculiar way. In the fall of 1854, Mr.

Clemson took three acres of land—all of the same quality, and sowed it with rye. There was no manure used of any kind whatever. The land was of medium quality. Part of the field was sowed with prepared seed—part with seed in a natural state, all the land treated alike. That part of the field which was sowed with unprepared seed yielded an exceedingly poor crop—thin on the ground—small heads, and small shriveled grain. That part with prepared seed yielded as fine a crop of rye as I ever saw. It was thick on the ground the heads long, full, and bearing down from the weight of the grain. In the spring of 1855, Clemson took nine acres of oats, the land of the same quality through its entire extent, and sowed 1 part with prepared—part with unprepared seed. The crop of oats was exceedingly heavy, and the differences between that from prepared seed and that from unprepared was [sic] very great. There was no manure used of any kind, and the entire nine acres treated in the same way.[42]

Clemson's findings on guano ran counter to the glowing reports from other farmers who had tried guano. The seabird fertilizer from Peru had become a craze among farmers in the 1850s. Exports rose to nearly 600,000 tons by the end of the 1860s.[43] With money to be made, exploitation followed. Over-harvesting quickly depleted the resource, and lower quality products flooded the market. Clemson conducted his research in the mid-1850s. His less-than-stellar results from guano may have been caused by low quality product, which often did not contain sufficient nitrogen to produce significant plant growth. If that were the case, Clemson was not alone in getting poor-quality guano. Still, by 1880, South Carolina, along with North Carolina, Georgia, Maryland, and Virginia, topped the South in fertilizer purchases, spending $14,094,000 combined.[44]

The demand for fertilizer led many to offer products that were of little or no use. Southeastern farmers lobbied state governments to hire geologists to analyze and certify the chemical content of fertilizers as a way to catch adulteration. In South Carolina, legislators established the Office of Inspector of Phosphates and Special Agents in 1872.

It is important to keep in mind that the South Carolina fertilizer certification office has played a financial role in the life of Clemson University. Since its founding in 1889, the college/university has overseen and been partly financed by state fertilizer assay fees and revenue. Today, the University's Regulatory Services division enforces fertilizer quality and safety laws for the state. The division's motto is "Regulation through Education," a fitting reminder of the essential link between Clemson, agriculture, and the public.

In 1857 Clemson's hopes for another posting abroad were raised when Belgian King Léopold I asked the Buchanan administration to again send Clemson to Belgium. The request was denied. Clemson continued to lobby for a post in Washington, conducting experiments, attending scientific meetings, and delivering research papers. He also became active in creating the Maryland Agricultural

College, which opened in 1859.[45] Domestic chores included adding a porch to The Home and making the residence hospitable to family and visitors.

New Year's 1860 was especially jubilant for Clemson. U.S. Secretary of the Interior Jacob Thompson invited him to fill the post of superintendent of agricultural affairs. The post officially started February 3, and it was just the tonic Clemson needed. His spirits buoyed by the new challenge, Clemson sought to make The Home a model farm.[46] Neither his good mood nor his post would last for long.

The Civil War derailed Clemson's return to prominence. He would serve as superintendent of agricultural affairs for slightly more than a year, resigning in March 1861, to follow his political beliefs and family sympathies south. During his thirteen-month tenure, Clemson set out clearly his vision for a federal department of agriculture. When Congress enacted legislation in 1862 that would lead to forming the department, Clemson's impact was clear to those who knew the man and understood the political times.[47]

Clemson assigned ownership of The Home to Anna, who, along with daughter Floride, stayed in Maryland, as Clemson and son Calhoun traveled to South Carolina and joined the Confederacy. Anna initially made a go of running the house and farm, staying in the house, despite the peril, to prevent the property from being seized by the Union army.[48]

Regarding the "peculiar institution" of slavery, Anna and Thomas Green Clemson seemed to agree, although during their years in Europe Anna's support of slavery had been more apparent in her letters and evidently in her conversations there. Her rationale was made clear in a letter from Anna to her father on January 24, 1846, while she was in Brussels. Anna wrote: "They talk of slavery. I never saw in all my life in the south, the amount of suffering and misery that one sees here in one month, and so I tell all who mention the subject to me…'make your working classes in Europe as happy as our slaves, then come back to me, and I will talk about the abolition of slavery.'"[49] Anna essentially put forth the classic sociopolitical comparison between chattel and wage slavery. During the Maryland years, in contrast, a number of the ever pragmatic Thomas Clemson's letters express pointedly negative judgments of slaves as expensive, unreliable, even "dangerous" workers.

By 1863, Anna and Floride could not continue the stress of living amid marauders and Union soldiers, and so Anna deeded the farm to Clemson's uncle Elias Baker with instructions to hold or sell. She rented a house in Beltsville, Maryland, where she and Floride lived until they were granted a pass through military lines in December 1864.[50] They arrived in Pendleton on December 31. The New Year would bring an end to war and the beginning of the daunting task of reconstruction.

**Deed of Conveyance of The Home property from Thomas Green Clemson to Anna Maria Calhoun Clemson, April 15, 1861. Thomas Green Clemson Papers, Special Collections, Clemson University Libraries.**

## *Immediately After the Civil War*

On June 25, 1865, Clemson's son Calhoun came home to Pendleton. Six days later his father arrived. Settling his family in with Mrs. Calhoun in Pendleton, Clemson observed: "This country is in a wretched condition, no money and nothing to sell. Existence is almost problematical. The negroes utterly demoralized. Murders and robberies common occurrences. I fear that a long time must elapse before the country arrives at a settled state. Every one is ruined, and those that can are leaving."[51] Floride, Clemson's daughter, noted the situation in her diary:

*Sep 2nd.* Gen. Wade Hampton & his wife, (Mary McDuffy that was) came to see us last Saturday. He is a fine looking man of fifty about with dark brown hair & beard still untinged with grey, & a fine dark blue eye. A very striking dashing look. He said nothing kept him in this country *but* a desire to pay his debts.

He was staying at Keowee, Hall Calhoun's [home], on his way to his place in Cassier's [Cashiers] valley. I have been very sick with sick headaches &c. lately, sometimes in bed for two or three days. *One* week had *four* sick headaches. Dr. Maxwell says the summer was too hot & did not agree with me. Am now a little better. They say the state of things in the low country is terrible. Men, formerly wealthy, have litterally [sic] not wherewithal to buy bread & many must starve. Lands which have been abandoned by their owners during the war, are confiscated to be divided by the 'freedmen's beaureau' [sic] among the negroes. An insurrection is much dreaded. All negroes have now asserted their freedom now. At Ft. Hill all have left but some fifteen hands. Jackson [former slave of Mrs. John C. Calhoun] has also quietly & amicably set up as shoemaker, & fidler [sic] for himself from here. An officer of negroes was shot at Walhalla a few days since. Negro garrisons are stationed at Anderson, & that place, but none here, though they pay us visits! Got a letter from Miss Olivia Buck today dated Aug. 3rd. She says among other things that Miss Lane is engaged to Mr. Henry Johnson of Baltimore. I believe this because she told me about him when I was there. He is a Southerner too. I am really glad to hear of it, for Mr. B. is a perfect tyrant to her. The Riggs are still in Europe. The Woods at their place. Mrs. Harvey in Scottland [sic]. All old friends are well. I would so love to go to see them all again. Billy Dundas is going to marry Miss Marron.[52]

The Clemsons and Calhouns were in slightly better financial shape than some of their neighbors. Clemson had a few investments that brought in cash. Mrs. Calhoun, however, had to auction Fort Hill equipment, stock, and produce in December 1865 to pay off her late son Andrew's debt. After the sale, she was able to buy two mules, two cows, 500 bushels of corn, fifty bushels of peas, a barn full of fodder, and a dozen hogs for $1,600, with a year's credit.[53]

Sorting out his business dealings preoccupied Clemson. While the final sale of The Home would not occur in his lifetime, he still found time to revive his interest in agricultural science and to promote an agricultural and mechanical college in South Carolina. He joined the Pendleton Farmers' Society and was elected as its president in 1868. He also served on its committee to found a college, but the effort failed. Discouraged, Clemson dropped out of the society, writing to James Edward Calhoun that he tried to set out a course for a better future and it had not been supported. He would retire, becoming a "mere looker on in Venice."[54] Clemson's dark mood notwithstanding, his vision for a college would become a reality two decades later.

In the meantime Clemson had a farm to run. With the death of Mrs. Calhoun in 1866, daughter Anna became heir to three-quarters of the Fort Hill holdings and her daughter, Floride Elizabeth, holder of the remainder. Ultimately the quarter title would come to Floride Isabella Lee, the daughter of Floride Elizabeth and Gideon Lee, who were married in 1869. Resolution of ownership of the property led to a bitter battle among the Calhouns, which took six years to settle. Before

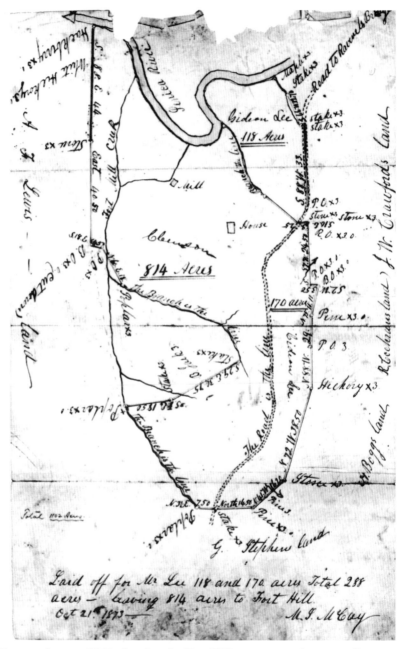

Surveyor's map, 1873, showing the Fort Hill property and surrounding areas.
Created for Gideon Lee, the father and legal representative of Floride Isabella
Lee, the Clemsons' granddaughter, the property division is indicated on the plat
by *Gideon Lee* and *Clemson*. Thomas Green Clemson Papers, Special Collections,
Clemson University Libraries.

that settlement was completed, tragedies struck the Clemsons: in 1871 they lost both of their children. Floride Elizabeth Clemson Lee died on July 23, and less than three weeks later, John Calhoun Clemson died on August 10.

### *Finally at Home at Fort Hill*

Anna and Thomas Clemson moved to Fort Hill in June 1872. The homecoming was a blessing for the couple. For Anna, who for so long had wanted a permanent home, Fort Hill would be where she completed her life.[55] For Clemson, Fort Hill would be both his home and his final act of commitment to improving educational conditions for his adopted state. First, however, the place needed a good cleaning.

Fort Hill had fallen into disrepair.[56] The property, except for the main house, had been rented out and allowed to become a shambles, with buildings and fences in poor condition. Conditions with the neighbors were also in disrepair. Clemson and his neighbor Andrew T. Lewis squabbled over boundaries, roaming livestock, fences, and a milldam on Clemson's land. In his final words to Lewis about the dam, Clemson wrote curtly: "When you demolish your dam, you may, with some show of reason, remonstrate with regard to mine. You must excuse me, if, in [the] future, I decline further correspondence on this subject."[57]

Roaming cattle exemplified a major postwar economic situation. Fences were no longer inexpensive to construct or maintain. Prior to the war, zigzag and split rail fences were common. Off-season, slaves would clear forests, cut timber, split rails, and set them up as a matter of course. The fences were legal boundaries for fields and kept cattle out of croplands, allowing them to otherwise roam free. Conditions changed dramatically after the war. The lack of timber and the necessity to hire workers made fencing cropland very costly. Growers in some southeastern states lobbied their state legislatures to reverse the situation by enacting laws that required cattlemen to fence in their animals instead of growers fencing in their crops. The reversal represented a major change of view. Without slave labor and abundant land, farmers now focused on preserving their cropland.[58]

Fences were a significant but local worry. A bigger problem was that South Carolina was trapped in a trade imbalance. With no capital—emancipation zeroed out a substantial asset—farmers depended on high-interest, short-term loans from the North, which went to buy manufactured goods produced outside the region. Southern planters fell back on a system they knew: they restored cotton to its throne and the South returned to a single cash crop. The southern Sisyphus lived again, having to "raise more cotton to buy more hay to feed more mules to raise more cotton."[59]

The Panic of 1873 and ensuing national depression bankrupted some and demoralized many more. In 1870 short-staple cotton sold for an average of twenty-four cents a pound. In 1876 the price had plunged to thirteen cents a pound.[60]

Freedmen headed to the cities, creating a farm labor shortage. State governments stepped in to regulate labor, agriculture, and commerce. Business—from factory to merchant—replaced cotton as the major revenue generator. The plantation economy and planter class were pushed aside, relics of a vanishing era. Good times there were long forgotten.

Meanwhile at Fort Hill, Anna Maria Clemson died of a heart attack on September 22, 1875, while Clemson was away from their home for a short time. Devastated, he became nearly a recluse, entertaining friends who would stop by, but otherwise rarely leaving Fort Hill. The end of his life was thirteen years away, during which Clemson finalized his bequest that would create "a high seminary of learning." Soon after his death on April 6, 1888, Clemson's Last Will and Testament set into motion an intense legislative and legal furor. On December 6, 1889, exactly twenty months after his death, the ratification of Clemson's bequest to the State of South Carolina was completed, and his vision became a posthumous reality: The Clemson Agricultural College of South Carolina.

Thomas Green Clemson's legacy is more than the university that bears his name. His agricultural experience in the South became a whetstone for sharpening his vision of what the region needed to prosper. Clemson's experience with agriculture showed him the folly of a cash-crop economy. He realized it was a risky business model. Prudent farmers grow a number of crops and raise cattle, hoping prices are up for some when they are down for others. The same holds true for cities, states, and nations. Diversity was vital to weathering the ebb and flow of economic cycles and to ensuring that the region could provide for many of its own needs. The South failed to diversify. Much of what it needed, ranging from hay mowers to cooking pots, had to be imported from either the North or abroad. The South was at the mercy of outsiders and was destroyed by those who had more and varied resources. This realization led Clemson to promote college education as a means to diversify the southern economy, thus generating industries and jobs for South Carolinians.

Slavery was pernicious, not only on moral but also on economic grounds. Clemson's passive acceptance of slavery would not have diverted his attention from the fact that it kept away foreign immigrants, who opposed slavery. The South was sparsely populated and needed more people to create communities and merchant economies. Nor would he have ignored the reality that hourly paid laborers were a superior work force to slaves. They were motivated to work to earn their pay; moreover, they did not have to be purchased, housed, or fed. The end of slavery freed not only men and women, but also capital. The question was: how best to put it to use?

Clemson knew the answer: knowledge is what creates change. Centers of learning were vital to revolutionizing the South, turning it away from a caste system and toward the ideal of self-sufficiency and civic virtue. The South's devotion to a religious and classical education could go a long way in building character, ethics, an appreciation of the arts, and a sense that history is prologue to the future. However, in that same classical education, one could find pragmatic warnings and mandates. One such example is Marcus Tullius Cicero's sage words: "*Cognito contemplatioque naturae manca quodam modo atque inchoata sit, si nulla actio rerum consequatur,*" that is, "Knowledge and the study of nature would somehow be weak and incomplete if it were not followed by practical results."[61]

Certainly, Clemson and even some of his nineteenth-century predecessors recognized that more was needed by most graduates than a classical education. As eminent southern scientist Matthew Fontaine Maury observed in 1836:

> When our young men leave college, most of them (some exceptions) are prepared as little for entering the world as they were when they entered college, the reason for this is that every young man is taught to believe Latin and Greek of the first importance; consequently everything that is solid and practical, such as mathematics, chemistry, and the like, is made to occupy a subordinate place and only a smattering of them is obtained.[62]

Clemson understood this as well as the meaning of the saying, "a farmer grows what a farmer knows." He grasped that putting science and technology to use was vital for farmer and industrialist alike. He was committed to seeing the blessings of science bestowed on the South. Through his planting experience, he knew that farmers would have to learn new ways to cultivate and restore their land. Intensive farming would have to replace land-consuming extensive farming.

Clemson also knew the power of agriculture and chemistry, a partnership that would lead to the most important discovery in modern history—the production of synthetic fertilizer. Make no mistake: it is neither the computer nor oil upon which our civilization continues. It is synthetic fertilizer, without which the world could not feed itself.[63]

Thomas Green Clemson was not a particularly successful farmer, but his knowledge, vision, and legacy ensured a future of successful farmers, as well as scientists and engineers, who continue to transform his adopted state and the global community.

### Notes

1.  Wayne David Rasmussen, ed., *Readings in the History of American Agriculture* (Urbana: University of Illinois Press, 1960), 110.
2.  Vaclav Smil, *Enriching the Earth: Fritz Haber, Carl Bosch, and the Transformation of World Food Production* (Cambridge, MA: MIT Press, 2001), 3; Lavoisier's contributions, notwithstanding, in 1794 he was guillotined in Paris during the Reign of Terror.
3.  Ibid., 4.
4.  Ibid., 5–12.

5.  Ibid., 5.
6.  Alester G. Holmes and George R. Sherrill, *Thomas Green Clemson: His Life and Work* (Richmond, VA: Garrett and Massie, 1937), 11.
7.  *The Journal of Chemical Education* 5: 4 (April 1928): 435.
8.  Holmes and Sherrill, *Thomas Green Clemson*, 17.
9.  Ernest McPherson Lander Jr., *The Calhoun Family and Thomas Green Clemson: The Decline of a Southern Patriarchy* (Columbia: University of South Carolina Press, 1983), 32.
10. Lewis Cecil Gray, *History of Agriculture in the Southern United States to 1860*, vol. 2 (Gloucester, MA: Peter Smith, 1958), 794.
11. Ibid., 788.
12. Lander, *Calhoun Family and Thomas Green Clemson*, 32.
13. Ibid.
14. John Solomon Otto, *Southern Agriculture during the Civil War Era, 1860-1880* (Westport, CT: Greenwood Press, 1994), 13.
15. Ibid., 2.
16. Daniel R. Goodloe, *Inquiry into the Causes Which Have Retarded the Accumulation of Wealth and Increase of Population in the Southern States: in Which the Question of Slavery is Considered in a Politico-Economical Point of View. By a Carolinian* (Washington, DC: W. Blanchard, 1846), 1-28.
17. Otto, *Southern Agriculture*, 84.
18. Holmes and Sherrill, *Thomas Green Clemson*, 93n5.
19. Smil, *Enriching the Earth*, 26.
20. Gray, *History of Agriculture*, 810.
21. Lou Ferleger, ed., *Agriculture and National Development: Views on the Nineteenth Century* (Ames: Iowa State University Press, 1990), 138–139.
22. Lander, *Calhoun Family and Thomas Green Clemson*, 9.
23. Ibid., 23.
24. Ibid., 27.
25. Ibid.
26. Ibid.
27. *Annual Report of the American Historical Association* (1929): 158–159; *American Historical Association Report* 2 (1899): 467, both cited in Holmes and Sherrill, *Thomas Green Clemson*, 92nn1–2.
28. *American Historical Association Report* 2 (1899): 473, cited in Holmes and Sherrill, *Thomas Green Clemson*, 93.
29. Gray, *History of Agriculture*, 793.
30. Holmes and Sherrill, *Thomas Green Clemson*, 93.
31. Gray, *History of Agriculture*, 904.
32. Holmes and Sherrill, *Thomas Green Clemson*, 94.
33. *American Historical Association Report* 2 (1899): 649, cited in Holmes and Sherrill, *Thomas Green Clemson*, 93–94n5.
34. Ibid., 627, cited in Holmes and Sherrill, *Thomas Green Clemson*, 95n10.
35. Lander, *Calhoun Family and Thomas Green Clemson*, 80.
36. Ibid., 85.
37. Ibid., 142.
38. Ibid.
39. Ibid., 15.
40. Holmes and Sherrill, *Thomas Green Clemson*, 109.
41. Otto, *Southern Agriculture*, 11.
42. See *American Farmer* 13, no. 4 (October 1857).
43. Smil, *Enriching the Earth*, 40.
44. Otto, *Southern Agriculture*, 84.
45. Holmes and Sherrill, *Thomas Green Clemson*, 97–121.
46. Lander, *Calhoun Family and Thomas Green Clemson*, 189.
47. Holmes and Sherrill, *Thomas Green Clemson*, 138–140.
48. Lander, *Calhoun Family and Thomas Green Clemson*, 208–209.

49. Ibid., 92.
50. Ibid., 218.
51. Ibid., 228.
52. Charles M. McGee Jr. and Ernest McPherson Lander Jr., eds., *A Rebel Came Home: The Diary and Letters of Floride Clemson 1863–1866*, revised edition (Columbia: University of South Carolina Press, 1989), 92–93.
53. Lander, *Calhoun Family and Thomas Green Clemson*, 228.
54. Ibid., 235.
55. Ibid., 240.
56. Ibid.
57. Ibid., 241.
58. Otto, *Southern Agriculture*, 80.
59. Philip M. Fravel, "A History of Agricultural Education in South Carolina with an Emphasis on the Public School Program," Dissertation (Blacksburg, VA: Virginia Polytechnic Institute & State University, February 2004), 20. See also http://scholar.lib.vt.edu/theses/available/etd-04242004-202220/.
60. Otto, *Southern Agriculture*, 76–77.
61. Marcus Tullius Cicero, *De Officiis*, 1: 43, cited in Smil, Preface, *Enriching the Earth*, v.
62. Ronald L. Numbers and Janet S. Numbers, "Science in the Old South: A Reappraisal," *Journal of Southern History* 48, no. 2 (May 1982): 179–180. See also http://www.jstor.org.
63. Smil, Preface, *Enriching the Earth*, xiii.

# Chapter 8

# RACE, RECONSTRUCTION, AND POST-BELLUM EDUCATION
### IN THOMAS GREEN CLEMSON'S
### LIFE AND WORLD

## *Abel A. Bartley*

**Rendering of Fort Hill, John C. Calhoun's plantation, with slave quarters and outbuildings identified. From 1938 drawing by Jack Tuttle. Ethel Mitchell Collection, Special Collections, Clemson University Libraries.**

An honest chronicler of the past faces many challenges. Historians, more often than not, are caught in the vortex of truth and consequences as they analyze past events, people, and movements. The best historians are those who can accurately, fairly, and realistically re-create the past from their research into the available evidence. At the same time, they attempt to reconstruct the past without interjecting their own personal, regional, or cultural biases. All history is propaganda, but not all propaganda is history. Thus any attempt to reconstruct Thomas Green Clemson's attitudes toward race, slavery, Reconstruction, and post-bellum South Carolina education mandates careful analysis, even trepidation. The first step in this chapter's attempt has been to place his attitudes and ideas in the context of nineteenth-century America and to understand that as a transplanted Yankee, who came South for personal and economic reasons, Clemson was probably influenced by the prevailing attitudes and ideas of that region and his desire to fit into his adopted state.

After careful study of Thomas Green Clemson's life, one thing is immediately clear: what we don't know about him far outdistances what we do know. For a man who lived through some of the most controversial and important times in American history, Clemson left very little in the way of personal recollections that would allow us to know what he thought about the major issues confronting Americans during his lifetime. Perhaps it is this lack of information that tells us the most about Clemson and the world in which he lived. Nevertheless, our task is to address the available facts.

### Starting in Philadelphia

Thomas Green Clemson was born on July 1, 1807, in Philadelphia, Pennsylvania. His father, Thomas Clemson III, and his mother, Elizabeth Baker Clemson, were able to establish a relatively comfortable existence for their family. There is continuing debate over whether or not the Clemsons were Quakers, but what is not debatable is that his father's side of the family did have traceable Quaker roots. Quakers were a religious sect, founded by George Fox in England during the seventeenth century and made up of disaffected Christians from various factions. Though small in numbers, they had pockets of strength in several North American regions such as Pennsylvania. They were especially prominent in Philadelphia where they established several meeting houses and societies and helped mold the city during Clemson's day. Though the Clemsons had been members of the group, it is clear they did not practice all of the faith's tenets. For example, several of the Clemsons served in the military during the American Revolution, a direct violation of the Quakers' pacifist teachings.[1]

Clemson's father apparently was kicked out of the Quaker fellowship after he married Elizabeth Baker, an Episcopalian. Subsequently, Clemson's father did not often attend religious services, although Elizabeth carefully ensured that her children attended church and reserved a pew for the family each Sunday at an Episcopal church, which probably had no black members.

At the turn of the century Philadelphia was a flourishing city and the center of economic development and political debate. It was also a center of early abolitionist activity where African Americans congregated and developed a thriving community. By the time Clemson was born, slavery was virtually a dead issue in

Pennsylvania. The state set in motion a gradual emancipation program in 1780. The law stated that no African Americans born on or after 1780 would be held in bondage after they became twenty-eight, after which they would be treated as indentured servants or apprentices. This opened the state for free-blacks who wanted to escape slavery. In 1790 there were still 3,707 black slaves in Pennsylvania, but some 6,531 were free-blacks.[2]

Because of Quaker influence, Philadelphia was also the center of a strong and relatively independent free-black population that made its mark on that society. Richard Allen and Absalom Jones, for instance, helped found the African Methodist Episcopal (AME) Church there in 1816—a church that became the first independent black Christian denomination in the world. Another free-black, Paul Cuffe, had a profitable sailmaking company, along with many others who rose to prominence and made black life in Philadelphia prosperous. There were also a number of black institutions in Philadelphia, such as the Free African Society, where blacks met and provided mutual aid. One such effort was the school they established for free-black children. During the same period, the Quakers established some of the first antislavery societies in the country and sponsored some of the first abolitionist lectures. In fact, they had been heavily involved in pro-black activities since before the revolution. Historian Howard Chudacoff writes, "By the 1820s in Philadelphia, African Americans had created an institutional life that was richer and more stable than that of lower-income whites with whom they shared neighborhoods." Therefore, Thomas Green Clemson was reared in a society where progressive free-blacks played a prominent and visible role. Whether or not he took notice of these blacks and their activities is unknown.[3]

In 1813 Clemson's young life changed when his father died. By the time of his death, the senior Clemson had amassed a fortune estimated at more than $100,000. His will dictated that his fortune be divided among his six children, with his three sons each receiving a $5,000 additional payment. In addition to his real property, Thomas Clemson III had two indentured servants: a black female and a German male. There is no record of what became of them, but young Clemson had an early personal awareness of black servitude within America.[4]

John B. Gest, a prominent Philadelphian and a cousin, was appointed the Clemson children's guardian after the elder Clemson's death. Gest ensured that the children received a proper education. Thomas Green Clemson attended schools in Philadelphia before going to the American Literary, Scientific, and Military Academy in Norwich, Vermont. There he became interested in studying chemistry. However, no schools in North America offered an advanced chemistry education, and so Clemson went to Paris where he studied chemistry and physics at the Sorbonne, audited a four-year course of study at the School of Mines, and earned a formal certificate as an assayer from the Royal Mint of Paris. While in

Paris, he also participated in the July 1830 revolts, which overthrew the King of France, Charles X, who had attempted to restore an absolute monarchy. Here we see the young Clemson participating in a social movement designed to overthrow a perceived tyrannical power.[5]

In the 1830s, when Clemson returned to Philadelphia, he was a well-educated and sophisticated gentleman who appreciated art and music, played the violin, and spoke several languages. Moreover, Clemson was a confirmed bachelor who, by all accounts, enjoyed his independence and single status. Clemson soon found a job in the Pennsylvania mining industry where he distinguished himself with his knowledge and ability to utilize technology. In addition, he joined the Geological Society of Philadelphia where he wrote and read papers, which helped to establish his intellectual credibility.[6]

In 1836 Clemson and Richard C. Taylor went to Cuba for a short time to investigate bituminous coal. This was one of the first rich coal veins to be discovered in the tropics. Clemson also was part owner of and technical advisor for the Mine LaMotte in Missouri. He found himself involved in a number of mining ventures during this period, which took him to several areas where he demonstrated his abilities and utilized his education. They certainly allowed him to see various groups of laborers in the mines. And some of these ventures were lucrative for him; presumably, Clemson earned $20,000 from a mining project in South America. There is little known about this adventure, but it is a claim that has not been disputed.[7]

### *Connecting with the South and Slavocracy*

During the first half of the 1830s—when he was not traveling or studying in Europe—Clemson lived in Philadelphia, even though he spent a great deal of time in Washington, D.C. There, in 1838, he was introduced to Anna Maria Calhoun, the eldest daughter of South Carolina politician and U.S. Senator John C. Calhoun. The meeting transformed Clemson's life and started him on a most dichotomous path. This descendent of Quakers and son of a wealthy merchant became a friend and son-in-law of one of the country's most notorious defenders of slavery and racial privilege. After their November 13, 1838, marriage on John Calhoun's plantation at Fort Hill, Clemson would be forever linked to the South, John C. Calhoun, and South Carolina. The state incrementally became Clemson's adopted home, and John C. Calhoun became his surrogate father and political patron. In 1839, after a year in Philadelphia, Thomas and Anna Clemson moved to South Carolina where they lived on John C. Calhoun's plantation. This gave Clemson his first experience in working with slaves and the regimented lifestyle of plantation life. If he had any personal animus against owning slaves, he did not initially express it in his letters or correspondences.[8]

The South Carolina Clemson moved to was a racial caldron of slavery and white privilege. South Carolina had a large black population which was mostly held in slavery and virtually cut off from the benefits of the society. Most of the state's residents had a relatively simple agricultural lifestyle. Moreover, in 1840 Pickens County had a population of only 14,356 people. It was nothing like the bustling metropolis he had known in Philadelphia.[9] Unlike the status of African Americans in Philadelphia, South Carolinian slaves were less than second-class citizens. They were considered disposable property to be used at the owner's whim and then sold when no longer useful. Both Pickens and Anderson Counties were regions dominated by the slavocracy and plantation system, and Clemson expressed no regrets for becoming a part of this society.

Between the fall of 1840 and spring of 1843, Clemson managed John Calhoun's Fort Hill Plantation. With his marriage to Anna, the South got an erudite northerner who had scientific and technical knowledge along with valuable international experience. The Clemsons lived in South Carolina for four years before moving to Europe to serve in the American diplomatic corps. Clemson's affection for his new home followed him to Europe where his views on slavery began to emerge. For example, while in Belgium, both Clemsons defended slavery as preferable to what they called the wage slavery of Europe. Their argument would have been welcomed by John C. Calhoun.[10]

Of course, by joining the Calhoun family, Clemson had connected himself to one of the South's most respected and powerful families. Moreover, John C. Calhoun was one of the South's most recognized political figures and its leading proponent of slavery. Calhoun had descended from a family with a long and distinguished reputation in the state. His great-grandfather Ezekiel Calhoun is reported to have introduced slavery into the Piedmont area when he arrived in the 1750s. He came to South Carolina from Virginia and joined a Scotch-Irish settlement in Abbeville. He had two sons—John Ewing and Patrick, John C. Calhoun's father—both of whom became active in politics and won legislative seats. For unknown reasons, John Ewing changed the spelling of his last name to Colhoun.[11]

John E. Colhoun married the daughter of a wealthy planter, got elected to the U.S. Senate, and had one of the largest holdings in the Pendleton, South Carolina, area. He accumulated a sizeable slave holding, establishing an early link between his wealth and slavery. He died while still a senator in 1802. After his death, Colhoun's estate was in limbo for several years, because his two surviving children were very young. When his daughter Floride married her cousin John C. Calhoun, she was given several slaves and some property. In 1836 Colhoun's estate was finally settled: John E. Colhoun Jr. got the Keowee plantation, and John E. Colhoun Sr.'s widow, also named Floride, got the plantation at Cold Springs. John C. Calhoun and Floride received a separate plantation at Fort Hill, the site today of Clemson University's campus. Calhoun increased his slave holdings through inheritance, after his father died. The same was true after his mother-in-law died and her estate was settled. Calhoun slowly built an estate through inheritance. He used his slaves at his Fort Hill plantation, his gold mines in Georgia, and also on his plantation in Alabama.[12]

John E. Colhoun Jr., on the other hand, ran up a considerable debt which forced him to sell some of his slaves. Colhoun had become a prominent citizen of Pendleton, serving as president of the Pendleton Farmers' Society. Hoping to diversify his holdings, he invested in a woolen factory. However, Colhoun was a big spender who lived beyond his means. Even with a plantation with eighty slaves, he could not create enough wealth to sustain his family's lifestyle. As a result he was frequently forced to face the embarrassing sale of his slaves and other property during the 1830s and 1840s to satisfy debts. In 1842, for instance, Thomas Green Clemson bought five of John Colhoun's slaves to work on his Edgefield plantation. Colhoun eventually settled most of his debt by selling his woolen factory and 800 acres of his plantation.[13]

In 1853 Martha Colhoun (John E. Jr.'s widow) died, leaving the Colhoun plantation at Keowee to be run by her two children. They still had seventy-seven slaves of varying ages and genders worth on average $425 each. According to the plantation ledger, the slaves ranged in value from $50 for an eighty-year-old man to $1,100 for some seventeen- to nineteen-year-old males. These were similar figures for slaves purchased by Andrew Calhoun, Anna Calhoun Clemson's brother, in 1854 for his plantation.[14]

John C. Calhoun ran his Fort Hill plantation like most other slave owners. Though most people referred to him as being "just and kind," he was nonetheless a person who owned other individuals and, like other southern men, was capable of using swift and decisive action to punish his slaves. Calhoun had no problem having his slaves whipped when the situation called for it. He also understood that slave owners who indulged their slaves generally had the most unruly slaves. John Calhoun owned between thirty and ninety slaves, depending on which records one cites.[15] He developed a plan whereby he constantly switched slaves with his son Andrew, who owned a plantation in Alabama, to make sure that the slaves would not be overworked in the hot environs of Alabama. This also allowed Calhoun to keep his slaves in the family.[16]

The plantation at Fort Hill was like other plantations. The slave quarters were one, long, single tenement about an eighth of a mile from the big house. Each slave family was allowed to have its own small garden where the slaves grew yams, greens, corn, and turnips. Calhoun also supplied meats and corn meal to supplement what the slaves grew. At Christmas the slaves received fresh meats and wheaten bread. Calhoun seemed to have been fascinated by the joviality of his slaves. He once wrote Clemson that the slaves danced until after midnight.

Susan Richardson (b. 1830, part Native American) was owned as a slave by John C. Calhoun in her younger years and then given to Anna Maria Calhoun Clemson as a personal maid. After the Civil War, she married Billy Richardson and moved near Saluda, S.C. Early twentieth-century photograph with Richardson holding young Byron Herlong. Fort Hill Collection, Clemson University.

However, he did not believe that African Americans had much in the way of intellectual maturity. He once wrote a friend, "Show me a Negro who can parse a Greek verb or solve a problem, in Euclid," and he would grant that he was the human equal of the white man.[17]

Clemson's association with John C. Calhoun forces researchers to wonder about his feelings toward African Americans. Calhoun, as mentioned earlier, was one of the most notorious racists toward African Americans of his period and one of the South's leading advocates for slavery. He did not believe that African Americans had the mental or intellectual capacity to live as free people in a white society. Calhoun argued that slavery was a sort of school for civilizing Africans and moving them toward greater development. In an 1837 speech he said, "I appeal to facts, never before has the black race…attained a condition so civilized and so improved not only physically, but morally and intellectually." He went on to say, "He came to us in a low, degraded, and savage condition and in the course of a few generations it has grown under the fostering care of our institutions."[18]

Former Calhoun slave Nancy Legree, photographed at age 106. She was given to Ransome Calhoun and taken to Columbia, S.C. Presumably, she returned to the Upstate after the Civil War. Black Heritage in the Upper Piedmont of South Carolina Project Collection, Special Collections, Clemson University Libraries.

**Former slaves Thomas Fruster and Frances Fruster, from a stereopticon photograph of Fort Hill during Thomas Clemson's last decade. Jane Prince, Clemson's caregiver, is seated on the porch, ca. 1880. Fort Hill Collection, Clemson University.**

Clemson spent time with Calhoun watching how he ran his plantation at Fort Hill. Clemson thus gained valuable knowledge about plantation management and life from the time he spent managing his father-in-law's plantation. Many of the things he did later when he became a plantation owner were modeled after what he saw Calhoun do. Still, Clemson believed that his own knowledge of scientific agriculture would be beneficial to any plantation.

During the early 1840s Clemson was looking for new areas in which to invest his money. As the iron industry and other ventures began to decline, he turned toward agriculture as a possible profit venue. John C. Calhoun suggested that he purchase a plantation. Not long after that, Clemson heard about a plantation in Edgefield owned by Arthur Simkins, the brother-in-law of Francis Pickens and James Edward Calhoun. Clemson, who was away on business in Pennsylvania, asked his father-in-law to investigate the plantation to see if it was worth purchasing. Calhoun encouraged him to make the purchase, but only after he looked the place over himself. On December 2, 1842, the two of them made an inspection of the plantation. Clemson named the property "Canebrake" in recognition of the thicket of canes on the bank of the river which ran through the lowlands. After inspection he decided to purchase the property and join the southern slavocracy. Clemson agreed to buy the 1,050-acre plantation for $24,000. The deal gave him more than 1,000 acres of land in Edgefield in Saluda County, South Carolina.[19]

Clemson's foray into slaveholding occurred during some of the heaviest periods of abolitionist activity. Both southerners and abolitionists were hardening their positions as the nation's leaders debated the peculiar institution. At the same time, the Second Great Awakening was once again pushing the notion of Christian Brotherhood and denouncing slavery as sinful, unbiblical, and immoral. Clemson chose to become a slaveholder during this crucial era, and there is no evidence that he considered the wider implications of slavery when he made his decision. Whatever the case, Clemson was not forced into slave ownership; it was a role he deliberately chose.[20]

Clemson immediately ran into problems with his new plantation. He had no slaves and immediately had to purchase them from his neighbors. He also did not have enough time to run the plantation personally, so he negotiated with Arthur Simkins to share the running of the plantation for the first year. In addition, the plantation was not in good shape, and the house was in ill-repair and weather-damaged. Clemson purchased a slave named William who had the responsibility of repairing their home and building other structures.[21]

Clemson knew that he was becoming a slave owner when he purchased Canebrake. He knew that the success of this investment was tied to getting good slaves who could help him turn a profit from the endeavor. In 1845, a year after the Clemsons had arrived in Belgium, John C. Calhoun wrote a letter informing Clemson that Canebrake was doing fine. The buildings were being repaired, the planting and plowing were nearly completed, the horses and mules were in reasonably good condition, and the crops consisted of 120 acres of cotton, 110 acres of corn, and seventy acres of oats. He also noted that the slaves were generally healthy, even though their housing remained in disrepair.[22]

Clemson did not own his plantation long. However, during that period he accumulated thirty-seven slaves, mainly through purchase. Clemson became a strong supporter of slavery. In 1845, he tried to sell his plantation for $13,000 while keeping his slaves to rent out. Clemson said of slaves, "they are the most valuable property in the South, being the basis of the whole southern fabric." He sold slaves when the situation called for it, once remarking, "My object is to get the most I can for the property….I care but little to whom and how the[y] are sold, whether together or separated…the affair should be kept as secret as possible on account of the Negroes." Clemson's personal correspondences have several allusions to purchasing and selling slaves. He was a businessman who wanted to make a profit from his investment. It is clear that Canebrake was not the economic success story he hoped for. Moreover, in 1854 when Clemson was living in Maryland, he was no longer convinced that slavery was a viable labor source. In a letter to Elias Baker dated July 19, 1854, he wrote, "Negroes I think will be the resort that I shall be compelled to—they are hazardous & give much trouble & require constant watching."[23]

## The War Years

During the period leading up to the Civil War, the Calhoun family was active in rallying South Carolinians. Andrew Calhoun tried to remain out of the spotlight even though he felt slighted that he was not in an important political position in the state. His mother, though worried, expressed support for the Confederacy. On December 3, 1860, she wrote, "We are living exciting times here since Lincoln has been elected....The South is now so wide awake that nothing could turn their course. The dissolution of the Union is inevitable, and I think nothing else will save us." Clemson did not support secession, but he also did not think the North should coerce the South. His major concern seemed to be finances as the war approached. On March 9, 1861, Clemson resigned from the government, and he and Anna quietly went south, leaving their children in Maryland.[24]

On April 4, 1861, President Abraham Lincoln met with a delegation of Virginia Unionists in the White House. This meeting convinced Lincoln that he could not negotiate with them to avoid conflict. This meeting also convinced him to re-supply Fort Sumter, but not to send large numbers of forces. He wanted to make it clear that the South was the aggressor. That was in essence the last day to avoid conflict. On that day Clemson was in Montgomery, Alabama, a center of southern secession. He clearly could see that conflict was coming. In a letter to his uncle Elias Baker, Clemson stated, "We are preparing for war, and if the North wants it and the black republicans force it upon us, they will surely have it and they will find out that war will not take place in this ground, it will be carried home to them until they cry peace."[25]

The Civil War began at 4:30 a.m. on April 12, 1861, when Confederate forces fired on Fort Sumter in Charleston. This event precipitated President Abraham Lincoln's call for forces to put down a rebellion in the South. Thomas and Anna Clemson quickly returned to Maryland to check on their children and business affairs. With the war starting, Clemson found himself in a strange position. He was a native northerner who had sworn he would never live in the South again. Also, he had several investments, including property, in the North. He transferred his property and finances into his wife's name, and he and his son Calhoun moved back to South Carolina.[26]

During the first two years of the Civil War, Clemson stayed with his mother-in-law in Pendleton, giving speeches and caring for the plantation at Fort Hill. In 1863, he chose to join ranks with his southern neighbors and participate in the war as a Confederate officer. Clemson's decision to join the Confederate cause must not have been an easy one. Notwithstanding his Pennsylvania roots, Clemson was already disappointed that the Confederate government had not created, as he advised, an Agricultural Department. His son Calhoun also joined the Confederate Army, first as an enlisted man but then quickly rose to the rank of second lieutenant. The Army initially stationed him close to his family in South Carolina.[27]

In the spring of 1863, Clemson and his son traveled to Richmond, Virginia, the capital of the Confederacy and where Clemson offered his service to the Confederacy. On May 7, 1863, he officially became a member of the Confederate military. Because of his extensive knowledge of science and technology, Clemson was assigned to a mining unit working at the Nitre and Mining Bureau, Trans-Mississippi Department. His son was later transferred to this same unit. One can assume that, by volunteering to serve in the Confederacy, Clemson was willing to fight and kill to preserve slavery. As James McPherson writes, "The Emancipation Proclamation announced a new war aim. Thenceforth, the Union army became officially an army of liberation. The North was now fighting to create a new Union, not to restore the old one."[28] By 1864 Clemson was in charge of ironworks in Texas and was building furnaces. In September he was transferred to an inspector role and given light duty.[29]

There were no meritorious distinctions associated with Clemson's military service. In fact, his contributions to the Confederacy were not significant. Like many others, he provided services and material aid to the Confederacy, but provided little in the way of military skills. Apparently, Clemson did not see any real military action. His age and technical knowledge probably precluded him from dangerous duties. He did suffer a broken arm from a wagon accident in January 1864. Calhoun Clemson, however, was captured and placed in a Union prison on Johnson's Island in Lake Erie. Eventually, Calhoun Clemson was released, and Thomas Clemson was paroled officially on June 9, 1865. This ended his military career.[30]

### *The Reconstruction Years*

After the Civil War, the Clemson family reunited and lived at the home of Anna's mother in Pendleton, South Carolina, a place that had been devastated by the war. Clemson became convinced that the only hope for the South was education, and especially scientific education on agriculture. He wrote, "There is, in my opinion, no hope for the South short of widespread scientific education. Our condition is wretched in the extreme. Everyone is in trouble, many ruined, and others are quitting the country in despair. The late harvests have been short, many are in want, and the State treasury is as empty as most of the inhabitants find their pockets and granaries."[31]

The Reconstruction years were very difficult for most South Carolinians. The state had been economically, socially, and politically devastated by the war. Agriculture was in disarray as the former slaves reveled in their newfound freedom. At the same time, the African American population steadily increased in South Carolina as blacks began to enjoy the fruits of their free labor. They began to move from rural areas to the rapidly developing urban areas of the state. Particularly in the coastal areas, where agriculture was still the dominant form of production, blacks outnumbered whites and had a freedom they did not have in more rural and western parts of the state.[32]

White southerners were insulted by notions of black equality and freedom. Many of the southern leaders had come to believe that the key to solving the chaos was returning African Americans to their familiar state of slavery. This would ensure a stable labor supply and also solve the race problem. Southerners believed that the attempt to transform their slaves into free people had been a complete failure. Taking advantage of the chaotic conditions of the postwar society, white politicians moved in to reestablish the existing social order under a different guise. Many were of the opinion that it was foolhardy to believe that they would ever treat their former laborers as equals. To ensure an orderly transition and also to establish some semblance of order, President Andrew Johnson appointed Benjamin Franklin Perry, a former Unionist from Greenville, as the provisional governor of the state.[33]

Perry seemed like a strange choice. Even though it was said that he wept like a baby at the state's choice to secede from the Union, he nevertheless served in the state legislature throughout the war. During the prewar debates he had expressed his support for the Union and his opposition to the political dominance of planters over the state. Being from Greenville, he represented the Upstate, supposedly a more progressive area. Nevertheless, Perry, a shrewd politician, chose to keep former Confederate officials in their positions of authority when he reorganized South Carolina's state government. Thus the staunchest rebels were able to maintain their political base under Perry. He hoped that by doing this he could placate the Lowcountry and the coastal planter class, which he believed were essential to his political career. These men would open Perry to the charge by his critics that he had, "put upon their legs a set of men who…like the Bourbons have learned nothing and forgotten nothing."[34]

In order for the state to be restored to the federal fold, Perry's duty was to call a convention so that South Carolinians could amend their constitution. The convention was supposed to define citizenship for the state, determine who could vote and hold office, and determine who could make the rules and laws governing the state. There was little discussion about African Americans' civil rights in the initial discussions. When Perry called the convention for September 13, 1865, in Columbia, most southerners continued to believe that the same status that governed free-blacks during slavery governed the former slaves after the war.[35]

Most of the delegates knew, of course, that they had to abolish slavery. Still, Governor Perry opened the debates on African American rights by pointing out his opposition to giving blacks the vote. His rationale was that, because of their widespread ignorance and degraded condition, they were incapable of making wise political decisions. The governor also stated, "This is a white man's government and intended for white men only." He went on to say, "The Supreme Court of the United States has decided that the Negro is not an American citizen under the Federal Constitution." Therefore the governor encouraged the delegates to "settle this grave question as the interest and honor of the State demanded."[36]

The constitution the leaders wrote did only the minimum as far as African American rights were concerned. It outlawed slavery, restricted the suffrage to white men aged twenty-one years or older, and specified that only voters could hold office. It specifically restricted officeholders in the state house of representatives or senate to free white men. The constitution further defined any one who had black blood either through birth or marriage as black. Blacks were not allowed to carry or keep a firearm, sword, or military weapon, without written permission from a judge. They could keep a shotgun or rifle used for hunting, but not a pistol, musket, or weapon appropriate for purposes of war. Blacks could not serve in the militia or own a distillery. Moreover, they could be arrested by any white person.[37]

In addition, black orphans were to be apprenticed out under contract. Blacks could not own or operate businesses unless they had a license. Vagrancy and idleness were punished with a term of hard labor. Taken together these laws represented the so-called black codes. George Tindall said of these, "This code was the first effort by whites of the state to redefine the relations of the races under the new conditions. The nature of the black codes indicates that white South Carolinians could not conceive of Negoes [sic] as truly free agents in their relationship to the economy of the state." White South Carolinians viewed the freed slaves as they viewed free-blacks under slavery.[38]

### Ante- and Post-bellum Education in South Carolina

African American leaders refused to sit idly by while their hard-fought struggle for inclusion was ignored. Fifty-two African American leaders met in November of 1865 to plan a strategy for gaining black rights. They demanded the full gamut of rights and privileges enjoyed by whites. They specifically demanded unhindered access to the franchise, free public education, the right to bear arms, serve on juries, establish newspapers, assemble peacefully, enter all venues of agriculture, commerce, and trade, and "develop our whole being by all the appliances that belong to civilized society."[39]

While many of the other demands could be slowly negotiated, African Americans demanded immediate access to education. White South Carolinians had demonstrated a reluctance to educate African Americans from the area's earliest days. After the Revolutionary War, when the Episcopal church attempted to form academies to teach African Americans to read and write, there was little initial objection. However, attitudes rapidly changed after the early 1800s with the Haitian Revolution, the Denmark Vesey conspiracy, and the Nat Turner rebellion. South Carolinians, like other southerners, came to believe that it was not wise to provide knowledge to the slaves. As one commentator noted, "In the face of earnest opposition of influential citizens, laws were then passed providing penalties for teaching slaves to read and write." Nevertheless, several African Americans were able to gain an education through various means.[40]

One thing that characterized early educational efforts for South Carolina was that very few people believed that the state should expend money educating their citizens. Therefore, education initially was the domain of religious institutions and private citizens. South Carolinians established a network of private schools which they used to educate the children of the most prominent citizens. As historian Henry Thompson has noted, "From the time of the founding of the colony up to the 1860's...the well to do in South Carolina patronized private schools, or employed tutors for their sons and governesses for their daughters." Children of wealthy white South Carolinians generally sent their children to northern or European universities for higher education. Even after South Carolina opened its colleges, wealthy parents continued to send their children elsewhere for advanced schooling. One British official said, "None of the British Provinces, in proportion to their numbers, sent so many of their sons to Europe for education as South Carolina."[41]

In 1811, when Thomas Green Clemson was a four-year-old boy living in Philadelphia, Stephen Elliott introduced legislation to spend $37,000 for developing a system of free schools open to all free white children in South Carolina. The legislation had the state providing $300 for each school in proportion to the number of delegates its district had. There was a long protracted battle to defend this nascent system. Several prominent and wealthy South Carolinians opposed the increased taxation to support the system. They also argued that education was not under the purview of the state but instead a private and parochial matter.[42]

Little action was taken to increase the number of public schools until the 1850s. During the so-called great American Common Schools movement, there was a drastic and rapid increase in the number of free schools. By 1852—a year after Thomas and Anna Clemson had returned to the United States from Belgium—South Carolina had increased its spending on public schools to $74,000. By 1861 the state had increased its annual expenditures on education to $200,000, and the enrollment had increased from 17,838 in 1850 to 20,000 by 1861.[43]

The establishment of a functional public school idea was slowed by the attitudes of both poor and wealthy whites. Wealthy whites were reluctant to send their children to these schools. They did not believe that they needed free schools, since they could send their children to private schools or hire private tutors for them. The poor also were hesitant to send their children to free schools. They were worried about the stigma that was often attached to these schools. Those who sent their children to these schools were identified as paupers. Because parents were loathe to be identified as poor, they generally chose to keep their children ignorant and at home. As one South Carolina official said, "Many men would deprive their children of the means of education in preference to having them branded at school as paupers."[44]

As a result of this opposition, South Carolinians slowly came to the opinion that public education was an unnecessary state expense, since those who desired an education could acquire one at their own expense. The attitudes of the upper class came to dominate the feelings of lower- and middle-class South Carolinians. The upper class argued that all the state had to do educationally was do something for the poor, and the 1811 school law fulfilled that requirement. They had established paupers' schools, and therefore any of the poor who wanted to educate their children could do so at one of those schools. There was another reason why public schools were not regarded as a necessity: no public clamor arose in favor of them. There were enough private schools to satisfy most people's thirst for public education.[45] Still in certain areas, people did make improvements in their public school systems. In Charleston, for example, C. G. Memminger implemented a plan for improving the city's schools. They hired trained teachers from the North who improved the curriculum and instituted an improved educational experience. The system worked so well that it attracted students from all classes.[46]

One of the most improbable occurrences of the period was the expansion of African American education in South Carolina. With whites generally being in the minority through much of the early history of South Carolina, there was constant fear that their slaves might revolt. After the 1822 Denmark Vesey conspiracy and the 1830s slave rebellions, many South Carolinians came to believe that the South had to take a defensive stance on slavery. They passed new rigidly enforced laws designed to protect slavery and enforce the prevailing racial etiquette. Nevertheless, a surprising number of African Americans were able to gain a rudimentary education. There were several free-black societies that ran schools. Some of these schools were partially funded by whites, and at least one white teacher was employed in one.[47]

Educational development and postwar Reconstruction went hand in hand. Many believed that the best way to rebuild the South was through innovative educational initiatives that transformed the former slaves into useful members of South Carolina's society. Since late 1861, when Union forces captured Hilton Head and some of the adjacent islands, there were efforts to bring education to average South Carolinians. After the white plantation owners abandoned their properties on the Sea Islands, in a desperate attempt to avoid Union forces, they left more than 9,000 African American slaves with no supervision. A Union general, serving in the area, appealed to northern entities for some advice and aid. In response, these northern philanthropists organized a series of what became known as freedmen's aid societies.[48]

Solomon Peck opened a school in 1862 on the Sea Islands at Port Royal. This attracted several teachers who came to the school to teach. With the help of the Pennsylvania Society, they helped found a series of schools on the islands. One of the most famous was the Penn School founded on St. Helena and named after the Pennsylvania Society. Several other schools were founded on the other islands, and an unorganized network of schools was established. There was early friction about what type of education was most pressing for the newly freed slaves. Many argued for an education that emphasized skills and trades which would arm the former slaves with the most needed skills and knowledge. Others believed that African Americans needed to be trained in the classics so that they could quickly dispel the racist notions about blacks.[49]

Education in South Carolina was clearly going through a period of transition during the post-bellum period. In 1865 Governor James L. Orr recommended ending school funding. However, this did not end the nascent efforts to bring free public education to South Carolinians. By 1866, the year in which Thomas Clemson was elected president of the Pendleton Farmers' Society and began efforts to establish a scientific institution in the Upstate, nearly half of South Carolina's school districts still had schools which were educating some 2,245 students. Nevertheless, the notion of universal education was not a fully developed concept in the minds of most South Carolinians. It was clear, however, that the state was moving in that direction.[50]

In 1867 an interracial delegation met and wrote a new constitution. There were seventy-six African Americans among the 124 delegates. Of those, fifty-seven had come from slavery. They wrote what most called the best state constitution the state had seen. Passed by a 70,558 to 27,288 vote, it was ratified on April 16, 1868. The new constitution created a biracial suffrage, cancelled debts incurred by purchasing slaves, provided a $1,000 homestead exemption from debts, and a $500 personal property exemption. It also included a provision requiring the General Assembly to establish a public school system.[51]

White South Carolinians exhibited a disdain for the 1868 state constitution. For all their bluster, however, they enjoyed the benefits and changes wrought by this document. One of the biggest changes was the introduction of universal education. This education was modeled on the theory that "the whole people shall establish, organize, support and supervise the educational training of all children and youth."[52] For the first time since 1834, African American children could legally receive an education in South Carolina. The 1868 state constitution was the first organic law which made mention of education in South Carolina. By enacting this new constitution, South Carolinians ushered in a new era, thus bypassing the old system of private schools and replacing it with a new educational system of free public schools open to all classes and races. It also created an elected state superintendent of education and provided for county school commissioners who would be elected biennially. The name of the latter position would eventually be changed to county superintendents of education. This system set up a State Board of Education which delineated the state superintendent of education as chairman and the local county superintendents as the board.[53]

The law called for the state legislature to "provide for a liberal and uniform system of free public schools throughout the State." The legislature was to divide the state into workable school districts, and each district was to have at least one school which was open at least six months of each year. The state also mandated compulsory attendance for all school-age children between the ages of six and eleven. The constitution outlined three revenue sources for funding these schools: an annual general appropriation from the state legislature, a one dollar poll tax levied on all able-bodied male citizens, and a voluntary local tax, levied on non-property owners. The money raised from these taxes was to be distributed to the various districts in proportion to the number of students attending the schools. The legislature also set aside money for supporting the University of South Carolina and for establishing an agricultural college; a school for the deaf, dumb, and blind; a state reform school; and, within five years, a State Normal School. The legislation also called for a clear separation between the church and state in school matters.[54]

Emphasizing the changed nature of the state, Section 10 of the 1868 state constitution stated, "All public schools, colleges and universities of this State, supported in whole or in part by public funds, shall be free and open to all the children and youths of the State, without regard to race or color."[55] South Carolina's first superintendent of education was Justus K. Jillison, a well-educated transplant from Massachusetts. He was a hard worker who went about his duty of establishing a school system with Yankee ardor. However, his efforts did not meet with the type of success that he wanted. The administrators misused funds, and the teachers suffered from constant harassment from whites who opposed educating blacks and were reluctant to pay for the schools.[56]

Jillison's first school reports were a precursor to the problems South Carolinians would have with public education. The system was chronically underfunded. The legislature provided only $50,000 for education, and many people refused to

# Constitution.

We, the People of the State of South Carolina, in Convention assembled, Grateful to Almighty God for this opportunity, deliberately and peaceably of entering into an explicit and solemn compact with each other, and forming a new Constitution of civil Government for ourselves and posterity, recognizing the necessity of the protection of the people in all that pertains to their freedom, safety and tranquility, and imploring the direction of the Great Legislator of the Universe, do agree upon, ordain and establish the following

Declaration of Rights and Form of Government as the Constitution of the Commonwealth of South Carolina.

## Article 1.
### Declaration of Rights.

Section 1. All men are born free and equal - endowed by their Creator with certain inalienable rights, among which are the rights of enjoying and defending their lives and liberties, of acquiring, possessing and protecting property, and of seeking and obtaining their safety and happiness.

Section 2. Slavery shall never exist in this State; neither shall involuntary servitude, except as a punishment for crime, whereof the party shall have been duly convicted.

Section 3. All political power is vested in and derived from the people only; therefore they have the right, at all times, to modify their form of government in such manner as they may deem expedient, when the public good demands.

Section 4. Every citizen of this State owes paramount allegiance to the Constitution

**Manuscript of Preamble and Article 1 of the original 1868 South Carolina Constitution. S.C. Department of Archives & History.**

# CONSTITUTION.

---

*We, the People of the State of South Carolina, in Convention assembled,* Grateful to Almighty God for this opportunity, deliberately and peaceably of entering into an explicit and solemn compact with each other, and forming a new Constitution of civil government for ourselves and posterity, recognizing the necessity of the protection of the people in all that pertains to their freedom, safety and tranquility, and imploring the direction of the Great Legislator of the Universe, do agree upon, ordain and establish the following

DECLARATION OF RIGHTS AND FORM OF GOVERNMENT AS THE CONSTITUTION OF THE COMMONWEALTH OF SOUTH CAROLINA.

## ARTICLE I.

### DECLARATION OF RIGHTS.

SECTION 1. All men are born free and equal—endowed by their Creator with certain inalienable rights, among which are the rights of enjoying and defending their lives and liberties, of acquiring, possessing and protecting property, and of seeking and obtaining their safety and happiness.

SECTION 2. Slavery shall never exist in this State; neither shall involuntary servitude, except as a punishment for crime, whereof the party shall have been duly convicted.

SECTION 3. All political power is vested in and derived from the people only; therefore they have the right, at all times, to modify their form of government in such manner as they may deem expedient, when the public good demands.

SECTION 4. Every citizen of this State owes paramount allegiance to the Constitution and Government of the United States, and no law or ordinance of this State in contravention or subversion thereof can have any binding force.

SECTION 5. This State shall ever remain a member of the American Union, and all attempts, from whatever source, or upon whatever pretext, to dissolve the said Union, shall be resisted with the whole power of the State.

SECTION 6. The right of the people peaceably to assembl consult for the common good, and to petition the Governmen any department thereof, shall never be abridged.

Published Preamble and Article 1 of the 1868 South Carolina Constitution.
S.C. Department of Archives & History.

pay the one dollar poll tax. White politicians expressed open hostility toward education, particularly as it related to African Americans. The superintendents were ill-prepared and overwhelmed by the problems. There was opposition from both black and white parents to integrated education. Moreover, there was a culture of poverty and ignorance that Jillison found difficult to overcome.[57]

While many were pressing for the development of free public education, Thomas Clemson was traveling the state pressing his case for scientific education. He used speeches, circulars, and town meetings to push his case. Clemson was convinced that the best way to foster economic and commercial development in South Carolina was through the expansion of scientific education. One writer said of him, "Clemson was very much in earnest about scientific education for South Carolina and for the South. In season and out he never missed an opportunity to urge its importance." While the state moved toward public education, Clemson made a strong case for scientific education.[58]

Clearly, the early enthusiasm for free public education came from the former slaves who had suffered so many years of ignorance and lack of opportunity. As scholar Lewis P. Jones notes, "To blacks, reading and writing were as much symbols of liberty as were the words forty acres and a mule."[59] Within five years of the end of slavery, literally thousands of African American children had been exposed to their first taste of education. It was these former slaves and their northern white allies who convinced ordinary citizens that education was beneficial to them and their children. White philanthropists combined their resources with the efforts of white missionaries, who came south, to set the stage for public education. The federal government, in the person of the Freedmen's Bureau, helped facilitate these efforts.

Nevertheless, white South Carolinians led by the state's governor had resisted these federal efforts since 1865. Undaunted, the federal initiatives continued. For instance, in early fall 1865, Reuben Tomlinson was named the state superintendent by the Freedmen's Bureau. His job was to coordinate and help facilitate the educational efforts.[60]

Tomlinson was a Pennsylvania Quaker who had worked with educational organizations on the Sea Island Experiment. He served as superintendent for three years bringing order to the chaotic educational scene. His coordination of the facilities and teachers helped to make sure that each school had an instructor and adequate facilities. Though the teachers were paid by private organizations, many of the facilities were funded by the Freedmen's Bureau. During the 1865-1868 period, whites demonstrated mixed feelings about the educational efforts. In some areas they supported educational efforts for blacks as long as the teachers were southern. They were adamantly opposed to Yankee teachers coming south and filling their children's heads with radical, Yankee ideas. By 1865 there were 6,000 predominantly black students being taught by 108 teachers. By 1867 most religious denominations had endorsed education for African Americans. Slowly, they were able to convince whites to support public education.[61]

Nevertheless, white opposition to African American education gradually began to solidify. Many white leaders began to see the potential dangers in having an educated black mass. While many supported elementary public education for blacks, they did not support providing secondary education to blacks. At the same time, there was a growing opposition to integrated education. Whites were also concerned about the type of education the African American children were receiving. They believed that a classical education which emphasized reading, writing, and arithmetic was inappropriate for their former slaves. They instead preferred a vocational education with heavy emphasis on skills like carpentry, agriculture, and homemaking.[62]

The northern missionaries who staffed the South Carolina schools had a totally different concept of education. They argued that they wanted "to educate, convert, and save" through their education. Therefore, they preached a heavy dose of religion and moral inspiration with their lessons. They also were dedicated to providing the former slaves with a classical education which would prepare them to become teachers, preachers, and leaders within their communities. They rejected the notion that African Americans needed only to learn how to farm, nail, or carry something. Instead, they provided instruction in classical literature, geography, philosophy, Latin, and mathematics. This was clearly the type of education that African Americans preferred.[63]

As white opposition began to congeal, there was a corresponding decrease in enthusiasm for public education. The teachers who had come south with such great hope were discouraged as they suffered harassment from local whites and suspicion from local blacks. The embryonic school system did educate some people and could boast of some victories. However, it never was able to reach the promise it held out. Schools like the Avery Institute in Charleston served as a shining example of what could have been. Founded in 1865 by the American Missionary Association and headed by Frank L. Cardoza, this was one of the best schools in South Carolina.[64]

Cardoza, a native, freeborn black, was the best-educated African American in the state. He was positive proof of the potential of education for African Americans. However, it was that potential which frightened white South Carolinians the most. It threatened to rob them of their work force and upset their delicate racial hierarchy. South Carolina's educational story was not a pretty story during the 1870-1876 period. The money dedicated to education was often squandered and never made its intended impact. Also, efforts to engage in the social experiment of integrating the schools led to the withdrawal of whites from public schools, with the added insult of many white leaders undermining the efforts. The state university system also saw a dramatic decrease in the number of white students as the state tried to implement integration.[65]

**Principal Benjamin F. Cox addressing a weekly chapel meeting at the Avery Institute. Reproduced from *The Pinnacle: A Book of the Class of 1916.* Avery Research Center for African American History and Culture, College of Charleston.**

During the 1871-1872 session, the state legislature approved $300,000 for education. Amazingly not one dollar of that money was used to pay teachers. Black students were able to sustain their educational efforts with the aid of benevolent societies. White children who were dependent on the state monies were disadvantaged. As researcher Henry Thompson writes, "The school sessions were irregular, the teachers became discouraged, the white taxpayers were naturally disgusted, and the entire system had sunk into a state of disrepute and worthlessness."[66]

By far the biggest challenge faced by South Carolinians was the rampant corruption, which characterized their system. The white political allies of African Americans proved to be more interested in lining their pockets than in establishing a workable school system. They often were associated with misappropriations of school funds. Blacks also were implicated in some of these scandals. Historian Alrutheus A. Taylor wrote, "Through inexperience and ignorance the dupes of designing rascals, the Negro legislators were led to sanction schemes of the despoilers and to that extent contributed to the failure to promote an efficient system of universal free education in South Carolina." However, the progress they made was remarkable, considering that for more than 200 years white South Carolinians had not been able to get that far.[67]

When Hugh S. Thompson took control of the educational system from Jillison in 1877, he found that a strong foundation had already been laid. The school attendance had been increased from 25,000 to 123,000. Several thousand schools were in operation and staffed by more than 3,000 teachers. In 1878 the state legislature passed a new school law which put control of the local school systems in the hands of district trustees, subject to the supervision of the county board of examiners. It also said that local poll taxes would be used in that area. The local management of schools meant that blacks could expect minimal attention to their educational needs. Moreover, the revised tax structure meant that black schools would be starved of funds because generally blacks did not pay the poll tax because of ignorance or poverty.[68]

The evidence is clear that once schools were removed from African American influence, whites received the lion's share of the benefits from public education. Certainly, there were improvements made by white school officials that aided both races, improvements such as greater efficiency of teachers, longer school terms, and an increasing number of schools open to both races. However, blacks in rural areas found that their school facilities were in a declining state. In cities like Charleston, blacks could still get a good education. In other urban areas, however, the schools were not much better than they were in rural areas where the school term rarely exceeded two and one-third months.

### *Clemson and South Carolina Education*

Though not initially a part of the educational debates, Thomas Green Clemson was one of the leading advocates for education in South Carolina. He spent much of his life advocating for agricultural education and the benefits of such an education in shaping American life. He was a particularly strong supporter of scientific education and the potential it showed for helping to build a state's economy. Clemson's advocacy of agricultural and scientific education was well-known. He had helped establish the Maryland Agricultural College and was one of the school's most vocal proponents. For example, prior to that college's establishment, Clemson often declared, "The only hope we have for the advancement of agriculture is through the sciences and yet there is not one single institution on this continent where proper scientific education can be obtained."[69] Another example, which was later published in the *American Farmer,* is a letter Clemson sent to James Earle, president of the Maryland Agricultural Society. In words that echoed many of his other statements, Clemson wrote, "The subject is one of momentous interest, one of light and darkness, poverty or wealth, and comparative degradation or elevation. The only possible hope for the advancement of the arts is through science."[70]

When educational proponents began to advocate in favor of a national system of land-grant colleges in each state, Clemson was a part of those discussions. The U.S. Agricultural Society was very active in pushing the country toward a system of agricultural and industrial colleges in each state. Organized in 1852, the Agricultural Society published a journal and organized exhibitions in each state. Justin Smith Morrill, a Whig representative from Vermont, became very interested in this movement. On December 14, 1857, Representative Morrill introduced the first bill calling for land-grant colleges. The so-called Morrill Land Grant Act was passed by both houses of Congress but was vetoed by President Buchanan. In 1862 Morrill, now a Republican, reintroduced the bill. Again it was passed by Congress; this time it was signed by President Abraham Lincoln on July 2, 1862. The new piece of legislation granted to each state 30,000 acres of public land for each U.S. senator and representative under apportionment based on the 1860 census. Proceeds from the sale of these lands were to be invested in a perpetual endowment fund which would support colleges of agriculture and mechanical arts in each of the states. This new law provided federal aid to states for establishing state agricultural colleges. It also ensured that farmers would have access to the latest scientific techniques for agriculture.[71]

Clemson, of course, had a long history of advocacy for education. However, there is no evidence that he was a supporter of integrated education. By the time Clemson was contemplating his school, segregated education was a recognized feature in South Carolina. During the early Reconstruction period, the University of South Carolina experimented with integrated education. The first blacks enrolled there in October 1873—William Dart even graduated. Their presence resulted in resignations by faculty and withdrawals by some students. Nevertheless, the university remained open until 1877, when the Democrats regained control and closed the institution. In 1880 the school was reopened, for whites only, as the South Carolina College of Agriculture and Mechanical Arts. The South Carolina Agricultural and Mechanics' Institute in Orangeburg had opened for African American students in 1872.[72]

Clemson seems to have remained aloof of the racial issues surrounding education. He clearly did not believe that white children would attend schools where black children were present. His focus remained on scientific education. In 1875 Clemson's wife suddenly died. Anna Calhoun Clemson left her share of the Fort Hill estate to Clemson. Her will specifically called for Clemson to establish a scientific institution which would serve the state of South Carolina. He dedicated the remainder of his life to creating this institution. Clemson fired off a letter to his old friend W. W. Corcoran enlisting his aid in establishing this school. Clemson wrote, "The necessity is paramount, and I have been solicited again to use my feeble exertions to convert Fort Hill into such a purpose, and thus save from desecration that beautiful hallowed spot, and pass it down for future time to the diffusion and investigation of the laws of the Creator."[73]

In the early 1880s Clemson began to put into place a plan to open an agricultural and technical college. He planned to endow the project through a gift from his will. Clemson proposed to give his 800-acre Fort Hill plantation to the state for this college. He wanted to make sure that South Carolina had trained farmers, scientists, and engineers. Much has been made about the will which left the bequest. For example, many argue that the bequest's not specifically barring African Americans or women from the college proves that Clemson was a progressive and well ahead of his time.

This argument, however, warrants closer examination. Clemson obviously did not believe that integrated education was viable. The state had outlawed such education a few years earlier. In 1873 Clemson's friend Henry Trescot wrote him a letter outlining the problems at the University of South Carolina. In this letter Trescot points out, "As far as white people of the state are concerned, the University may be considered as closed for whether such prejudice be natural or artificial, right or wrong, wise or foolish, it is eradicable that where the black scholar goes, the white will not."[74] He went on to suggest that Clemson needed to start a new school to save education in South Carolina.[75]

The other issue that must be considered is that Benjamin Tillman was one of the people consulted when the school was proposed. Tillman, one of the leading anti-black proponents in the state, would not have had any part in a plan to open a school where integrated education was allowed. A powerful politician who represented Clemson's part of the state, Tillman had built his reputation on his opposition to black people. This was no secret, and if Clemson had wanted to advocate for a progressive style of education, he would not have consulted such a conservative politician. Clemson's goal was unwavering: "My purpose is to establish an Agricultural College which will afford useful information to the farmers and mechanics."[76] That purpose did not include fostering a social revolution.

Certainly, it is always difficult to judge a man after the fact. Thomas Green Clemson, in particular, is a difficult man to understand. His life and work were a series of contradictions. For instance, this descendent of Quakers owned, sold, and traded in slaves. He volunteered to join the war effort, becoming an officer in the Confederate Army. Even though he was born and reared in the North, he somehow developed a greater affinity for the South. Clemson, an internationalist who participated in social revolutions, fought to maintain the conservative southern oligarchy of which he had become a part.

Even as a slaveholder he is difficult to understand. His letters never mention developing strong personal ties with any of his servants. He never wrote any personal treatises about his views on slavery, even though he was friends with some

of the most vocal racists and defenders of slavery. In other words, Thomas Green
Clemson became a white southerner whose racial views seem no different from
those he befriended. Of course he was different in the visionary passion that drove
his bequest for the establishment of Clemson Agricultural College. To achieve
that goal he was an old-line pragmatist on the difficulty of integrating colleges in
South Carolina. Even though his correspondences with friends, such as Henry
Trescot, indicated that they discussed the racial difficulties for South Carolina's
colleges, Clemson's final decision was limited by what was possible at the time.
Nevertheless, Clemson was a man who chose to do what African Americans and
many others would have called the wrong things when the right things were presented to him.

## Notes

1.   *Thomas Green Clemson Farsighted Farmer: An Adopted South Carolinian Who Served the Palmetto State*, American Guide Series, Compiled by the Federal Writers' Project, Work Projects
Administration (Columbia: State Department of Education South Carolina, ca. 1935–1937),
5; for information on the Quakers, see Jean Soderlund, *Quakers and Slavery: A Divided Spirit*
(Princeton: Princeton University Press, 1985), 28–29, 57–66.
2.   For information on Clemson's father and family, see Jerome Reel's entries in Chapters 1 and
2; Leon Litwack, *North of Slavery: The Negro in the Free States 1790–1860.* 7ᵗʰ ed. (Chicago:
University of Chicago Press, 1961), 3; John Hope Franklin and Alfred Moss, *From Slavery to
Freedom: A History of African Americans* (New York: McGraw-Hill, 1994), 81, 85.
3.   Carter G. Woodson, *The Negro in Our Times* (Washington, DC: Associated Publishers, 1922),
147–151; Darlene Clark Hines et al. *African American Odyssey* (Upper Saddle River, NJ: Pearson Prentice Hall, 2006), 115–117; Howard Chudacoff and Judith Smith, *The Evolution of
American Urban Society.* 6ᵗʰ ed. (Upper Saddle River, NJ: Pearson Prentice Hall, 2005), 69.
4.   Alester Holmes and George Sherrill, *Thomas Green Clemson: His Life and Work* (Richmond,
VA.: Garrett and Massie, 1937), 2.
5.   Holmes and Sherrill, *Thomas Green Clemson*, 1; *Thomas Green Clemson Farsighted Farmer*, 6.
6.   Ibid., 11.
7.   Ibid.
8.   Holmes and Sherrill, *Thomas Green Clemson*, 11.
9.   1840 U.S. Census.
10.  *Thomas Green Clemson Farsighted Farmer*, 7.
11.  William J. Megginson, *African American Life in South Carolina's Upper Piedmont 1780–1900*
(Columbia: University of South Carolina Press, 2006), 148.
12.  Ibid., 150.
13.  Ibid., 150–151.
14.  Ibid., 151.
15.  Margaret Coit, *John C. Calhoun: American Portrait* (Columbia: University of South Carolina
Press, 1991), 285–286.
16.  Ibid.
17.  Ibid., 287.
18.  Paul Finkleman, *Defending Slavery: Proslavery Thought in the Old South: A History with Documents* (New York: Bedford/St Martin's Press, 2003), 58.
19.  Holmes and Sherrill, *Thomas Green Clemson*, 93.
20.  Franklin and Moss, *From Slavery to Freedom*, 173–176.
21.  Ernest McPherson Lander Jr., *The Calhoun Family and Thomas Green Clemson: The Decline of
a Southern Patriarchy* (Columbia: University of South Carolina Press, 1983), 59.

22. Ibid., 94–95.
23. Lander, *Calhoun Family and Thomas Green Clemson*, 90–92; Walter Johnson, *Soul to Soul: Life Inside the Antebellum Slave Market* (Cambridge: Harvard University Press, 2001), 39; TGC to Elias Baker, 19 July 1854, Clemson Papers, MSS 2, Special Collections, Clemson University Libraries (hereafter cited as SCCUL).
24. Lander, *Calhoun Family and Thomas Green Clemson*, 200, 203–204.
25. James McPherson, *Ordeal By Fire: The Civil War and Reconstruction*, 2nd ed. (New York: McGraw-Hill, 1992), 148; TGC to Elias Baker 4 April 1861, Clemson Papers, MSS 2, SCCUL.
26. McPherson, *Ordeal By Fire*, 149, 207.
27. Lander, *Calhoun Family and Thomas Green Clemson*, 210.
28. McPherson, *Ordeal By Fire*, 297.
29. Ibid., 212–213, 297.
30. Lander, *Calhoun Family and Thomas Green Clemson*, 212–214; Parole of Thomas G. Clemson Issued by U.S. Government, 9 June 1865, Clemson Papers, SCCUL.
31. *Thomas Green Clemson Farsighted Farmer*, 11.
32. Alrutheus A. Taylor, *The Negro in the Reconstruction of South Carolina* (New York: AMS Press, 1924), 4–6.
33. Ibid., 40–41.
34. Eric Foner, *Reconstruction: America's Unfinished Revolution 1863–1877* (New York: Harper and Row, 1988), 187–188.
35. Taylor, *Negro in the Reconstruction*, 40–41; George Tindall, *South Carolina Negroes 1877–1900* (Baton Rouge: Louisiana State University Press, 1952), 7–8.
36. Taylor, *Negro in the Reconstruction*, 42.
37. Ibid., 42–46.
38. Ibid; Tindall, *South Carolina Negroes*, 7.
39. Foner, *Reconstruction*, 113.
40. Henry T. Thompson, *The Establishment of the Public School System of South Carolina* (Columbia, SC: R. L. Bryan Company, 1927), 2.
41. Ibid., 3.
42. Ibid., 5–6.
43. Ibid., 7.
44. Ibid., 8.
45. Ibid.
46. Ibid., 8–9.
47. Lewis P. Jones, "History of Public Education in South Carolina," *Public Education in South Carolina: Historical, Political, and Legal Perspectives*, ed. Thomas McDaniel (Spartanburg, SC: Converse College, 1984), 14.
48. Taylor, *Negro in the Reconstruction*, 82.
49. Ibid., 84.
50. Jones, *History of Public Education in South Carolina*, 15.
51. Tindall, *South Carolina Negroes*, 8–9.
52. Thompson, *Establishment of Public Schools in South Carolina*, 9.
53. Ibid., 9–10.
54. Ibid., 9.
55. Ibid., 11.
56. Ibid., 11–12.
57. Taylor, *Negro in the Reconstruction*, 100; Holmes and Sherrill, *Thomas Green Clemson*, 147.
58. Jones, *History of Public Education in South Carolina*, 14.
59. Ibid.; Luther P. Jackson, "The Educational Efforts of the Freedmen's Bureau and Freedmen's Aid Societies in South Carolina," *Journal of Negro History* 8, no. 1 (January 1923): 14. This article provides a good look at early educational activities among the former slaves in South Carolina.
60. Jones, *History of Public Education in South Carolina*, 16.
61. Ibid., 17.
62. Ibid.

63. Ibid., 18.
64. Ibid., 19.
65. Thompson, *Establishment of the Public School System of South Carolina*, 12–13.
66. Taylor, *Negro in the Reconstruction*, 101.
67. Ibid., 102; Thompson, *Establishment of the Public School System of South Carolina*, 19–21.
68. Holmes and Sherrill, *Thomas Green Clemson*, 124.
69. Ibid., 124–125.
70. Ibid.
71. Tindall, *South Carolina Negroes*, 227.
72. Holmes and Sherrill, *Thomas Green Clemson*, 152–153.
73. Henry Trescot to TGC, 19 October 1873, Clemson Papers, MSS 2, SCCUL.
74. Ibid.
75. Ibid.
76. Holmes and Sherrill, *Thomas Green Clemson*, 160.

# Chapter 9

## Thomas Green Clemson:
### Art Collector and Artist

## *William David Hiott*

Thomas Green Clemson's self-portrait, ca. 1845, and a portrait of his brother Rev. Baker Clemson are the only extant family portraits by Clemson. Oil on canvas. Fort Hill Collection, Clemson University.

Thomas Green Clemson's affection for the arts is poignantly described in his address entitled "The Beautiful Arts—the magic bonds which unite all ages and Nations." His lecture, presented at the Second Festival of the Washington Art Association in 1859, gives a synopsis of Clemson's views on art. At the festival, according to an account in *The National Intelligencer*, Clemson's remarkable lecture addressed, among other things:

the universality of the creations and influences of art. All organized beings, he asserted, were artists—from the minute creature that built up the coral islands and twined coral wreaths around the world up to man. Every work of art, as well as every act of man, would have a universal and perpetual influence; therefore they should be benignant and true. If we attempt to represent the history, the life, the genius of our country in art, it should be done with truth, and not with pretense—as in the case of the old Capitol, which had to be whitewashed to save it from perdition. There was ample evidence that our national artists were competent to perform the requirements of this period in respect to the illustration of the national history, and they ought to be permitted to do it, so that of what is done the question may not in the future be asked in derision, 'Was that the condition of American art in 1859?' Mr. Clemson illustrated his views by free and discursive allusion to ancient and modern, European and American life, circumstances, and scenery, drawing enforcement to his position from moral, mental and physical science alike.[1]

Thus Thomas Green Clemson—scientist, agriculturist, and diplomat—revealed an enlightened view of the arts, a view that supports his being considered a Renaissance man of the mid-nineteenth century. One of the pronounced manifestations of this acquired passion was his scholarly connoisseurship of oil paintings. In 1888, the "Appraised Bill of the Property of the Estate of Thomas G. Clemson" featured an itemized list of Clemson's personal property at Fort Hill that included: "39 oil paintings; no means of valuing," followed in the next line by, "9 family portraits; no means of valuing."[2] While many items in his estate were commonplace, the executors were understandably stumped by the art appraisal. Nevertheless, in 1888 the forty-eight paintings and family portraits became known collectively as the Thomas Green Clemson Art Collection.

## *Thomas Clemson—Art Collector*

Thomas Clemson collected works that pleased him and hung on his walls both at The Home in Maryland and later at Fort Hill in South Carolina. Still, the magnitude and scope of the collection are impressive not merely by nineteenth-century standards, but by today's art scholarship and appreciation as well. As directed in his last will and testament, Thomas Clemson specified that his paintings were to adorn the walls of Fort Hill in perpetuity after his death; however, most of the family portraits were to go to his granddaughter Floride Isabella Lee. Another painting was to be chosen by his attorney and executor James H. Rion as a memento. Because Rion predeceased Clemson, Richard W. Simpson, his new attorney and executor, was given a choice of the paintings as well as Clemson's personal sealing ring—a carved equestrian representation of Marcus Aurelius Antoninus Augustus, the Roman emperor and Stoic philosopher.

Historically, the earliest extant record of the collection is Anna Maria Calhoun Clemson's handwritten "Catalogue of Pictures" from 1852.[3] The listing was an inventory of the art that had been shipped to the United States from Belgium, where the Clemson family lived during Thomas G. Clemson's tenure as chargé d'affaires to the court of King Léopold I of Belgium. The Clemsons stayed for a brief time on the Island of Dosoris near Glen Cove, Long Island.[4] Anna Clemson's "Catalogue," which bears the word *Dosoris*, lists forty-seven enumerated paintings, which include eight family portraits. These forty-seven paintings, which Anna Calhoun Clemson first cataloged in 1852, are essentially the same collection Clemson bequeathed to the State of South Carolina in his 1888 will. The Thomas G. Clemson collection of fine art today totals nearly fifty paintings divided into five distinct categories: Old Master paintings, original mid-nineteenth-century artworks, mid-nineteenth-century copies of original paintings, portraits of the Calhoun and Clemson families commissioned in Belgium, and finally works of art by Thomas G. Clemson.

The Old Master paintings, the oldest works in the Clemson Art Collection, are from the seventeenth century. The Clemson collection now contains eight of the original eleven Old Master paintings which Thomas Clemson collected.[5] These remaining Old Master paintings are four biblical works, two genre portraits, and two pastoral landscapes. Clemson considered most significant the three paintings attributed respectively to Rubens, Rembrandt, and Velasquez, which would have already been considered antique during Clemson's time, having been painted nearly two hundred years earlier.

A *Virgin and Child*[6] was the first painting in Anna Clemson's art inventory and which she attributed to the artist "P. P. Rubens" and annotated, "Painted for a friend's cha-

Anna Calhoun Clemson's catalog of the paintings they had shipped home from Belgium begins with "No. 1 Virgin and Child—P. P. Rubens." Attributed then to Peter Paul Rubens, it has since been attributed to the school of Rubens and specifically to his protégée Cornelis Schut. Oil on canvas. Fort Hill Collection, Clemson University.

pel."[7] The provenance that Anna evidently also recorded on a paper label was that the Virgin and Child picture was "painted for a friend's chapel in 1600. Purchased from the family of Rubens's friend by M. Tielens (a Catholic priest) and bought from him by T. G. Clemson, A.D. 1849."[8] This small painting, although similar to works by Rubens, closely resembles the work of one of Rubens's students and has been attributed most often to Cornelis Schut,[9] whose "skill in interpreting the themes of the Counter-Reformation led to his being much in demand for commissions in churches and monasteries."[10] The painting consists of the Virgin and Child arranged in the center of the composition with elaborate cherubim encircling the subjects.

Anna Clemson identified *Flower Piece*, a vibrantly colored still-life painting, as an artwork by "Zeghers (the Jesuit) & medallion by Tenniers."[11] The still life of flowers by Daniel Seghers encircles a centerpiece, attributed to David Teniers, of a religious figure of a child with a lamb.[12] The figure portrayed is of a standing child with a camel-hair loincloth next to a lamb in the foreground and a large tree in the background. The iconography appears to be a rendition of the young John the Baptist with a lamb, illustrating, for a private altarpiece, the verse "Behold! The Lamb of God who takes away the sins of the world!" However, the subject matter also has been thought to depict Jesus as the Christ Child. The cartouche by David Teniers is, as Anna Clemson described, a medallion in the larger work. The elaborate floral still life, attributed to Daniel Seghers, utilized bold primary colors for the large wreath of tulips and peonies, representative of Seghers's signed works.[13]

Another sacred painting in the collection is the *Adoration of the Magi* indexed as "Adoration (on copper)—Franck," which depicts the Three Kings bringing gifts to the Christ Child. The small painting on copper is richly adorned in jewel tones portraying the Magi of the orient bringing gold, frankincense, and myrrh.[14] The painting, attributed to Frans Francken, vividly presents the Magi—sometimes singled out as Caspar, Melchior, and Balthasar, with the latter showing African features. Although unsigned, the *Adoration* has on the reverse the seal of the Antwerp Guild in which Francken held membership.[15]

Thomas Clemson's Old Master painting collection includes two works of portraiture. "Head by Velasquez"[16] in Anna Clemson's "Catalogue" is a small bust portrait of a young boy. He is fashionably dressed in a starched rounded collar and fringed and buttoned attire, a fashion popularized by the famous Spanish painter, Diego Rodríguez de Silva y Velázquez. The oil on wood panel, which is inscribed in the upper left corner with *Act. 14, A 1616*, has been more recently attributed to the school of Otto van Veen.[17] Perhaps the most realistic Old Master work that Clemson owned is "Peasant with Soup—Frans Hals."[18] The painting is a genre scene of a young girl in peasant dress eating porridge from a soup bowl, and it does resemble such famous paintings as the *Gypsy Girl* by Frans Hals in the Louvre.[19] The work bears the stylistic artistry of the Hals family of painters and has been attributed to either Harmen Hals or Jans Hals, both sons of Frans Hals.[20] The two remaining Old Master paintings are landscapes on wooden panels. List-ed by Anna Clemson as "Landscape by Poussin"[21] and "Landscape,"[22] both have been attributed to either Nicolas Poussin or Claude Lorraine. The landscapes are similar—one with a tavern and the other with the ruins of Roman columns—and are generally cited as the school of Claude Lorraine.

One painting had been set aside for the executor of Clemson's estate who was originally James Rion and, following his death, Richard W. Simpson. Simpson chose the painting that Clemson considered the Rembrandt, which was listed in Anna's Catalogue as: "[No.] 11 The Philosopher (supposed to be Rembrandt or Ferdinand Bols)." The painting, also known as a painting of St. Paul, was passed down through the Simpson family until it was acquired in 2007 for the Fort Hill museum from a descendent of Richard W. Simpson. While the attribution is unlikely, the painting bears a striking similarity to Rembrandt Harmenszoon van Rijn's series of self-portraits portraying the artist as St. Paul. The large painting is framed in an elaborately hand-carved vine frame, most likely of Belgium origin, which Clemson chose for his most prized work.[23]

Anna Calhoun Clemson's inventory listed this large painting as "[No.] 11 The Philosopher (supposed to be Rembrandt or Ferdinand Bols)." Also called *St. Paul*, it bears a striking resemblance to self-portraits of Rembrandt Harmenszoon van Rijn. Oil on canvas. Acquisition from Richard W. Simpson's heirs. Fort Hill Collection, Clemson University.

In addition to the eight Old Masters in the collection today, Thomas Clemson originally owned three other Old Masters itemized in Anna Clemson's 1852 "Catalogue of Pictures." One painting listed as "Virgin, Child, and St. Joseph in a garland of fruit by Jordaens" is speculated to have been destroyed in transit during Clemson's lifetime. Also in the collection and in existence through the mid-twentieth century were two still-life paintings which Anna Clemson identified as "Fruit, by De Heem"[24] and "Student's Repast by Van Son."[25] The still-life paintings had hung at Fort Hill in 1893 and had later hung in the Old Museum in the Sikes Hall library through the mid-1950s. The subsequent attribution for *Fruit* has varied between Jan Jansz van de Velde and Jurien van Streeck.[26] The painting was described as a "Still life with wineglass, lemons, Ming dish, olives, etc."[27] The second intriguing artwork, *Student's Repast*, was identified as a "still life with herrings, pipes, oysters, etc" and is attributed to Pieter Claesz.[28] Both paintings were inventoried in poor condition in the late 1950s; after 1960, the whereabouts of the two artworks are unknown.[29] Jurien van Streeck and Pieter Claesz were masterful still-life artists. Their works appear in major international collections today. Unfortunately no clear photographs of these two works in Clemson's collection have been uncovered. One black and white photograph was found of the "Fruit" painting; however, no clear image exists of "Repast" except for a grainy image hanging on the wall of Fort Hill in 1893 with the art collection.[30]

Thomas G. Clemson's own collection of contemporary works acquired during his travels abroad appear artistically to show that he was particularly drawn to the Belgian artists of the Barbizon school of realism. The painting "Titian Placing his Model—Eeckhout"[31] shows the great Renaissance painter called Titian or Tiziano Vecellio in his studio positioning a fashionably dressed noblewoman.[32] Although the painting is quite small, the attention to detail is a hallmark of the works of Jacob Joseph Eeckhout (spelled *Eeckhart* by Thomas Clemson). Another small yet moving painting, identified as

**Anna Calhoun Clemson's inventory listed the painting as "Titian Placing his Model—Eeckhout." Oil on canvas. Fort Hill Collection, Clemson University.**

"Poverty & Suffering—DeBlock," is by Eugene DeBlock who painted the portraits of Mr. and Mrs. John C. Calhoun.[33] The painting's depiction of a parent caring for an ailing child may have become increasingly poignant to the Clemsons after the deaths of their children: Cornelia (Nina) Clemson at age three and later Calhoun Clemson and Floride Elizabeth Clemson Lee.

Louis Robbe is the artist most widely represented in the Clemson Collection. Thomas Clemson collected several original pastoral scenes by the Belgian painter and also commissioned Robbe to copy paintings. Anna Clemson identified the three original Robbe landscapes as "Cattle—L. Robbe,"[34] "Goats & Sheep—L. Robbe,"[35] and "Group of Lambs—Robbe."[36] Landscapes formed a prominent place in Clemson's collecting and in some ways provide insight into his appreciation for livestock, animal husbandry, and more general agricultural pursuits.

Likewise, Thomas Clemson prized the two seascapes—"Landscapes by Fearnley a Swedish painter"[37]—which were ambassadorial gifts. This pair of landscapes by Thomas Fearnley has been individually titled *Castle of Kronborg*[38] and *Castle of Elsinore*[39] from Shakespeare's *Hamlet* and "were presented to T. G. Clemson by Count de Woyna, the Austrian Ambassador at Brussels, A.D. 1848."[40] Anna Clemson listed another picturesque seascape in the collection as "Marine view in Holland—Francia."[41] Windmills and a coastal village highlight this work by François Louis Thomas Francia. Two cityscape travel paintings in the Clemson collection are architectural renderings: "Scene in Spain—Bossuet," attributed to François Bossuet,[42] and "Gateway—Tavernier,"[43] which is illustrative of Andrea Tavernier's urban motifs and subjects.

There are six original artworks which feature human subjects. A painting listed by Anna Clemson as "Magdalene—Van Schendael" is perhaps the most powerful painting in the collection for its iconographic representation of *The Repentant Magdalen* at the tomb with a cross in the right shadow. Mary Magdalene's

The painting, identified by Anna Calhoun Clemson as "Magdalene—Van Schendael," is the work of Belgian artist Petrus Van Schendel. Oil on canvas. Fort Hill Collection, Clemson University.

crumpled figure is shown holding a skull.[44] This painting is lighted by a single candlelight, a trademark of Belgian artist Petrus Van Schendel. He "specialized in genre scenes and interiors lit by moonlight or candlelight," particularly village market or cottage interior scenes,[45] and was known as a painter of light somewhat in the fashion of the modern, consumer-oriented artist Thomas Kinkade.

The contemporary, nineteenth-century original artworks which Clemson collected vary in size and subject matter. A *Head*, by Jean Baptiste Greuze, is a small, profile-image bust portrait of a young boy, identified as "Head—Study by Greuge."[46] In contrast is the much larger painting which Anna Clemson cataloged simply as "Boy Mending Pen—Spanish."[47] The painting, attributed to the Spanish Bodegón School, is a sophisticated yet simple painting of a young man with a knife whittling down the point of a quill pen. Perhaps because Anna Clemson listed no artist for the work, it has sometimes been assumed that this painting is a copy. However, the placement of this painting as No. 10 on her list, between the Old Master paintings and the original artworks, aids the speculation that the life-size "Boy Mending Pen" portrait is an original work.

*The Quarrel* and *Reconciliation* are paired genre paintings: first, a couple with their backs to each other; second, a smiling couple. The painting *Two Old Men*, although not related to the prior set of two paintings, may have been a part of multi-panel episodes in a serial form by the Belgian artist Charles Karel Ferdinand Venneman.[48] His strength as an artist was his ability to capture in a realistic fashion the expressions of peasant folk around the hearthside.

Thomas Green Clemson supplemented his art collection with what might be considered museum copies, and of the original ten copies, nine remain in his collection.[49] Clemson's reproductions were in some ways the equivalent of the highest quality art poster of today. The nineteenth-century museum copy, "Tasso in Prison visited by Montaigne (original in King Leopold's Gallery) Copy after Gallait,"[50] is the largest of the canvases in the Clemson Art Collection. The painting depicts essayist Michel Eyquem de Montaigne visiting Italian Renaissance poet Torquato Tasso in an insane asylum, where the famous Counter-Reformation author of the epic poem *Jerusalem Delivered* spent many years, due to bouts of depression.[51] Thomas Clemson, in an 1876 letter to the curator of the Corcoran Gallery of Art, stated that this painting was a "Copy after Gallait a celebrated painting in the King's private gallery."[52] The original image of *Montaigne Visiting Tasso in Prison*, painted by Belgian artist Louis Gallait, is still in the Royal Museum of Belgium.[53]

*A Portrait of the Queen of England, after Landseer* was the title Thomas G. Clemson submitted to the Washington Art Association, when he loaned the work for exhibition, along with three other paintings (including two portraits), for the association's Fourth Annual Exhibition in Washington, D.C., in 1860.[54] Anna Clemson had earlier listed this painting of a seated brunette holding two King

Charles spaniels as: "Girl of Antwerp with two dogs (original in King Leopold's gallery), Copy after Landseer."[55] In Thomas Clemson's handwriting, in 1876, he further annotated that the painting was "representing Queen Victoria, original in the Gallery of King of Belgium."[56] The subject, wearing a lace veil and an ornate crucifix, certainly does appear to be someone of royalty, and King Léopold I, in fact, was the uncle and principal advisor to his niece Queen Victoria, the daughter of Léopold's sister Princess Victoria of Saxe-Cobourgh-Saalfeld. Sir Edwin Landseer painted many portraits of Queen Victoria with dogs and horses, including numerous paintings and engravings with her prized King Charles spaniel named Dash.

"Magdalene Study after Murillo—DeBlock"[57] is a captivating portrait of Mary Magdalene based upon Bartolome Esteban Murillo's moving paintings of *The Penitent Magdalen*. Eugene DeBlock, in what has been described as a very sensual painting of Mary Magdalene, captures Murillo's paintings of a beautiful Magdalene with attractive feminine features highlighted by long, flowing hair and alabaster skin. DeBlock's painting of Mary, like his portraits, has a dark background but also creates a sense of realism and contemplation.

Identified by Anna Clemson as "Waterfall—Copy of Auchenbach by L. Robbe," this is one of two such copies Louis Robbe painted for Thomas Clemson. Oil on canvas. Fort Hill Collection, Clemson University.

Louis Robbe copied for Clemson two paintings by fellow contemporary artists which Anna Clemson cataloged as "Landscape—Copy of Koekoek by Louis Robbe"[58] and "Waterfall—Copy of Auchenbach by L. Robbe."[59] The Marinus Adrianus Koekkoek landscape reproduced by Louis Robbe has elements of Robbe's original compositions of pastoral landscapes.[60] The Robbe copy after Achenbach (spelled *Auchenbach* by the Clemsons) is actually a second copy that Clemson commissioned of the *Waterfall* painting. Clemson wrote to W. W. Corcoran that he had acquired for him "a copy of a painting by Auchenbach, and is in all respects equal to the original, as you will see it is signed by Robbe after Auchenbach. This picture is so charming that I am sure you will be pleased with it. I thought it so much so that I had a copy made for myself which now hangs in my salon."[61] Unfortunately, in 1979 the Corcoran Gallery deaccessioned this painting, along with two others known to have been collected for Corcoran by Clemson.[62] The painting listed in the 1979 Corcoran auction catalog as "'A Cascade' by Louis Robbe after Andreas Achenbach" is the exact twin of the painting on view at Fort Hill.

Anna Clemson identified one reproduction that Thomas Clemson greatly admired as "Old Man Smoking—Copy after Leys,"[63] which depicts a gentleman in Baroque Flemish costume. The artist Henri Leys had revered the earlier works of the Old Masters, and his treatment harkens back to that era. Thomas Clemson himself created his own copy, which is discussed later. In Clemson's version, the man is seated in an elaborately carved chair, possibly representing one Clemson had seen or owned in Belgium.

An interesting pair of scenic paintings includes "Peasant Girl Crossing the Water"[64] and the "Gate of the Alhambra." The first work is a picturesque painting of a young girl walking along the shore with her pet spaniel. One can imagine her stopping briefly to pick wildflowers which are shown overflowing her apron. The only annotation given by Anna Clemson was that "Peasant Girl" was *after a painter of Antwerp.*" No attribution to either the original artist or the creator of the copy is known. The second of these copies in Clemson's collection is an architectural rendering, like a postcard image, of the "Gate of the Alhambra—Copy of Boussuet."[65] This is of the famous Spanish arched gate and is similar to the two other gated street scenes in the collection, which together form a unique trio of Spanish cityscapes. The Mell "Catalogue" lists both paintings as copies "by T. G. Clemson taken at Brussels, A.D. 1848," but neither Anna nor Thomas Clemson himself ever listed these two paintings as his own works.

Last but certainly not least of the paintings that Thomas Clemson had a copy of was an infamous image, which Anna listed simply as "Beatrice Cenci (Very old Copy)."[66] This museum copy of a Beatrice Cenci painting after Guido Reni is probably the most recognizable of all the paintings in Clemson's collection. The much-reproduced image of the young girl with the turban has had a far-reaching impact on western art and has inspired numerous writers, including the Romantic poet Percy Shelley. The gaze of the teenager and the story of the abusive family experience that resulted in her murder of her father give a powerful context to her expressionless face. The image of innocence lost is as recognizable to most as is Johannes Vermeer's painting of the *Girl with the Pearl Earring.* These copies, which represent museum studies of famous paintings both earlier than and contemporary to Clemson's era, helped round out his art collection. Something within their imagery or subject matter appealed to Clemson, even though he would have been aware that they were—at that time—of little value as an investment, with the possible exception of the Cenci copy.

## Family Portraits Commissioned by Thomas Clemson

Thomas Clemson's interest in art extended beyond acquiring oil paintings of sacred art, landscapes, seascapes, and various genre paintings of one form or another. He personalized his interest in art by commissioning a series of family portraits. These paintings were closely monitored by Clemson, and indeed some paintings, such as the life-size painting of Anna, which hangs in the parlor at Fort Hill, were individually considered as exemplary European artworks. Jacobs Joseph Eeckhout's individual portraits of Thomas Clemson's immediate family (the couple and their two children) and Eugene DeBlock's paintings of his Calhoun in-laws are the best known of the renderings. The Clemsons had portraits painted of both Senator and Mrs. John C. Calhoun. The Belgium family portraits commissioned by Clemson originally accounted for eight paintings of which five are on view at Fort Hill today.[67] Another pair of portraits of the Clemsons is still in family hands, including a portrait of Anna Clemson which she identified as having been painted by Henri Jean Baptiste Jolly and a painting of Clemson which is either by DeBlock or Eeckhout.[68]

Perhaps the most impressive of all of the portraits is the life-size portrait of Anna Calhoun Clemson. Thomas Clemson's close friend and associate, Henry Gourdin of Charleston, offered to Clemson his glowing accolades for the Clemson family paintings upon first seeing them: "I was delighted with Eeckhout's portraits of Mrs. Clemson and your two interesting children. The former is a magnificent picture as a work of art as well as for the taste in the arrangement and its fidelity as a likeness." Henry Gourdin went on to say that "the portrait of your little boy, with his dog, is unsurpassed in simplicity and beauty by anything that I have ever seen." Of the portrait of Clemson himself, his friend noted that the "picture of yourself, is not only an excellent painting, but a commendable likeness as well."

The only art criticism that Clemson's colleague made note of is directed at the portrait of Clemson's daughter, Floride Elizabeth Clemson: "The picture of the little girl is also very beautiful, but a canary, in the place of so huge a bird as a parrot, would have been better. The bird is about as long as the child, and I have little doubt that in France this would be the most attractive portion of the picture, but with me, I confess I should have preferred something less conspicuous, and of a more pleasing character than so noisy a pet."[69] The painting of Floride with her cockatoo still remains an intriguing painting. Close examination following recent conservation shows that the cockatoo's head originally turned toward the right and was retouched to turn toward the girl's neckline.

The Clemson portraits had been shipped with the entire Clemson family when they came back to the United States in November 1848 for an extended visit through the spring of 1849. The Clemsons divided their time—which coincided with an anticipated regime change with the election of President Zachary Taylor—between Philadelphia visiting Clemson's mother and South Carolina. During this period, Anna wrote to her father, John C. Calhoun, about their Belgian portraits:

> We have had our portraits opened since we came. They are perfectly safe, & everyone says they have never seen such likenesses & such painting. The director of the Academy of Fine Arts [in Philadelphia] has laid violent hand on them & insists on placing them in the Academy for a month that persons may see what good paintings are. We have consented, as we know the artist who painted them is anxious to come to America, at least for a time, & if they are seen, he may receive encouragement to do so. He promised at the end of that time to see them sent to Charleston himself, so the delay will not be long, & they may perhaps get to Pendleton as soon as if they went now, as there are perhaps but few wagons at this busy season.[70]

The entire grouping of the Clemson family portraits did make their way to Fort Hill prior to Calhoun's death.

Before the Clemsons left Belgium, they also commissioned several portraits of Senator and Mrs. Calhoun. Just how this was accomplished Clemson described in a letter to his brother-in-law, James Edward Calhoun: "they were copies as I informed you from the portrait and daguerreotype which I left for the purpose."[71] The daguerreotype by Matthew Brady that Clemson had taken to Belgium was one of the last photographic images of John C. Calhoun. Anna seemed very impressed by the completed portrait by Belgian artist Eugene DeBlock when she wrote to her father, "I wish you could see your portrait. I think you would be pleased with it. You are in the same position as in Brady's Daguerreotype & look as if you had just finished a speech in the Senate. We have had a magnificent frame made for it, & it is not only a fine portrait but a work of art."

Anna went on to ask her father, "How do you like our portraits? I suppose from what mother says they have arrived before this."[72] Clemson noted in one letter to his brother-in-law, "My portrait of your father was considered a very fine likeness by all who saw it and Mr. DeBlock appears to have copied it as nearly as possible." Clemson went on to say that "everything was done that could be done by me and my friend an artist who superintended the execution."[73] Henry Gourdin wrote to Clemson somewhat critically about his impression of the Calhoun painting: "Mr. Calhoun while it is commendable as a likeness, did not strike me as being a particularly good painting."[74] The last Brady photograph of Calhoun unfortunately shows the senator sick and frail nearing the end of his life.

The painting of Floride Calhoun was based on a miniature image by Charleston artist Charles Fraser. This miniature had a special place in the Clemsons' life while they were living in Belgium. As Anna wrote in a letter to her father, her children, "constantly ask to kiss their grandmother's miniature—your likeness, being only engraving, does not strike them so much. I do wish, if it be possible, you would have a good likeness of yourself taken for me, about the size of mother's. I need not tell you how I should prize it."[75] Anna did get her wish of a small miniature of John C. Calhoun by Mueller.

The portraiture commissioned by Clemson in Belgium, especially those by Eeckhout and DeBlock, are in the Fort Hill Collection. These Belgium portraits include the massive "Portrait of Mrs. Anna C. Clemson—Eeckhart,"[76] along with the children's paintings: "Portrait of John Calhoun Clemson"[77] and "Portrait of Floride E. Clemson."[78] The Clemson portraits hang at Fort Hill in the Formal Parlor. Both paintings of Senator and Mrs. John C. Calhoun also hang in the State Dining Room at Fort Hill. Anna listed them respectively as "J. C. Calhoun by DeBlock"[79] and "Portrait of Mrs. J. C. Calhoun."[80] The remaining Clemson family portraits, which Anna Clemson listed as "Portrait of T. G. Clemson"[81] and "Portrait of Mrs. Clemson,"[82] are still in private hands, but eventually will return to Fort Hill. Thus, the nine family paintings listed in the 1888 "Appraisal of the Estate of Thomas Clemson" most certainly included the same paintings listed some thirty years earlier in 1852 by Anna in her "Catalogue."

### Thomas Clemson—Painter

In addition to the paintings and portraits either collected or commissioned by Thomas G. Clemson, the story of his interest in art would be incomplete without taking into consideration his own paintings which also are represented in the collection. Collecting art and painting art are certainly not always synonymous avocations; however, Thomas Clemson evidently transitioned quite smoothly from collector to artist. He himself produced art ranging from original works and copies to portraiture. At Fort Hill today are five full-scale paintings that are attributed to Thomas Clemson. One of his paintings is a landscape, commonly called *Chickens*,[83] which features a Rhode Island rooster and a hen in a barnyard with two pigeons in the loft. This painting in many ways captures the realistic spirit of the Robbe paintings and borrows the manger background and side illumination of sun streaming in a triangular opening from Robbe's *Barnyard Scene*.

The four other paintings attributed to Clemson are human figurative paintings, including a copy of a Madonna and Child and a copy of the *Old Man Smoking*[84] in his collection. Clemson creatively signed the Madonna and Child painting, probably using a reverse mirror. He also made his own copy of *Old Man Smoking*, but he took the liberty to paint the bearded subject with facial features similar to his own. Clemson's version is a copy of a small painting in his collection, "Old

**Thomas Green Clemson's painting of a Madonna and Child may best represent his art talents. The holy mother's facial features resemble Anna. The painting was photographed in the Fort Hill parlor in the 1880s. Oil on canvas. Fort Hill Collection, Clemson University.**

Man Smoking—after Leys," which is a copy of an original painting by Henri Leys.

In letters, Thomas Clemson mentions painting portraits, the most important of which is his self-portrait.[85] As with any artist, Clemson's self-portrait must have been a daunting task. It is a dark painting in somber colors and devoid of background. One might imagine how he might have looked at his reflection and concentrated on how he saw himself. Another of his full-length paintings, also at Fort Hill, is Clemson's portrait of his brother Baker Clemson[86] who has very similar facial features to his own. There are no good records of exactly how many paintings Thomas Clemson produced. However Anna did write to her father in 1849 that "while in Virginia Mr. C. took four portraits. Three were excellent, & his sister's (Mrs. Washington) was one of the best he has ever done."[87] Incidentally only one artist-board portrait study is in existence—a delicate woman's hand with the wedding band of his wife Anna.

In addition to Clemson's completed works, several of his studies on artist board are extant: one study of a goat's head and two studies of goat knee joints. These show that Clemson the scientist closely studied the articulated leg, knee cap, and hoof to get the details as anatomically correct and lifelike as possible. They bear a resemblance to the Robbe landscapes which he greatly admired. The works by Clemson are an intriguing handful of paintings and studies. Still, the longevity of Clemson's painting period is somewhat unknown. There are indications that by the end of 1857 he probably had stopped painting; for example, in a letter to Floride, which queries her daughter's interest in painting, Anna Clemson notes, "Katie must indeed be improving rapidly in painting, & must have quite a talent for it. Would you like to learn? When you got through the drudgery, your father could aid you, & he has all the necessary implements & materials, which I suppose he will never use much more." Anna adds, perhaps having seen Thomas's painting hobby, "Do not spend time, however, at that or any other accomplishment, unless you have a decided taste for it.[88]

Thomas Green Clemson's mahogany artist palette. Fort Hill Collection, Clemson University.

### *Thomas Clemson—Promoter of the Fine Arts*

For Thomas G. Clemson, a multitalented and multifaceted individual, his personal art collection and painting were intrinsic parts of his artistic interests and activities. However, his personal impact on the mid-nineteenth-century American art scene should be assessed as well, because he was not only an art collector, but also a promoter of the fine arts in both private correspondence and public exhibitions. Thomas Clemson's circle of contemporaries included two very significant entrepreneurs in the nation's most prominent metropolitan areas—Washington, D.C., and New York. In his efforts to collect European art, he found several allies in the United States, most notably William Wilson Corcoran, founder of the Corcoran Gallery in Washington, D.C.; this art collection profited from Clemson's artistic eye and his brokering purchases of Flemish art.[89] For instance, as mentioned earlier, he shipped to Corcoran three oil paintings in 1850, and explained in a letter: "The largest is a landscape of the same size as the painting before sent, by Robbe. The next largest is an old picture of flowers by the celebrated French artist Baptiste. The third is a copy of a painting by Auchenbach."[90] Clemson's copy of *Waterfall* still exists, as noted earlier; however, its twin, known as "Corcoran's Cascade," was deaccessioned in the late 1970s. In fact, all three of the paintings which W. W. Corcoran had worked with Clemson to acquire were later considered undesirable by Corcoran's namesake art gallery, although today's curators lament their sale.

**William Wilson Corcoran, founder of the Corcoran Gallery in Washington, D.C., by Abraham Bogardus and Daniel and David Bendann, photographers, ca. 1871-1873. The Historical Society of Washington, D.C.**

Clemson went on to tell Corcoran that "Lys, Gallait & Wappers are the first painters of Belgium. Their pictures are as much esteemed as any of the ancient masters, but they charge high prices for their work. You can not have a collection of modern pictures without having of their works & if you wish something very fine I would advise you to get of their works."[91] This letter is also important because it includes one instance in which Clemson talks about art as an investment: "persons that have money here in Europe think it a good investment to purchase paintings of either of the artists, as they increase in value with time."[92]

Another contemporary in Clemson's art endeavors was Charles Leupp of New York. Leupp was involved in the New York art scene and especially with the Gallery for the National Academy of Design and the New York Gallery of the

**Miniature portrait of Charles Leupp of New York. Oil on ivory. Gift of Mr. & Mrs. Creighton Lee Calhoun. Fort Hill Collection, Clemson University.**

Fine Arts. For the opening of the new Gallery of the Academy in 1850, Leupp wrote to Clemson that he expected to show "Eeckhouts picture of the 'Trilitte' and also the two by Robbe should they arrive in time."[93] Leupp commented on art appreciation in New York, stating to Clemson: "I am happy to say a love for Art is beginning to be felt among the people in this country but it is as yet confined to cheap pictures."[94] Leupp went on to observe, "all true lovers of art are instinctively friends."[95] Not only were Charles Leupp and Clemson friends, but Leupp's wife was one of the children of an early mayor of New York City, Gideon Lee Sr., the father of D. W. Lee and Gideon Lee Jr., the future son-in-law of Thomas Clemson.

As to the status of art in New York, Leupp lamented to Clemson, "Yourself standing at a distance and surrounded by art and its worshipers imagines that the world feels, as you do, the real degree of having established Galleria of pictures and of sculptures among us. I confess with shame and a feeling of indignation that we only care here for money and the semblance of things artistic—the shadow not the substance."[96] Substance in art was Thomas Clemson's ultimate goal.

## *Tracking the Thomas Clemson Art Collection Since 1852*

The Clemson Art Collection has a long-storied and well-traveled history. Thomas G. Clemson shipped his paintings from Belgium first to Dosoris Island adjacent to New York's Long Island. There Anna first recorded her "Catalogue" of the collection. The paintings later hung in The Home in Bladensburg, Maryland. The large collection of various sizes was a challenge to hang. Anna, in one letter to her daughter away at school, wrote, "Under my picture stands the lounge. The corner table stands under where your grandfather hung but Tasso hangs there now, & you & Calhoun have changed sides, each with your small pictures. On the carved table are the 'Armour Captis' & the 2 flat vases forming the chimney-piece. The étagère is between the windows, & in the corner where the secretary was, are my work table, & green chair & above hangs your grandfather."[97]

On the eve of the Civil War, Thomas Clemson had the entire collection packed up and shipped to his uncle Elias Baker in Altoona, Pennsylvania, for safekeeping. It took well after the end of the Civil War to regain the collection, and, though accounts somewhat differ, a couple of the paintings were destroyed in transit. Annie White Mell recorded in 1903 that the paintings were "finally sent to Fort Hill a few years before the death of Mr. Clemson. When they arrived some of the pictures were found to be badly damaged by careless packing and one or two were entirely destroyed, greatly to Mr. Clemson's regret."[98] There is another tradition from Alester Holmes that "Two of the outstanding works originally in the collection were left at the University of Virginia for some unknown reason when the others were shipped South during the Civil War." Exactly when, how, and if one or two ended up at the University of Virginia is a mystery, and Holmes found no definitive proof; moreover, no record of the paintings exists at the University of Virginia today.[99]

The whereabouts of four of the paintings listed in Anna Clemson's "Catalogue" are unknown, and they are presumed destroyed. From the 1852 "Catalogue" list, the following paintings were never part of the 1888 bequest: "Virgin, Child, and St. Joseph in a garland of fruit by Jordaens,"[100] "Flowers—Robie,"[101] "Mother Teaching Child—Copy,"[102] and "Landscape—Robbe."[103] While the actual composition of these four paintings is unknown, they would appear to be the Holy Family, a still life, a composition of two figures, and a landscape.

The history of this portion of the Thomas Clemson Art Collection since the opening of Clemson College is another intriguing story. As the College opened in

1893, the paintings were shown hanging in the Fort Hill Parlor, literally covering the walls and even doors.[104] One grouping of paintings was moved to the library in the main building (now Tillman Hall), but thankfully after the early fire in the main building. The earliest attempt to catalog the paintings at the College and to disseminate information about them was done by Annie White Mell, wife of Clemson College President Patrick Hues Mell. In 1903, Mrs. Mell, who was very interested in history, wrote an article on the collection for the *Clemson Chronicle* entitled "The Clemson Collection of Paintings: Donated to Clemson Agricultural College." She relied heavily on the 1852 "Catalogue" of Anna Clemson. The Mell Catalogue lists thirty-four paintings.[105]

Photograph showing paintings from the Clemson painting collection on display in the reception room of Tillman Hall at Clemson University, ca. 1896. Clemson University Photographs, Special Collections, Clemson University Libraries.

After Sikes Hall was renovated following a fire that gutted its interior, it was reconfigured in 1927 by campus architect Rudolph Lee to house the expanding library. The majority of the paintings were moved to the library with a collection of other campus historical artifacts. Photos from the 1940s show the paintings hanging on the walls of the balcony surrounding the Lee-designed reading room of the library. By most accounts there were thirty-four paintings hanging in the Old Library.

In 1941, the Clemson Art Collection was described in the publication *South Carolina: A Guide to the Palmetto State*, commonly referred to as the WPA Guide to South Carolina, which was compiled by the Writers' Program of the Work Projects Administration in the State of South Carolina. In the section on the Upstate, the text describes Clemson College's library as housing, in addition to its books, some "35 paintings collected or copied by Clemson in Brussels. W. W. Corcoran, founder of Corcoran Art Gallery in Washington, had commissioned him to purchase pictures. Clemson believed he had acquired for his own collection two Rubens, a Velasquez, and a Rembrandt. But there is some doubt about their authenticity. One of the Rubens, a Virgin and Child, and the Velasquez Head are in the library here as well as Peasant's Repast, Frans Hals, and Study of a head by Greuze."[106]

**Photograph of the Clemson Art Collection hanging above the Sikes Hall Library's main reading room, ca. 1930. J. C. Littlejohn Collection, Special Collections, Clemson University Libraries.**

The paintings were exhibited on the walls of the second-floor gallery overlooking the main reading room. As longtime librarian Mary Stevenson wrote in 1963, "When I first came to Clemson College in 1927 (as assistant librarian), most of the paintings were hung around the balcony of the library.... When visitors came to the library we gave them copies of Mrs. Mell's list." Stevenson went on to write that "as the library became more and more crowded through the years, I feel sure that some of the paintings were moved and placed in storage to make room for shelving, etc. In 1954, the paintings were moved to the Architecture Dept.," then Riggs Hall, which was the home of the School of Architecture prior to Lee Hall.[107] The Clemson Art Collection had been exhibited as part of the Clemson College museum collection which was discontinued in the library in the 1950s because of room needed for collection and library activities. The library outgrew its building prior to moving to the new library building in 1966. The paintings were put in storage and soon forgotten. They were rediscovered tucked away in Riggs Hall, including a portion in the attic and another portion in the boiler room, in the late 1950s by architecture professors and students.

Dr. Harold N. Cooledge, professor of art and architectural history, and others worked tirelessly throughout the 1960s to have the remaining paintings restored. Eventually by the early 1970s they were conserved, with support from the Clemson Alumni Association. Unfortunately, two still-life paintings were later listed as missing from the collection.[108] Cooledge composed a short brochure entitled "Thom. G. Clemson Painting Collection" and numbered the collection at twenty-five paintings. Cooledge, however, overlooked the oil painting of Beatrice Cenci, maybe because it was a copy, and did not take into consideration the seven paintings remaining at Fort Hill. Thus, the total of on-campus paintings was, in fact, thirty-three. Both Annie White Mell and Cooledge always counted the *Chickens* painting by Clemson in their listings; however, Anna Clemson had never enumerated it or Thomas Clemson's other works.

For the last quarter of the twentieth century, the majority of the collection hung in the Board Room and offices of Sikes Hall before coming home again to adorn the walls of Fort Hill after its restoration in 2003. With their reinstallation in Fort Hill, this group of paintings rejoined a smaller grouping of seven paintings—*Marine View in Holland, Archway, Landscape-Robbe after Keokoek, Goats and Sheep, Group of Lambs, Mary Magdalene,* and *Old Man Smoking*—which had remained at Fort Hill. One noticeable distinction between these two groups of paintings is that the frames of paintings that had remained at Fort Hill were relatively intact, whereas the frames of the paintings that had been moved often and stored for an extended period of time were almost entirely destroyed. A few of the original frames exist for conservation and reproduction.[109]

## An Assessment of Thomas Clemson's Passion for Art

Thomas Green Clemson's art collection is an eclectic compilation representing biblical motifs, icons from antiquity, allegories of literature, landscapes, and portraiture. Clemson's art ranges the gamut of mid-nineteenth-century European visual arts collecting. No one knows exactly what the cost of his collecting hobby

**PLATE 1.** *Thomas G. Clemson* by Joseph Bayas Ord (American, 1805-1865), ca. 1830. Oil on canvas, 33 ½ x 26 ¾ in. Fort Hill Collection, Clemson University.

**Plate 2.** *Anna Maria Calhoun Clemson* by Jacobus Joseph Eeckhout (Belgian, 1793-1861), 1848. Oil on canvas, 72 x 61 ¼ in. Fort Hill Collection, Clemson University.

**PLATE 3.** *John Calhoun Clemson* by Jacobus Joseph Eeckhout (Belgian, 1793-1861), 1848. Oil on canvas, 28 ½ x 22 ½ in. Fort Hill Collection, Clemson University.

**PLATE 4.** *Floride Elizabeth Clemson* by Jacobus Joseph Eeckhout (Belgian, 1793-1861), 1848. Oil on canvas, 28 x 22 in. Fort Hill Collection, Clemson University.

**PLATE 5.** *John C. Calhoun* by Eugenius F. DeBlock (Belgian, later American, 1812-1893) was based on an 1844 daguerreotype by Matthew Brady. Oil on canvas, 38 ½ x 31 ¾ in. Fort Hill Collection, Clemson University.

**PLATE 6.** *Floride Colhoun Calhoun* by Eugenius F. DeBlock (Belgian, later American, 1812-1893). Oil on canvas, 38 ½ x 31 ¾ in. Fort Hill Collection, Clemson University.

**PLATE 7.** *Old Man Smoking* by Thomas Green Clemson (1807-1888) was his copy of a museum study of a painting by Henri Leys (Belgian, 1815-1869). Oil on canvas, 36 x 28 ½ in. Fort Hill Collection, Clemson University.

**PLATE 8.** *Chickens* by Thomas Green Clemson (1807-1888) was inspired by the *Goats and Sheep* painting by Louis Robbe (Belgian, 1806-1887). Oil on canvas, 14 x 17 in. Fort Hill Collection, Clemson University.

**PLATE 9.** *Virgin and Child* by Cornelis Schut III (Flemish, 1629-1685). Attributed during nineteenth century to Peter Paul Rubens (1577-1640), it is now attributed to his protégée Cornelis Schut. Oil on cradled wood, 16 ½ x 12 ½ in. Fort Hill Collection, Clemson University.

PLATE 10. *Flower Piece* is the work of two Flemish artists: Daniel Seghers (1590-1661) painted the floral still life; David Teniers (1610-1690) created the inner medallion cartouche. Oil on canvas, 22 ½ x 26 in. Fort Hill Collection, Clemson University.

**PLATE 11.** *Adoration* by Frans Francken II (Flemish, 1581-1642). Oil on copper, 10 ½ x 7 ¾ in. Fort Hill Collection, Clemson University.

**PLATE 12.** "The Philosopher (Supposed to be Rembrandt or Ferdinand Bol)," as Anna Clemson described it, was a prized painting in their collection. It is probably a 19th-century copy after a *St. Paul* painting by Rembrandt Harmenszoon van Rijn (1606-1669). Oil on canvas, 29 ½ x 23 ¾ in. Fort Hill Collection, Clemson University.

**PLATE 13.** *Goats and Sheep* by Louis Marie Dominique Robbe (Belgian, 1806-1887). Oil on canvas, 18 ½ x 23 ¼ in. Fort Hill Collection, Clemson University.

**PLATE 14.** *The Castle of Elsinore* by Thomas Fearnley (Swedish, 1802-1842). Oil on canvas, 13 x 20 in. Fort Hill Collection, Clemson University.

**PLATE 15.** *Tasso in Prison Visited by Montaigne* by Louis Gallait (Belgian, 1810-1887). Copy after Gallait's painting in the King Léopold of Belgium gallery. Oil on canvas, 40 ⅛ x 33 ¼ in. Fort Hill Collection, Clemson University.

**PLATE 16.** *Girl of Antwerp with Two Dogs*, museum copy by unknown artist after Sir Edwin Landseer's painting of a young Queen Victoria, the niece of King Léopold I of Belgium. Oil on canvas, 27 x 21 ¾ in. Fort Hill Collection, Clemson University.

was in terms of 1840s and 1850s dollars. In some ways it must have been a considerable investment from a diplomat's stipend. However, Clemson never simply looked at his collection as monetary assets that might appreciate and later be sold at a profit. Moreover, the reproductions within his collection appealed to him and were the means of his having museum-quality reproductions of fine art to decorate his home. Likewise, some paintings were models for his personal study and his personal art craft.

Thomas G. Clemson's passion for the fine arts provides an invaluable glimpse into Thomas Clemson the man. After all, this is the person who, in 1859, insisted, "All organized beings [are] artists—from the minute creature that built up the coral islands and twined coral wreaths around the world up to man." In art as in other segments of his career, he was an enlightened man ahead of his time. His collecting art is a conspicuous case in point of that enlightenment. When few of his American contemporaries were doing so, he began to collect representative samples of seventeenth-century and nineteenth-century European paintings. He rounded out his collection by commissioning original portraits as well as museum-grade copies of impressive paintings he had seen or studied. When his own paintings were added to that effort, the result was an oil painting collection that would have rivaled any personal art collection in America at his time.

Today, the Thomas Green Clemson Art Collection is remarkably intact.[110] It is also remarkable that, by specifically giving most of that collection to Fort Hill, Clemson established an artistic legacy for his namesake institution of higher learning as well as a tangible and highly personal link with its founder.

## Notes

1. *The National Intelligencer,* 6 April 1859, cited in Alester G. Holmes and George R. Sherrill, *Thomas Green Clemson: His Life and Work* (Richmond, VA: Garrett & Massie, 1937), 36–37. The Washington (DC) Art Association had been founded in 1857 by William Wilson Corcoran in support of the arts. Clemson's reference to the Capitol preservation was a very controversial and political decision.
2. "Appraised Bill of the Property of The Estate of Thomas G. Clemson, Deceased" (1888), Clemson Papers, Special Collections, Clemson University Libraries (hereafter cited as SCCUL).
3. Anna Maria Calhoun Clemson, "Catalogue of Paintings," in "An Inventory of furniture, pictures, etc. Taken at Dosoris, December 1, 1852. Added to and regulated August 1853" [by Anna Calhoun Clemson], Fort Hill Collection, Clemson University.
4. Ernest McPherson Lander Jr., *The Calhoun Family and Thomas Green Clemson: The Decline of a Southern Patriarchy* (Columbia: University of South Carolina Press, 1983), 139.
5. The remaining three Old Master paintings acquired by Thomas G. Clemson (and not in the current Clemson Collection) were listed in Anna Clemson's "Catalogue" as follows: paintings "No. 6 Fruit by DeHeem" and "No. 7 Student's Repast by Van Son" are missing; painting "No. 5 Virgin, Child, & St. Joseph in a Garland of fruit by Jordaens" is one of the paintings unaccounted for and presumed destroyed in transit in the 1880s.
6. "Virgin and Child" (No. 1), Cornelis Schut III (Flemish, 1629–1685), oil on cradled wood, 16 ½ x 12 ½ in. (40.64 x 30.48 cm.). In this portrayal the Virgin Mary is holding the Christ

Child nestled within her arms. Mary has porcelain, fair skin and wears a red garment, whereas the nude Christ Child is shown with blond hair. The margins are filled with renditions of cherubim including one cherub that is placing a garland wreath of flowers on Mary's head.

7. Anna Calhoun Clemson, "Catalogue of Paintings" (1852), Fort Hill Collection, Clemson University.

8. Quoted in Annie White Mell, "The Clemson Collection of Paintings: Donated to Clemson Agricultural College" (1903), Clemson Papers, SCCUL.

9. W. R. Valentiner to C. Wallace Lott, 2 July 1957, in Clemson Papers, SCCUL. Valentiner was director of the North Carolina Museum of Art in Raleigh, NC, in the late 1950s. He was a well-respected art historian and examined the entire Clemson collection. C. Wallace Lott had enlisted student assistance in conducting documentation and measurements of the collection. As H. Glenn McGee stated, in "the summer of Nineteen Fifty-six I took four of the paintings to Miss Margaretta M. Salinger of the Metropolitan Museum of Art who suggested that we take the entire collection to Dr. W. R. Valentiner." H. Glenn McGee to National Art Gallery, 8 April 1958. The response from David E. Finley to C. Wallace Lott was that "most of the paintings would be of greater interest and more suitable shown in Mr. Clemson's house, as they were bought by him I assume, for that purpose." David E. Finley to C. Wallace Lott, 16 June 1958. RG—Record of the Curatorial Department—General Curatorial Subject File, 1941–1971, National Gallery of Art. See Marline Jutsen, National Gallery Archives, National Gallery of Art, to William Hiott, 20 September 2006, Fort Hill Collection, Clemson University.

10. Cornelis Schut I (b. Antwerp, 13 May 1597–d. Antwerp, 29 April 1655). See Hans Vlieghe, "Schut, Cornelis, I," *Grove Art Online*, Oxford University Press 2006.

11. "Flower Piece" (No. 4), Daniel Seghers (Flemish, 1590–1661), oil on canvas, 22 ½ x 26 in. (55.88 x 66.04 cm.). The painting actually combines two works. The inner medallion forms a cartouche that contains the image of the young child and a lamb. The child more than likely represents a young St. John the Baptist, not the Christ Child. The boy is seated on the ground and holds a staff in his left hand, while his right rests on the back of the lamb, most likely representing Jesus. The outer section of the painting is a large, polychrome floral wreath composed of peonies, tulips, roses, and miscellaneous wildflowers. See Irene Haberland, "Seghers, Daniel," *Grove Art Online*, Oxford University Press, 2006. See also Hans Vlieghe, "Teniers: David Teniers II," *Grove Art Online*, Oxford University Press, 2006.

12. See letter of W. R. Valentiner to C. Wallace Lott, July 1957, Clemson Papers, SCCUL, in which Valentiner considered the medallion the work of Jan Lievens (1607–1674), a Dutch Baroque Era painter.

13. Verse is from John 1:29. For an example, see *Garland of Flowers with the Holy Family*, San Diego Museum of Art, Online Catalogue, http://www.sdmart.org/exhibition-secular.html#still.

14. "Adoration of the Kings" (No. 9), Frans Francken II (Flemish, 1581–1642), oil on copper, 10 ½ x 7 ¾ in. (25.4 x 17.78 cm.). Depicted in the painting is a manger scene with the Holy Family. The first king, dressed in a rose-colored robe and offering gold, is kneeling before the Christ Child. Standing to the right are the other two kings, one Moorish in royal blue garments and a white turban followed by another king in purple. The "star of Bethlehem" shines in the upper right margin and above four other figures including Joseph, two soldiers, and a laborer or shepherd. This work is executed in rich jewel tones. The back of the copper plate contains the incised monogram signature, which is one of the "Francken" families of painters.

15. Frans Francken II (Flemish, 1581–1642). See "Francken; Frans Francken II," *Grove Art Online*, Oxford University Press, 2006.

16. "Head by Velasquez" (No. 2), School of Otto Van Veen (early seventeenth century), oil on cradled wood panel, 12 x 10 in. (30.48 x 24.4 cm.). The subject is wearing a black jacket and a pleated white starched collar.

17. W. R. Valentiner to C. Wallace Lott, 2 July 1957. Otto van Veen (b. Leiden, ca. 1556–d. Brussels, 6 May 1629). See "Veen, Otto van," *Grove Art Online*, Oxford University Press, 2006.

18. "Peasant with Soup—Frans Hals" (No. 8), attribution to the Hals school of painters (it has been considered the work of either Harmen Hals or Jan Hals, both sons of Frans Hals, the seventeenth-century Dutch master), oil on cradled wood, 19 ¾ x 14 in. (48.26 x 35.56 cm.). In 1876, Thomas Clemson referred to this painting as "Peasant Eating Soup"; sometimes it has been labeled as "Girl Eating Soup" because of its depictions of a young woman eating porridge

or soup in a genre action scene. The subject is wearing a white cap, white shawl, red shirt, dark skirt, and white apron.

19. See letter of W. R. Valentiner to C. Wallace Lott, 2 July 1957, Clemson Papers, SCCUL, in which Valentiner attributes the work to Harmen Hals (b. Haarlem, 1611–d. 1669), son of Frans Hals.

20. Creighton Gilbert to President Robert C. Edwards, 26 April 1961, SCCUL: "In the case of the Girl Eating Soup, the traditional label of Frans Hals is, in fact, too optimistic; Dr. Valentiner's suggestion of his son Harmen Hals is simply a polite way of saying that it is by a minor member of the Hals school, which it is." When contacted in 2006, Creighton Gilbert, now a distinguished emeritus professor of art at Yale University, remembered viewing the photographs of the paintings while he was working at the Ringling Museum of Art in 1961. In a recent exhaustive search, the archivists of the Ringling Museum were able to locate one black & white photograph of the *Fruit* painting (No. 6). The only image found to date of the *Repast* painting (No. 7) is a grainy illustration in the 1896 Clemson College Catalogue in a photograph entitled "Relic Room." The *Repast*, placed on the bottom row second from the left, is directly under the Beatrice Cenci painting.

21. "Landscape by Poussin" (No. 3), attribution to Nicolas Poussin (1594–1665), but generally attributed to the Dutch School (seventeenth/eighteenth century), oil on wood panel, image 17 x 25 in. (43.18 x 63.5 cm.). Depicted in this image is a wayside tavern in a forested area. The tavern yard contains travelers, and one figure is approaching on horseback. Tall stately trees dominate the landscape. See Hugh Brigstocke, "Poussin, Nicolas," *Grove Art Online*, Oxford University Press, 2006.

22. "Landscape" (No. 42), attribution to Claude Lorraine (1605–1682), but generally attributed to the Italian School (seventeenth/eighteenth century), oil on cradled wood panel, 11 ⅞ x 14 ⅜ in. (27.94 x 35.56 cm.). Depicted in this image is a "Romantic" landscape with pillared ruins dominating the left margin. Noblemen in conversation are in the midforeground. There is a body of water in the right foreground and a hillside city in the right midground with a sky filled with gray-tinted clouds.

23. The painting's canvas, 29½ x 22¾ in., is placed in a mid-nineteenth-century frame and may well have been custom-made for the Clemsons in Belgium where intricately carved frames and furniture were highly prized.

24. "Fruit, by De Heem" (No. 6), attribution to Jan Davidsz De Heem (1606–1684). The dimensions of the painting were recorded as 16 ¼ x 25 ¾ in. (40.64 x 63.5 cm.) and annotated as "Missing from Collection" in a two-page listing of the "Thomas G. Clemson Collection," dated 9 June 1970, by Michael Holden. See "Heem, de: (1) Jan Davidsz. De Heem," *Grove Art Online*, Oxford University Press, 2006.

25. "Student's repast by Van Son" (No. 7), attribution to Pieter Claesz (b. Steinfurt in Westphalia, 1597–98; worked in Haarlem; d. Spaarne, 1661). The dimensions of this painting were recorded as 20 ⅛ x 14 ¾ in. (50.8 x 35.56 cm.) and annotated as "Missing from Collection" in Michael Holden, "Thomas G. Clemson Collection," 9 June 1970. See Pieter Biesboer, et alia, *Pieter Claesz: Master of Haarlem Still Life* (Zwolle: Waanders Publishers, n.d.). This exhaustive catalog for a three-city exhibition, including the National Gallery of Art in Washington, DC, features numerous examples and includes the attribute of a "still life with herrings, pipes, oysters, etc."

26. Jan Jansz van de Velde (b. Amsterdam, 1620–d. 1660). See Gilbert Creighton letter to President Edwards, 26 April 1961, SCCUL.

27. W. R. Valentiner to C. Wallace Lott, 2 July 1957, SCCUL.

28. "Student's Repast," Pieter Claesz. See note 25.

29. "Flowers—Robie" (No. 13), Jean-Baptiste Robie (Belgian, 1821–1910). He was famous for his floral still-life paintings. His "Flowers" (No. 13) and Louis Robbe's "Landscape" (No. 16) are unaccounted for and presumed destroyed in transit in the 1880s.

30. One still life appeared in a photograph of the parlor at Fort Hill in 1893.

31. "Titian Placing His Model" (No. 21), Jacobus Josephus Eeckhout (Belgian, 1793–1861), oil on wood panel, 17 ⅜ x 9 ¾ in. (43.18 x 22.86 cm.). The image depicts the artist Titian as an older man standing and holding an artist's palette in his left hand. The female subject, dressed

in royal gold clothing, is seated next to a table with a green tablecloth and a silver tea service. An artist's apprentice is in the background.

32. The subject is Titian (Tiziano Vecellio), a Venetian Renaissance painter (1485–1576).

33. "Poverty & Suffering—DeBlock" (No. 27), Eugene DeBlock, nineteenth century, oil on canvas, 15 ¼ x 18 ⅜ in. (38.1 x 45.72 cm.). The depiction is an interior room scene showing a female alongside the bed of a sick child. Another young boy sits on the floor at the head of the bed. The family in grief and poverty is executed in dark, somber colors.

34. "Cattle" (No. 14), Louis Marie Dominique Romain Robbe (Belgian, 1806–1887), oil on canvas, 30 x 40 ½ in. (76.2 x 101.6 cm.). The central subjects are three long-horned dairy cattle drinking from a small pond surrounded by a pair of ducks and five ducklings. Beyond, a herd grazes on the lush green meadow framed by distant rolling hills and a pale blue sky filled with pastel clouds.

35. "Goats & Sheep—L. Robbe" (No. 15), Louis Marie Dominique Robbe (Belgian, 1806–1887), oil on canvas, 18 ½ x 23 ¼ in. (45.72 x 58.42 cm.). The barnyard scene is of one horned goat and four sheep inside a barn stall covered with straw. The image is reminiscent of a manger scene with sunlight piercing the left side of the scene. The blue sky is seen through a small hole in the wall. The painting is signed *Robbe* in the lower right image.

36. "Group of Lambs" (No. 28), unsigned but attributed by Anna Calhoun Clemson to Robbe, oil on canvas, 14 ¼ x 19 in. (35.56 x 48.26 cm.) stretcher size, 22 ½ x 28 in. (55.88 x 71.12 cm.) framed. The painting depicts three sheep at rest in a meadow with a shepherd and herd in the background.

37. "Landscapes by Fearnley—a Swedish painter." These landscapes are known respectively as *Castle of Kronborg* and *Castle of Elsinore*. They are incorrectly attributed, in some sources, to John E. Fernley Sr. (English, 1781–1860).

38. "The Castle of Kronborg" (No. 18), Thomas Fearnley (1802–1842), oil on canvas, 13 x 20 in. (33.02 x 50.8 cm.). The painting is referred to as *Kronborg*, the name of the city, which is sometimes misspelled as *Kronberg*. In this depiction the castle is set in the distance with a body of water in the foreground with cattle grazing. It is signed and dated 1825 at the base midmargin.

39. "The Castle of Elsinore" (No. 19), Thomas Fearnley (1802–1842), oil on canvas, 13 x 20 in. (33.02 x 50.8 cm.). This painting is referred to as *Elsinore* (sometimes misspelled as *Elsenor*), the name of the castle from Shakespeare's *Hamlet*. The castle is situated in midground with two sailboats approaching shore. The sky is overcast with a rough lapping sea. The painting is signed and dated 1825 in the lower right margin.

40. Annie White Mell, "The Clemson Collection of Paintings: Donated to Clemson Agricultural College" (1903), Clemson Papers, SCCUL.

41. "Marine view in Holland—Francia" (No. 26), oil on canvas, 10 ¼ x 12 ½ in. (25.4 x 30.48 cm.) image size, 16 ½ x 18 ¾ in. (40.64 x 45.72 cm.) gilt frame. This seascape includes sailing boats off shore, windmills, a man, and a small boat. It is signed *Ancia*.

42. "Scene in Spain—Bossuet" (No. 25), François Bossuet (1800–1889), oil on canvas, 15 x 12 ½ in. (38.1 x 30.48 cm.). The cityscape image is viewed through an archway with a church in the background and with figures and a person riding a donkey in the foreground. The painting is signed and dated in the lower left *F. Bossuet 1851*.

43. "Gateway—Tavernier" (No. 20), Andrea Tavernier (Italian, 1858–1931). The painting depicts two men drinking from a bottle of wine and standing next to a wheelbarrow under an arched gate. In the background are mountains, a rocky coastline, and a deep blue sky. It is signed in the lower right corner.

44. "Magdalene by—Van Schendael" (No. 17), Petrus Van Schendel (Belgian, 1806–1870), oil on panel, 7 ¾ x 9 ⅜ in. (17.78 x 22.86 cm.) image, 12 ¾ x 14 ⅜ in. (30.48 x 35.56 cm.) frame. The moonlight night scene represents a woman at a shire with a cross hanging nearby. The painting is lit with one single candle casting its shadow on her face and clasped hands as she gazes upward to the heavens. In her hands is a book with a human skull resting on it. The painting is signed *P. Van Schendel*.

45. Wiepke F. Loos, "Schendel, Petrus van," *Grove Art Online*, Oxford University Press, 2006.

46. "Head—Study by Greuge" (No. 12), Jean Baptiste Greuze (French, 1725–1805), oil on canvas, 10 ⅜ x 8 ⅜ in. (25.4 x 20.32 cm.). The image depicts a silhouette of a small bust portrait

of a young man with curly long blond hair and wearing a yellow scarf and red shirt. See "Greuze, Jean-Baptiste," *Grove Art Online*, Oxford University Press, 2006.

47. "Boy Mending Pen—Spanish" (No. 10), Spanish Bodegon School, nineteenth century, oil on canvas, 27 x 23 in. (68.58 x 58.42 cm.). Depicted in this image is a boy sharpening a quill pen. In the left midmargin is a small oil lamp.

48. Charles Karel Ferdinand Venneman (Belgian, 1802–1875).

49. "Mother Teaching Child—copy" (No. 40) is unaccounted for and presumed destroyed during transit in the 1880s.

50. "Tasso in Prison visited by Montaigne (original in King Leopold's Gallery), Copy after Gallait" (No. 32), Louis Gallait (1810–1887), Spanish School, oil on canvas, 40 ⅛ x 33 ¼ in. (101.6 x 83.82 cm.). This portrait of *Tasso in Prison* depicts the subject Torquato Tasso (1544–1595) seated at a table with illuminated manuscripts and visited by a Dominican monk and Montaigne. It is executed in dark and somber colors.

51. *Le Tasse dans sa prison visité par Montaigne*, Musées Royaux des Beaux-Arts de Belgique.

52. TGC to W. Macleod, 18 January 1876, Corcoran Gallery of Art Archives, Washington, DC.

53. Louis Gallait's painting of *Tasso in Prison* is similar to a painting by Eugene Delacroix entitled *Tasso in the Hospital of St. Anne Ferrara*. Delacroix's Tasso is pictured along with an eerie scene of fellow inmates reaching their arms through the left window's bars, whereas Gallait used a vine creeping through the bars in their place.

54. Washington Art Association (4th Annual Exhibition), Washington, DC, 1860. See Smithsonian American Art Museum, Pre-1877 Art Exhibition Catalogue Index, online at: siris-artexhibition.si.edu.

55. "Girl of Antwerp with two dogs (original in King Leopold's gallery), Copy after Landseer" (No. 34), [Sir Edwin Landseer], oil on canvas museum copy, 27 x 21 ¾ in. (68.58 x 53.34 cm.). The girl of Antwerp is seated and wears a red velvet shawl with fur trim, a white lace mantilla, and gold cross suspended from a black ribbon. In her lap the subject is holding two King Charles spaniels.

56. TGC to W. Macleod, 18 January 1876. Corcoran Gallery of Art Archives.

57. "Magdalene Study after Murillo—DeBlock" (No. 33), "Magdalene" European School, oil on canvas museum study, 20 ¾ x 20 ¼ in. (50.8 x 50.8 cm.). In this painting, Mary Magdalene is looking toward heaven. The subject is wearing a white gown beneath a dark robe and is gazing upward and to her left.

58. "Landscape—Copy of Koekeek by Louis Robbe" (No. 35), Louis Marie Dominique Romain Robbe (Belgian, 1806–1887), oil on canvas copy, 16 ½ x 20 ½ in. (40.64 x 50.8 cm.) panel, 25 x 29 in. (63.5 x 73.66 cm.) frame. The pastoral landscape with cows, a herder, a dog, trees, and a stream is signed *Robbe* in the lower right.

59. "Waterfall—Copy of Auchenbach by L. Robbe" (No. 36), Louis Marie Dominique Romain Robbe (Belgian, 1806–1887), oil on canvas copy "after Andreas Achenbach," 17 ⅝ x 15 ½ in. (43.18 x 38.1 cm.). Depicted in this image is a white-water river in a gorge creating a waterfall cascading in the foreground. A small building is left of the gorge, and a small cabin with a sod roof is on the hill to the right. A man on a horse is pictured approaching the cabin, while the sky is filled with storm clouds.

60. Marinus Adrianus Koekkoek (1807–1868).

61. TGC to W. W. Corcoran, 24 August 1850. A copy of this letter from the Library of Congress Manuscript Division is in Clemson Papers, SCCUL.

62. Marisa Bourgoin to William Hiott, 15 November 2006, Fort Hill Collection, Clemson University. The correspondence is in regard to the Corcoran paintings in the collection of the Gallery. See "19th Century European Paintings from the Collection of the Corcoran Gallery of Art," Auction Catalogue, Sotheby Parke Bernet, 3 May 1979, in the Fort Hill Collection.

63. "Old Man Smoking—Copy after Leys" (No. 43), nineteenth-century copy after Henri Leys (1815–1869), oil on canvas, 11 x 9 in. (27.94 x 22.86 cm.) stretcher size, 17 ⅝ x 16 in. (43.18 x 40.64 cm.) frame. The subject is an old man in Flemish attire and hat. He is seated at a table with a ceramic wine jug and is pictured smoking a pipe while reading.

64. "Peasant girl crossing the water" (No. 37), attributed to François Antoine Bossuet (Belgian, 1800–1889), oil on canvas, 20 ¼ x 16 in. (50.8 x 40.64 cm.). This is a genre scene of a girl walking along a shore's edge with wildflowers gathered in her apron. She is holding a bucket in

her right hand and a basket with a bottle of wine in her left hand. A spaniel follows along, and in the landscape background are a pale blue sky and fluffy white clouds.

65. "The Gate of Alhambra" (No. 38), attributed to Francois Basseret (French, nineteenth century), oil on canvas, 20 x 16 in. (50.8 x 40.64 cm.). This painting shows a procession of revelers, possibly leaving a wedding, passing through the arched gateway while two musicians play guitars. The flanking buildings are decorated, and the details are executed in rich jewel tones.

66. "Beatrice Cenci (Very old Copy)" (No. 39), nineteenth-century museum study after Guido Reni, oil on canvas, 20 ¾ x 16 ¼ in. (50.8 x 40.64 cm.). This is a portrait of Beatrice Cenci depicted as a young girl dressed in a white shawl and turban. With her back to the viewer, the figure is looking back.

67. "Portrait of Mr. T. G. Clemson—DeBlock" (No. 30) and "Portrait of Mrs. Clemson—Jolly" (No. 31), attributed to Henri Jean Baptiste Jolly (Belgian, 1812–1853), have been on loan to Fort Hill in the past and are owned by Thomas Clemson's descendents. The tradition passed down to Lee Calhoun is that the painting, which will eventually come to Fort Hill, is by DeBlock. The family tradition also holds that the original canvas was much larger, but, due to damage, it was cut down to a bust-sized portrait of the same size as the Jolly painting of Anna. Any indication of a signature is therefore lost.

68. "Portrait of Mr. T. G. Clemson—Eeckhout" (No. 47) is unknown and may have been destroyed in transit in the 1880s. Only one Belgian-era portrait of TGC is extant. The existing painting of Thomas G. Clemson is attributed by the family to DeBlock (No. 30) though artistically it has similarities to both DeBlock and Eeckhout.

69. Henry Gourdin to TGC, 26 August 1852, Clemson Papers, SCCUL. The painting of J. Calhoun Clemson shows a youth wearing a red jacket and a lace collar. The boy is sitting and holding his pet dog which resembles a small greyhound or a whippet. A seascape is in the right background.

70. Anna Clemson to John C. Calhoun, 15 April 1849, SCCUL. See also edited copy of letter in Julia Wright Sublette, "The Letters of Anna Calhoun Clemson, 1833–1873" (Ph.D. dissertation, Florida State University, 1993), 448 (hereafter cited as Sublette). Dr. Julia Wright Sublette (13 September 1927–27 January 2009) spent many years transcribing the correspondence of Anna Clemson. See also Lander, *The Calhoun Family and Thomas Green Clemson*, 114, for more about the Clemsons' visit to the United States in 1848–1849.

71. TGC to James Edward Calhoun, 19 March 1852, Clemson Papers, SCCUL.

72. Anna C. Clemson to John C. Calhoun, in Sublette, 458.

73. TGC to James Edward Calhoun, 19 March 1852, Clemson Papers, SCCUL.

74. Henry Gourdin to TGC, 31 January 1852, Clemson Papers, SCCUL.

75. Anna Clemson to John C. Calhoun, 11 April 1847, in Sublette, 422.

76. *Anna Calhoun Clemson* (No. 44), Jacobus Joseph Eeckhout (1793–1861), oil on canvas, 56 x 45 ¼ in. (142.24 x 114.3 cm.) image size, 72 x 61 ¼ in. (182.88 x 154.94 cm.) frame. The subject is wearing a black empire gown and holding a lady's fan. In the left foreground is a white marble top table with ornate carvings. On the table is a long-stemmed flower in a porcelain vase. A scarlet garment is draped on the subject's right. The background features an opening onto a balustrade and distant landscape. A red-colored drape frames the right side opening. The portrait is signed *J. J. Eeckhout 1848* in the lower left.

77. *John Calhoun Clemson* (No. 45), Jacobus Joseph Eeckhout, oil on canvas, 28 ½ x 22 ½ in. (71.12 x 55.88 cm.) image size, 38 ½ x 33 ¼ in. (96.52 x 83.82 cm.) frame. This portrait of Calhoun Clemson as a youth is signed *J. J. Eeckhout 1848* in the upper right.

78. *Floride Clemson* (No. 46), Jacobus Joseph Eeckhout, oil on canvas, 28 x 22 in. (71.12 x 55.88 cm.) image size, 38 ⅝ x 33 in. (96.52 x 83.82 cm.) framed. This portrait shows Floride Elizabeth Clemson as a young girl dressed in a green dress with red ribbons in her braided hair. On the girl's right arm is a large cockatoo whose head has been turned inward to face the subject. This portrait is signed *J. J. Eeckhout 1848* in the lower right.

79. "Portrait of John C. Calhoun" (No. 29), Eugenius F. DeBlock [from a Daguerreotype by Mathew Brady], oil on canvas, 38 ½ x 31 ¾ in. (96.52 x 78.74 cm.). The subject is wearing a crimson frock coat with a black overcoat. The background is muted and devoid of ornamentation. Thomas G. Clemson stated of the image, "this Photograph is of a Daguerreotype taken in 1844, when Mr. Calhoun was Secretary of State, and sent to Europe, from which were

painted the Portraits by Eeckhart and de Block. This is the *best likeness* extant. I carried the Daguerreotype to Europe when Chargé d'Affaires to Belgium." Annotated by James H. Rion: "the above is written on the back of my copy by Mr. Clemson, Mr. Calhoun's son-in-law." Fort Hill Collection, Clemson University.

80. "Portrait of Mrs. John C. Calhoun" (No. 41), attributed to Eugenius F. DeBlock, oil on canvas, 38 ½ x 31 ¾ in. (96.52 x 78.74 cm.). The subject is seated on a sofa and dressed in a black gown with white lace trim. To her left is a table with a single red flower in a vase.

81. "Portrait of Thomas Green Clemson" (No. 30).

82. Anna Maria Calhoun Clemson, "Catalogue of Paintings," Fort Hill Collection, Clemson University.

83. *Chickens*, Thomas Green Clemson, oil on canvas, 14 x 17 in. (35.56 x 43.18 cm.). This painting, set in the interior of a barn, features a Rhode Island Red rooster and a White Leghorn hen, with a background of two pigeons at rest. Its setting replicates the interior barnyard scene in the *Goats and Sheep* by Louis Robbe, not only in subject matter but also in the triangular side light and wall background; only the animals are different.

84. *Old Man Smoking* (ca. 1844–1860), Thomas Green Clemson, oil on canvas, 36 x 28 ½ in. (91.44 x 71.12 cm.). This painting is a copy of the small painting which itself is a museum study of a painting by "Lys." Clemson appears to have painted himself in as the subject, and there are some changes in the impedimenta of the painting.

85. *Thomas Green Clemson* (self-portrait), Thomas Green Clemson, oil on canvas, 29 x 22 in. (73.66 x 55.88 cm.) image with a four-inch wide molding frame. The subject is dressed in a coat with a brown collar and a black tie.

86. *Baker Clemson,* Thomas Green Clemson, oil on canvas, 29 ½ x 25 in. (73.66 x 63.5 cm.). The subject, Thomas Clemson's brother, is dressed in a high-collar shirt.

87. Anna C. Clemson to John C. Calhoun, 15 April 1849, Clemson Papers, SCCUL. See edited copy of letter no. 124 in Sublette, 448.

88. Anna C. Clemson to Floride Clemson, 21 December 1856, in Sublette, 538.

89. Charles M. Leupp to TGC, 10 December 1849, Clemson Papers, SCCUL.

90. TGC to W. W. Corcoran, 24 August 1850. A copy of letter from the Library of Congress Manuscript Division is in Clemson Papers, SCCUL.

91. Ibid.

92. Ibid.

93. Charles M. Leupp to TGC, 19 February 1850, Clemson Papers, SCCUL.

94. Ibid.

95. Charles M. Leupp to TGC, 10 December 1849, Clemson Papers, SCCUL.

96. Ibid.

97. Anna Clemson to Floride Clemson [Philadelphia], 25 October 1857, edited letter No. 179 in Sublette.

98. Annie White Mell, "Clemson Collection of Paintings: Donated to Clemson Agricultural College" (1903), SCCUL. Copy in Mary Stevenson, "Thomas G. Clemson's Collection of Paintings," Clemson College Library, Clemson, SC, 1963.

99. See Holmes and Sherrill, *Thomas Green Clemson*, 35. See also Suzanne Culbertson, "The Clemson Art Collection: $1500 Needed To Restore Paintings," *The Tiger* (Clemson University), 14 May 1965, SCCUL.

100. "Virgin, Child, and St. Joseph in a garland of fruit by Jordaens" (No. 5). The title alludes to the Holy Family set in a cartouche or medallion of a floral piece wreath. There are numerous extant paintings of the Holy Family by Jacob Jordaens; however, none have that exact composition. Five fragments of an oil-on-canvas painting exist in the Fort Hill Collection. The largest is approximately 4 x 2 inches and appears to be a piece of a neckline with white lace on a red and blue cloak. The four smaller fragments are dark background elements, possible furniture details.

101. "Flowers—Robie" (No. 13). Presumably this painting was a floral still life by Jean-Baptiste Robie, a prominent, nineteenth-century, Belgian still-life artist.

102. "Mother Teaching Child—Copy" (No. 40). Unlike the other three paintings, Anna Clemson did not list either the original artist or the copyist. Thomas Clemson offered a slightly different title for the work: "Mother Teaching Son—Copy." There are too many paintings with similar

titles from antiquity and the nineteenth century to determine anything conclusive about the image.

103. "Landscape—Robbe" (No. 16). The painting was more than likely another similar Louis Robbe landscape with a pastoral scene.

104. Photograph of Relic Room of Fort Hill, Fort Hill Collection, Clemson University.

105. The thirty-four paintings are listed by Annie White Mell. See also *Twelfth Annual Report of the Board of Trustees of Clemson Agricultural College* (Columbia, SC: 1901), which referenced the "measures to be taken to renovate the valuable collection of paintings bequeathed by the Hon. T. G. Clemson to Clemson College. A distinguished artist in Washington writes: 'I am very much astonished to find such a galaxy of names of fine old masters are represented in the United States in a single collection. Many of these pictures will be priceless if in good condition.' While they are in fairly good condition now, we ought not to allow them to decay or deteriorate through neglect."

106. Writers' Program, Work Projects Administration, *South Carolina: A Guide to the Palmetto State* (New York: Oxford University Press, 1941), 412.

107. Culbertson, "The Clemson Art Collection: $1,500 Needed to Restore Paintings," *The Tiger* (Clemson University), 14 May 1965, SCCUL. Mary Stevenson, "Thomas G. Clemson's Collection of Paintings," Clemson, SC: Clemson College Library, 1962. Stevenson had a long interest in the art collection and compiled a collection of copies of pertinent correspondence from the Clemson Papers relating to the art, a compilation that was preceded by a three-page introduction.

108. Mary Stevenson to Dr. Harold Cooledge, 4 July 1973, SCCUL. Mary Stevenson took some exception to the text of the brochure regarding the loss of the paintings while under the watch of the library. She went on to ask, "Have the college security officers been notified about the two missing paintings? I don't think that their loss should be vaguely blamed on those responsible for the paintings before 1957, because no paintings at all have ever been lost by the Library or by Fort Hill." After she congratulated him on his hard work on the project, Stevenson reiterated, "I do think that the college authorities should make a very strong effort to locate the two missing pictures."

See also: "Clemson Art Collection Exhibit Set," *Columbia Record* (Columbia, SC), 5 June 1973; "Thomas G. Clemson's Art Collection To Be Exhibited," *Anderson Independent* (Anderson, SC), 6 June 1973; "Thomas Clemson Painting Now Displayed At Clemson," *Anderson Daily Mail* (Anderson, SC), 11 June 1973; "Clemson Art is on Display," *The State* (Columbia, SC), 17 June 1973 ; and Lynne Lucas, "Clemson's hobby yields prize art," *Greenville News and Piedmont* (Greenville, SC), 10 September 1978, SCCUL.

109. Mary Stevenson, "Old Frames at Ashtabula," 1973, SCCUL. The bulk of the art collection was restored in the early 1970s and reframed. The original frames were stored for many years at Ashtabula in Pendleton, SC, with the assistance of longtime librarian and local historian, Mary Stevenson. As she wrote, "In 1973, when I noticed that the paintings collected by Thomas G. Clemson *had been reframed* when they were restored by the Clemson Alumni Association…I was afraid they [original frames] had been destroyed or given to the people who restored the paintings." Mary Stevenson had the frames brought to Ashtabula where some were used to frame other pictures. Nine of the original frames were reacquired by Fort Hill in 1999. Although a costly procedure, some of the original frames are restorable. While others are beyond repair, they provide an example for appropriate reproduction frames for the collection, since Thomas Clemson often had custom-made frames for his artwork.

110. The appraisal bill more than likely listed Clemson's *Madonna and Child*, *Old Man Smoking*, *Chickens*, and possibly the *Baker Clemson* portrait in place of the other four paintings that were missing earlier from Anna Clemson's list. The grand total of paintings in the five categories would actually come to fifty-two paintings. Fort Hill houses other family portraits and art, such as Hiram Powers's marble bust of Cornelia (Nina) Clemson and a portrait of Thomas G. Clemson as a young man in France, painted by James Ord. Other busts and paintings attributed to American artists, along with art that John C. Calhoun collected, are omitted from the discussion here, which is specifically related to the Thomas Green Clemson Art Collection.

The author is indebted to the century and a half of scholarship on the Thomas G. Clemson Art Collection, most notably the Catalogue of Anna Clemson in 1852, Thomas G. Clemson's listing in 1876, Annie White Mell's listing in 1910, and, more recently, to Dr. W. R. Valentiner's descriptions in 1958, Mary Stevenson's descriptions in 1963, Dr. Harold Cooledge's catalogue in 1973, and subsequent insurance appraisals by the late William S. Belser and Frank A. Sarnowski Jr., beginning in 1993, and painting conservation assessments and restoration by Craig Crawford, AIC, beginning in 2005, which were funded by a Save America's Treasures Grant.

Anna Calhoun Clemson's 1852 "Catalogue of Pictures"

**About the Appendix:** This transcription of Anna Clemson's "Catalogue of Pictures" maintains her attributions, spellings, and punctuations. Entries 5, 7, 13, 16, 40, and 47 are missing from the collection. Thomas Clemson's own paintings, not included in Anna's 1852 catalogue, appear on page 222.

> 1852
> Catalogue of Pictures
> No. 1 Virgin & Child by P.P. Ruben, Painted for a friend's chapel
> 2 Head by Velasquez
> 3 Landscape by Poupin
> 4 Flower Piece by Zeghers (the Jesuit) Medallion by Teniers
> 5 Virgin, Child, & St Joseph in a garland of fruit by Jordaen
> 6 Fruit &c &c by De Heem
> 7 Students Repast Van Son
> 8 Peasant with soup Frank...
> 9 Adoration (on copper) Franck
> 10 Boy mending pen Spanish
> 11 The Philosopher (supposed to be Rembrandt or Ferdinand Bol?)
> 12 Head — Study by Grenze
> 13 Flowers Robie
> 14 Cattle L. Robbe
> 15 Goats & Sheep ditto
> 16 Landscape ditto

# CATALOGUE TRANSCRIPTION, WITH THUMBNAILS OF PAINTINGS

## 1852
## Catalogue of Pictures

1. Virgin & Child by P. P. Rubens. Painted for a friend's chapel.

2. Head by Velasquez

3. Landscape by Poussin

4. Flower Piece by Zeghers (the Jesuit) Medallion by Teniers

5. Virgin, Child, & St. Joseph in a Garland of Fruit by Jordain

6. Fruit by DeHeem

7. Student's Repast— Van Son

8. Peasant with Soup— Frank Hals

9. Adoration (on copper)—Franck

10. Boy Mending Pen— Spanish

11. The Philosopher (supposed to be Rembrandt or Ferdinand Bols)

12. Head—Study by Greuze

13. Flowers—Robie

14. Cattle—L. Robbe

15. Goats & Sheep—Ditto

16. Landscape—Ditto

1.

2.

3.

4.

5. *[Missing]*

6.

7. *[Missing]*

8.

9.

10.

11.

12.

13. *[Missing]*

14.

15.

16. *[Missing]*

| No | | |
|---|---|---|
| 17 | Magdalen | Van Schendael |
| 18 | Landscapes by Fearnley | |
| 19 | a Swedish painter | |
| 20 | Gate Way — | Tavernier |
| 21 | Titian & lacing his model | Eeckhout |
| 22 | The Quarrel & Reconcilia- | |
| 23 | tion | Vennerman |
| 24 | Two Old men | Ditto |
| 25 | Scene in Spain | Bosuet |
| 26 | Marine view in Holland — | Francia |
| 27 | Poverty & Suffering | De Block |
| 28 | Group of Lambs | Robbe |
| 29 | Portrait of Hon. J.C. Calhoun | De Block |
| 30 | Portrait of T.G Clemson | ditto |
| 31 | " of Mrs Clemson | Jolly |
| 32 | Tasso in prison visited by Montaigne | |
|  | (original in King Leopolds Gallery) | |
|  | Copy after Gallait | |
| 33 | Magdalen Study after Murillo | De Block |
| 34 | Girl of Antwerp with two dogs | |
|  | (original) in KingLeopolds gallery) | |
|  | Copy after Landseer | |

17. Magdalen—Van Schendael

18. Landscape by Fearnley

19. Landscape by Fearnley

20. Gateway—Tavernier

21. Titian Placing his Model—Eeckhout

22. The Quarrel—Venneman

23. The Reconciliation—Venneman

24. Two Old Men—Ditto

25. Scene in Spain—Bossuet

26. Marine View in Holland—Francia

27. Poverty and Suffering—DeBlock

28. Group of Lambs—Robbe

29. Portrait of Hon. J. C. Calhoun—DeBlock

30. Portrait of T. G. Clemson—Ditto

31. Portrait of Mrs. Clemson—Jolly

32. Tasso in Prison visited by Montaigne (Original in King Leopold's Gallery)—Copy after Gallait

33. Magdalen Study after Murillo DeBlock

34. Girl of Antwerp with two dogs (Original in King Leopold's Gallery)—Copy after Landseer

17.

18.

19.

20.

21.

22.

23.

24.

25.

26.

27.

28.

29.

30.

31.

32.

33.

34.

| No. 35 | Landscape Copy of Koekoek by Louis Robbe |
| 36 | Water Fall Copy of Auchenbach by L. Robbe |
| 37 | Peasant girl crossing the water |
| 38 | Gate of the Alhambra - Copy of Bisprut |
| 39 | Beatrice Cenci - very old Copy |
| 40 | Mother teaching child - Copy |
| 41 | Portrait of Mr J. C. Calhoun |
| 42 | Landscape |
| 43 | Old Man Smoking Copy after Leys |
| 44 | Portrait of Mrs Anna C. Clemson Eckhart |
| 45 | " of John Calhoun Clemson - ditto |
| 46 | " of Floride E. Clemson ditto |
| 47 | " of Mr T. G. Clemson ditto |

35. Landscape Copy of Koekoek by Louis Robbe

36. Waterfall Copy of Auchenbach by L. Robbe

37. Peasant Girl Crossing the Water

38. Gate of the Alhambra —Copy of Bossuet

39. Beatrice Cenci (Very old Copy)

40. Mother Teaching Child—Copy

41. Portrait of Mrs. J. C. Calhoun

42. Landscape

43. Old Man Smoking— Copy after Leys

44. Portrait of Mrs. Anna C. Clemson— Eeckhout

45. Portrait of John Calhoun Clemson— ditto

46. Portrait of Floride E. Clemson—ditto

47. Portrait of Mr. T. G. Clemson—ditto

35.

36.

37.

38.

39.

40. *[Missing]*

41.

42.

43.

44.

45.

46.

47. *[Missing; see page 212, note 68]*

### Addition to the Appendix

Anna Clemson's 1852 "Catalogue of Pictures" did not include Thomas Clemson's own works of art. His extant paintings are as follows:

**Thomas Green Clemson
self-portrait**

**Baker Clemson
portrait**

*Chickens*

*Madonna and Child*

*Old Man Smoking*

# Chapter 10

# MUSIC IN THE LIFE AND WORLD OF THOMAS GREEN CLEMSON

## *Andrew Levin*

Rob,

Enjoy! Our
founder was
a musician!
(of sorts)

Andrew Levin

**Violin of Richard W. Simpson, Thomas Green Clemson's friend, attorney, and executor of his estate. Originally, the instrument may have belonged to Clemson. Fort Hill Collection, Clemson University. Gift of the Simpson family.**

Although a good deal is known about Clemson's painting and interest in art through his correspondence and collection, there is little in his letters or papers that directly addresses his interest or participation in music.

Scholars have mentioned in passing that he attended the opera, played the violin, married into a musical family, and encouraged music-making in his own home. But is there more to know? This chapter, with the help of diaries, journals, and other sources, will attempt to answer that question by first establishing a context of classical, popular, and dance music in the locales and times in which the Clemsons lived, and then by examining the musical Calhouns, Colhouns, and Clemson family itself. The final part of the answer will be found in a study of Thomas Green Clemson as a violinist and composer of simple tunes.

## Paris

There are no extant records that describe Clemson's attendance at musical performances in Paris (1826–1831, 1832–1837) or Brussels (1844–1851). However, given his love for music and his later participation in music-making at home, it is probable that he attended musical events in these large, culturally active cities.

Paris had a mature, vibrant operatic and concert life during Clemson's years in the city. Opera was especially popular, with the city supporting a number of production companies. These included the Paris Opéra, specializing in dramatic works and developing the new grand opera genre; the Théâtre (National) de l'Opéra-Comique, featuring comic opera; the Théâtre Italien, instituted some years earlier by Napoleon himself, due to his interest in Italian opera; and a number of smaller companies. The Italian opera composer Rossini, who spent most of his later years in France, directed the Théâtre Italien from 1824 to 1826. His final opera, *Guillaume Tell*, was commissioned by and premiered at the Opéra in 1829.[1]

Scholar Julia Wright Sublette, editor of Anna Calhoun Clemson's letters, suggests that Clemson courted Anna Calhoun at the opera in Washington, D.C., in 1838, comparing the local production to what he had seen in Europe. Whatever the case, it is intriguing to think he may have witnessed the original production of *Guillaume Tell* while a student in Paris.

Orchestral music in Paris was not as fully supported as opera during these years, with various concert series coming and going over the decades. But in 1828 a concert series was initiated by the new Société des Concerts du Conservatoire. This ensemble was composed of former and current students of the Paris Conservatory and in its first few concerts devoted entire programs to Beethoven, thus establishing Beethoven's presence in France.[2] It was this orchestra that premiered a most radical work for its time, Hector Berlioz's *Symphonie fantastique*. The year was 1830, when Clemson was living in Paris and during which he participated in the July 1830 revolts that brought down the King of France. Again, it is exciting to think he may have attended an early performance of this famous work.

## Brussels

Brussels also had an active musical scene when the Clemsons lived in this capital city. Orchestral concerts took place at the Conservatoire Royal de Musique and the Koninklijk Muziekconservatorium and featured classical music and conservative contemporary works. There were also presentations of "historical concerts" featuring music of the sixteenth, seventeenth, and eighteenth centuries, as well as concerts featuring certain genres, such as church music, dance music, and choral music.[3]

Opera was also quite popular, with productions centered around the opera house La Monnaie. Many operas of Italian masters were performed there, often in their first French-language productions; these included works by Rossini, Bellini, Donizetti, and Verdi. The company also performed works by the German Meyerbeer as well as French and Belgian composers.[4] Given their past experiences and interest in opera, and the likely expectation that government officials attend cultural events, one assumes the Clemsons attended the opera in Brussels.

## Classical Music in the New World

Both the Calhoun and Clemson families were patrons of and participants in classical music in America. In colonial times this music was class entertainment, just as it was in England. It was cultivated in the homes of educated Americans, as something expected from wealthy, sophisticated persons. This was true especially in the large cities and in the South. Southern families patterned much of their behavior on English models, and with classical music this was no different: they favored English composers, English performers, and even patterned concert events after the English. Charleston, South Carolina, for example, replicated the Vauxhall Gardens of London.

From early on Charleston was a center of commerce and culture, and it was home to the second known public concert (1732) and the first opera performance (1735) to take place in the colonies. Among the few but highly skilled musicians in Charleston was Charles Theodore Pachelbel, son of Johann Pachelbel, the famous organist and composer of the now ubiquitous *Canon in D*. Thus, long before the Civil War, Charleston had an active cultural calendar, which included concerts, balls, and theatrical productions. Many famous European musicians performed in Charleston on their concert tours, including the Norwegian violinist Ole Bull, the "Swedish Nightingale" Jenny Lind, the Italian opera singer Adelina Patti, and the German piano virtuoso Sigismond Thalberg.[5]

Philip Vickers Fithian, a known diarist and tutor at a Virginia plantation, wrote in the 1770s about the skills required of educated young men. He noted that "any young Gentleman traveling through the Colony...is presum'd to be ac-

quainted with Dancing, Boxing, playing the Fiddle, & Small-Sword, & Cards."[6]
Of the women he wrote:

> She has but lately had opportunity of Instruction in Dancing, yet she moves
> with propriety when she dances a Minuet & without any *Flirts* or vulgar *Ca-*
> *pers.…*.She plays well on the Harpsichord, & Spinet; understands the principles
> of Musick, & therefore performs her Tunes in perfect time, a Neglect of which
> always makes music intolerable,…She sings likewise to her instrument, has a
> strong, full voice, & a well-judging Ear.[7]

Such musical education was often provided by itinerant music teachers. Writing
in 1858 to her daughter Floride of some neighborhood girls in Maryland, Anna
Clemson notes, "They have a music master, to come out & give them lessons."[8]

In light of this tradition of music lessons and at-home performances, it is
interesting to remember that many of our famous, early statesmen were also amateur musicians. Examples include Thomas Jefferson (violin and voice), Patrick
Henry (violin), Governor Penn of Philadelphia (violin), Benjamin Franklin (guitar and harp), and the first Secretary of the Navy Francis Hopkinson (organ and
harpsichord).

In the nineteenth century, German and Italian opera became very popular in
the States, replacing the favor formerly shown to English music. At first, this complicated European music was made more palatable to its audiences: it was sung in
English translation, the sung recitative was converted to spoken dialogue, and the
music itself was simplified. However, as the Civil War approached, opera was presented in a manner closer to its initial conception, with fewer simplifications and
in the original language. But as with other types of classical music, its very cost
kept the lower classes away, and opera was enjoyed mostly by those of wealth.

Classical music also found its way into the parlors of the middle and upper
classes. With the Industrial Revolution came an explosion of piano manufacturing; quality instruments were built in this country at a price wealthier families
could afford. Thus learning piano became *de rigueur* for educated young ladies.
The music publishing industry responded, releasing large quantities of sheet music, such as popular tunes, dance melodies, original classical music, arrangements
of opera, and more.[9]

### *Dance Music in the United States*

Social dancing was very important to the wealthy class. The Calhouns and
Clemsons all danced or were trained in social dancing. Young people were instructed by visiting or local dance masters, enabling them to learn the steps and
grace to mix in polite society. Balls were held in public places, such as hotels, at
travel destinations like hot springs, and even in large homes.

Dance music in the United States was patterned after the European model. For instance, the waltz came from Vienna, the quadrille and cotillion from Paris, and the polka from Bohemia in eastern Europe. Contradances were danced to jigs, hornpipes, and reels from England, Ireland, and Scotland. Social dancing underwent considerable change in the course of the nineteenth century: early on, dancers gathered into either four-couple groups or two opposing lines and moved to prescribed dance steps. However, as the century progressed, more dances were executed as couples' dances, when the intimacy required of them was increasingly tolerated.

In the early part of the century dances were accompanied by just a violin or two. As the piano gained in popularity, it took a part in providing dance music, either alone or with the violin. But as the venues became larger, dance bands likewise became larger.[10] A typical ensemble would include two violins, flute, clarinet, cornet, and a bass instrument (usually a cello), with optional piano or harp.[11]

Many people of wealth "took the waters": they vacationed at hot springs for health reasons and for pleasure. In addition to the springs themselves, these establishments also offered a variety of social activities, including music and dance. Popular resort areas in the South included Glen (or Glenn) Springs, South Carolina; Warm Springs in Buncombe County, North Carolina (now called Hot Springs); and Warm Springs and White Sulphur Springs in Virginia. Many South Carolina planters "figured prominently in the attempt to develop spas and mountain resorts in the up country."[12]

Floride Colhoun Calhoun (Anna Calhoun's mother, Mrs. J. C. Calhoun) frequented a number of these springs. Her favorite was Glen Springs, just fifteen miles south of Spartanburg,[13] but she also took the cure at White Sulphur Springs.[14] Different businesses offered different amenities, including dancing, billiards, music, hunting, and fishing.[15] Often there was informal music-making after dinner as well as evening performances by amateurs or itinerant professionals. Later at night, guests could attend a ball, where they might dance "the German cotillion, Spanish dance, Virginia reel, quadrille, and waltz. The number of musicians varied from a single Negro fiddler to a full band or orchestra."[16]

A great deal of dance music was arranged for piano and would likely have been played by the young Anna Calhoun and later her daughter Floride. Anna's cousin Martha Colhoun played piano and, as will be discussed later, even published two sets of waltzes.

## Popular Music in the United States

The Calhouns and Clemsons also enjoyed popular music, as noted in various letters and diary entries. One form that was very popular, both at home and on the stage, was minstrel music. Before the Civil War, minstrel singers toured the country (mostly in the North), presenting a sort of vaudeville show. White singers, usually Northerners, performed various sketches and songs in blackface. Minstrel songs, often called "Ethiopian melodies," were simple, catchy melodies in a lively, dance-like tempo. While the performers portrayed slaves, the music they sang was not based on actual slave melodies. In fact, before the Civil War, most minstrel songs were based on decidedly Anglo-American music: popular tunes, traditional folk tunes, and even Italian opera melodies. A number of Stephen Foster's songs are of this style, including *Old Folks at Home* and *Old Uncle Ned*,[17] two songs Thomas Clemson is known to have played on his violin.

Songs created in nineteenth-century America became an important part of the American landscape, played at home and performed on stage. As scholar Michael Hamm points out, many of the songs written in the post-Civil Wars years

> that poured from the American presses in the second half of the nineteenth century are direct descendants of Thomas Moore's *Irish Melodies* and Stephen Foster's plantation songs. Their sentiment is personal, their musical means are simple enough to allow amateur singers and pianists to give a decent account of them, [and] they are verse-chorus songs with a prevailing mood of gentle nostalgia….American songs of the mid-nineteenth century were widely sung, reprinted, and imitated in England and elsewhere in Europe. They were one of this country's contributions to the style and spirit of what came to be known as the Victorian era.[18]

As will be discussed later in more detail, Anna Calhoun Clemson's letters and Floride Clemson's diary make many references to popular songs they heard or played, showing the importance of this music in their lives.

### Classical Music in Washington, D.C.

When Anna Calhoun attended performances of Rossini's *Il Barbiere di Siviglia* and Bellini's *La Somnambula* in 1838, she witnessed a fairly new phenomenon: European opera in the United States capital city. Rossini's *Barbiere* was the first, performed in 1836 and in English translation. The operas were produced at the National Theatre and featured works in the *bel canto* style, mostly by the Italians Rossini, Bellini, and Donizetti. In the second half of the century the fare expanded to include operettas, musical comedies, and grand opera.[19] During the Civil War years Anna and Floride Clemson attended the opera in Washington, D.C., many times, hearing works by Verdi, Mozart, Bellini, Donizetti, and perhaps more.[20]

In addition to opera, music lovers in the nation's capital also had the pleasure of hearing musical fireworks by traveling piano virtuosi, Mozart's *Requiem* by choral societies, and fine music in churches—all of which the Clemsons did when they lived in Maryland in the 1850s and 1860s.[21]

## *The Upstate of South Carolina*

Patrons of classical music in nineteenth-century America had many opportunities to hear fine music, but these usually took place in the larger cities. Members of the Calhoun and Clemson families enjoyed the opera and concert music in Paris, Brussels, Washington, D.C., and Charleston; however, there were far fewer opportunities for such activities in upstate South Carolina. Still, due to the unusual qualities of Pendleton, South Carolina, its residents and visitors were able to enjoy such music, though on a much smaller scale. The Pendleton area boasted many residents of wealth and culture, who brought to the region a love of classical and popular music as well as dance. Since the early eighteenth century, lowcountry planters had been attracted to the Pendleton area for a respite from summer heat and disease. They purchased farms and built large, sumptuous residences. Some were so attracted to the area that they made it their permanent home. These new residents not only farmed but also contributed to the emerging society. As Samuel Gaillard Stoney explained in 1938:

> The Piedmont villages of Pendleton, Greenville, Spartanburg, and Winnsboro owed much to these planter sojourners, who not only contributed to their population and society but also patronized and helped to establish some of their institutions and facilities, such as schools, churches, hotels and public houses, roads and stage lines.[22]

Pendleton became a "sparkling, cosmopolitan and intellectually stimulating society, moving in the surroundings of luxury and culture. There were afternoon parties, lavish dinners and spectacular balls."[23] In time Pendleton developed "a extended reputation for elegance, refinement and hospitality second to very few places in the State."[24]

Social dancing was important to Pendleton residents. For example, members of the Pendleton Dancing Club, taught by an English dancing master, held many balls in such places as the Pendleton Hotel, the Blue Ridge House, the Dickenson Hotel, and, perhaps most memorably, the Tom Cherry Hotel.[25] In 1891, writing of times fifty years earlier, David U. Sloan reminisced, "and who of her old citizens do not remember the long ball-room in the old Tom Cherry Hotel, and the beautiful young girls who once skimmed like swallows over those well-waxed floors?"[26]

Wealthy families in Pendleton, like those in other parts of the country, must have valued music-making among its youth, as evidenced by music teachers who lived in the area. Among those buried in the graveyard of St. Paul's Episcopal Church in Pendleton is a Madam Girard, perhaps a Polish countess. It is said she was the first woman to play violin on the American stage; she also sang opera.

Known as Mrs. Pinkind (by her second marriage), she lived in the area at the time of the Civil War until her death.[27]

When passing through the area in 1837, George W. Featherstonhaugh, a noted British geologist and traveler, commented in his diary about an entertaining evening enriched by some home music-making:

> After partaking of an excellent dinner we adjourned for the evening to the portico where by the aid of a guitar accompanied by a pleasing voice and some capital curds and cream, we prolonged a most agreeable conversazione until a late hour.[28]

For upstate residents desiring a higher quality music and theatre, they could travel as close as Greenville and Spartanburg, where traveling companies of musicians and actors performed.[29]

### *Music in the Calhoun and Colhoun Families*

Within these international, national, regional, and local contexts, the place of music in the Calhoun, Colhoun, and Clemson families can be viewed more clearly and in greater detail. For example, Floride Colhoun Calhoun, John C. Calhoun's wife, was a pianist and organist of some skill. She played the organ at

Floride Colhoun Calhoun's grand square piano was manufactured by H. Worcester of New York and purchased from B. Newhouse & Co. in Mobile, Alabama. Displayed on the piano is a waltz from *Keowee Waltzes* composed by Mrs. Calhoun's niece, Martha Maria Colhoun. Fort Hill Collection, Clemson University.

Trinity Episcopal Church during summers in Newport, Rhode Island.[30] She also apparently led a subscription effort to purchase an organ for St. Paul's Episcopal Church in Pendleton, "because she bacame [sic] tired of having to 'lift' a tune with the aid of a tuning fork."[31] In addition, the two pianos now in the Fort Hill mansion were both hers. As Frank A. Dickson points out, "One feature of the parlor is the rosewood spinet, which, made in England, was acquired by Mrs. Calhoun in her girlhood, and with it is her music book that has her name inscribed in it." Regarding the second piano, Dickson continues, "Mrs. Calhoun's large square grand piano was contributed to Fort Hill by the heirs of Mrs. T. J. Mauldin of Pickens. It was sold after Mrs. Calhoun's death in 1866 to Mrs. Mauldin's father, a resident of Charleston."[32]

When South Carolina seceded from the union, Floride Colhoun Calhoun was concerned not only for her family still in Maryland, but for their finer possessions as well. As Julia Wright Sublette notes, "A flurry of letters from Floride Colhoun Calhoun urged the Clemsons at Bladensburg to lock up their silver, to send Floride's piano south, and to bring the whole family on to Pendleton while it was still possible."[33]

The Calhouns' eldest daughter Anna was a well-educated woman who, before she married, assisted her father, U.S. Senator John C. Calhoun, in his activities in Washington, D.C. Her parents sent her, at age fourteen,[34] to Barhamville, formally known as the South Carolina Female Collegiate Institute, located just outside of Columbia, South Carolina. Established in 1826, it counted as its graduates Ann Pamela Cunningham, the founder of the Mount Vernon Association, and Martha ("Mittie") Bulloch [Roosevelt], the mother of President Theodore Roosevelt. It boasted a four-year curriculum and a faculty that included European teachers. The music program was especially known for its creativity. Its music teachers were arrangers, composers, and performers, who taught piano, guitar, and singing, if not more. The school closed its doors in 1865 when the women were evacuated for their own safety in advance of Sherman's army. The school never reopened.[35]

The sixteen-year-old Anna Calhoun wrote to her school friend Maria Simkins in 1833, speaking of her own guitar playing: "I have improved a good deal and learnt several very pretty tunes since I saw you but do not intend to play for any person at least this summer so you will have that pleasure all to yourself."[36] She also learned about guitar playing from one of her uncles (perhaps James) and requested help from her brother James Edward Calhoun. Writing to him in 1833 she requested, "I also want your assistance on my guitar, though they tell me I am much improved since you heard me; and I want your opinion on my new guitar stand, which I think quite pretty."[37] Anna was also concerned about very practical musical matters: purchasing new strings for her instrument. In 1837 she reminded her friend Maria, "dont [sic] forget your guitar and the strings I wrote to ask you to get for I am now on my last set and Uncle James says he had none to

Left and below: *Barhamville, Valse Brillante pour le Piano* by Manuel M. Párraga, who taught at Barhamville. (New York: William Hall & Son, 1854). Library of Congress, sm1854 240360.

bring me and I dont [sic] know what we shall do if you forget to bring some."[38]

Anna's social activities in Washington, D.C., included music and dance. At one party she "spent the evening very merrily in waltzing playing magical music and hearing Miss Slakum and Mr. May sing duetts [sic], which they do quite prettily."[39] She also attended the opera in the nation's capital. She wrote to both Maria Simkins and her brother Patrick about the two operas she saw in one week: Rossini's *Il Barbiere di Siviglia* and Bellini's *La Somnambula*. To Maria she wrote that she thoroughly enjoyed herself, for the "wit and merriment" of the former and the "fine singing and

music" in both of them. Specifically, she noted that one singer "was said to be well sustained, by those who are judges of such matters" and that she does not wonder "at the passion for operas, in Europe, where they are so much better got up, when even this inferior specimen gave me so much delight."[40]

A week later in Washington, Anna was serenaded by a harpist in the evening. Julia Wright Sublette suspects Clemson's participation in both the serenade and the evenings at the opera:

> It is highly probable that the serenade was arranged by Thomas G. Clemson, whose courtship of Anna would have had to be well under way by this time. Anna's guarded references are consistent with the tone of the two letters which precede this one, in which she refers with enthusiasm to her evenings at the opera, 'so much better got up in Europe' (probably a reflection of Clemson's critique, based on his extensive European experience, which he would almost surely have discussed with Anna).[41]

Anna was not the only one in the Calhoun family who played music and danced. Anna's brothers took dancing lessons from a dancing master in Pendleton in 1840,[42] her brother William played fiddle, and her brother James Edward played guitar. William Lowndes Calhoun must have been a real lover of music. In writing to her brother Patrick of the Christmas activities in 1839, Anna noted that William played *Come Haste to the Wedding* "(the only tune he knows)...on the fiddle, marvelously out of tune, & time, but it answered the purpose as well as better music would have done, with the children."[43] But he would also go to great lengths to hear fine singing. In writing to her daughter Anna, Floride mentioned that "Willy was just on the eve of going to Charleston, to hear Jenny Lind sing, he said he would hear her, if it broke him."[44] It is not known if he actually attended the event.

Special mention must be made of Martha Maria ("Cuddy" or "Coody") Colhoun, daughter of Col. John Ewing Colhoun and first cousin of Anna Calhoun Clemson. Martha was an extraordinarily talented young lady who made a strong impression upon her family and friends, but then died of the family scourge (tuberculosis) at the age of twenty-seven. She was a welcome and frequent guest at Fort Hill and "high-spirited and sociable, was greatly loved by the Fort Hillians and welcomed on any occasion."[45] According to Col. James T. Bacon, editor of the *Edgefield Chronicle* and an accomplished musician,

> She was an enthusiastic, fearless, inimitable horse woman—the lightest and airiest of waltzers—she played beautifully on the piano! People would assemble on the piazza late in the afternoon to see Miss Cuddie ride off on horse back. People would assemble in the ball room to see Miss Cuddie waltz. People would gather around the piano at all hours to hear Miss Cuddie play. She had composed and published a set of very pretty waltzes named *Keowee Waltzes*, in honor of her na-

tive river, and all the men whistled them. In those days women—ladies—did not whistle; they would as soon have thought of whistling as chewing gum![46]

Her waltzes were published in two "setts," each set containing a handful of waltzes and other dances. Each dance is named after a nearby place name, such as "Jocassee," "Tallulah," etc., and are, as a whole, quite charming. They were published in Charleston in 1847 with an engraving on the cover that likely portrays the John Ewing Colhoun family plantation known as Keowee. Also on the cover are the title and author of the work: *Keowee Waltzes, composed and arranged for the Pianoforte by a Lady of South Carolina.* Although it cannot be known for certain, it is tempting to credit Martha Colhoun with two other pieces composed by "A Lady of South Carolina": the *Jasper Guards March* (1849), which was dedicated to the Officers and Members of the Jasper Guards of Charleston, South Carolina, and the *Volunteer March* (1847), dedicated to the Palmetto Regiment.[47]

**Keowee Waltzes by Martha Maria ("Cuddy") Colhoun (Charleston, S.C.: George Oates, 1847). Special Collections, Clemson University Libraries.**

## *Music in the Clemson Family*

Anna continued to play piano as she approached her marriage. After return-ing to Fort Hill in 1838, Anna wrote to her friend Maria of the "most superb piano" given to her by her uncle James: "It graces the drawing room, and I, for the present, grace it, for some time every day, endeavoring to recall all the little knowl-edge I formerly possessed."[48] This is in odd contradiction to an account given by Floride Calhoun. She wrote to her daughter-in-law Margaret Calhoun about the activities at the newlywed Clemsons' new home: "They bought a splendid piano. Maria [Simkins] told me they intend setting out in style."[49] Perhaps Floride did not know the piano was a gift from her son James.

As the Clemson children grew older they too began to learn music and so-cial dancing. When the family resided in Brussels, Anna enrolled her children in dancing lessons. Calhoun was eight at the time and Floride was six.[50] The children were also encouraged in this activity by their uncle William, who wrote: "I would like so much to hear you & little Sissy sing, and see you dance. You must learn all the European dances, and teach them to me when you come home, for a great many of them we never see."[51]

Floride Clemson showed a real affinity for music, excelling in both piano and singing. Much can be learned about music-making in the Clemson family from Anna's 1850s letters to her daughter, who at the time was attending school in Pennsylvania. In an 1858 letter Anna encouraged Floride to practice her music, in order to please her mother: "I shall expect to see you much improved, when you come home....You know how fond I am of music, & when you think what pleasure you can give me, particularly in singing, I am sure you will take the trouble to be prepared to give me that pleasure."[52] In another letter Anna explains why Floride should apply herself to her musical studies. In developing her voice and understanding of music, she will be able to "give pleasure to others, under all circumstances, & if necessary may make you independent, by becoming a means of supporting yourself."[53]

Floride returned from school in the summer of 1857 and apparently played music often. At the time the Clemsons' youngest daughter Cornelia ("Nina")—who also showed some musical aptitude—was not even two years old. Yet after Floride returned to school in September, Anna wrote her daughter that Nina "often talks of you but cannot be induced to touch the piano herself or let me do so, since you left. Is it not singular?"[54]

As noted earlier, educated young ladies learned to accompany themselves sing-ing, either on the piano or guitar. Floride must have been learning this skill, for in 1858 Anna wrote to her daughter, "I shall expect to see you much improved, when you come home, especially I expect you will be able to accompany yourself, (in some of your songs at least,) that I may have the pleasure of hearing your voice, which others praise so highly."[55] Floride, in turn, enjoyed sharing her music with family and friends. While visiting her grandmother and namesake Floride Colhoun Calhoun in 1859 and 1860, she entertained her by playing piano several hours a day and singing for her.[56]

Not just music but dancing also occupied Anna's thoughts. As the Clemsons made improvements to their Maryland house in 1858, she noted the size of the new piazza, measuring thirty-seven by twelve feet, "& as the floor is beautiful, it will be a fine place to dance—two quadrilles could easily be formed in it, or a *very long Virginia reel.*"[57]

With the arrival of the Civil War, both Thomas Green and son Calhoun Clemson joined the Confederate cause; however, this did not temper especially Floride's musical activities. During this time, while still in Maryland, she continued to sing and play for others. She wrote often about her singing and others' impressions of it: "My singing is much liked, especially in Southern songs. All are Southern here almost."[58] And with the war raging, Floride attended the opera in Washington, D.C., as her mother had twenty-five years earlier. Both mother and daughter attended performances of Mozart's *Don Giovanni* and Verdi's *Il Trovatore*, accompanied by D. Williamson Lee, a financial advisor of Thomas Clemson and a brother of Gideon Lee Jr., Floride's future husband. Floride wrote in her diary of the performances: "The house was wretched, & the scenery worse. The singing very good. The roads were dreadful, & the nights dark. I enjoyed it exceedingly."[59] Three nights later she attended a performance of Bellini's *Norma* (the third time she had seen this opera). Four days after that, she heard the American piano virtuoso Louis Moreau Gottschalk and, after another four days, attended a performance of Donizetti's *Lucia di Lammermoor.*[60] A busy schedule indeed!

Floride's dancing lessons also served her well at this time, as dancing was an important component of her social activities. As she wrote in her diary: "The night before last, I went to the Commencement ball, & to the commencement in the morning. I was dressed in a white spotted muslin, & danced every set. We got to bed at 5 o'clock in the broad day-light!"[61]

Floride sang not just alone but in church choirs as well. During the war she sang in choirs in Baltimore and Beltsville, Maryland, then later in Pendleton after the war. She also enjoyed listening to fine choral singing, as evidenced by her attending a performance of Mozart's *Requiem* in Washington, D.C.[62]

Floride's mother, Anna Clemson, had a fine ear for music, and when played badly she could not keep from noting it. She wrote to her daughter in 1863 of some soldiers and their music at two nearby places of entertainment:

> There is quite (an almost nightly) nuisance, in the shape of that execrable band from Ft. Lincoln, which comes to make night hideous, for several hours, at Yosts & Barney's. No two instruments accord, & they neither play in time or tune, nor any tune worth hearing, so the only effect they produce is setting one's teeth on edge.[63]

The years following the Civil War were very difficult for upcountry residents, both personally and financially. It is unbelievable to read, then, that a month after the surrender at Appomattox, as marauding Union soldiers marched through the Pendleton area and with Thomas Clemson and his son still away, Anna Clemson bought her daughter a piano! Floride recorded in her diary:

> Mother got me a piano last Monday from Mr. Groaning's, one of Hazelton's [a New York piano manufacturer]. 7 1/4 octaves. The treble is very sweet, but the base [sic] not very full. It is much handsomer than my Steinvoch, but not so fine, as an instrument. *A bird in the* &c. I have also a nice carved music stand, & stool, with it. All for $350 gold.[64]

Floride wasn't the only Clemson child with musical talent. Writing in 1865 after her brother returned from the war, she wrote that Calhoun's "voice is musical in speaking, but he does not sing much although he has more ear than I have."[65] No small praise by a young lady who often spoke highly of her own good singing.

### *Thomas Green Clemson's Music*

In summing up Clemson's "hobby" of music, Holmes and Sherrill, in their 1937 biography *Thomas Green Clemson: His Life and Work*, make a claim regarding Clemson's skills and interests in music: "Nothing whatsoever is known about his skill and accomplishment as a musician, but one would judge from the very nature of the man that he would either be interested in the old masters and the classics or that he would not be interested at all."[66] This contention, however, is hard to support. While Clemson apparently enjoyed attending the opera and supported his daughter's musical studies, he also enjoyed various aspects of popular music: he danced; he played minstrel songs, other popular songs, and church hymns on his violin; and he wrote a few polkas and a "national air"—hardly music of the "old masters"!

In his middle teens Clemson had studied at The American Literary, Scientific, and Military Academy (now Norwich University) in Norwich, Vermont. While essentially a military school, it also provided its students with a technical and classical education. Not much is known about its musical offerings, except that in 1820 (its second academic year and two years before Clemson attended) the school formed a band, now the oldest collegiate band in the nation.[67]

When Clemson first traveled to Europe, he was a young man of some means, so one could imagine his attending musical events according to his interests. However, no record of such attendance exists. He did note in his Private Pocket Journal, though, that he "commenced dancing" in both 1832 and 1834.[68]

Later on, Clemson and his daughter exchanged very few letters, and he was sometimes uncommunicative. But while *he* may not have expressed his feelings about her music directly to her, his wife did, writing to Floride that "your father…

seems pleased with your progress, particularly in singing."[69] He may not have expressed himself with words, but he did support her music in other ways. As Floride wrote in her diary in 1866, "Father returned from his two months' visit to the North, the night before last. He looks well. The boxes are on the way. He brought me some 15 pieces of music, a white dress &c. &c."[70]

Whereas Clemson enjoyed attending musical events, supported his daughter's activities, and danced, he also participated in music directly: he played the violin. It is not known when Clemson began to play, but he certainly could by his fiftieth year when he played to amuse Nina, his fourth-born child. To their daughter Floride, Anna wrote in 1856, "Nina is sitting on the floor clapping her hands, while your father plays on the violon [sic]. She is very fond of music."[71]

There is one known account of Clemson's skill on the violin, and that comes from his daughter Floride. Writing in her diary shortly after her father's return from the war, she commented that "Father has wonderfully improved in playing on the violin, & really composes some quite good common place tunes."[72] Clemson apparently enjoyed playing for friends as well as family. In 1937 Holmes and Sherrill wrote that "Some of the older people in the community now recall the visits which they made with their parents to hear Clemson play the violin when they were small children."[73]

Forty years after Clemson's death, Alester Holmes interviewed Mrs. Jane Prince—Clemson's last caregiver—and her daughter Hester ("Essie") Prince Boggs. In response to the question about whether Clemson played the violin, Mrs. Prince answered, "Yes, sir; beautifully." Mrs. Boggs, who was a young girl during Clemson's last years, noted the pieces that Clemson played on his violin: *All is Quiet Along the Potomac Tonight, Auld Lang Syne, Come and Let Us Worship, Old Uncle Ned, The Anna Polka, Sewanee* [sic] *River, Comin' Thru the Rye,* and *Rosin the Beau.*[74]

Much can be gained by looking at this list of works. The first, *All is Quiet Along the Potomac Tonight,* with music by John Hill Hewitt and words by Ethel Lynn Beers, refers to official telegrams reporting "all is quiet tonight" to the Union secretary of war by Major-General George B. McClellan.[75] As with many songs of the Civil War, this one was sung by soldiers on both sides of the conflict. The poet was a northerner; the composer, though born in the North, spent many years, including the war years, in the South.[76] The song is simple and understated, much like the poetry that inspired it. *Auld Lang Syne* is a Scottish folk melody with words added by the poet Robert Burns. This song was quite popular in the States. There are many songs with titles close to *Come and Let Us Worship,* so it is difficult to ascertain which version is the one that Clemson played. However, it is undoubtedly a church hymn. Stephen Foster wrote *Old Uncle Ned* for the Christy Minstrels for public performance. In some arrangements it is called an "Ethiopian

Tune," that is, a minstrel song. It has an engaging melody, but the words would be considered offensive today in its reference to African Americans.

Clemson himself wrote *Anna's Polka*, probably in 1862.[77] It is a bouncy, attractive dance tune written as a melody with no accompaniment. However, because of the many errors in music notation, it is unfortunately difficult to know just how it should sound. Given that he played it himself, he may have simply notated the tune in shorthand, for his own use.

Original manuscript of *Anna's Polka*, composed by Thomas Green Clemson, ca. 1862. (Musical notation on the second, fourth, and sixth staves has bled through from the manuscript's other side.) Thomas Green Clemson Papers, Special Collections, Clemson University Libraries.

*Anna's Polka*, realized by Andrew Levin, 2007, Clemson University.

Regarding other tunes that Clemson liked to perform on the violin, the name *Sewanee River* is what Stephen Foster's *Old Folks at Home* is often called. (Foster, however, used a "Swanee" spelling for the Suwannee River in southern Georgia and northern Florida.) *Comin' Thro' the Rye*, like *Auld Lang Syne*, is an old Scottish folk song with added words by Robert Burns. Internationally known singer Jenny Lind often included this song in her performances when touring this country. *Rosin the Beau* and *Rosin the Bow* are both spellings of this Irish tune that has been set to a variety of words. It has a long and colorful history. As scholar William R. Ward explains:

> This is one of those ubiquitous tunes which was popular with the American people for at least half-a-century—popping up in all sorts of places—as the vehicle for political campaign songs (at least eight of them); for alcoholic reform (though in its original version, it is a drinking song); for the unofficial state song of Washington; for a Civil War song; for a Southern folk hymn; and for a comic opera air. It is a captivating tune of Irish origin introduced in the 1830's as a rollicking drinking song.[78]

It was widely published—sometimes in collections, such as *Ethiopian Melodies No. 5.*[79] The perky tune would be sung many times to account for all of its verses.

In addition to the melodies he enjoyed playing and his piece *Anna's Polka*, Clemson composed seven other tunes. One of these is *Johnstone's Polka*, composed in

**Manuscript of *Johnstone's Polka* by Thomas Green Clemson, 1862. Thomas Green Clemson Papers, Special Collections, Clemson University Libraries.**

1862 and perhaps named for General Joe Johnston of the Confederate Army. It was handwritten on the back of the sheet of music that contains his *Anna's Polka*. The paper itself shows water damage from a fire at Fort Hill, where the piece had been in storage. A few small holes also obscure some notes, but they can be ascertained with near certainty when compared with parallel passages elsewhere in the tune. The music is scored in two staves—treble and bass clefs—presumably for piano, although it is not known that Clemson played the piano. It has a catchy melody and very simple chords in accompaniment. Some of the rhythms are hard to decipher, so the tune could be realized in a few different ways.[80] However, the overall shape is easy to distinguish, and one can easily imagine dancers moving to this tune.

A third work by Clemson is his *Carolina Forever: National Air*.[81] Composed in 1862, it is scored as a simple tune without accompaniment. Of the eight Clemson compositions, it is the best written. The notation is clear and accurate, and the four, four-bar phrases are well-balanced and pleasing to the ear. It has an attractive, melodic shape, and, in calling it an "air," he might have thought it appropriate for singing, perhaps as a Confederate anthem. However, it would not serve this purpose well, as it has a very wide range, the same as that in the *Star-Spangled Banner*.

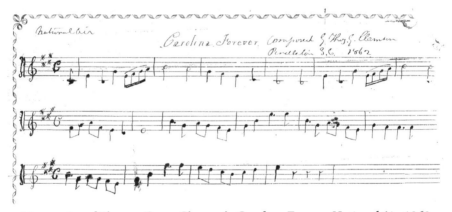

**Manuscript of Thomas Green Clemson's *Carolina Forever: National Air*, 1862. Fort Hill Collection, Clemson University.**

Compared to the inaccurate and hard-to-decipher notation of the previous three tunes by Clemson, the remaining five were written out very cleanly on two sides of a single sheet of music manuscript paper which, like the previous works, show some water damage and paper tears. Even though these five works, all written for piano, still contain a few obvious errors and some oddities in rhythmic notation, overall they are quite easy to read.[82]

The first of the five is the *Palmetto Polka*, a lively tune in 12/8 time, incorrectly notated as 2/4 time. Oddly, the piece is ten measures long, which is very unusual for dance music. Most music of this sort is composed in four-measure phrases, so either

Clemson had a special dance choreographed to this tune or he intended it just for listening. The *Hampton's Legion Polka* was named for General Wade Hampton and his private army. It too is a ten-measure dance, with very simple harmonies and left-hand accompaniment. A more regular, eight-bar tune is Clemson's *Mi Casa Quick Step*, named after Mrs. John C. Calhoun's Pendleton home, which also was the home of the Clemson family at the end of the war. It is a sprightly tune with a little more rhythmic variety than the other melodies. The longest and most sophisticated of the five tunes is his *Calhoun March*. Its twenty measures not only have the most rhythmic variety, but they also make up the only piece that modulates to a different key, providing welcome harmonic relief. The final work of these five is the *Confederate Dance*, an engaging, eight-bar melody with simple chordal accompaniment.

Clemson repeatedly used a particular melodic shape in his music. It is interesting in that it bears more than a passing resemblance to the opening of Thomas Moore's *The Minstrel Boy*, a song that was popular with both the northern and southern soldiers during the Civil War. Perhaps Clemson included this melodic fragment unconsciously.[83] Note below the similarities between the top excerpt from *The Minstrel Boy* and the lower five excerpts from other Thomas G. Clemson melodies:

**Comparison of *The Minstrel Boy* with several Clemson tunes.**

It is clear that Clemson was not a trained musician. In addition to rhythmic inaccuracies, phrases of odd lengths, and considerable repetition of melodic, rhythmic, and harmonic ideas, all eight of his tunes are in the same key of E major. Still, they are attractive pieces, written probably for his own pleasure and that of his friends and family. While they do contain imperfections, they are also spontaneous and joyful, highlighting a side of Clemson's personality not often portrayed.

As Clemson neared the end of his life he desired to see once more his granddaughter, Floride Isabella Lee, who lived in Carmel, New York. He wrote to her in 1887 asking her to come to Fort Hill to visit him and enticing her with a potential new friend in his housekeeper's daughter, Hester ("Essie") Prince. He wrote that "Hester has her organ and plays quite well, by the time you come, she will play very well. Hester is smart, has a good music talent, and is remarkably well educated. I think you would be well pleased with her if you knew her."[84]

After Clemson's death in 1888, his last will and testament offered the state the means to build a mechanical and agricultural school to aid in the recovery of the South. He also referred to the future school as a "high seminary of learning." While Clemson did not envision its becoming a general liberal arts college, it is instructive to note just how important the arts were to the well-educated, well-rounded man who made such a college possible. It is also instructive—and appropriate—to note just how important the arts have become at Clemson University. Moreover, Thomas Clemson's own music is finding a new audience in the twenty-first century. For instance, Andrew Levin's full orchestra and string quartet arrangements of *Carolina Forever*, which were premiered in 2007, will also be performed periodically in future seasons. More recently, a recording by Levin and other music faculty members will allow visitors to the Fort Hill mansion or viewers of video productions about Clemson—the man and the university—to hear several of Clemson's compositions, as well as tunes he loved to play on the violin. Thus, at his "high seminary of learning," one can rediscover Thomas Green Clemson, lover of music.

## Notes

1. Charles Pitt, "Paris," *The New Grove Dictionary of Opera*, http://sys.lib.clemson.edu:2286/shared/views/article.html?section=opera.005519#opera.005519.
2. David Charlton, John Trevitt, and Guy Gosselin, "Paris," *Grove Music Online*, http://sys.lib.clemson.edu:2286/shared/views/article.html?section=music.40089#music.40089.
3. Robert Wangermé and Henri Vanhulst. "Brussels," *Grove Music Online*, http://sys.lib.clemson.edu:2286/shared/views/article.html?section=music.04203#music.04203.
4. Charles Pitt, "Brussels," *The New Grove Dictionary of Opera*, http://sys.lib.clemson.edu:2286/shared/views/article.html?section=opera.900679#opera.900679.
5. John Joseph Hindman and Douglas Ashley, "Charleston," *Grove Music Online*, http://sys.lib.clemson.edu:2286/shared/views/article.html?section=music.05462#music.05462.

6.  Hunter Dickinson Farish, ed., *Journal and Letters of Philip Vickers Fithian, 1773–1774: A Plantation Tutor of the Old Dominion* (Williamsburg, VA: Colonial Williamsburg, 1943), 212.
7.  Ibid., 163.
8.  Anna Clemson to Floride Clemson, 4 April 1858, Clemson Papers, MSS 2, Special Collections, Clemson University Libraries, Clemson, South Carolina (hereafter cited as SCCUL).
9.  The Library of Congress makes available an extremely large collection of nineteenth-century sheet music for free download at http://frontiers.loc.gov/ammem/mussmquery.html.
10. Charles Hamm, *Music in the New World* (New York and London: W. W. Norton, 1983), 302.
11. Elias Howe, *Complete Ball-Room Hand Book* (Boston: Oliver Ditson, 1858), n.p., cited in Hamm, 302.
12. Lawrence Fay Brewster, *Summer Migrations and Resorts of South Carolina Low-Country Planters*, Historical Papers of the Trinity College Historical Society, Series 26 (Durham, NC: Duke University Press: 1947), 106–107.
13. Ernest McPherson Lander Jr., *The Calhoun Family and Thomas Green Clemson: The Decline of a Southern Patriarchy* (Columbia: University of South Carolina Press, 1983), 88.
14. Ibid., 101.
15. Brewster, *Summer Migrations and Resorts*, 88.
16. Ibid., 106–107.
17. Hamm, *Music in the New World*, 187–188.
18. Ibid., 254.
19. Katherine K. Preston, "Washington DC," *Grove Music Online*, ed. Laura Macy, http://www.grovemusic.com.
20. Anna Maria Calhoun to Maria Simkins, 21 May 1838, Clemson Papers, MSS 2, SCCUL; Floride Clemson, diary entry, 20 April 1863, Clemson Papers, Ibid.
21. Floride Clemson, diary entries, 17 July 1863, 1 May 1863, Clemson Papers, Ibid.
22. Samuel Gaillard Stoney, *Plantations in the Carolina Low Country* (Charleston: Carolina Art Association, 1938), 35, cited in Brewster, *Summer Migrations and Resorts*, 114.
23. Beth Ann Klosky, *The Pendleton Legacy* (Columbia, SC: Sandlapper Press, 1971), 48.
24. Richard White Simpson, *History of Old Pendleton District, with a Genealogy of the Leading Families of the District* (Anderson, SC: Oulla Printing & Binding Company, 1913), 18.
25. Klosky, *Pendleton Legacy*, 63.
26. Dave U. Sloan, *Fogy Days, and How; or, The World has Changed* (Atlanta, GA: n.p., 1891), 57; copies of these reminiscences were made by the Clemson College Library in 1963.
27. Klosky, *Pendleton Legacy*, 27.
28. George W. Featherstonhaugh, *A Canoe Voyage up the Minnay Sotor: with an Account of the Lead and Copper Deposits in Wisconsin; of the Gold Region in the Cherokee Country; and Sketches of Popular Manners*, vol. 2, reprint edition (St. Paul, MN: Minnesota Historical Society, St. Paul, 1970), 267; this account was first published by Richard Bentley of London, England, in 1847.
29. Rosser H. Taylor, *Ante-Bellum South Carolina: A Social and Cultural History* (New York: Da Capo Press, 1970), 135; it was originally published by the University of North Carolina Press, Chapel Hill, NC, in 1942.
30. Interview with William David Hiott, Clemson University Director of Historic Properties (5 October 2006).
31. Klosky, *Pendleton Legacy*, 27.
32. Frank A. Dickson, *Journeys into the Past: The Anderson Region's Heritage*, sponsored by the Anderson County Bicentennial Committee (n.p., privately published, 1975), 65, 68.
33. Julia Wright Sublette, "The Letters of Anna Calhoun Clemson, 1833–1873," Ph.D. dissertation, Florida State University (Ann Arbor, MI: UMI Dissertation Services, 1993), n806.
34. Lander, *Calhoun Family and Thomas Green Clemson*, 4.
35. Sarah H. Rembert, "Barhamville, A Columbia Antebellum Girls' School," *South Carolina History Illustrated* 1, no. 1 (Columbia, SC: Sandlapper Press, February 1970), 44–48.
36. Anna Calhoun to Maria Simkins, 2 May 1833, Clemson Papers, MSS 2, SCCUL.
37. Anna Calhoun to James Edward Calhoun, 4 July 1833, Clemson Papers, Ibid.
38. Anna Calhoun to Maria Simkins, 8 August 1837, Clemson Papers, Ibid.
39. Anna Calhoun to Maria Simkins, 4 July 1836, Clemson Papers, Ibid.

40. Anna Calhoun to Maria Simkins, 21 May 1838, Clemson Papers, Ibid.
41. Sublette, "Letters of Anna Calhoun Clemson," n175.
42. Anna Calhoun Clemson to John C. Calhoun, 21 December 1840, Clemson Papers, MSS 2, SCCUL.
43. Anna Calhoun Clemson to Patrick Calhoun, 4 January 1840, Clemson Papers, Ibid.
44. Floride Calhoun to Anna Calhoun, 1 January 1851, Clemson Papers, Ibid.
45. Lander, *Calhoun Family and Thomas Green Clemson*, 154.
46. Mary Stevenson, ed. *The Diary of Clarissa Adger Bowen, Ashtabula Plantation, 1865, with Excerpts from Other Family Diaries and Comments by Her Granddaughter, Clarissa Walton Taylor, and Many Other Accounts of The Pendleton Clemson Area, South Carolina, 1776–1889* (Pendleton, SC: Research and Publication Committee Foundation for Historic Restoration in Pendleton Area, 1973), 17; its source was an undated newspaper clipping.
47. Martha Colhoun (attr.), *Keowee Waltzes* (Charleston, SC: George Oates, 1847). Interestingly, two other works were published at nearly the same time "by a Lady of South Carolina": *The Volunteer March, composed and respectfully dedicated to the Palmetto Regiment* (1847) and *Jasper Guards' March, composed and dedicated to the Officers & Members of the Jasper Guards of Charleston, S.C.* (1848). There is no evidence to support or deny a claim that Martha Colhoun wrote either of these other songs.
48. Anna Calhoun to Maria Simkins, 2 August 1838, Clemson Papers, MSS 2, SCCUL.
49. Floride Colhoun Calhoun to Margaret Calhoun, 15 December 1838, Clemson Papers, Ibid.
50. Charles M. McGee Jr. and Ernest M. Lander Jr., eds., *A Rebel Came Home: The diary of Floride Clemson tells of her wartime adventures in Yankeeland, 1863–64, her trip home to South Carolina, and life in the South during the last few months of the Civil War and the year following* (Columbia: University of South Carolina Press, 1961), 5.
51. William Calhoun to Calhoun Clemson, 13 February 1848, Clemson Papers, SCCUL.
52. Anna Calhoun Clemson to Floride Clemson, 14 March 1858, Clemson Papers, Ibid.
53. Anna Calhoun Clemson to Floride Clemson, 9 November 1856, Clemson Papers, Ibid.
54. Anna Calhoun Clemson to Floride Clemson, 27 September 1857, Clemson Papers, Ibid.
55. Anna Calhoun Clemson to Floride Clemson, 14 March 1858, Clemson Papers, Ibid.
56. McGee and Lander, eds., *Rebel Came Home*, 19.
57. Anna Calhoun Clemson to Floride Clemson, 4 April 1858, Clemson Papers, MSS 2, SCCUL.
58. Floride Clemson, diary entry, 1 January 1863, Clemson Papers, Ibid.
59. Floride Clemson, diary entry, 20 April 1863, Clemson Papers, Ibid.
60. Floride Clemson, diary entry, 1 May 1863, Clemson Papers, Ibid.
61. Floride Clemson, diary entry, 28 June 1863, Clemson Papers, Ibid.
62. Floride Clemson, diary entries, 17 July 1863, 28 December 1863, 6 February 1864, and 30 June 1864, Clemson Papers, Ibid.; also cited in McGee and Lander, eds., *Rebel Came Home*, 37, 46, 48–49, 55–56.
63. Anna Calhoun Clemson to Floride Clemson, 16 August 1863, Clemson Papers, MSS 2, SCCUL.
64. Floride Clemson, diary entry, 13 May 1865, Clemson Papers, Ibid.
65. Floride Clemson, diary entry, 26 June 1865, Clemson Papers, Ibid.
66. Alester G. Holmes and George R. Sherrill, *Thomas Green Clemson: His Life and Work* (Richmond, VA: Garrett and Massie, 1937), 37.
67. Norwich University, *History of Norwich University*, http://www.norwich.edu/about/history.html.
68. Thomas Green Clemson, "Private Pocket Journal," 10, Clemson Papers, MSS 2, SCCUL.
69. Anna Calhoun Clemson to Floride Clemson, 31 May 1857, Clemson Papers, Ibid.
70. Floride Clemson, diary entry, 22 June 1866, Clemson Papers, Ibid.
71. Anna Calhoun Clemson to Floride Clemson, 21 December 1856, Clemson Papers, Ibid.
72. Floride Clemson, diary entry, 17 July 1865, Clemson Papers, Ibid.
73. Holmes and Sherrill, *Thomas Green Clemson*, 37.
74. Alester Holmes, ed., *Reminiscences of Mrs. Prince in re. Thomas G. Clemson*, Interview with Alester Holmes, typewritten, 9 March 1928, Clemson Papers, MSS 2, SCCUL; the Princes moved in at Fort Hill in 1881 or early 1882, when Hester (Essie) was eight years old. As William Hiott explains, "She was in many ways a surrogate granddaughter to Clemson. He saw to her education and bought her a small pump organ. She continued to live in the house with her mother and was actually married in Fort Hill in 1892 or 3" when she was around 21 years old.

(Interview with William David Hiott, Clemson University Director of Historic Properties, 3 November 2006).

75. "All Quiet Along the Potomac Tonight," *Wikipedia, The Free Encyclopedia*, http://en.wikipedia. org/wiki/All Quiet Along the Potomac Tonight.

76. "John Hill Hewitt," *Wikipedia, The Free Encyclopedia*, http://en.wikipedia.org/wiki/John_Hill_ Hewitt. Interestingly, Hewitt took a teaching position in 1824 at the Baptist Female Academy in Greenville, SC. Later, when a rival suggested that Hewitt was a mulatto, his private students left him. John C. Calhoun wrote a letter on his behalf to contest this accusation.

77. Thomas Green Clemson, *Anna's Polka*, 1862, Clemson Papers, MSS 2, SCCUL.

78. William R. Ward, ed., *The American Bicentennial Songbook, Volume 1: 1770–1870s* (New York: Charles Hanson Music & Books, 1975), 163.

79. *Ethiopian Melodies No. 5: Jim along Josey, Old Rosin the bow, The Log Hut, Arranged for the Piano Forte* (Baltimore: F. D. Benteen, and New Orleans: W. T. Mayo, 1852).

80. Thomas Green Clemson, *Johnstone's Polka*, 1862, Clemson Papers, MSS 2, SCCUL.

81. Thomas Green Clemson, *Carolina Forever: National Air*, 1862, Clemson Papers, Ibid.

82. Thomas Green Clemson, *Palmetto Polka, Hampton's Legion Polka, Mi Casa Quick Step, Calhoun March*, and *Confederate Dance*, Clemson Papers, Ibid.

83. Around 1812, Thomas Moore had written the two-verse poem, "The Minstrel Boy," describing a minstrel boy who dies in a war, and set it to the melody of *The Moreen*, an old Irish folk song. Fifty years later, during the Civil War, an anonymous American poet added a third verse, describing the return of the boy and the end of all wars—a sentiment shared by soldiers on both sides, certainly.

84. Thomas Green Clemson to Floride Isabella Lee, 26 April 1887, Clemson Papers, MSS 2, SCCUL.

# Chapter 11

## THE FORT HILL YEARS

### *William David Hiott*

**In this stereopticon photograph, Thomas Clemson is shown seated in a rocking chair on the east lawn of Fort Hill, ca. 1880. Fort Hill Collection, Clemson University.**

Thomas Green Clemson was associated with Fort Hill for nearly half a century. From his marriage to Anna Maria Calhoun in the parlor on November 13, 1838, until his death in the master bedroom some fifty years later on April 6, 1888, Fort Hill was never far from his mind, even if he was a continent away. Thomas Clemson personally occupied Fort Hill for nearly twenty years at two distinct periods of his life. As newlyweds he and Anna lived at Fort Hill for almost four years, beginning in 1839. Later in 1872, Thomas and Anna retired to Fort Hill where they both died, Anna in 1875 and Thomas some thirteen years later in 1888.

There is certainly a marked contrast from the optimistic outlook of Thomas Clemson at Fort Hill in the late 1830s, when he began his family life, as compared to his return to Fort Hill in 1872, the year after the deaths of their two adult children. The couple only had three years together back at Fort Hill before his beloved Anna passed away.

### *Early Married Life at Fort Hill*

Thomas Clemson's first years at Fort Hill were a time of transition from bachelorhood to married life. Following his marriage to Anna Maria Calhoun at Fort Hill, the Clemsons returned to Philadelphia to establish a household. Anna evidently did not like the northern city life, and soon they returned to Fort Hill. The estate played an important part in Thomas Clemson's career as the place where he first saw agricultural production up close. Moreover, as Calhoun's dutiful son-in-law, Clemson oversaw much of the day-to-day management of the estate. His letters to Calhoun during this period are some of the best firsthand descriptions of life on the plantation. Furthermore he took a special interest in Calhoun's gold mine in Dahlonega, Georgia, where Clemson put his geological and mining studies into practice.

The first years at Fort Hill also saw the births of the Clemsons' first three children. Their first child, whose name is unknown, died as an infant in 1839. The next two children—John Calhoun Clemson born in 1841 and Floride Elizabeth Clemson born in 1842—were both named for their grandparents, and both lived to adulthood. The Clemsons' last child, Cornelia (Nina), was born over a dozen years later in Maryland.[1]

At Fort Hill, the Clemsons occupied Anna's bedroom and the two adjacent rooms as a suite, with one acting as their nursery.[2] Anna had been born in 1817, so she was less than ten years old when the Calhouns moved to Fort Hill. While her father was in Washington for months each year, it was Anna who was his eyes and ears, recording the family events, weather, crops, and the local gossip from Pendleton. Fort Hill was a special place for Anna; her bedroom was in the middle of the second floor and was colorfully decorated with floral striped wallpaper topped with an intricately matching border.[3] Anna's room also afforded panoramic views of the mountains in the distance toward Keowee Heights, their Cousin Colhoun's plantation to the north, and to the south, it overlooked her father's columned study and the formal garden planted for her sister Cornelia.

Clemson's marrying into this family and plantation also became special. After all, Anna was considered to be John C. Calhoun's favorite child, and Clemson was his only son-in-law. As a result of these circumstances and perhaps due to Clemson's father having died when he was only six years old, Clemson became a protégé of the statesman. In addition to gaining agricultural experience, Clemson, with Calhoun's help, acquired an estate, Canebrake, near Saluda where the Clemsons lived briefly prior to going abroad to Belgium. And throughout their years in Europe and later in Maryland, Fort Hill was not far from his mind. The influence of Anna's father, both during and after Calhoun's lifetime, made the Fort Hill estate a crucial place in Clemson's memories and his deeds. Moreover, as Ben Robertson, the twentieth-century local folklorist, noted in his *Upcountry Memoir*, there was something about the red hills and cotton fields that drew Clemson to this particular vicinity.

### Post-War Years in Pendleton, South Carolina

Thomas Clemson's later years at Fort Hill are an intriguing era in American history. The collapse of the southern economy following the Civil War and the turmoil of the Reconstruction era in South Carolina were the backdrop for his determination to rebuild his adopted state through scientific education. It is a heroic story of perseverance through overwhelming odds toward his lifetime goal to help rebuild the state.

Out of the ashes like the phoenix, South Carolina needed to reconstruct itself, and, in response, Thomas Clemson would eventually make a significant difference in the economic course of the state. Although born a Philadelphian, Clemson had cast his lot with the South.[4] Now, its infrastructure and educational systems were in a shambles. However, Clemson's lifelong study of science and agriculture had equipped him with the skills to provide invaluable leadership at this crucial moment.

His return to the Pendleton District following the Civil War was not directly to Fort Hill. The Clemson family reunion on July 1, 1865, coincidentally marking Thomas's fifty-eighth birthday, took place near the village green of Pendleton at Mi Casa, the home of his mother-in-law, Floride Calhoun (Mrs. John C. Calhoun). As Clemson's daughter Floride recorded in her diary, her father "looks pretty well, but is about iron grey now, though not bald, which is pretty well for a man well on to 60." Just a few days later, Floride noted, "Father has wonderfully improved in playing on the violin & really composes some quite good common place tunes. He does look so well, & has given up smoking. He is a dear old fellow."[5]

Unlike other older war veterans might have done, this "dear old fellow" did not retire or rest on his laurels for past honors and activities. In fact, his transition from citizen soldier of the lost cause to an advocate for his adopted state makes one think of Cincinnatus, the ancient Roman farmer-dictator. Clemson also saw the benefits of the Palmetto State's reconstructing itself by turning swords into plowshares. His lifelong goals of scientific agriculture and public education were again on his mind. The Morrill Land Grant Act, which Clemson had supported, had finally been passed by Congress in 1862, but the timing wasn't right for either Thomas Clemson or South Carolina.

His most pressing immediate tasks were to check on how his financial holdings had fared during his absence. Clemson relied on a host of financial advisors during his career. Many of them are a who's who of national and local business leaders. Some were lifelong friends, some were relatives, and some also had been advisors to Calhoun. Leading the list of financial advisors were Charles Leupp and William Wilson Corcoran. Fortuitously, both Leupp and Corcoran were fellow art collectors, which provided close personal relationships as well.

Charles Leupp represented Clemson's finances on a national level from his offices in New York. Incidentally, Leupp's wife was Isabella Lee, daughter of an early New York mayor, Gideon Lee Sr. Leupp's brother-in-law, D. W. Lee, would also represent Clemson's assets. Interestingly, Leupp's other brother-in-law, Gideon Lee Jr., would later marry Clemson's daughter, Floride Elizabeth Clemson. Charles Leupp was a partner in several enterprises with financier Jay Gould for many years. Tragically, Leupp took his own life, but the Leupp firm continued investments for Clemson. Corcoran likewise had been Clemson's longtime friend and from his offices in the Washington area also handled investments which remained secure during the war. An intriguing part of the story is that, through many shrewd financial moves, Thomas Clemson was able to shelter his finances during the Civil War years and likewise to hold on to the majority of his assets throughout the turbulent Reconstruction era. In other words, his financial dealings throughout his life were often very calculated and astute.

His assets, including his Bladensburg home, had been managed as well as could be expected. He asserted to his friend Tazewell Taylor, "my name has been tabooed by the powers that be" and went on to say that "I would go to Maryland if I was not apprehensive that my presence there would excite them to further vindictiveness all of which I desire to avoid."[6] In a follow-up letter to Taylor some six months later, Clemson confided, "It would appear from what my friends tell me that before I can have citizenship, that it would at least be polite to secure a pardon."[7] As Clemson relayed to his uncle by marriage James Edward Calhoun, "the North is no place for a Confederate."[8] Clemson had made his choice to support the Confederacy. Now the consequences of the conflict were evident everywhere, and Clemson was determined to use his scientific and agricultural talents in the rebuilding of South Carolina.

Clemson was elected president of the Pendleton Farmers' Society on October 8, 1868,[9] and one of the duties of the society under Clemson's leadership was to promote "aid to found an institution for the diffusion of scientific knowledge, that our civilization may advance, and that we may once more become a happy and prosperous people."[10] In a letter to Professor Joseph Henry of the Smithsonian Institution, Clemson stated bluntly, "There is in my opinion no hope for the

South short of wide spread scientific education. Our condition is wretched in the extreme."[11] Clemson's appraisal of South Carolina is not flattering when he writes of the "lethargic epidemic, which appears to have fallen upon all the population of the state."[12]

**Photograph, ca. 1890, of Farmers Hall, constructed 1826-1828, in Pendleton, S.C. Fort Hill Collection, Clemson University.**

One longtime supporter of Clemson, D. W. Lee, wrote to Clemson that "the great misery which the South is suffering is arousing a strong feeling of sympathy," and he goes on to echo Clemson's thinking: "as you say the remedy lies mainly in an improved system of Agriculture." However the current political situation in Washington was grim. Lee observed that "the quarrel between congress and the President [Johnson] is most unfortunate, but there is here no belief that the latter will be successfully impeached, or indeed impeached at all. This movement of the extreme republicans would only add another element to the existing confusion."[13] Indeed the rifts in politics of the Reconstruction era were both extremely unfortunate and confused.

While Clemson began promoting agriculture on a state and national level, Fort Hill was also in dire straits. The Civil War occupants of Fort Hill had been Andrew Pickens Calhoun, eldest son of the statesman, and his family. Andrew had been in the process of purchasing the estate from his mother; however, he had not paid off the mortgage. Thus with his death began a curious and complicated course of events that eventually would result in the foreclosure on the Fort Hill mortgage initiated by Floride Calhoun against the estate of her daughter-in-law Margaret Calhoun. The intricacies of the details of the various legal proceedings and resulting animosity between the family of Andrew Pickens Calhoun and the Clemsons are all well documented.[14]

The ongoing feud between Floride Calhoun and her eldest son Andrew is also captured in the family letters. One of the more poignant letters during this episode was from Anna to her brother:

> Mother is very ill, my brother, & has been for months, a great sufferer. She is now confined to her room & almost constantly to her bed, & tho I do not consider the disease, under which she labors, so serious, still, the intense pains, & consequent wear on her constitution, make us anxious about her. She, herself, thinks she will never recover, & under the influence of this feeling said yesterday—'I wish Andrew would come & see me. I should like to be reconciled to my only son before I die.'

Anna went on to state pleadingly that "you will feel & appreciate the motives which have activated me, & believe in the sincere desire to establish family harmony, felt by your sister Anna."[15]

**Photograph of Andrew Pickens Calhoun, ca. 1865, the year he died. Fort Hill Collection, Clemson University.**

Ironically, it was Andrew who predeceased his mother in the spring of 1865. That left his widow Margaret Calhoun to face the Union forces who eventually made their way to the Pendleton District.[16] Floride Clemson recounted in her diary on Sunday, May 28, that "a thousand Yankees under General Brown passed through this place" in Pendleton and noted, "they were at Fort Hill, & took Johnny's fine horse, & others I believe, did little or no other damage."[17] Fort Hill had survived the war, but there was some doubt about whether the estate would survive the peace intact.[18] Floride Calhoun, Mrs. John C. Calhoun, died prior to the closure on the contract, which placed the financial matter in Clemson's lap, since Anna Calhoun Clemson was the last of the Calhouns' children and to whom Mrs. Calhoun had willed the bulk of her estate.[19]

Clemson, in one way or another, soon became involved in the everyday events at Fort Hill. On January 1, 1868, Clemson signed a contract with the sharecroppers and tenant farmers working the place. The subsequent "Articles of Agreement between Thos. G. Clemson and the Freedmen and women of Fort Hill Plantation" was signed with fifteen workmen.[20] As the end of 1868 drew near, Clemson recounted the previous three years: "When Mrs. Clemson and my daughter arrived in Pendleton before the surrender at the commencement of 1865 they found Mrs. Calhoun (J. C.) my wife's mother entirely destitute and it became her duty (Mrs. Clemson) to find the means of support. At that time there was living in the house Mrs. Kate Calhoun two children and servant make six in family. I supported them for fully a year until my means were exhausted."[21]

Thomas and Anna had the additional expenses in 1869 for the wedding of their daughter Floride Elizabeth Clemson to Gideon Lee Jr. of Carmel, New York. Thomas and Anna Clemson gained a son-in-law on August 1, 1869, when Floride Elizabeth Clemson became Mrs. Gideon Lee in a ceremony at St. Paul's Episcopal Church in Pendleton. As chronicled in her personal diary, she had lived a busy life as a young debutant prior to the war. However, the Civil War had diminished the number of eligible bachelors of her own age. Now, perhaps for financial security, she had chosen to marry a Mexican War veteran whose family had had lengthy financial dealings with Clemson. As mentioned earlier, Gideon Lee's brother, D. W. Lee, had handled Clemson's investments as had their brother-in-law Charles Leupp. Gideon Lee's father, a politician, had been an early mayor of New York. Thus, the wealthy northern groom could provide much which the war-torn South could not. Still, Thomas Clemson was not entirely supportive of Floride's marrying a man nearly twenty years older than she.

Anna had other reservations about the marriage. She had become very close to her daughter during the war years, both by lengthy letters and their cohabitation in Maryland and at Mi Casa. As Anna wrote about the impending marriage of her daughter Floride to Gideon Lee of Carmel, New York, "I feel very sad at parting with F., for I shall have very little inclination to go north to visit her, & shall have to depend on her coming here. We live together like sisters, & companions, & I shall miss her greatly."[22]

Gideon and Floride Lee's marriage was, in fact, tragically short. A daughter christened Floride Isabella was born to the couple on May 15, 1870. A little over a year later, Gideon Lee became a widower when his wife Floride died suddenly on July 23, 1871. The cause of her death was most likely tuberculosis. The Clemsons later blamed her poor health, in part, to an early misdiagnosis and her untreated condition while she studied at her aunt's boarding school in Baltimore before the war. Anna wrote, "Her father & myself have never doubted she owed her confirmed ill health and early death to the shock her system received during the two years spent at Mrs. Barton's." She added that when Floride finally did go to the doctor, he "said she had a severe attack of inflammation of the lungs which *from neglect* had become *serious*."[23]

A little over two weeks after Floride's death, John Calhoun Clemson was killed in a train wreck in Seneca.[24] A picture ca. 1870 of Calhoun Clemson shows a handsome young man with a mustache similar to his father. He also was a tall man, nearly 6 feet 4 inches—just two inches shorter than Clemson and two inches taller than his grandfather John C. Calhoun, for whom he had been named. Calhoun Clemson, who had survived the Civil War and imprisonment in a POW camp, had not married and left no heirs.[25]

*Left to right:* Photographs of Floride Elizabeth Clemson Lee and her brother, John Calhoun Clemson, ca. 1870, the year before both died. Fort Hill Collection, Clemson University.

*Left:* Floride Isabella Lee, young daughter of Floride Elizabeth Clemson and Gideon Lee Jr. *Right:* Gideon Lee Jr. Photographs are ca. 1873 and ca. 1880, respectively. Fort Hill Collection, Clemson University.

## *The Later Years at Fort Hill*

This tragic chain of events took an emotional toll on the Clemsons. They finally returned to take up residence in Fort Hill in 1872. But how different the old home place must have felt to both of them. The sights and sounds of Fort Hill were a marked contrast to their earlier occupation in the antebellum years. They were now not only alone, but also childless following the tragic deaths of Floride and Calhoun in 1871 and the earlier death in 1858 of their three-year-old daughter Cornelia (Nina).

In many ways their thoughts about Fort Hill might be transposed to Margaret Mitchell's epic novel of the Reconstruction era where the father of the novel's protagonist, Scarlett O'Hara, exclaims, "Why, the land is the only thing in the world worth workin' for, worth fightin' for, worth dyin' for, because it's the only thing that lasts." And the same was true with Fort Hill: the land mattered to the Clemsons as a part of their heritage and history, and they sought to ensure that it would last, if not for their own children, then perhaps for others'. Scores of young South Carolinians needed assistance to break out of subsistence farming. Thus, Thomas and Anna Clemson determined that they would collectively make education-related plans for the estate after their deaths.

In 1873, Clemson returned steadfastly to the encouragement of agricultural education. In response to a letter from Clemson, William Henry Trescot wrote: "I have thought a good deal over our conversation at my last visit to Fort Hill and am of the opinion that a better opportunity will not again occur to urge upon the state the adoption of your suggestion." Trescot goes on to insist, "Some vigorous effort must be made to establish a new institution." Pendletonian Trescot ended his letter to Clemson with an interesting comparison: "You have noticed I suppose that Ashland Mr. Clay's home has been converted into a college for Kentucky."[26] Clemson might have surmised that if Clay's estate was utilized as a college, why not Calhoun's? Reminders of the Great Triumvirate abounded at Fort Hill, including Henry Clay's gift of a sideboard made of wood from the *U.S.S. Constitution*, the famous ship affectionately called "Old Ironsides."

In 1874, Clemson was again calling upon old friends and colleagues for support of his educational vision. One such respondent to his cause was Joseph Henry of the Smithsonian, who wrote to Clemson, "It will give me much pleasure to do anything in my power to assist in developing your commendable project of establishing a first class institution of learning in South Carolina." Henry offers some advice when he asked of Clemson, "Could something be done for the enterprise through the Peabody bequest?"[27] He goes on to state, "I have just read a work by Pike, on the state of South Carolina under its present rulers and am much import with its deplorable condition. Nothing but education and immigration can apparently assist you but the result of these will require time to become apparent."[28] Finally, Henry offers his assistance "to indorse your proposition as fully as you may desire."[29] Such assistance and Clemson's efforts faced even further obstacles. South Carolina's conditions during postwar Reconstruction, especially what contemporaries and historians have referred to as the radical or republican Reconstruction, were known for corruptions, especially in the eyes of white Carolinians.

In all of his agricultural and educational efforts, Thomas G. Clemson had found a willing partner in his wife. Tragically, on September 22, 1875, Anna Maria Calhoun Clemson died. Her funeral service was held at St. Paul's two days later.[30] Clemson was understandably shaken by her sudden death from a heart attack. Anna, in her last years, no longer had the girlish figure shown in her Belgium portrait, and photographs show her as being noticeably overweight in the 1870s, probably contributing to her untimely death. Clemson's confidant and family friend James Rion emotionally expressed his condolences to Clemson: "You have lost a wife, who was in every sense of the word a companion for you not only worthy of affection but the highest esteem. Her good nature, high spirit, elegance of manner, extensive information and reading, fine intellect, and all the more valuable female accomplishments fitted her to be a wife worthy of any man that has ever lived."

**Photograph of Anna Calhoun Clemson, ca. 1875, the year of her death. Fort Hill Collection, Clemson University.**

Rion continued to reminisce about Anna, "I well remember how her father's eyes would brighten up, when he would speak of 'Anna.' In reading over his letters it is very touching to see with what pride he wrote of her, when a mere child. She was by all properly regarded as the child who inherited more of her father's great talents than any other of his children. 'His children,'— They are now all gone!"[31]

Following the death of Anna, Thomas Clemson's determination toward his goal became a more singular passion. His renewed impetus included the enlistment of William Wilson Corcoran. In a letter to Corcoran, Clemson recounts a history of his ambitions, but, more important, fully defines his current objectives:

Since the surrender an effort has been making in South Carolina to establish an institution for teaching the Sciences and Arts, theoretical & practical, & thus raise the people of the state from ignorance & demoralization to prosperity the hope of the well born. Had the intentions first—formed by our mutual friend Mr. Peabody,[32] been carried out the State of South Carolina would have been in a very different condition from her present status. Up to present writing our efforts have been without avail.

For sometime it was hoped that funds would be raised for founding such an institution at Fort Hill, the former residence of Hon. J. C. Calhoun. Either from ignorance or poverty the necessity and importance of the project was not realized. Last winter a proposition came before the legislature of So[uth] Carolina to organize a University at Columbia but for like causes it failed.

The efforts, which we made at the Smithsonian Institution before the war to found such institutions in each state was passed in 1862, donating to each state, land scrip for the purpose....

The necessity is paramount, and I have been solicited again to use my feeble exertions to convert Fort Hill into such as purpose, and thus save from desecration that beautiful hallowed spot, and pass it down for future time to the diffusion & investigation of the laws of the Creator.

When the subject was first agitated we—Mrs. Clemson and self, were willing to donate sixty or eighty acres, but it was thought that the entire place would be necessary to carry out the project, in a manner commensurate with its importance...

Independent of the historical sentiments attached to Fort Hill it has been much favored by nature. It has an exceptional position for health at the junction of two rivers the Seneca & 12 mile. In this Piedmont region with a climate unsurpassed having a magnificent panoramic view of the highest mountains east of the Mississippi. In the language of our friend Professor Henry, 'this upper Carolina is the garden spot of the North American Continent.'

Fort Hill has come to be a second Mecca and is visited by thousands, who come to catch an inspiration from its history. We have kept the place from desecration.

If the project here presented should go into operation it would insure the prosperity of the State and be an additional light to the world, and be surely counted to its founders in that life which we hope to realize hereafter....

When Thomas Jefferson was requested to know what inscription he desired to be inscribed upon his tomb he answered 'Founder of the Charlottesville University [University of Virginia]; author of the Declaration of Independence and mover of the statute for religious freedom.'[33]

Thomas Clemson, in his later years, saw himself as an elder agricultural statesman of sorts and even let it be known to the administration of President Grover Cleveland that he still had a desire to finish what he considered unfinished business in regards to agriculture on a national level. Clemson's confidant Rion noted to Clemson that "it would not be wise in Mr. Cleveland, to appoint a son-in-law of John C. Calhoun and especially one who left his Office at Washington (even though at the point of the bayonet, and with a halter in view) and joined the Rebellion and kept the Trans-Mississippi Department a-going until the close of the war. But if Cleveland will have the independence to make the appointment so much more to his credit."[34] However, William Henry Trescot who was ever the politician in Washington informed Clemson that South Carolina was pushing Mr. Aiken as the "probable appointment to the Agriculture Bureau were Democrats ever restored to power."[35] Clemson did not get the appointment; instead he refocused his energies on agriculture at Fort Hill.

Clemson's own management of the Fort Hill estate extended well beyond the tenant farmers who contracted with him. He continued his personal experimentation with agriculture and even spawned an interest in aquaculture. For instance, after having been shipped California salmon from the Maryland Commission of Fish and Fisheries, he made additional requests for carp.[36] There are further Fort Hill accounts of his feuding with neighbors over roaming cattle and stagnant water in millponds.

During his last years, Thomas Clemson also began tying up what he saw as loose ends related to money and property. It would be going too far to say that Clemson was in the mold of Dickens's famous character Ebenezer Scrooge. However Clemson did have a long memory when it came to loans. One particular account is insightful. In a sharp letter to George North, who was a brother-in-law, Clemson wrote,

> As a man advances in life he naturally feels a desire to square accounts with this world, and as I loaned you money more than the third of a century since, on your honor supposing you were an honest man…Some persons are forgetful of moneyed obligations. Not imposing that a conscientious Christian man desires to shirk a moral obligation. I now remind you that the money, which you have used for your own benefit and at the expense of myself and family, is needed, and as no reasoning, time can absolve you from paying a debt I think it high time for you to think of paying me what is justly due. There also is another small matter which however small I demand the return of an original letter by General G. Washington loaned to you long since, which you may have forgotten.[37]

Obviously, Clemson also had a long memory in regards to objects. One such object that Clemson obsessed about was another Washington memento—this time a gold medal that he once had in his possession. As Clemson recounted,

> I purchased the gold medal at public auction of my own volition and without instruction of any kind or form. The medal was one, which was presented to General George Washington and inherited by Samuel Walter Washington and sold at Harewood to increase the aspect of his estate. Considering that after the

sale, regrets were expressed at the relics leaving the family, I left it at Harewood having no recollection of having given it to any one. My conduct was motivated by a sentiment of feeling. Further I advanced many thousands of dollars, in gifts and loans and that I have stood between the family of the widow of Samuel Walter Washington and utter destitution now for near half a century.[38]

Clemson sought restitution for his loss, but, as his attorney noted, he had waited too long on this matter. Clemson also had acquired from and left with his sister Louisa Clemson Washington a Windsor chair that supposedly belonged to President Washington and a unique sofa that has an eagle motif from their Harewood estate. For these and other objects, Clemson did not agree with any statute of limitations on recovery of his prewar funds or possessions.

Fortunately, Clemson was more successful in keeping ownership of his art collection, which had been shipped at the start of the Civil War to his uncle Elias Baker in Altoona, Pennsylvania. At the urging of his attorney, Clemson was instructed to request of his uncle's son "a list of your paintings in his charge in order to have in black and white an acknowledgment of ownership." Rion had a personal interest in the paintings beginning in 1883, as he also wanted Clemson to clearly "write me a letter and in it have an offer to give me one of your pictures at Mr. Bakers." Clemson's own annotation on the back of the letter noted the subject as "concerning my pictures which my dear uncle had boxed up when I was driven from Washington & when my wife and daughter were left alone surrounded with northern troops on my place."[39] It is interesting to note that in 1876, after having visited the Corcoran Gallery of Art, Clemson had made some overtures for the sale of these paintings to Mr. MacLeod, the curator of the Corcoran Gallery.[40] MacLeod, however, had to decline the offer because he had no funds for acquisition. Nevertheless, this collection of oil paintings meant much more to Clemson than an investment, and he worked tirelessly until the artworks were retrieved.

The last decade of Thomas Clemson's life was spent, in his own words, as a hermit. In response to Clemson's personal commentary, his close friend attorney James Rion shot back, "You say you are living the life of a hermit, and wishing to visit among those who have left this world. I must say you are a very *comfortable* hermit, with a splendid estate, elegant home and a faithful and intelligent housekeeper, your income greater than you can use, with books French and English to read and with good friends scattered about it is true." As Clemson grew older, he grew more lonely and reclusive. Suffering from depression, he also longed for the company of those who had passed on. Rion, not attuned to Clemson's interests in what was known as spiritualism in the nineteenth century, then lamented, "It is true however that you can not visit those on 'the other side,' except in thought and dream, but you have many friends on *this side*, who you can visit."[41]

Thomas Clemson was not known as an outwardly religious person. Indeed there is very little known about his personal beliefs. Whatever the case, both Anna and Thomas, who had been raised as Episcopalians, had some interest in the nineteenth-century forms of spiritualism.[42] Clemson sent a copy of a vision that Anna had recorded to John Gray who responded to Clemson, "I have no doubt whatever of the fact that Mr. Calhoun appeared to & spoke with his daughter, as related by her."[43] Whether Clemson had similar revelations is impossible to know. However, Clemson did correspond with others about spiritualism and was referred to works including "Cromwell Modern Spiritualism and Ancient Christianity."[44] In Clemson's last years, Jane Prince, his caregiver and housekeeper, said only of Clemson's spiritual life that he was often visited by a traveling Methodist minister and read the Bible.

*Left:* **Jane Prince, Thomas Clemson's caregiver for the last seven years of his life. Fort Hill Collection, Clemson University.** *Right:* **Jane Prince's daughter Hester ("Essie") and Hal Boggs at their May 1888 wedding at Fort Hill. Fort Hill Collection, Clemson University.**

Jane Prince and her daughter Hester "Essie" Prince were much more than simply employees; they had become an adopted family while Clemson's only grandchild Floride Isabella Lee was growing up in Carmel, New York. Floride Isabella kept up a regular correspondence with her Grandfather Clemson. She wrote about everyday life growing up with her father and her stepmother, Ella Lorton, formerly of Pendleton, who had been a childhood friend of Floride Elizabeth Clemson. Her daughter Floride Isabella's letters to her grandfather are full of accounts of the weather and the seasons as the years passed without her being able to make the trek to Fort Hill. Floride, in answering one of her grandfather's letters, says,

> I am very sorry that you are so lonely. I should like to go south every winter to see you, but if Papa can not go, & you know I can not go alone. It is not my fault. I remember you very distinctly and besides I have your nice photograph which you sent me some time ago. Your dogs must be very pretty; I should like to see them. You say you have but one cat, I wish you might have some of ours. We have about eight of them. One is an immense fellow the largest cat I ever saw. He is striped black & gray and we call him Tiger…I am glad Jane and Hester Prince take such good care of you.[45]

Often Floride recounts books she was reading, including *Twenty Thousand Leagues under the Sea* and *Around the World in Eighty Days* by Jules Verne. While Clemson made provisions for his granddaughter in versions of his will, he had other plans for Fort Hill.

Thomas G. Clemson's last years were also marked by a burning desire to preserve the legacy of his illustrious father-in-law. Clemson spearheaded the commissioning of a biography on Calhoun, kept an eye on efforts of the Calhoun Monument Association in Charleston for erecting a monument at Marion Square in front of the Old Citadel, and even attempted to have Calhoun's body exhumed for reburial either at St. Paul's next to Floride or at Fort Hill, in addition to making provisions for the historic preservation of Fort Hill in drafts of his will.

Thomas Clemson had greatly admired his father-in-law, who was an important influence on Clemson. Therefore he sought in many ways to preserve Calhoun's legacy. His efforts in that regard ranged from his preservation of Fort Hill and its contents to preserving the papers of John C. Calhoun for scholars. One of those efforts was the commissioning of a biography of John C. Calhoun. Although this was a time-consuming effort for Clemson to underwrite, this activity eventually proved unsuccessful through the course of three authors. Thomas Clemson first engaged the services of R. M. T. Hunter[46] and later W. P. Starke. James H. Rion even offered that he "could write two Chapters—'Mr. Calhoun on Slavery' & 'Mr. Calhoun.'"[47]

Robert Mercer Taliaferro Hunter had been a politician, congressman, and U.S. senator from Virginia. With Hunter's close working knowledge of John C. Calhoun, Clemson thought he would be able to fashion a biography of his father-in-law. Often working at a distance from Fort Hill beginning in 1876, Hunter spent an extensive amount of his research digging through the speeches and public addresses of Calhoun. His downfall may have been that he got bogged down in his research after completing what he considered a first volume on Calhoun. The great delays caused consternation for Clemson, and Hunter eventually withdrew his services.

Clemson went on to hire William Pinckney Starke who lived at Fort Hill from 1883 to 1886 and created a manuscript in shorthand before he died after a swim in the river. Starke's shorthand was utilized by later scholars, including Professor Franklin Jameson with whom Clemson corresponded. Jameson later noted that the collection "embraced 430 letters written by Calhoun, a certain amount of miscellaneous manuscripts. And about 2,300 letters written to him."[48] Clemson's preservation of Calhoun's correspondence has been useful for generations of scholars.

Thomas Clemson's wish to have his father-in-law's body moved from Charleston to the Upstate had become a sore point with the next generation of Calhouns and was looked upon somewhat disapprovingly by the Charleston newspaper, the *News and Courier*. In particular, the grandsons, in negative editorials in the paper, alluded to Clemson's wish to remove Calhoun's body for burial at Fort Hill as a conspiracy to inflate the worth of his estate and make his property more valuable for sale.

Simpson, in response to Clemson's request to include this stipulation as a provision of his bequest, pointed out to him, "I desire very much to talk with you about the removal of the remains of Mr. Calhoun. There are some difficulties in the accomplishment of this object, which I desire to state to you and in order that you may fully comprehend them I will be plain and unreserved. The only representatives left to Mr. Calhoun are the grandchildren and yourself, who is not a blood relation. Of this number you are in favor of the removal, and the others are opposed to it."

Simpson went on however to applaud the entire concept of Clemson's vision for an institution when he remarked,

> I never felt more relieved in my life and were you to do this act of public spirited generosity—that instant every slander and lie that have been uttered against you would be stamped as false and baseless fabrications. That moment you would pass in the minds of the people from a money-seeking individual to a liberal patriotic and public-spirited citizen. Every slander against you would be brushed away, and for all time to come your name will be linked with the name of Mr. Calhoun and the memories which cluster around Fort Hill.[49]

In addition to the final revisions of his will, Clemson's later years were devoted to seeing to fruition several avenues of preserving the legacy of his father-in-law, John C. Calhoun, beginning with the preservation of Fort Hill. It had become, as Clemson had hoped, a tourist attraction following Calhoun's death, and Clemson referred to Fort Hill as a Mecca for pilgrimages. Clemson promoted the house through articles and photographs. Perhaps the most widely circulated article (a travel description) about Fort Hill during the Clemson period was published in the *Scribner's Monthly* in 1883, for which Clemson was interviewed:

Everything is substantially as Mr. Calhoun left it, and all is plain and worn. The old-fashioned side-board was constructed of historic wood, and besides much family plate, it was ornamented by two great polished horns of African oxen, handsomely mounted in gold, a gilt clock of the time of Louis XVI, and other lesser articles of virtu, all gifts to Mr. Calhoun. Another interesting relic was the old straight-backed, sprawl-legged armchair, which Washington used at Trenton. In the more reserved 'parlor,' beyond this room are many family portraits in antique frames, including a queer one of Mrs. Calhoun's mother when a girl, with her hair done up in an inconceivably bushy manner.

This stereopticon photograph, ca. 1880, of the formal dining room at Fort Hill includes the *U.S.S. Constitution* ("Old Ironsides") sideboard, given to John C. Calhoun by Henry Clay. Fort Hill Collection, Clemson University.

The author goes on to write,

The library has its sides filled with bookshelves, and these are packed with volumes of every description, though largely the literature of the law and the rostrum....A marble bust of the senator occupies a pedestal in the corner, and here are the table at which he wrote, the chair in which he sat, the pictures that please his taste. It is a dark and somber room, though; there is not a bit of brightness or light to relieve the sober array of books, the heavy furniture, the dark paint and dull, grained ceiling.

*Above:* Stereopticon photograph, ca. 1880, showing Thomas Clemson seated
on front porch of Fort Hill. Fort Hill Collection, Clemson University.
*Below:* Relic Room of Fort Hill, showing a portion of Thomas Green Clemson's
art collection, ca. 1896. Fort Hill Collection, Clemson University.

The article concludes, "It still remains in the family, but a purchaser for the larger part if not the whole, would probably be welcomed."[50] Although Clemson had considered sale earlier, his plans with Anna for a college precluded considering a sale again.

The best photographs of Fort Hill during Clemson's later years were a series of stereopticon slides, which were produced with Clemson's blessing and with the goal to share images of Fort Hill with a wider audience. The series included the now famous black and white images of Clemson around Fort Hill. It may have been one of the conditions of the photo shoot that Clemson pose in front of each façade of the house. The famous photograph of Clemson seated on the north portico was part of this series, as were one in his rocking chair on the east lawn and another lying down, as sunbathers do today, on the south lawn of Fort Hill.

Two interior photographs were also shot. The first, which includes the Constitution Sideboard, pans the state dining room, which was also used by Mr. Clemson as his sitting room. The corresponding photographic image is of the parlor and aimed toward the right side of the mantel. This photograph shows a very crowded room in the vein of many other Victorian parlors. It appears as if the photographer asked Clemson to place many of his most prized possessions in that side of the room, which may have been enhanced by the depth of field of the stereoscope. In this corner of the room is the Clark Mills bust of John C. Calhoun, a porcelain bust after the Hiram Powers bust of Calhoun. The photo

**Stereopticon photograph of the Fort Hill Parlor, ca. 1880.**
**Fort Hill Collection, Clemson University.**

also shows the miniature painting of Clemson as a young man in Paris and the marble bust of his deceased daughter Cornelia (Nina) Clemson by Hiram Powers from a death mask. The furnishings in the image include his King Léopold Chair, the étagère in the corner, and Clemson's own painting of the Madonna and Child to the right of the fireplace.

In that same year (1883) and five years before his death, Clemson offered this assessment of his state of affairs: "I am growing old; I have been bereaved of all my family and live on a plantation some what isolated distant four miles from the town of Pendleton in Anderson Co., S.C. I live in the County of Oconee on the Seneca River." He went on to say, "This is a beautiful place & having been the residence of J. C. Calhoun is much visited & is become a kind of Mecca, much in some respects like Mt. Vernon."[51]

Thomas G. Clemson often drew a parallel between Fort Hill and Mt. Vernon in his desire to preserve the dwelling house as a museum. It is interesting to note that Anna Calhoun's roommate in the Barhamville finishing school was Anna Pamela Cunningham who devoted herself to the preservation of Mt. Vernon. It is then not surprising that one of Clemson's proposals regarding Fort Hill was that if the state did not accept his bequest he wanted the estate donated "to the women of South Carolina who by some legally constituted association such as now holds possession of Mt. Vernon may act as trustee for the preservation of the home of the illustrious man who spent his life in the public service of his country and who dignified a State which so long trusted and honored him."[52]

The revisions to his will by both James H. Rion and Richard W. Simpson honored Clemson's wishes that Fort Hill remain intact and, following his death, open for the inspection of visitors.

In other ways, his attorneys sought to keep him mindful of the chain of title of Fort Hill when Clemson was nearly eighty years old; Clemson understandably became forgetful of the chain of title to Fort Hill or perhaps the forgetfulness was calculated wishful thinking on Clemson's part. His longtime attorney James Rion in one very lengthy letter sought once and for all to set him straight. What follows in Rion's chronology was the convoluted and complicated deed history of Fort Hill which went to the root of the issue. The later animosity between Clemson and his son-in-law Gideon Lee made Clemson's granddaughter Floride Isabella an unwilling pawn in a chess game between two stubborn old men miles apart which essentially would end in a draw. Lee did not allow his daughter to visit the old man, but eventually she did receive the portion of Fort Hill land (not the home site), which Anna had set aside cordially with Gideon years earlier.

Rion's tone with Clemson in the following is abrupt and directly to the point. As a close family friend and a protégé of Calhoun, Rion was justifiably direct: after all, Anna had been as close as a sister to him. He begins with Clemson by reciting the land transactions: "*You never bought* Fort Hill, *nor paid* one cent for it. Mr.

Lee never bid for you or any one. *No one* ever *paid a cent* for the place. I will *again* explain it to you and I hope this will be finally satisfactory. I fear every day, of your having a difficulty with Mr. Lee (about as for whom, I have no concern, except I don't like him.) on account of your *unjust* charges against him." Rion's uneasiness regarding Lee's intentions would later come to fruition.

Then, somewhat out of frustration with Clemson whose memory may have been fogged by advanced age, James Rion succinctly goes through the course of events of the chain of title. He outlines them as follows:

1. John C. Calhoun owned Fort Hill.
2. Mrs. Floride Calhoun owned Fort Hill.
3. She sold the place to Andrew P. Calhoun.
4. Andrew mortgages the place to secure purchase money.
5. Mrs. Calhoun brought actions against Andrew to foreclose the mortgage. The court decided he owed $45,000 and decreed the place sold to foreclose the mortgage.
6. Mrs. Calhoun *willed* ¾ of the mortgage to Mrs. Clemson and ¼ to her daughter or if dead her child (now Floride Isabella Lee *your* granddaughter)—Mrs. Calhoun died.
7. Then at sale under Order of Court at Walhalla Jan 1872 the place was bid in so as to conform to Mrs. Calhoun's will ¾ for Mrs. Clemson and ¼ for Mrs. Lee.
8. You did not attend sale, Mr. Lee did not attend sale, Edward Noble as Attorney only attended sale,—no money was paid (except a small amount for costs) no money could have been paid—the title so says—the place was *bid in* for the debt, and those to whom the debt were willed by Mrs. Calhoun thereby owned the place.
9. You never did or *could* have bought or *paid* for the place.
10. Mrs. Clemson and Mr. Lee (for his daughter) desiring to divide the place according to their interests, on 5 November 1873, E. B. Colhoun for Mrs. Clemson [and] M. L. McCay for *Miss* Lee divided the land 818 acres for *your wife*, and 288 for Mr. Lee as guardian for his daughter. Now observe all this time *you* have no interest in Fort Hill, owning not a *square inch*, nor having *paid one cent*.
11. Mrs. Clemson made a will and gave you Fort Hill or her 818 acres.
12. On Mrs. Clemson's death you inherited Fort Hill as the Devisee of your wife.

All this is of Record, and you *must* understand it, and *never again* claim that you bought or paid for Fort Hill. When you do so, you not only accuse Mr. Lee;—but you claim that *Mrs. Clemson* to the day of her death claimed to own, what *you* had bought and paid for. You *grieve* me when you adhere to such *mistaken* notions.[53]

Having clarified the chain of title and written his last will and testament under the direction of James H. Rion with later revisions by Richard W. Simpson,[54] Thomas Clemson penned very few letters during his last two years of life. Near his death, he was confined to the first floor of Fort Hill because he could no longer go up the staircase. Clemson's dying wish was to see his long absent granddaughter. One of his enticements was to have her come see his paintings. And he assures young Floride that she would have someone her own age as a companion: "I would like you to see Fort Hill now that I have my paintings. Hester has her organ and plays quite well, by the time you come, she will play very well....Hester is smart, has a good music talent, and is remarkably well educated. I think you would be well pleased with her if you know her."[55]

The Prince family, both Essie and her mother Jane Prince, were very much a surrogate family for Thomas Clemson. While Essie was like an adopted granddaughter, Jane Prince, faithfully and dutifully, almost as a daughter taking care of an ailing elderly parent, saw to his day-to-day needs.[56] Right before Clemson's death, one of the most poignant letters sent from Fort Hill to his granddaughter was authored not by Clemson, but by his housekeeper's daughter Essie Prince, a teenager, who was writing to another teenager, Floride Isabella Lee, in Carmel, N.Y.:

Mr. Clemson received you & your father's letter a few days since, he rec'd his dressing gown & pajamas some weeks ago. The poor old gentleman has been very ill. We have been looking for him to die. We are all sorry to hear of Mr. Lee being sick, but if he could only hear his prayers or realize how he longs to see you surely you would come & see him. He appears better but we don't think he can possibly get well. The Dr. has been coming every day and says that Mr. Clemson has bronchitis. The dear old man said the other day that he has almost given up all hope of seeing you in this life. In the dead hours of night he often cries out, 'O Lord is it possible I will have to die without ever again seeing my only grandchild.' He has prayed to be spared to see you, but unless you come very soon I fear you will not gaze on him in life, but sad to say it will be in death. My mother stays by him night & day and does every thing she can for his comfort in fact he will not permit anyone to wait on him but her. We have stood faithfully to him for seven long years & intend to remain so to the end.
I am with respect
Yours very truly,
Essie Prince.[57]

And what Essie had predicted soon came true. A newspaper article, entitled "A Glorious Gift: Thomas G. Clemson's Bequest to the Farmers of South Carolina," noted:

Miss Lee, a very young lady, the dead man's only grandchild and great grand-daughter of Mr. Calhoun. Miss Lee has not been to Fort Hill before since she was a small child, and there was a very picturesque scene soon after her arrival when the old family servants, some of them with snow white hair and beard, gathered in the old fashioned, moss covered porch of the homestead to see and pay their loyal respects to the youngest representative of the family with which they have been identified so long.[58]

As historian Ernest Lander so aptly surmised, "The meeting was no consolation for Thomas Green Clemson."[59] Floride Isabella Lee was provided in Clemson's last will and testament what had been agreed upon years earlier by Anna and Gideon: essentially 288 acres, family portraits, silver, etc. Although Gideon Lee disagreed with the will, Clemson was very specific that the Fort Hill home be preserved as a part of the "high seminary of learning." Ironically, Clemson's granddaughter and only heir would soon meet and several years later marry her cousin, Andrew Pickens Calhoun II, son of Duff Green Calhoun and grandson of Andrew Pickens Calhoun—Anna Calhoun Clemson's eldest brother and the firstborn of John C. Calhoun. As the family Prayer Book editorialized about their marriage, "so ended the feud."[60]

Thomas Clemson handpicked the original life trustees for the institution that he envisioned. Many of them, such as Simpson, had known Clemson for a long time and knew his wishes for the institution to bear his name and for the preservation of Fort Hill. Clemson knew that others, like Benjamin Tillman, had similar objectives for the farmers of the state. And even others, like D. K. Norris, had strong ties to industry and particularly textiles. The first organizational meeting of the constituted Board of Trustees was held in the shadow of Fort Hill under an old oak tree where provisions of the will were read and agreed upon.

Although he did not live to see the scientific institution that bears his name, Clemson had certainly envisioned the college. Mary Rion, widow of James Rion, wrote to R. W. Simpson just a month after Clemson's death and related, "he took me out on the Hill top of the farm in front of Fort Hill and said Mrs. Rion I want the building which I wish erected for education purposes located right here & wish a monument to Mr. Calhoun in front of it so that both can be seen from the R.R."[61]

A newspaper account, entitled "The Old Calhoun Home," highlights many of the items that Clemson left in his will for the Fort Hill museum. The article describes it all in great detail:

> The point towards which the visitor at Fort Hill turns with most interest is the stately old mansion on the hill, where Calhoun lived and worked. The house must have been impressive in its day, and it still wears the air of some ancient ancestral hall. It is a frame building with tall-whitewashed brick columns sup-

porting the roofs of two spacious verandas, the one facing northward, the other to the east. The walls are white, relieved by blinds of green. Inside, everything is practically as it was in Calhoun's day. The rooms are papered and furnished with heavy, cumbersome, old fashioned furniture, which, with the low ceiling and narrow doorways and passages, give the interior a not over cheerful aspect.

A long, narrow apartment opening on the east front of the house is the art gallery, containing a rare collection of pictures and bric-a-brac. Here are a chair given to Mr. Clemson by the King of Belgians, another chair said to have been used by George Washington, a sideboard made from the hull of the old frigate "Constitution" presented to Calhoun by Henry Clay, to whom it was given by the officers of the frigate, and other quaint souvenirs of Calhoun's life. This room will be fitted up and retained as a museum of Calhoun's relics...Calhoun's old library is a little, single room house in the yard a few steps from the mansion. Its tables and shelves, with many of the books—some of them are relics in themselves—are those used by the great statesman in his daily labors. The desk he wrote on is still there, and in one of its drawers are the remains of his supply of goose quill pens.[62]

**Sketch of John C. Calhoun's office, from an illustrated article on Fort Hill in *Scribner's* magazine, ca. 1883. Fort Hill Collection, Clemson University.**

The preservation of Fort Hill is stated specifically in Thomas Clemson's last will and testament: "it is my desire that the dwelling house on Fort Hill shall never be torn down or altered, but shall be kept in repair, with all the articles of furniture and vesture which I hereinafter give for that purpose and shall always be open for the inspection of visitors." Clemson goes on to say that "for the purpose of adorning the Fort Hill residence as provided in Item 4 of my will, all of my permanent furniture, relics and articles of vesture, pictures and painting, including the large painting or picture of John C. Calhoun now hanging in my sitting room and not otherwise disposed of herein, and all of my books."[63]

In his codicil, Clemson further notes that he specifies the "executor to employ such person as he may deem necessary to take charge of the Fort Hill dwelling house and the articles therein donated" and finally, "I authorize and empower my executor to expend such sums of money as he may deem necessary to keep the Fort Hill dwelling house and premises in repair."

Simpson and the trustees saw to it that the old main building was built on the hill a short distance from Fort Hill.[64] Today, Fort Hill is preserved, and the old main building, later named Tillman Hall, sits on the hill. However, instead of a monument of Mr. Calhoun in front of Tillman Hall, a bronze statue of Thomas Green Clemson greets visitors to the Clemson University campus some 200 years after his birth in Philadelphia. This is a fitting memorial to Clemson and his vision of a "high seminary of learning" for his adopted state of South Carolina.

## Notes

1. Ernest McPherson Lander Jr., *The Calhoun Family and Thomas Green Clemson: The Decline of a Southern Patriarchy* (Columbia: University of South Carolina Press, 1983), 35; the book's frontispiece displays the Calhoun-Colhoun-Clemson family tree. Thomas and Anna Clemson's first child was a daughter. Very little is known of this infant girl born on 13 August 1839. She died within a month, and her burial location is unknown. However, Thomas Clemson's caregiver, Jane Prince, noted that she was told the daughter was buried at the Old Stone Church in Pendleton, SC, but no baptismal records, gravestone, or cemetery records with her name have been found. The second child of the Clemsons was their only son John Calhoun Clemson. He was born at Fort Hill on 17 July 1841, died on 10 August 1871, and is buried at St. Paul's in Pendleton. A Civil War veteran, he was thirty at the time of his death and unmarried. The Clemsons' third child was Floride Elizabeth Clemson, born on 29 December 1842. She married Gideon Lee Jr. and had one daughter, Floride Isabella Lee. Floride Elizabeth died on 23 July 1871, and is buried in Carmel, NY. The fourth child of the Clemsons was Cornelia Clemson, born 3 October 1855. She died at age 3 in Maryland at The Home on 20 December 1858. A bust of Cornelia Clemson is in the parlor at Fort Hill. Named for her aunt and Anna's sister Cornelia Calhoun, she was fondly called Nina by her parents. In 1872, her body was moved to the Rock Creek Cemetery in Washington, DC, where she was listed as age 3 years, 2 months, and 17 days and having died on 20 December 1858 of scarlet fever in Prince George's County, MD. Her burial site was owned by Anna Calhoun Clemson, along with seven vacant sites that were never used. See Correspondence, 24 February 2000, Fort Hill Collection, Clemson University, Clemson, SC.
2. Susan Clemson Richardson recounted that she had been a slave at Fort Hill and had been given by Calhoun to the Clemsons as Anna's personal maid. She recounted sleeping in a room adjacent to the Clemsons so she could be awakened to care for the small children. See Fort Hill Collection, Clemson University.
3. The wallpaper and the matching border were reproduced in 2003.
4. Thomas G. Clemson and Robert E. Lee were both 54 in 1861 and, like Lee, TGC made a similar decision to resign from his federal job with the Department of the Interior Patent Office and his post as superintendent of agricultural affairs in order to enlist with the Confederacy.

5.  Charles M. McGee Jr. and Ernest McPherson Lander Jr., eds., *A Rebel Came Home: The Diary and Letters of Floride Calhoun 1863–1866*, revised edition (Columbia: University of South Carolina Press, 1989), 90.
6.  TGC to Tazewell Taylor, 18 October 1865, Clemson Papers, Special Collections, Clemson University Libraries, Clemson, SC (hereafter cited as SCCUL).
7.  TGC to Tazewell Taylor, 28 May 1866, Clemson Papers, SCCUL.
8.  TGC to James Edward Calhoun [aka James Edward Colhoun], 24 June 1866, Ibid.
9.  Minutes of the Pendleton Farmers' Society, 8 October 1868, Ibid.
10. Alester G. Holmes and George R. Sherrill, *Thomas Green Clemson: His Life and Work* (Richmond, VA: Garrett & Massie, 1937), 146.
11. Ibid., 146.
12. TGC to Jas. Ed. Colhoun, 14 March 1867, Clemson Papers, SCCUL.
13. D. W. Lee to TGC, 29 January 1867, Ibid.
14. See Lander, *Calhoun Family and Thomas Green Clemson*, for the unpleasant effects that the events had on the family. The family animosity began with the overindulgence of John Calhoun with financing Andrew's Alabama estate also called Cane Brake in which Clemson invested—an investment he came to regret bitterly. Local lore recounts a rift between Floride Calhoun and her daughter-in-law Margaret; there is even one story of Mrs. Calhoun's being served tea at Fort Hill with a piece of her own china but from a cracked cup.
15. Anna Calhoun Clemson to Andrew Pickens Calhoun, 10 March 1865, Clemson Papers, SCCUL.
16. Mildred Calhoun Wick provides a dramatic account as related to her by her father, Pat Calhoun: her grandmother Margaret "turned to Father and Rasmas, the young black boy assigned to be Father's constant companion. 'Pat, Rasmas,' she said, 'you run deep into the woods and hide until the soldiers leave and it's safe for you to come out.'…Unknown to her, they left the safety of the wood and hid behind some trees near the house…They [soldiers] took food, liquor and money, and put small objects into their pockets." Pat Calhoun, then eight years, old related in later life, "it was the most terrifying experience of my life." Mildred Calhoun Wick, *Living with Love* (Newport, DE: Serendipity Press, 1986), 18.
17. McGee and Lander, eds., *A Rebel Came Home*, 87.
18. While Fort Hill, John C. Calhoun's estate, had survived the tumultuous Civil War, his mortal remains in Charleston had been relocated to an unmarked grave for safekeeping by the rector of St. Phillip's in Charleston.
19. Floride Calhoun was buried in St. Paul's Episcopal Church graveyard in Pendleton, SC.
20. The freedmen and women signing this 1868 document were: Felix Collins, Pinckney Cunningham, Cato Sherman, Jessie Mickleburg, Daniel Coscam, Edward Reed, Quash Richardson, Bob Pedigrew, Jonas Coscam, John Lagree, Frank Spencer, Jonas Jackson, Osborn Preston, Ben Brown, Wash., H., Stephen Green, and Thomas C. Abbot. Clemson Papers, SCCUL. The corner of the document is torn and is missing; only the first name "Wash." remains. The contracts survive for only three years: 1868, 1869, and 1871. The numbers of tenants or sharecroppers ranged from fifteen to twenty employees. Several of the freedmen continued for multiple years. The Reid, Greenlee, and Fruster families are not listed as employees at this point. However, Bill Greenlee, along with Jim and Francis Fruster, would be African American employees at the time of Clemson's death years later. It is interesting to note that the slave last name of "Calhoun" appears nowhere after the war; however, numerous African American Calhouns trace their roots to Fort Hill.
21. TGC to R. W. Simpson, 16 December 1868, Clemson Papers, SCCUL.
22. Anna Calhoun Clemson to James Edward Calhoun, 8 June 1869, Ibid.
23. Anna Calhoun Clemson to Louisa Washington, 7 March 1873, Ibid. A transcription of the letter is included in Julia Wright Sublette, "The Letters of Anna Calhoun Clemson, 1833–1873" (Ph.D. dissertation, Florida State University, 1993), 892.
24. A newspaper account entitled "Fatal Accident" relates, "A terrible accident occurred at Hunnicut's Crossing on the Blue Ridge Railroad last Thursday evening resulting in the death of Mr. John Calhoun Clemson, grandson of Hon. John C. Calhoun and only son of Hon. Thos. G. Clemson of Pendleton. It appears from the testimony taken at the inquest…that a lumber train belonging to the Greenville Railroad ran into the passenger train of the Blue Ridge Road at the place designated and that Mr. Clemson in attempting to get into the second class car

was thrown violently against the facing of the car door and fatally injured in the region of the heart one of his ribs penetrating that organ." Clemson Papers, SCCUL.

25. There is a tradition that John Calhoun Clemson was married to Jane Prince and that her daughter Essie was the offspring of John Calhoun Clemson. This tradition is especially recounted in the documents and oral tradition of the Boggs family. See family genealogy typescript of 14 September 1871 in Aaron Boggs Papers, SCCUL. The typescript has a notation on page 2 that "John Calhoun Clemson married Jane 1870. Hester a daughter of John Calhoun Clemson & Jane born April 14, 1871 at Mi Casa, Pendleton, S.C." Anna Clemson's correspondence is silent for the year of 1871.

26. William Henry Trescot to TGC, 19 October 1873, Clemson Papers, SCCUL.

27. Cited in Franklin Parker, "George Peabody, 1795–1869: His Influence on Educational Philanthropy," *Peabody Journal of Education* 49, no. 2 (January 1972): 139; original source is a letter from George Peabody to the Trustees of the Peabody Education Fund, 7 February 1867, Archives of George Peabody College (now Vanderbilt University), Nashville, TN. In his bequest the philanthropist established the Peabody Education Fund to "encourage the intellectual, moral, and industrial education of the destitute children of the southern States."

28. James Shepherd Pike (8 September 1811–29 November 1882). Pike authored a series of articles for the *New York Tribune*, which was published as *The Prostrate State: South Carolina under Negro Government* (New York: n.p., 1874).

29. Joseph Henry to TGC, 10 September 1874, Clemson Papers, SCCUL.

30. The funeral notice simply states, "The Friends and acquaintances of Mr. & Mrs. Thomas G. Clemson are invited to attend the funeral services of the latter at St. Paul's church today at 3 o'clock P.M. Sept. 24, 1875," Ibid.

31. James H. Rion, 25 September 1875, Ibid.

32. George Peabody of New York.

33. TGC to W. W. Corcoran, 29 October 1878, Clemson Papers, SCCUL; see also Holmes and Sherrill, *Thomas Green Clemson*, 152–153.

34. James H. Rion to TGC, 18 December 1884, Clemson Papers, SCCUL.

35. William Henry Trescot to TGC, 21 December 1884, Ibid.

36. J. B. Ferguson, Maryland Commission of Fish & Fisheries, to TGC, 3 January 1879, Ibid.

37. TGC to George North, 21 January 1871, Ibid.

38. TGC to those whom it may concern, 19 February 1877, Ibid.

39. James H. Rion to TGC, 19 August 1883, Ibid.

40. TGC to William MacLeod, 18 January 1876, William MacLeod Papers, Corcoran Gallery of Art, Washington, DC. A copy of the letter is in the Fort Hill Collection, Clemson University. Clemson's offer of the paintings for sale received a response that MacLeod, on behalf of the newly established Corcoran Gallery of Art, was not at liberty to expend funds for acquisition.

41. James H. Rion to TGC, 6 November 1883, Clemson Papers, SCCUL.

42. A record of a vision Anna C. Clemson had of her father, John C. Calhoun, ten years after his death, was transcribed by Ernest Lander and appears in McGee and Lander, eds., *A Rebel Came Home*, Appendix IV, 173.

43. John Gray to TGC, 28 December 1875, Clemson Papers, SCCUL.

44. N. B. Wolfe to TGC, 20 February 1878, Ibid.

45. Floride Lee to TGC, 30 January 1886, Ibid.

46. Robert Mercer Taliaferro Hunter, 1809–1887, *Biographical Directory of the United States Congress Online*.

47. W. P. Starke to TGC, 29 January 1883, Clemson Papers, SCCUL. Starke quotes from a letter that Rion had written asking him to take up the Calhoun biography project following Hunter's dismissal.

48. Franklin Jameson, *Correspondence of John C. Calhoun*, Fourth Report of the Manuscripts Commission, American Historical Association, 1900, 12.

49. R. W. Simpson to TGC, 11 January 1882, Clemson Papers, SCCUL; see also Holmes and Sherrill, *Thomas Green Clemson*, 155.

50. Ernest Ingersoll, "The Calhoun Summer Home," *Scribner's Monthly* (Century), 21 (1881): 893–895. This article includes two hand-drawn sketches: one of the exterior of the house and office showing the detached kitchen and one important sketch of the interior of Calhoun's

office which attest to the fact that Clemson kept the house very much as a museum to his father-in-law even during Clemson's lifetime.

51. TGC to W. P. Jackson and George Seufferle, 8 August 1883, Clemson Papers, SCCUL. Jackson and Seufferle were acting as agents for Clemson in regard to the rental of The Home in Maryland.

52. Holmes and Sherrill, *Thomas Green Clemson*, 157.

53. James H. Rion to TGC, 16 July 1886, Clemson Papers, SCCUL.

54. James H. Rion devoted much of his life and career to assisting both Anna and Thomas Clemson. As a young protégé of John C. Calhoun, he essentially grew up at Fort Hill and felt a great debt and duty to repay Thomas Clemson in managing his estate. Rion is the author of Thomas Clemson's original will and testament. An attorney in Winnsboro, he predeceased Clemson when he died suddenly on 12 December 1886. Clemson received a telegram the next day, 13 December. The following day, Thomas Clemson wrote a short one-page letter to Richard Simpson noting that "it may be impossible that the death of so distinguished a man should have passed away so suddenly without your knowledge. It now becomes necessary that I should see you." See TGC to Richard Simpson, 14 December 1886, Clemson Papers, SCCUL.

55. TGC to Floride Lee, 26 April 1887, Ibid.

56. Both Jane Prince and her daughter Essie were well provided for in Clemson's will. When interviewed by Alester Holmes on 9 March 1928, Mrs. Prince stated of Fort Hill, "I went there in January 1881. I was there all told, eleven years, but during his life I was there seven years, then the state retained me on....The Mr. J. F. Calhoun wanted something to do with the college." Here Jane Prince makes reference to the family of James Francis Calhoun who moved into the west side of the house and whose family and daughters' (particularly Ida Calhoun) duties were to show visitors through the segregated museum relic rooms. In 1928, President Sikes's interpretation of the will was to open the entire house as a museum. The second restoration began in 2000 and was completed in 2003.

57. Essie Prince to Floride Lee, 25 February 1888, Clemson Papers, SCCUL. Essie Prince was, in the words of her mother, special to Mr. Clemson: "the apple of his eye and the bane of his existence." He doted on the young girl. He personally taught her French, violin, piano, and organ lessons. Thomas Clemson's pump organ is currently on loan to Woodburn Plantation in Pendleton. Essie Prince married Hal Boggs at Fort Hill in May 1888. Jane Prince was provided for in Clemson's estate. See newspaper article by Earl Mazo, "Former Fort Hill Housekeeper Cherished Relics Left Her by Thomas G. Clemson," *The Tiger* (Clemson University), March 1938, and Earl Mazo, "Clemson Praised by Housekeeper," *Greenville News* (Greenville, SC), 8 March 1938, Fort Hill Collection, Clemson University.

58. See "A Glorious Gift: Thomas G. Clemson's Bequest to the Farmers of South Carolina," newspaper clipping in the Clemson Papers, SCCUL.

59. Lander, *Calhoun Family and Thomas Green Clemson*, 257.

60. Calhoun Family Prayer Book, Fort Hill Collection, Clemson University.

61. Mary C. Rion to R. W. Simpson, 7 May 1888, Simpson Papers, Clemson University, Special Collections, Clemson University Libraries. Mary C. Rion (1829–1901) was very close to Clemson as had been her husband. An avid gardener, her book *Ladies' Southern Florist* was published in 1860.

62. "A Glorious Gift: Thomas G. Clemson's Bequest," newspaper clipping in the Clemson Papers, SCCUL.

63. Last Will and Testament of Thomas Green Clemson.

64. Tillman Hall, formerly known as Main Hall, was named for Benjamin Ryan Tillman in 1943 on the fiftieth anniversary of the opening of the college. A full-length painting of Tillman was commissioned for the renamed building.

# Chapter 12

## CLEMSON'S LAST WILL AND TESTAMENT

### *Clayton D. Steadman*

Thomas Green Clemson, ca. 1880. This tinted photograph hangs in the
Clemson bedroom at Fort Hill. Fort Hill Collection, Clemson University.

Thomas Green Clemson died on April 6, 1888, leaving his Last Will and
Testament to direct the disposition of his worldly assets. These consisted
primarily of the approximately 800 acres of land and his estate at Fort
Hill, South Carolina, valued at $80,000, plus numerous personal and household

items of minimal value. Certainly there was nothing particularly unusual about a relatively prosperous individual like Clemson leaving a will; the probate records of Oconee County, South Carolina, contain many such documents from the last two decades of the nineteenth century. But Clemson's Last Will and Testament is not like the typical will of its time.[1] It is a unique document in many ways, but it is most unique in two major respects: the nature of his bequests and the manner in which those bequests are to be managed. This iconoclastic document is a reflection of its author and benefactor and the unusual, sometimes competing, amalgam of his own peculiar personality. Finally, the Last Will and Testament is the foundation for Clemson University, an institution whose creation and continued existence as a result of the will has had a profound and lasting effect on the people of the State of South Carolina.

## *The Long Evolution of a Dream*

It is impossible to state when Clemson first formulated the concept of donating the bulk of his estate for the establishment of a college primarily focused upon providing education for the benefit of "farmers and mechanics," but it was a natural outgrowth of an interest in scientific education and especially agricultural education that spanned most of his professional career.

In 1856, while a resident of Prince George's County in Maryland, Clemson was an early and outspoken advocate of the establishment of an agricultural college in that state. He wrote numerous letters and articles supporting the creation of what was to become the University of Maryland and actively solicited donations to the endowment that was a necessary condition of legislative appropriations for the college's operations.[2] Later, as the superintendent of agricultural affairs, Clemson supported the concept of donating federal lands to the various states for the purpose of establishing colleges for the study of agriculture and the mechanical arts. As discussed fully in Chapters 5 and 7, this idea was eventually embodied in the Morrill Act which created the federal land-grant college system, and which was passed into law in July 1862 after the onset of the Civil War and Clemson's resignation as the first United States Superintendent of Agricultural Affairs. Upon his return to South Carolina, he resumed his advocacy of agricultural education, urging the establishment of a department of agriculture within the Confederate government and the sponsorship of agricultural education within the Confederacy as a whole and South Carolina in particular.[3]

After the end of the Civil War, Clemson's interest in fostering agricultural education seems to have intensified. It took on the added dimension of being a possible panacea for South Carolina's dire economic condition. In 1866, Clemson was elected president of the Pendleton Farmers' Society and undertook to establish a school for the education of South Carolinians in science and specifically in the scientific study of agriculture. This plan seems to incorporate the intent of establishing a land-grant college that would qualify for federal largesse under the terms of the Morrill Act. A formal resolution adopted by the society in November of 1869 memorializes this intention and is another reflection of Clemson's long-standing and abiding interest in agricultural education.

It is about this time that two other themes begin to emerge that relate to Clemson's desire to found an agricultural college. One was his increasingly frustrated, critical, and sometimes hostile attitude toward South Carolina's elected officials. His writings refer to the failure of the legislature to appreciate the need for better education of its citizens and its "indifference" and "stolid apathy" in rejecting proposals to create an agricultural college in the state.[4] Clemson bemoaned the fact that the legislature habitually would "meet in conventions, pass resolutions, disperse and things remain in status quo…to the exclusion of that kind of information, for the want of which, the people are fast sinking in despair."[5] Some of his hostility and mistrust is typical of the recently dispossessed southern gentry's (a category into which Clemson does not necessarily fit, in all respects) attitude toward the Reconstruction governments imposed by federal law. For instance, his cynical references to Governor Daniel H. Chamberlain and H. H. Kimpton, the New York financier whose bond deals nearly wrecked the state treasury,[6] are consistent with the anti-carpetbagger sentiments of his contemporaries. But these kinds of comments continue to appear in Clemson's correspondence and writings long after the end of the Reconstruction governments in 1876. This fundamental mistrust of governmental officials to recognize the value of practical, mechanical, and agricultural education, and his perception of a legislative penchant for acting more for the benefit of the "well born" than of the majority of South Carolina's citizens will be reflected in Clemson's will and the governance structure of the institution thereby created.

The second theme to emerge from Clemson's writings at this time is an appreciation that the benefits of scientific education are not just theoretical, but functional as well. He notes in numerous passages that education, and scientific education in particular, is the surest means to economic prosperity.[7] This concept of education as a driver in economic development is another theme that will be played out in more detail in Clemson's will.

The earliest indication we have of Clemson's idea of donating Fort Hill to the State of South Carolina for the purpose of establishing an agricultural college was sometime in 1871, when he and his wife executed mutual wills with the intent of having the Fort Hill property go to the state upon the death of the surviving partner. No copies of these wills exist, but they are referred to in testimony contained in the record of the later lawsuit contesting Clemson's Last Will and Testament.[8] These references make it clear that the primary purpose of this bequest was to further Clemson's interest in agricultural education and to engender the economic benefits for the region that he believed would flow from the creation of such an institution. But it also is clear that a secondary purpose of such a bequest was to honor the memory of his father-in-law, John C. Calhoun. Clemson had always shown great admiration for Calhoun on several levels: first, as the father of his wife, Anna Calhoun Clemson, to whom both Calhoun and Clemson were devoted; second, as a thinker to whose political philosophy and intellectual curiosity Clemson responded avidly; and finally, as the mentor responsible for promoting Clemson's own diplomatic and governmental career. One does not get the sense that Clemson was beholden to Calhoun, but rather had a deep and sincere affection for the man which he sought to demonstrate through some lasting tribute.[9]

When Anna Calhoun Clemson died in 1875, Clemson became the sole owner of Fort Hill. All of his and Anna's children had predeceased them, and the only surviving heir was his granddaughter, Floride Isabella Lee. His and Anna's shared vision of creating an agricultural college at Fort Hill remained with him, and in 1878 he wrote to W. W. Corcoran, his old acquaintance from Washington, D.C., and outlined his plans for such an institution. He notes that creating a purely private college would be ideal—since as such it would be "untrammeled" by legislative interference—and seems to be making a thinly veiled pitch to Corcoran (whom Clemson acknowledges as "among the foremost philanthropists of the world") to determine his interest in contributing to such a project. We have no record of Corcoran's reply, and there is no record that he ever responded with a donation. Clemson goes on in the letter to note that, in the absence of private donations sufficient to establish and operate a college, it could be more inexpensive and expeditious to donate the land to the state in exchange for the state's making an appropriation sufficient "to carry the project into execution."[10]

James Henry Rion (1828–1886), Thomas Clemson's attorney, advisor, and a resident of Winnsboro, South Carolina, ca. 1885. George Valentine, photographer. South Caroliniana Library, University of South Carolina.

Sometime prior to 1883, Clemson instructed James H. Rion to draw up a will which included a provision for the donation of the bulk of his estate to the creation of an agricultural college. Rion, Clemson's attorney and a resident of Winnsboro, South Carolina, was born in Montreal, Canada, but grew up in Pendleton, South Carolina, where he attended school and actually lived for a time at Fort Hill. He graduated from South Carolina College in 1850; four years later he began practicing law in Winnsboro, where he remained until his death.[11] No copy of that original will exists, but we can ascertain the main components based upon a letter Clemson wrote to Rion on April 27 of 1883, suggesting changes to the draft he had prepared and forwarded to Clemson. In his letter, Clemson outlines his desire to create an institution that will instruct students in mathematics, geology and mineralogy, chemistry, and modern languages. He specifies that all of the Fort Hill property, consisting of over 800 acres of cultivated land, will be donated to this purpose and states that he hopes he does not "underestimate the intelligence of the legislature of a State ever distinguished for its liberality in assuming that such appropriations will be made as may be necessary" to operate the college he proposes.[12] He also notes that he intends to give the legislature a deadline—he proposes seven years in this letter and that time frame is shortened over subsequent drafts to five years and ultimately to three years—for accepting and funding his bequest or he directs that his estate should go to the establishment of a trust to preserve Fort Hill in much the same manner as George Washington's estate at Mount Vernon was preserved.

**Col. Richard Wright Simpson (1840–1912), who served as a member and first president of the original Board of Trustees of Clemson College, was a longtime friend, advisor, attorney, and executor of the estate of Thomas Clemson. Photograph from the 1907 *TAPS* yearbook, Clemson College.**

There is anecdotal evidence that Clemson originally proposed the name of "Calhoun-Clemson College" and that the original 1883 will referred to it as "Fort Hill Scientific Institute."[13] R. W. Simpson states in his testimony in the lawsuit over the probate of Clemson's will that he convinced Clemson to name the college "The Clemson Agricultural College of South Carolina."[14] Apparently, Clemson agreed with Simpson's recommendation, since the will states that the proposed school shall be known by that name.

Clemson appears to have been very thoughtful in drafting his will. In addition to Rion's input, he sought the advice of numerous other friends regarding his plans.[15] In the fall of 1886, Clemson invited South Carolina political leader B. R. Tillman, along with D. K. Norris and Clemson's attorney friend R. W. Simpson, to his home at Fort Hill to seek their counsel on his project. By this time, Simpson had eclipsed Rion as Clemson's primary legal counselor, due apparently to Rion's advanced age and declining health (he was to pass away on December

12, 1886). Simpson was a longtime friend and advisor to Clemson and a close neighbor, living in Pendleton, South Carolina, just a few miles from Fort Hill. Simpson was born in Pendleton in 1840 and graduated from Wofford College in Spartanburg before returning to the Pendleton area to pursue the practice of law and a legislative career. He also devoted himself to agricultural pursuits, and it was in this capacity that he and Clemson became friends. Simpson was the executor of Clemson's estate and was the named defendant in the lawsuit brought by Clemson's son-in-law, Gideon Lee, in an attempt to invalidate the will. Simpson also served as a member of the original board of trustees of Clemson College and was elected as its first president. He died on July 11, 1912.

**Daniel Keating Norris (1845–1905), a member of Clemson College's Board of Trustees from 1889 to 1905, was a friend and advisor to Thomas Clemson. This portrait hangs in Sikes Hall, Clemson University. Clemson University Artwork Photographs, Special Collections, Clemson University Libraries.**

**Benjamin Ryan Tillman (1847–1918), a populist politician, governor of South Carolina, and U.S. senator, championed the founding of Clemson College and served on its original Board of Trustees. Clemson University Photographs, Special Collections, Clemson University Libraries.**

At this convocation at Fort Hill in 1886, Clemson sought the advice and best thinking of this group of trusted advisors regarding the structure and tactics for fulfilling his dream of an agricultural college for South Carolina's youth. The exact details of that discussion are unknown since there are no contemporaneous notes of the meeting. Clemson makes no direct reference to it in any extant papers. The only accounts to have survived are an interview Ben Tillman gave in 1909,[16] the testimony R. W. Simpson gave during the Lee v. Simpson trial in 1889, and a newspaper interview Simpson gave in 1891.[17] Not only are these accounts recorded a number of years after the fact, but they are also inconsistent. All that is known for certain is that these four gentlemen—Rion, Simpson, Norris, and Tillman—met for the express purpose of discussing Clemson's plans for a bequest to create an agricultural college at Fort Hill. As a result of this meeting, Clemson gave Simpson a copy of the original will drafted by Rion (which Simpson was unaware of until that moment) and asked him to make certain changes based upon the comments he had received from his advisors. Simpson incorporated those changes, and a revised will was executed by Clemson on November 6, 1886. This is the final version of the will, although Clemson added a "codicil" dated April 20, 1887. The will[18] outlines the creation, purpose, and governance of Clemson College.

## No Ordinary Last Will and Testament

There are a number of specific provisions in the will that bear directly on the governance and operation of Clemson University, and it may be helpful to summarize the more notable of them. For example, Item 1 of the will contains the basic devise of Clemson's estate to the State of South Carolina for the express purpose of establishing an agricultural college at that location. The gift is conditioned upon the South Carolina Legislature affirmatively accepting the gift, including all terms and conditions stated in the will, within a period of three years from the probate of the will. This section also specifies that the property is to be held by the state "so long as it, in good faith, devotes said property to the purposes of the donation."

Item 2 describes the selection and duties of the board of trustees that is to govern the affairs of the institution created by the will. Seven initial trustees are named by Clemson, and these "life trustees" are expressly empowered to fill all vacancies among their members. Additionally, the will allows the S.C. Legislature to appoint up to six additional trustees in the event it accepts the gift in the manner prescribed in the will. Item 2 clearly states that the board of trustees shall never increase to a number greater than thirteen, making it clear that the life trustees are always to be in the majority, thereby allowing the legislature to influence but not control the governance of the college. This particular provision renders Clemson University's current governance structure unique among public universities and created the first "public-private" governing body for a public university with the added distinction of ensuring that the "private" life trustees would always be in the majority. This fact was to engender some opposition in the South Carolina Legislature and in the press during the debate over the acceptance of the will.

Photograph of the first Board of Trustees of Clemson Agricultural College of South
Carolina, ca. 1890. *Inset row at top:* Mauldin, Craighead, Wanamaker, Stackhouse.
*Middle row:* Donaldson, Sloan, Simpson, Bradley, Redfern, Tindall, Bowen.
*Front row:* Jefferies, Norris, Tillman, Hardin. Clemson University
Photographs, Special Collections, Clemson University Libraries.

Clemson University Board of Trustees gathers in 2007 under the Trustee Oak
on the Fort Hill lawn to commemorate the bicentennial anniversary of the
birth of Thomas Green Clemson. *From left to right:* E. Smyth McKissick III,
Louis B. Lynn, Thomas B. McTeer Jr., David H. Wilkins, Joseph D. Swann,
John J. Britton, Thomas C. Lynch Jr., Leon J. Hendrix Jr., Leslie G. McCraw,
Patricia Herring McAbee, Robert L. Peeler, William C. Smith Jr. (Bill L. Amick
not pictured). Clemson University Department of Creative Services.

Item 2 also states that the rights of the board of trustees shall never be "taken away or conferred upon any other man or body of men." The preamble to the will confers on the board "the full authority and power to regulate all matters pertaining to said institution." The will goes on to enumerate some of these specific powers as the right to "fix the course of studies, to make rules for the government" of the institution and to change the rules "as in their judgment, experience may prove necessary." The power thus delegated to the board is without limitation or exception.

Finally, in Item 3, the will provides for an alternative disposition of Clemson's estate in the event that the legislature fails to accept his donation in the manner mandated in the will. In the event of such a default, his land and other property—exclusive of some minor bequests to friends and family—would go to a trust for the establishment and operation of a school for the youth of South Carolina. The details of this alternative bequest are of limited interest given the fact that the legislature did in fact accept Clemson's bequest. However, the fact that an alternative was explicitly included in the will is important in analyzing the seriousness with which he considered the conditions his will places upon the state's acceptance of his proposed gift.

It is perhaps also useful to consider the legal implications of the will's form and structure, beginning with the fact that it created a charitable trust. To qualify as a charitable trust, it must be established that the donor's intent was charitable and that the beneficiaries are an indefinite group composed of society as a whole or a reasonably large segment of society as a whole. Clemson clearly expresses the charitable intent of his gift when he states in the will that his "purpose is to establish an agricultural college which will afford useful information to the farmers and mechanics" of the State of South Carolina. Similarly, the "farmers and mechanics" of South Carolina would meet the test of an indefinite group composed of a reasonably large segment of society as a whole. Thus, the will conforms to the accepted legal definition of a charitable trust.

Charitable trusts are accorded particular favor, and courts will construe them, if at all possible, so as to carry out the general intent of the donor. Generally, once a charitable trust is created, it cannot be modified. However, South Carolina courts have recognized a concept known as administrative or equitable deviation which authorizes a court to make changes in the administration of the trust provided certain, very narrow criteria are met.

For a court to apply equitable deviation, it must first be proven that the intent of the trust is impractical or illegal to enforce. Second, it must be established that the provision which is alleged to be impractical or illegal is due to circumstances not known or anticipated by the donor at the time the gift was made. In the case of the will, the intent is very simply to establish a college to be governed by a board of trustees with full authority and power to regulate all matters pertaining to its governance. The fact that Clemson University has existed and thrived for over one hundred years pursuant to this form of governance would seem to offer conclusive evidence that it is not "impractical" to continue enforcing the terms of the will as it is written. Furthermore, there is currently no law which would make it "illegal" for Clemson University to be governed by a board of trustees as provided in the will.

At the time of the will's drafting, and at the time it was probated and its terms accepted by the state, the possibility of the state governing the administration of the proposed college to be created was fully known to Clemson. His reference in the will to the governing structure of the "Agricultural College of Mississippi" (now Mississippi State University), his specific direction that the authority of the board never be taken away or abridged by the legislature, and the stipulation for an alternative bequest in the event that the legislature did not accept his gift with all of its conditions demonstrate Clemson's knowledge of the possibility of some form of governance which would usurp the power he specifically delegates to the board in his will.

Based upon an analysis of the terms and their probable construction in the event of a legal challenge, it seems virtually certain that the will would be deemed to be a charitable trust, duly established according to the laws of South Carolina. Furthermore, any challenge to the application of the will, insofar as the power and authority of the board of trustees to govern in all matters pertaining to the university, would not likely succeed on the basis of equitable deviation.

As noted at the outset, the will conditioned the gift of Clemson's property to the State of South Carolina upon several specific occurrences. These include the establishment of an agricultural college on the real property conveyed by the will, the application of all other assets (essentially cash) for the creation and operation of the college, and the governance of the college entrusted to a board of trustees appointed and perpetuated according to the terms contained therein. Finally, the creation of the trust was contingent upon the S.C. Legislature formally accepting the gift and all of its conditions no later than three years after the death of Clemson.

The language of the will is so clear and unambiguous as to leave no doubt of the validity of the trust thereby created. However, it is much less clear what legally enforceable obligations the state has assumed by virtue of its acceptance of the will. The only reference in the will to an ongoing obligation of the state to support the university is a reference in the preamble where Clemson says that he hopes he does not "overrate the intelligence of the legislature of South Carolina…in assuming that such appropriations will be made as are necessary to supplement the fund resulting from the bequest herein made." The will does not contain any requirement that the state provide any specific financial or other support for the creation or operation of the school. It is possible that an argument could be made that the language in Item 1 (e.g., "the State of South Carolina may accept said property as a donation from me, for the purpose of thereupon founding an agricultural college" and that the gift is to be held by the state "so long as it, in good faith, devotes said property to the purposes of the donation") implies an obligation on the part of the state to provide financial support for the college. It is also possible that an argument could be made that there is an implied obligation of the state to provide some minimal level of funding and other support by virtue of its acceptance of the gift. This issue has never arisen, other than as a hypothetical question, as the level of state funding since the establishment of Clemson College has always exceeded an amount that could be fairly characterized as "minimal."

Although the board has unlimited authority relative to the governance of Clemson University, it is not necessarily compelled to exercise that power. Again, the will is very clear that the board shall have "full power and authority" regarding all matters pertaining to the institution. They are expressly authorized to make decisions and to change them, bound only by their own collective judgment. Implicit in this authority is the right to not exercise their authority or to delegate it to some other person or body. The board has delegated many of the routine, administrative tasks of the university to the president and others, including the faculty. These delegations neither diminish nor abridge the powers of the board, nor are they irrevocable. The board may at any time revoke or amend any such delegation of authority "as in their judgment, experience may prove necessary."

Thomas Green Clemson's signet ring, used for embossing his seal on documents. The antique ring features an intaglio equestrian image of Marcus Aurelius Antoninus, Roman emperor and Stoic philosopher. Fort Hill Collection, Clemson University. Gift of J. G. Simpson, grandson of Col. R. W. Simpson.

### *The Furor Erupts*

Clemson's concerns about the South Carolina Legislature's lack of enthusiasm for his project proved to be well-founded. On April 20, 1888, the will was submitted to probate by Simpson, and the three-year deadline specified by Clemson added urgency to the will's supporters to maneuver quickly through the legislative and legal maze necessary for the will's terms to be ratified. Almost immediately, opposition to Clemson's plan arose, and the objections coalesced around two main themes. There were those who opposed the concept of a new, public college

**Descendant Chart for**
**Anna Maria Calhoun and Thomas Green Clemson**

**Prepared by Jerome V. Reel**

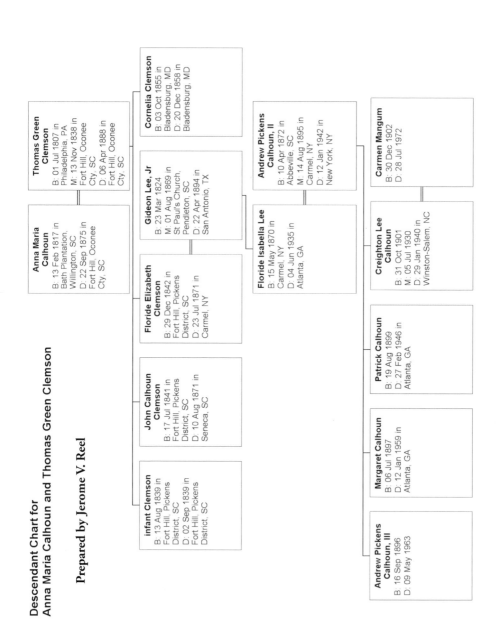

**Thomas Green Clemson**
B: 01 Jul 1807 in Philadelphia, PA
M: 13 Nov 1838 in Fort Hill, Oconee Cty, SC
D: 06 Apr 1888 in Fort Hill, Oconee Cty, SC

**Anna Maria Calhoun**
B: 13 Feb 1817 in Bath Plantation, Willington, SC
D: 22 Sep 1875 in Fort Hill, Oconee Cty, SC

**Cornelia Clemson**
B: 03 Oct 1855 in Bladensburg, MD
D: 20 Dec 1858 in Bladensburg, MD

**Gideon Lee, Jr**
B: 23 Mar 1824
M: 01 Aug 1869 in St Paul's Church, Pendleton, SC
D: 22 Apr 1894 in San Antonio, TX

**Floride Elizabeth Clemson**
B: 29 Dec 1842 in Fort Hill, Pickens District, SC
D: 23 Jul 1871 in Carmel, NY

**John Calhoun Clemson**
B: 17 Jul 1841 in Fort Hill, Pickens District, SC
D: 10 Aug 1871 in Seneca, SC

**infant Clemson**
B: 13 Aug 1839 in Fort Hill, Pickens District, SC
D: 02 Sep 1839 in Fort Hill, Pickens District, SC

**Andrew Pickens Calhoun, II**
B: 10 Apr 1872 in Abbeville, SC
M: 14 Aug 1895 in Carmel, NY
D: 12 Jan 1942 in New York, NY

**Floride Isabella Lee**
B: 15 May 1870 in Carmel, NY
D: 04 Jun 1935 in Atlanta, GA

**Carmen Mangum**
B: 30 Dec 1902
D: 28 Jul 1972

**Creighton Lee Calhoun**
B: 31 Oct 1901
M: 05 Jul 1930
D: 29 Jan 1940 in Winston-Salem, NC

**Patrick Calhoun**
B: 19 Aug 1899
D: 27 Feb 1946 in Atlanta, GA

**Margaret Calhoun**
B: 06 Jul 1897
D: 12 Jan 1959 in Atlanta, GA

**Andrew Pickens Calhoun, III**
B: 16 Sep 1896
D: 09 May 1963

in South Carolina devoted to agriculture and practical applications of scientific knowledge. Their argument was that there were already agriculture departments at the University of South Carolina and at Claflin College (for African American students). These opponents, in the press and the legislature, argued that creation of a new college for the primary purpose of agricultural education would be a duplication of effort and would drain scarce resources from the other public colleges.[19]

The second major objection seized upon by opponents to the college relate to a legal challenge filed by Gideon Lee on behalf of his daughter, Floride Isabella Lee, the only child of Clemson's deceased daughter, Floride Elizabeth, and Clemson's only surviving heir. Clemson had made provision for a bequest of certain personal effects and the sum of fifteen thousand dollars. Apparently, Clemson foresaw such a challenge in his codicil to the will, dated March 26, 1887, and he added two separate items dealing with this bequest. The first item cataloged the other bequests that Isabella had already received directly through her mother's (i.e., Floride Elizabeth Clemson Lee) estate, and the second specified in very unambiguous terms that, in the event of any legal challenge to the validity of the will and to the establishment of an agricultural college in particular, her bequest would be revoked. These provisions obviously belie some feelings of ill will or, at the least, mistrust with regard to Gideon Lee, Clemson's son-in-law. True to form, Lee began to agitate against the will almost immediately.

Floride Isabella Lee Calhoun (1870–1935), Clemson's granddaughter, who married a cousin, Andrew Pickens Calhoun II. Fort Hill Collection, Clemson University. Gift of Mr. and Mrs. Creighton Lee Calhoun Jr.

A late photograph of Gideon Lee Jr. (1824–1894), father of Floride Isabella Lee and son-in-law of Thomas Clemson. Fort Hill Collection, Clemson University. Gift of Mr. and Mrs. Creighton Lee Calhoun Jr.

Gideon Lee's first salvoes were in the press and not in the courts. He penned two letters, both of which were published in the Charleston *News and Courier*, and both of which challenged the legality of the will, excoriated Clemson as vainglorious and demented, and alleged that the State of South Carolina was abetting Clemson in cheating John C. Calhoun's great-granddaughter out of her rightful inheritance.[20] On November 26, 1888, concerned that there might be sufficient legislative support to gain acceptance of the will, Gideon Lee filed a lawsuit against Simpson, as executor of Clemson's will, in the U.S. District Court for the District of South Carolina.[21] Lee's contentions found favor with some legislators and members of the press who seized upon the possible delay and expense associated with a prolonged legal battle, not to mention what was seen by some as an unseemly position for the state to take in fighting over ownership of a child's family home, as reason to reject Clemson's gift. However, opinion was not one-sided, and other elected officials and statewide newspapers ridiculed Lee's position. They pointed out that, with a $15,000 bequest plus the inheritance she had already received from her mother's death, Isabella was hardly left destitute. Supporters of the will also noted that it is a long-recognized and accepted right that an individual is free to dispose of his or her assets upon death in the manner he or she chooses. Clemson's will was very clear as to his intent in bequeathing the bulk of his estate for the establishment of an agricultural college, and it was pointed out that it would dishonor him and the Calhoun family to ignore those wishes.[22]

It is interesting that the debate over Clemson's will divided fairly predictably along geographic and socioeconomic lines, with the newspapers and legislators of the Lowcountry generally in opposition, while those in the Upstate supported it. In many ways, the establishment of an agricultural school, primarily for the benefit of the poorer, less genteel yeomanry of the Upstate and in competition with the established colleges in Charleston and Columbia, prompted a rehashing of sectional and social conflicts that had played out over the previous course of South Carolina history. The key legislative supporter of the creation of a college at Fort Hill was Ben Tillman, the Populist politician from rural Edgefield County who, perhaps more than any other contemporary South Carolina political figure, represented the rural poor of the state. His outspoken advocacy of the will was to some extent a two-edged sword in that his association with the project galvanized some of the opposition to its acceptance.

Ultimately, Lee's legal challenge to the will's validity was unsuccessful, and the Circuit Court dealt with his arguments in a fairly perfunctory way. Lee's appeal to the public in the form of letters to various South Carolina papers was primarily one of sympathy for the financial security of Calhoun's great-granddaughter which, he argued, would be fatally compromised if the bulk of the Fort Hill estate went to the proposed agricultural school. Since such an argument has no real legal merit, it did not figure prominently in his legal pleadings. Those documents staked his position on the more technical argument that Clemson's Last Will and Testament and the subsequent codicil were void, due to preemption of earlier bequests by Calhoun's widow and by Anna Calhoun Clemson.[23] More specifically, Lee argued that the Fort Hill property did not belong to Clemson at all and that title to the property had passed from Calhoun's widow to her only surviving heir, Anna Clemson, and later to her only living heir, Isabella, Mr. Lee's daughter and ward. It was a tenuous argument dependent upon the courts' ignoring a series of previous decisions by probate courts (settling the estates of Mrs. Calhoun and Mrs. Clemson), as well as other miscellaneous transactions regarding the payment of taxes and liens on the property by Clemson. Ultimately, the Circuit Court (Fourth District) was not persuaded and issued its opinion on May 21, 1889, dismissing Lee's claims and affirming the terms of the will.[24]

With the final decision of the courts regarding the validity of the will, the legislative debate over its acceptance was reinvigorated. W. C. Benet, a member of the House of Representatives from Abbeville, led the fight for acceptance, and the opposition was spearheaded by J. C. Haskell and B. L. Abney from Richland County, along with W. H. Brawley from Charleston County. In the Senate, the chief supporter was B. W. Edwards of Darlington County. A bill to accept the bequest had been introduced in the House by Benet on December 6, 1888, and was approved on December 15 of that same session by a vote of 67 to 48, with the majority of votes against coming from the Lowcountry districts and Richland County (home to the University of South Carolina).[25] The House vote came prior to the resolution of Lee's lawsuit, and the Senate fight over acceptance was fueled by continuing speculation as to the outcome of the case. The case was still not resolved when the Senate took up the proposed bill, and opposition in the Senate was more spirited than in the House. The legislative debate and the concurrent court case invigorated the public debate, and the state newspapers, particularly the Charleston *News and Courier*, enthusiastically reported the legislative skirmishing and frequently published editorials on the issue, as well. The Senate vote on acceptance of the will was a dead heat, and Lieutenant Governor W. L. Mauldin of Greenville was called upon to cast the deciding vote for acceptance.[26]

Despite the victories in the House and Senate, acceptance of the will was not complete. The Bill of Acceptance was sent to Governor Richardson for signature, but Richardson exercised his right to employ a "pocket veto" and declined to act on the bill until the next legislative session.[27] Richardson's stated reason was to allow Gideon Lee's lawsuit to have been decided by the courts, thereby obviating the possibility of the state becoming embroiled in a potentially protracted and expensive legal imbroglio. But it should be noted that others questioned Richardson's true motives in not signing the bill, citing his lack of enthusiasm for Clemson's proposed college from the time it was first proposed.[28]

The decision of the Circuit Court in May of 1889 removed the rationale for Governor Richardson's hesitation in signing the Bill of Acceptance, and upon the convening of the 1889 session of the General Assembly, Richardson acquiesced and formally approved the Act of Acceptance on November 27 of that year.

## *The Dream Becomes a Posthumous Reality*

There was still one final step before Clemson's bequest was complete and that was for the chief justice of the South Carolina Supreme Court to issue an opinion confirming that the legislature and the governor had taken all steps necessary for the state to accept the terms of the will. That formality of ratification was satisfied on December 6, 1889, upon the issuance of an "Opinion of Chief Justice" by S.C. Supreme Court Chief Justice W. D. Simpson (no relation to R. W. Simpson) which stated simply that the legislature and the governor had acted appropriately to accept Clemson's bequest, subject to all of the terms and conditions set forth in the will. It seems fair to say that, with all legal and political prerequisites having been satisfied, this was the moment at which Clemson College came into being.

The promotion of scientific inquiry, the application of scientific principles to all aspects of human existence, and most especially, the establishment of an agricultural college for the benefit of the people of the State of South Carolina had long been Thomas Green Clemson's dream. It evolved into almost an obsession in his later years, consuming the bulk of his time and energy, as reflected in his surviving correspondence. One cannot help but wonder what Clemson believed was the likelihood that his dream of a college at Fort Hill would ever become a reality. Given his long record of failure and frustration in convincing the people and politicians of South Carolina of the educational and economic benefits of such an institution, only a true optimist could have had faith in the ultimate success of his dream. And it is a sad irony that by providing for the establishment of the college in his Last Will and Testament, he ensured that he would never live to see the ultimate outcome. It is a tribute to his persistence, foresight, and generosity, reflected in the instrument of its creation, that the institution now titled Clemson University came into being.

### Notes

1.  The standard last will and testament recorded in the probate records of Upstate South Carolina counties was usually not longer than a standard paragraph and consisted of a few basic elements: the name of the executor; a bequest of real estate, almost always to the surviving spouse

and children; and an occasional, specific gift of one or two particularly cherished or valuable items of personal property.

2. TGC to W. W. Corcoran, 3 January 1857, Corcoran Papers VI, MSS 61440, Library of Congress, Washington, DC; *American Farmer* 12 (1856): 69.

3. *De Bows Review* 7 (1862): 87ff. Given the themes of patriotism—for one's state, of course—individuality, and that peculiar form of democracy adored by the adherents of the Confederacy and which dominated the rhetoric of those heady, early weeks of Secession, it is probably not surprising that Clemson's rallying cry of agricultural education went largely unnoticed.

4. C. L. Newmann and J. C. Stribling, *Pendleton Farmers' Society* (Atlanta, GA: Foote & Dawes, 1908), 72; *Rural Carolinian* 1 (1870): 492.

5. *Rural Carolinian* 2, no. 1 (1870): 1.

6. TGC to W. W. Corcoran, 29 October 1878, Clemson Papers, Special Collections, Clemson University Libraries, Clemson, SC (hereafter cited as SCCUL).

7. See "The Minutes of the South Carolina Agricultural and Mechanical Society" (1869): 37.

8. 39 *Federal Reporter* 235, 1890; and District Court of South Carolina, Fourth Circuit, *Lee v. Simpson*, "Exhibits and Statements of Fact," testimony of R. W. Simpson.

9. Thomas Clemson eventually became embroiled in the statewide dispute over disposition of the final remains of John C. Calhoun. The statesman was interred in Charleston, the traditional locus of South Carolina political, economic, and social power, and Clemson allied himself with proponents of having Calhoun's remains removed to Fort Hill. Like many of Clemson's other passionately held positions, he found himself on the less popular and ultimately losing side of the argument. See Alester G. Holmes and George R. Sherrill, *Thomas Green Clemson, His Life and Work* (Richmond, VA: Garrett and Massie, 1937), 154–155.

10. TGC to W. W. Corcoran, 29 October 1878, Clemson Papers, SCCUL. Interestingly, at this point Clemson is willing to donate the property immediately, as opposed to a testamentary bequest to take effect upon his death. He offers to donate the property and to capture all or a portion of the interest on the principal for his living expenses until his own demise. He also states that he would be willing to place himself at the disposal of the governing body of any college thereby created, should they find his services to be useful.

11. *News and Herald* (Winnsboro, SC), 25 May 1910.

12. TGC to J. H. Rion, 27 April 1883, Clemson Papers, SCCUL. It is difficult not to detect the sarcasm in this reference, especially in light of Clemson's two decades of futilely imploring South Carolina's elected officials to fund such an institution. Interestingly, this language appears almost verbatim in the final version of the will. It may have been a sarcastic comment, but Clemson was utterly sincere in his concern about the legislature's commitment to provide adequate funding for his college.

13. Holmes and Sherrill, *Thomas Green Clemson*, 157.

14. District of South Carolina, Fourth Circuit, *Lee v. Simpson*, "Exhibits and Statements of Fact," testimony of R. W. Simpson.

15. Holmes and Sherrill, *Thomas Green Clemson*, 157.

16. *The State* (Columbia, SC), 21 June 1909.

17. Circuit Court of South Carolina, Fourth Circuit, *Lee v. Simpson*, "Testimony and Statements of Fact," testimony of R. W. Simpson.

18. Hereafter, the term "will" shall include the Last Will and Testament of Thomas Green Clemson, dated 6 November 1886, and the Codicil, dated 20 April 1887, unless otherwise specified.

19. See comments of Governor John Peter Richardson III, in *Journal of the House of Representatives of the General Assembly of the State of South Carolina* (1888): 40; also quoted in *News and Courier* (Charleston, SC), 8 September 1888.

20. *News and Courier* (Charleston, SC), 26 April 1888, and 2 May 1888.

21. Probate matters are generally within the jurisdiction of state courts; however, in this case, Gideon Lee and his daughter, Isabella, were both residents of the State of New York. This provided them the option of bringing the lawsuit in federal court based on diversity of jurisdiction, i.e., the fact that the adversarial parties were residents of different states. It is also likely that Lee chose federal court as his forum in the assumption that his arguments would receive a more impartial hearing than in a local, South Carolina court.

22. *Greenville News* (Greenville, SC), 3 May 1888.
23. Circuit Court of South Carolina, Fourth Circuit, *Lee v. Simpson*, "Exhibits and Statements of Fact," petition of Gideon Lee.
24. 39 *Federal Reporter* 235, 1890. Gideon Lee appealed the Circuit Court decision to the U.S. Supreme Court, which affirmed the decision of the lower court in a decision issued on 7 April 1890, thus ending the legal challenge to the will. See 134 U. S. 572, 1890.
25. Holmes and Sherrill, *Thomas Green Clemson*, 181–184; *Journal of the South Carolina House of Representatives* (1888), 250. Unfortunately, the House Journal is very sparse for this session and merely records the text of the Act of Acceptance and the vote. None of the legislative debate surrounding the legislation was captured, and we must rely solely on newspaper accounts for what little knowledge of the discourse we have.
26. Ibid., 263.
27. *Constitution of the State of South Carolina* (1868), Article III, Section 22.
28. *News and Courier* (Charleston, SC), 24 December 1888, and 27 December 1888; *Greenville News* (Greenville, SC), 30 December 1888.

**Opening of Thomas Green Clemson's Last Will and Testament, November 6, 1886. Probate Court Records of Walhalla, S.C. Will Book: 234-244.**

# Chapter 13

# PASSING IN REVIEW:
## THOMAS GREEN CLEMSON'S LIFE AND LEGACY

## *Verna Gardner Howell and Jerome V. Reel*

Detail of bronze seated sculpture of Thomas Green Clemson, located
in front of Tillman Hall, Clemson University. Sculpted in 1966 by
A. Wolfe Davidson (1903-1981), who also sculpted the *Littlejohn
Tiger*. Clemson University Department of Creative Services.

I n his time, Thomas Green Clemson was a person of note. He was born into a
family of privilege, educated both in the United States and Europe, and married into the prominent family of John C. Calhoun. Clemson distinguished
himself as a published scientist, a U.S. diplomat, and a leader in the agricultural

The Clemson Agricultural College of South Carolina's entering class of 1893. The students, still in civilian clothes, are lined up in military formation near the unfinished Main Hall (now Tillman Hall). Clemson University Photographs, Special Collections, Clemson University Libraries.

This May 1894 photograph is the earliest known picture of Clemson Agriculture College's entire student body in cadet formation. The original barracks building is in the left background. Clemson University Photographs, Special Collections, Clemson University Libraries.

community. He was thus well-educated, well-traveled, and well-connected. Yet his marks on history might have been lost if not for the achievement of what would become his lifetime ambition: the establishment of a college.

Clemson's vision of an agricultural and scientific college for South Carolina was born out of a complex array of personal and political circumstances. These circumstances—some of his own choosing and temperament, many of fate—compelled Clemson to make the bequest that continues to impact all of South Carolina and far beyond. In short, the founding of the Clemson Agricultural College of South Carolina (now Clemson University) secured Thomas Green Clemson's place in history and his influence upon untold generations.

Certainly, his path to that place in history was anything but smooth. Like the nineteenth century itself, Clemson's life (1807–1888) was an amalgam of great ambitions, frustrations, innovations, hard work, art, experiments, warfare, pragmatism, music, racism, persistence, loyalties, and tragedies. The amalgam becomes more and more evident as one moves through the preceding twelve chapters, each of which focuses on particular facets of Clemson's life and work. Now, the multifaceted components will be brought together in a final overview of that life and work and the ways in which Thomas Green Clemson's legacy has evolved in the twentieth and early twenty-first centuries.

### A Life in Review

The seeds of Clemson's destiny were sown in his youth, when he was enrolled in the American Literary, Scientific, and Military Academy at Norwich, Vermont.[1] Founded by Alden Partridge in 1819, the school offered instruction in mathematics and the sciences, including chemistry, botany, geology, and mineralogy. The academy also included physical training and a structured student life designed to keep students productively occupied.[2] Because Partridge—a professor of engineering turned Army captain, turned schoolmaster—firmly believed in the value of a broader, more practical education, students at Norwich were offered not just knowledge, but also the real-life application of that knowledge. Clemson, as an impressionable youth, was no doubt deeply influenced by Partridge's commitment to practical education, a commitment well ahead of its time. And Clemson was not alone. Senator Justin Morrill, who subsequently would sponsor the land-grant colleges act, lived about twelve miles from Norwich and was acquainted with Partridge and his school. To what degree Partridge inspired both Morrill and Clemson in their respective educational legacies is unknown, but the two were undeniably bound by Partridge's influences.[3]

After his time at the Norwich Academy, Clemson's hunger for scientific knowledge led him to Paris, France, where he continued his studies at the Sorbonne (University of Paris), the Royal College of France, and the School of Mines, and where he eventually received a certificate as an assayer of mines from the Royal Mint in Paris.[4] While in Paris, Clemson distinguished himself as a student.[5] He had the opportunity to learn from and conduct research beside some of the greatest scientists of the time. Here the foundation of Clemson's dedication was firmly set. Decades later, arguing for the necessity of scientific education, Clemson would write, "The only possible hope for the advancement of the arts is through science. The latter is the foundation upon which the former are built.... Science is the correct practice, an authentic, unerring history of all that has been discovered and invented since the creation of man."[6] His conviction on the value of science to humanity would fuel Clemson's future vision.

After Clemson received his assayer's certificate in 1831, he returned to Philadelphia, and even though he would often visit Europe during the next few years, he soon began to make a name for himself as a consulting and mining engineer in the United States. While consulting in Washington, D.C., he met Anna Maria Calhoun, the eldest daughter of prominent statesman John C. Calhoun. A confirmed bachelor, Clemson was duly smitten, soon addressing Anna as his "very much beloved, dear Anna" and referring to her as his "blessed idol." The thirty-one-year-old Clemson married twenty-one-year-old Anna on November 13, 1838, at the Calhoun estate of Fort Hill, South Carolina.[7]

Until Thomas Clemson appeared, the undisputed object of Anna Calhoun's affection had been her father. Both father and daughter were highly intelligent and politically aware, enjoying a very close relationship characterized by mutual affection and respect. Anna's marriage to Clemson in no way diminished her relationship with her father, but rather expanded it to include Clemson, himself a man of keen intellect and vision. Although there was no way to know it at the time, the marriage of Thomas Green Clemson and Anna Maria Calhoun represented a remarkable convergence of resources, intelligence, imagination, opportunity, and will that would one day make the Clemson legacy possible.[8]

Following their wedding, Clemson and Anna lived briefly in Philadelphia. When a tentative offer from the governor of Pennsylvania for Clemson to become the state geologist fell through, the couple moved to the Calhouns' home in South Carolina. In a matter of months, tragedy struck in the form of a fever epidemic. Among its casualties was Thomas and Anna Clemson's first child, an unnamed infant daughter only three weeks old.[9]

Living in South Carolina between 1840 and 1844, Clemson received a practical introduction to the business of agriculture. First, he briefly managed a plantation in the Abbeville District owned by James Edward Calhoun, brother of Mrs. John C. Calhoun. In the winter and spring of 1840–1841, Clemson managed his father-in-law's plantation, Fort Hill, while Senator Calhoun was in Washington. Clemson was apparently a quick study, and Calhoun enthusiastically approved of his work. Finally, in 1843 Clemson purchased his own plantation in the Edgefield District of South Carolina, which he named Canebrake.[10]

These first years in South Carolina were crucial in shaping Clemson's life. He experienced firsthand the daily challenges faced by farmers, even in the best of times. He had the opportunity to experiment with a scientific approach to agriculture and to imagine how such an approach could benefit not only the individual landowner, but also the broader economy of the region. His family grew, as Anna Maria gave birth to two more children—John Calhoun ("Calhoun") in 1841 and Floride Elizabeth in 1842. And he developed an attachment to the region, and to the Fort Hill estate in particular, that would significantly impact his future decisions.[11]

Clemson's diplomatic appointment in 1844 as chargé d'affaires to Belgium diverted his attention from farming and life in the South and gave him another welcomed opportunity to live abroad. While in Belgium, as in France earlier, Clemson observed firsthand the progress of science and education in Europe, and he would have been aware that, during the eighteenth century, numerous agricultural societies and schools featuring practical agricultural education had been established across Europe. Predictably, this period in European history was also marked by significant growth in the knowledge base for the natural sciences and their applications.[12] These facts were not lost on Clemson, who would later lament the lack of similar opportunities in America as he pleaded for action in support of scientific education.[13]

In March of 1850, while Clemson and his family were still in Belgium, John C. Calhoun died. Calhoun's ownership of about 600 acres adjacent to the Fort Hill estate passed to his widow, Floride Colhoun Calhoun, who owned the Fort Hill home and 500 acres. Canebrake, the farm Clemson had purchased in Edgefield District, had not fared well in the care of overseers and was sold by Clemson in 1850, during his and his family's short visit to the United States, after which they returned to Brussels. A year and a half later, in 1851—after serving under U.S. Presidents Tyler, Polk, and Taylor and now without the political influence of John C. Calhoun—Thomas Clemson was recalled by President Fillmore from his diplomatic post in Belgium.[14]

The Clemsons returned to the United States in 1851 and soon purchased and settled on a small farm, which they called The Home, outside of Bladensburg, Maryland. There their fourth and last child, Cornelia ("Nina"), was born in October of 1855. Clemson doted on Nina. Her untimely death in 1858 from scarlet fever devastated both parents and left Clemson depressed for months.[15] In contrast, it was also during this time that Clemson renewed his scientific career, performing experiments on his farm, writing articles for scientific and agricultural journals, and presenting articles and papers at scientific meetings.[16]

When the Clemsons moved to Bladensburg in 1853, they landed in the midst of an active educational movement that would echo in Clemson's future efforts on behalf of agricultural education for the state of South Carolina. As early as 1830, the Maryland Agricultural Society and the Maryland state legislature had been engaged in dialogue related to agricultural education in the state. In 1848, the society formed a committee to study the possibility of establishing an agricultural college. In October of 1854, the group publicly proposed to secure a farm to use for the Agricultural Society's exhibitions and as a location for an agricultural school and model farm. The school was to be funded through private donations and located within ten miles of Baltimore. Maryland Governor Thomas Ligon appealed to the state legislature for support of the proposal.[17]

By this time, Clemson's dedication to science had evolved into a fervent belief in the value of scientific, specifically agricultural, education. This conviction found voice in his support for Governor Ligon and the founding of the Maryland Agricultural College. In 1856, Clemson wrote, "The only hope we have for the advancement of agriculture is through the sciences and yet there is not one single institution on the continent where a proper scientific education can be obtained. Those who wish to cultivate science are compelled to resort to institutions maintained by the monarchical governments of Europe."[18] Clemson's fierce commitment to the value of scientific education would continue to motivate him until his last years.

The Maryland Agricultural College was established by act of the state legislature on March 6, 1856. But the success of that endeavor only fueled Clemson's passion for the greater cause of scientific education in the United States. In December of the following year, Justin Morrill introduced the first college land-grant bill, enjoining the Congress to establish a national educational system of agricultural education.[19] Over the next several years, Clemson would speak eloquently and passionately in favor of scientific education, as in this excerpt from his 1859 paper on "The Necessity and Value of Scientific Instruction":

> I have long been of the opinion that the time would surely come, when in this country, more than in any other, the demand for scientific instruction, and that in its highest grade, would be imperative. I have seen the subject rolling on and gathering daily strength, with the diffusion of general information....The want of adequate scientific instruction is everywhere felt more and more, and as population increases, and as our once fertile lands are exhausted, it will become a necessity. When nature's bank refuses to honor the drafts of the population of meat and bread the resources of science will be appealed to, and it will be discovered that there is no hope out of it; nay, it is a fact already known to many, that science is the only sure foundation upon which we can depend for the increase of facts or for the recuperation of exhausted lands, or sustaining the fertility of those that are tilled.[20]

Morrill's land-grant bill narrowly passed both houses of Congress in 1859, only to be vetoed by President Buchanan. Realizing that Buchanan's time in office was limited, supporters of the bill continued to lobby for its passage.[21] During this same time period, Clemson's active participation in national agricultural and political circles was rewarded by his appointment in 1860 as the first superintendent of agricultural affairs under the auspices of the Department of the Interior. While continuing to advocate for federally sponsored agricultural education, Clemson began to appeal for the creation of a cabinet-level Department of Agriculture.[22]

Both the Morrill Act and the proposal for a Department of Agriculture would eventually meet success, but not during Clemson's time in Washington. After barely a year in office, Clemson resigned his post in Agricultural Affairs as the threat of civil war became real. Sympathetic to the Confederate cause, the Pennsylvania-born scientist left Anna and Floride in Maryland under the watch of family and friends, granted Anna power of attorney over his northern property and investments, and moved to South Carolina. Their son, John Calhoun Clemson, enlisted in the Confederate army in 1861; his father followed suit in 1863. Thomas Clemson was assigned to the Nitre and Mining Bureau in Texas, where his scientific knowledge could benefit the Confederate cause. Calhoun Clemson was eventually captured and imprisoned on Johnson's Island in Lake Erie, Ohio.[23]

As the war neared its end, Anna secured passes for Floride and her to journey south in December of 1864. They traveled to Mi Casa, Mrs. John C. (Floride) Calhoun's home in Pendleton, South Carolina. They were joined there in the summer of 1865 by Calhoun and, six days later, Thomas Green Clemson. After four years of separation, the family was together once more.[24]

While Clemson and his immediate family emerged from the war physically and financially unscathed, it left them estranged from their Maryland home. The war's economic toll on the southern states was severe, and poverty and deprivation defined their new homeland. In the fall of 1865 Clemson wrote, "This country is in a wretched condition, no money and nothing to sell. Existence is almost problematical....I fear that a long time must elapse before the country arrives at a settled state. Every one is ruined, and those that can are leaving."[25] Clemson was eventually able to secure a pardon and reclaim his Maryland property, but the North would never again be his home.[26]

In the years immediately following the war, Clemson renewed his crusade for scientific education. Back in November of 1861, before his enlistment, Clemson had urged the establishment of a department of agriculture within the government of the Confederacy, a department that would develop improvements in farming technique and disseminate that new knowledge to farms throughout the South.[27] With the fall of the Confederacy, Clemson saw the needs of South Carolina and the South become even more urgent, thus motivating him once again to action.

Clemson joined the Pendleton Farmers' Society and was chosen to serve as its president in 1866.[28] In November of that year, the society appointed a three-man committee to solicit support to establish an agricultural college. The committee published a circular which characterized the condition of agriculture in the South as "wretched," noting "undeveloped" natural resources, and proclaiming "ignorance is the cause of our destitution." Clemson circulated the publication widely, along with his personal appeals for philanthropic help.[29] One of Clemson's most poignant appeals was contained in an article he wrote on "The Principles of Agriculture," published in *The Land We Love* in February of 1867: "Our condition is critical, our inheritance is in jeopardy, and we can not expect to retain it without a radical change from the past....Science will open up new avenues for profitable occupation to individuals which will redound to the power of the state; resources now lying dormant, will give occupation and wealth to unborn millions."[30]

Clemson did more than speak out for scientific education. He persuaded James Edward Calhoun to offer 1,000 acres of land in the Pickens (now Oconee) District for the purpose of establishing a college.[31] Clemson campaigned ardently for aid to finance the undertaking, but was unsuccessful. In 1870, he resigned from the Pendleton Farmers' Society and wrote James Edward Calhoun in frustration, saying, "the people are too ignorant or too apathetic to understand and too shortsighted to venture a dollar to make thousands."[32]

Unbeknownst to them, the disappointment that Clemson felt in 1870 would pale in comparison to the emotional devastation he and Anna would suffer the following year. Their daughter Floride Elizabeth had married Gideon Lee Jr. of Carmel, New York, on August 1, 1869, and had given birth to Floride Isabella the following spring. On July 23, 1871, the twenty-eight-year-old Floride died, apparently from tuberculosis. Seventeen days later the unthinkable happened: the Clemsons' thirty-year-old son Calhoun was killed instantly in a train wreck near Seneca, South Carolina. The unexpected tragedies left Thomas and Anna Clemson shocked, grief-stricken, and bereft of offspring save for their young granddaughter Floride Isabella Lee in Carmel, New York.[33]

Since returning to South Carolina after the Civil War, the Clemsons had made their home with Anna's mother at Mi Casa. Four years after her husband's death, Mrs. Calhoun had sold Fort Hill to their son Andrew, but Andrew died suddenly in 1865, having paid only a small portion of the debt. Thus the mortgage was still in Mrs. Calhoun's possession when she died in July of 1866, after a painful battle with cancer. In her will, Mrs. Calhoun left three-fourths of the Fort Hill mortgage to her daughter Anna and one-fourth to her granddaughter Floride Elizabeth Clemson. Andrew's family contested the will, but after a lengthy court battle, the matter was finally settled in January of 1872, when Anna and Floride Isabella Lee (Floride Elizabeth's heir) were awarded the property. On November 5, 1873, Anna and Gideon Lee (Floride Isabella's father and legal guardian) met and agreed to divide the estate: 288 acres for Floride Isabella Lee; 814 acres and the residence for Anna Calhoun Clemson.[34]

When Anna and Thomas Clemson took possession of Fort Hill in 1872, their lives had been undeniably altered by the deaths of their children. It was Anna who first emerged from the despair that had enveloped them. She had long shared her husband's vision of an agricultural and mechanical college for South Carolina, and she now saw an opportunity to promote that vision while honoring the Calhoun and Clemson family names. On September 29, 1871, Anna Calhoun Clemson executed a will leaving her "entire property and estate" to Thomas Clemson. With Anna's support, Clemson resumed his efforts to garner financial support for an agricultural college for South Carolina.[35]

In 1874, Anna, now an active partner in the campaign, personally selected a committee to produce an updated circular, once again seeking statewide support for "a Scientific School which would prepare youth of the State to become intelligent workers in the material development of the State." This time the cause was promoted as a tribute to the esteemed name of John C. Calhoun, and the proposed site for the institution was Fort Hill. Unfortunately, even with the Calhoun name attached, the effort failed once again.[36]

By now Clemson was in his mid-sixties, and Anna, her mid-fifties. Both had health problems—Anna was overweight with a heart condition, and Clemson complained of rheumatism. Even so, it was a shock to Clemson when, on September 22, 1875, Anna died of a heart attack at Fort Hill while he was away. Clemson's devastation was complete.[37] Shortly after Anna's death, he poured out his grief in a letter to his friend and advisor Henry Gourdin, "How to write you I scarce know. I am crushed, sick in mind, sick in body....What an extraordinarily and exemplary woman has gone to her long home. How disconsolate and wretched I feel it is impossible for anyone to imagine."[38]

Clemson lived almost thirteen years after Anna's death, during which time he remained emotionally "disconsolate and wretched." But just as Anna had supported Clemson in life, so also she did in death. By her will, Clemson inherited the Fort Hill property "absolutely and in fee simple." Her bequest provided Clemson the land necessary to realize their shared dream of an agricultural college in South Carolina; to the land and a small amount of money in Anna's bequest, Clemson's own estate would posthumously add some $80,000 in stocks and securities. Meanwhile, contentment eluded the lonely old man, now living a reclusive life at Fort Hill, but he eventually resumed his quest toward that dream.[39]

On October 29, 1878, Clemson made another plea for financial support— this time to W. W. Corcoran, an old friend and advisor from Washington, D.C. In his letter to Corcoran, Clemson summarized his mission and the progress toward it in this way: "Since the surrender an effort has been making in South Carolina to establish an institution for teaching the Sciences and Arts, theoretical and practical, and thus raise the people of the state from ignorance and demoralization to prosperity and the hope of the well born....Up to the present writing our efforts have been without avail."[40] Clemson's vision was now in sharp focus: The economic prosperity of the state of South Carolina depended on education—specifically scientific, practical education—and on his success in establishing a college for that purpose.

Clemson's plea to Corcoran yielded no resources. Clemson, who was by this time over seventy years old, decided to try another approach. Sometime between 1880 and 1882, he discussed his desire to donate Fort Hill to the State of South Carolina for the purpose of an agricultural institution with Pendleton neighbor R. W. Simpson, then a member of the South Carolina Legislature. He asked Simpson to delineate "what steps were necessary for him to take to accomplish his purpose." After consulting fellow legislators, Simpson encouraged Clemson's ambition, advising him by letter to "execute a deed of the property to the State *to take effect at your death* provided the State will agree to erect and maintain an Agricultural College thereon within five years after your death."[41]

Following Simpson's advice, Clemson enlisted his attorney James H. Rion to draft a will bequeathing his portion of the Fort Hill estate to the State of South Carolina to establish a college that was to be named "Fort Hill Scientific Institute." Clemson's instructions to Rion included a list of the specific areas of instruction to be taught at the institute: mathematics, geology and mineralogy (with emphases on mining), chemistry (with emphases on agricultural applications), and modern languages. The will, unfortunately not preserved, was executed on August 14, 1883.[42]

Clemson later shared his will and plans with some well-placed advisors, including B. R. Tillman, D. K. Norris, and R. W. Simpson. They consulted as a group, and the result was a new will drafted by Simpson and executed on November 6, 1886. In this final version, Clemson left $15,000 and some personal belongings to his only surviving relative, his granddaughter Floride Isabella Lee. The rest of his estate, including the Fort Hill property, plus the balance of his assets valued at approximately $80,000, he left to the State of South Carolina for the establishment of an agricultural college. As Clemson wrote in his will, "To accomplish this purpose is now the one great desire of my life."[43]

Clemson's will was the product of deep personal conviction and years of unfulfilled effort. With poetic simplicity, it conveyed Clemson's motivation ("Feeling a great sympathy for the farmers of this State, and believing that there can be no permanent improvement in agriculture without knowledge of those sciences which pertain particularly thereto") and his purpose ("to establish an agricultural college which should afford…thorough instruction in agriculture and the natural sciences…[and] should combine, if practicable, physical and intellectual education, and should be a high seminary of learning"). It plainly reiterated Clemson's conviction that scientific education is the key to economic prosperity: "I trust I do not exaggerate the importance of such an institution for developing the material resources of the State by affording its youth the advantages of scientific culture."[44]

The will was also the product of an astute and progressive mind. Clemson understood that his college would have to adapt to serve the educational needs of the future, needs that were beyond his present imagining. Yet he was determined to ensure that his motivation and purpose in founding the institution should be respected and preserved. To this end, he prescribed a thirteen-member board of trustees for the institution, seven of whom he appointed by name, and six appointed or elected by the legislature. Of the seven, he declared that they and their successors "shall always have the right...to fill all vacancies which may occur in their number by death, resignation, refusal to act, or otherwise." He further guaranteed to perpetuate his vision by insisting that "the State, if it accepts the donation, shall never increase the Board of Trustees to a number greater than thirteen in all, nor shall the duties of said board be taken away or conferred upon any other man or body of men."[45]

Clemson conferred enormous trust and responsibility on his board of trustees: "I desire to state plainly that I wish the trustees of said institution to have full authority and power to regulate all matters pertaining to said institution—to fix the course of studies, to make rules for the government of the same, and to change them, as in their judgment, experience may prove necessary, but to always bear in mind that the benefits herein sought to be bestowed are intended to benefit the agricultural and mechanical industries."[46] In doing so, he allowed for Clemson Agricultural College, now Clemson University, to adapt and evolve to meet her founder's purpose in the context of rapidly changing times.

While committed to securing the future of South Carolina, Clemson also wanted to preserve some of her past. In his will, he plainly directed that "the dwelling house on Fort Hill shall never be torn down or altered, but shall be kept in repair, with all the articles of furniture and vesture which I hereinafter give for that purpose, and shall always be open for the inspection of visitors."[47] By safeguarding the home of his cherished wife and illustrious father-in-law, Clemson paid tribute to the Calhoun family, ensuring that their connection to Clemson Agricultural College would not be lost to future generations.

On April 6, 1888, just a few months shy of his eighty-first birthday, Thomas Green Clemson died of pneumonia at his home at Fort Hill. He was buried beside his beloved Anna in the churchyard of St. Paul's Episcopal Church in Pendleton.[48]

However eloquently written, Clemson's will and the gifts it contained were not immediately embraced by all. In a case that traveled to the United States Supreme Court, Gideon Lee (on behalf of his daughter Floride Isabella) challenged Clemson's ownership of the Fort Hill property. R. W. Simpson, executor of Clemson's will, represented Clemson's interests and was ultimately successful. Meanwhile, the bill to accept Clemson's bequest and to establish Clemson Agricultural College was actively debated in the South Carolina General Assembly. Although the votes were divided in both Houses, the bill was passed in December 1888, but Governor John Richardson delayed signing the bill until the outcome of Gideon Lee's suit became apparent.[49] On November 27, 1889, Richardson signed into law the Act "To accept the Devise and Bequest of Thomas G. Clemson, and to Establish an Agricultural College in Connection Therewith." A few days later, on December 6, the act was finalized when W. D. Simpson, the S.C. Supreme Court justice, issued the required, confirming opinion. Finally, Clemson's legacy was secured.[50]

THOMAS GREEN CLEMSON'S GRAVE/ST. PAUL'S                    J. BARKER  12/24/01

*Thomas Green Clemson's Grave/St. Paul's* **by Clemson University President James F. Barker. Sketch made on December 24, 2001. Pen and ink. President's Office, Clemson University.**

### *A Legacy in Review*

The legacy of Clemson's will began to emerge rather quickly. The first results were agricultural. Within three years of Clemson's death, agriculturalists at his college were setting out new varieties of pecan trees. In rapid succession, cattle and poultry were brought by train to the former Fort Hill plantation, after convicts had fenced the fields. Then more wooded lots were cut (some timber for structural use), and overgrown fields were cleared, tilled, and planted in crops. An orchard was set out with fruit trees, and plans were made for botanical gardens. Frame houses for potential faculty and staff and brick homes for the faculty chairs were rushed along. Soon these scientists and scholars began to arrive.[51]

Among the first were the chemists who undertook the analysis of all fertilizers sold in South Carolina, thus ensuring the quality of that product for the 85% of the people actively engaged in agriculture for their lives and livelihoods. This service, informed by careful research in and experimentation with fertilizers, was communicated to the citizenry through regular printed reports written in lay language. Fifteen faculty members, most selected by the trustees on the suggestion of Clemson's first president, were carrying out these important tasks. A well-known Atlanta, Georgia, architectural firm designed the principal buildings, while the granite for their foundations was being hauled by train and mule-drawn wagons from the South Carolina mountains. Using the granite, timbers from the Clemson-Calhoun farm, and bricks made on site from the farm's clay, the convicts and their supervisors slowly erected the main buildings, while faculty members designed the water supply, the sanitation system, and the steam and electric power plants. People who lived around the area rode over on Sundays to watch as the College emerged from the soil. In the meantime, the faculty, working from the trustees' suggestions and the experiences of four other land-grant colleges, created the two curricula: agriculture and engineering.

**Groundbreaking work on the Ft. Hill estate for Clemson Agricultural College's original buildings, which were constructed by convicts. Clemson University Photographs, Special Collections, Clemson University Libraries.**

In July 1893, three and a half years after the governor and the Supreme Court justice signed the Act of Acceptance, the Clemson Agricultural College of South Carolina opened its doors to 446 students and fifteen faculty members. This first cadre of students stepped from train cars and marched with their faculty "drill sergeants" to the College. Of these students, about a third were placed by examination in the preparatory division (called the "fitting school"), while a number, transferring from other schools, were designated second-year men. The majority of the rest of the students became first-year men.[52]

For most students, this would be their first experience away from home and their first with flush toilets and electricity. (The 1900 census revealed that only 4% of all households in the United States had indoor plumbing or electricity.) All the faculty and students were white males, and all the students were from South Carolina. The College's lone secretary/stenographer was a man, but a woman was on the infirmary staff and another served as the "matron of the barracks." The first Clemson graduation was held in December 1896, when the College's second president awarded rings, diplomas, and degrees in agriculture or engineering to thirty-seven cadets who had entered the school in 1893 as transfer sophomores.

Fifteen years would pass as did two more presidents of Clemson College. Life in South Carolina was improving. The mule was still the primary beast of burden, but the horse and buggy were giving way to the automobile, while the railways stretched into most South Carolina communities for distance travel and hauling. The single telephone in the Clemson College president's office had not taken the place of the letter and telegram for communication. And if South Carolina was changing, Clemson was changing even more. Textiles, still a very small industry in the state, had been introduced in 1898 as the school's third curriculum.

While the student body remained all-male, it was becoming more diverse. No longer were all students from South Carolina. When the 1895 fall term began, for instance, one student from Atlanta was in the lower preparatory class and another, from Washington, D.C., was a freshman. By the autumn of 1897, fourteen students from four other states and the District of Columbia also were enrolled. Records for that year included religious affiliations: 66% of the students were listed as American Protestants (Methodist and Baptist); 26% were Protestants of European origin (Presbyterian, Episcopal, and Lutheran); and 1% were either Catholic (four) or Jewish (one, who, at that time was listed as "Israelite").[53]

By the 1911 graduation, the change in curricula was conspicuous as Clemson awarded bachelor of science degrees in agriculture, agricultural chemistry, husbandry, civil engineering, electrical engineering, mechanical engineering, and textiles. All but one degree field, textiles, were actually divisions of the original two fields. That they were able to be so divided indicated that the entering Clemson students were better prepared than their predecessors. Of course, the lower schools were becoming much more accessible to the public, and in towns and some counties, schools now went through the tenth grade. Financially better-off families all over the nation were also sending sons away to boarding schools for further preparation.

That there were only 742 Clemson graduates from all graduating classes by 1911 was the result of a serious shortage of space in student barracks and in classrooms, rather than a lack of demand for education. The graduates were almost evenly divided between engineering and agriculture, with a small number in textiles. The largest employer segment for the graduates was in the various power companies, such as General Electric and Westinghouse. The second largest group became schoolteachers in the sciences and agriculture, while the third went directly into farming. A few ministers, lawyers, and physicians, who had done their undergraduate work at Clemson, continued their studies in professional schools. Another small number went on to graduate schools for advanced research training. And although the majority (62%) lived in South Carolina, Clemson graduates could be found around the nation, with a sizeable number in the East and Midwest, in addition to the South. For example, clusters of graduates were residing in New York City, Schenectady, Pittsburgh, Washington, D.C., Atlanta, and Birmingham. On the other hand, some graduates were assigned military postings to the Canal Zone, Puerto Rico, and the Philippines; others worked in various government divisions, such as the Army (particularly in its engineering division), the Department of the Interior, or the Department of Agriculture.

During this same period, the Clemson faculty had grown to forty-nine, four of whom held the relatively new degree of Ph.D. Two others were veterinarians, and another nine held master's degrees. The remaining two-thirds of the faculty held baccalaureate degrees, but in some skill areas, a few had no degrees. Only one woman, the librarian, was on the professional staff. Three other women served as stenographers, but a man was the president's secretary. The College's professional staff also had grown. The Experiment Station, for instance, included nine men, one of whom was at the Coast Land Station between Summerville and Jedburg.

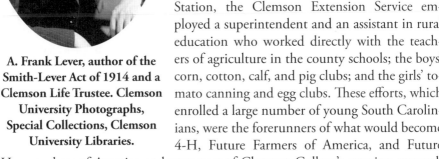

A. Frank Lever, author of the Smith-Lever Act of 1914 and a Clemson Life Trustee. Clemson University Photographs, Special Collections, Clemson University Libraries.

Originally a subdivision of the Experiment Station, the Clemson Extension Service employed a superintendent and an assistant in rural education who worked directly with the teachers of agriculture in the county schools; the boys' corn, cotton, calf, and pig clubs; and the girls' tomato canning and egg clubs. These efforts, which enrolled a large number of young South Carolinians, were the forerunners of what would become 4-H, Future Farmers of America, and Future Homemakers of America and were part of Clemson College's growing outreach and public service. With the signing of the Smith-Lever Act of 1914, the Extension Service was spread nationwide.[54]

One of the most interesting ways Clemson reached out across the state was through the so-called "Clemson Extension Train." Three times a year—in late autumn, in the winter, and in the spring (always between the academic sessions)— between twelve and fifteen faculty members rode the train, which was in two cars (a sitting car and a sleeping car) pulled by an engine and tender, for a week at a time. The circuits would cover the state in one year, rotating so that, after three years, each faculty group had toured each section in each season. Plant specialists dealt with fertilization, introducing new crops, giving field talks on terracing, tilling, and planting, while husbandry men and veterinarians worked with cattle, horses, sheep, and goats. An engineer would talk on local construction and roads, while the architectural engineer's focus was frequently on small public designs, such as for clinics and schools. In the early evenings on every tour, a historian or literature professor addressed the audience on topics of history or "good books." It was a rolling "Chautauqua" of sorts. One of the topics always featured in these circuits was home sanitation. Placement of wells and privies, earth closets, and the use or disposal of waste were important in the improvement of community health. These activities were not unique to Clemson or South Carolina, but were being carried out in the few states that were experimenting with extension service.

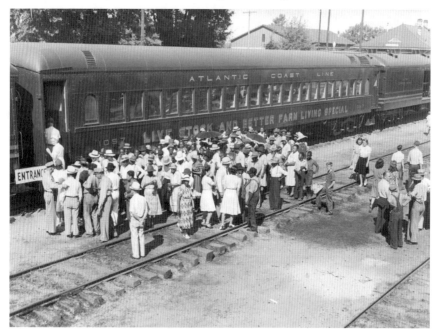

**The Extension Train was one of many successful ways in which Clemson College shared new agricultural methods and other valuable assistance with farmers and communities throughout South Carolina. Clemson University Photographs, Special Collections, Clemson University Libraries.**

These same years were also years of change for the United States and its foreign relations. The Spanish-American War, coming immediately after Clemson College's first graduations, drew young graduates into the war. None were killed, but afterward graduates served as specialists and teachers in Puerto Rico, Cuba, and the Philippines. Those became the liaisons, the sources of Clemson's early international students, the first of whom were enrolled in 1912–1913.

By 1912, Clemson had added architectural engineering to its degrees. In addition, short summer courses in textiles and cotton grading were joined by "one-year agriculture" or "OYA." Designed for young men past the ages of boys' clubs and who, for whatever reason, were unable to commit to a four-year college degree, the OYA program attracted students to a twelve-month course on the successful operation of a family farm. Their tutors occasionally were seniors who showed a gift for teaching or "irregular" and "special" students who already had received their baccalaureates and were now preparing for graduate studies, usually in the Midwest.

Another foreign war, World War I (1914–1918), fought primarily in Europe but with combat on other continents, affected Clemson, which was a military college and a land-grant college, and among the first to have a Reserve Officers Training Corps. When the United States declared war on the Central Powers (the Austro-Hungarian Empire, the Second German Reich, and the Ottoman Empire), a striking number of Clemson's 15,000 alumni—including both 1,000 graduates and other former students—were among the first to sign up for service. As a result, they were among the first to be sent across the Atlantic. A total of 1,549 Clemson men served in all branches of and in multiple capacities for the U.S. military. Of these 1,549, twenty-four lost their lives and two received Congressional Medals of Honor.[55]

In the two-decade hiatus between the world wars, Clemson College continued to broaden its teaching fields, outreach, and research. It was still hampered by a lack of student bed space and a shortage of laboratory space. That problem would be worsened by fires that destroyed the 1893 mechanical hall and the 1904 agricultural hall. Insurance and a loan from the state allowed the rebuilding of what had been the mechanical building as a larger facility for engineering and architecture. But the agriculture building, which had been gutted and which was inadequate for the laboratories now needed, was rebuilt as Clemson's first free-standing library, leaving agriculture teaching and research to smaller, poorly designed and equipped buildings. It would be a decade before agriculture would again be housed together.

Another set of economic population shifts was redefining South Carolina. Younger African Americans had begun migrating out of South Carolina as the need for soldiers and workers—for the war and the war effort—allowed them to join the new industrial assembly lines in the Midwest, where they were offered better pay, better schooling, and, hopefully, better lives. This labor loss in South Carolina encouraged Clemson College to introduce other agricultural products in the hopes of diversification. The raising of poultry and cattle was encouraged and met with some positive results. Successful experiments also were made with fruit trees. However, the new textile mills attracted the more able men and women to them. Fields were left idle and began to grow up in trees. When Clemson's trustees asked the legislature to fund a new program in forestry, the request was denied, due to lack of money, and South Carolina rapidly became less productive.

When the Depression began in 1929 and, in spite of the great hardships the world was facing, Clemson continued to grow. Between 1919 and 1940, its student body rose from just less than 1,000 to 2,300. With the aid of the federal government, five new barracks, a new agriculture building, a large textile school, and a field house were built, and the student athletes added luster to the name of the College and the state, by winning conference sports championships and an intersectional bowl game. Clemson agricultural, civil engineering, and mechanical engineers laid out better roads (some even hard-surfaced) and strung electric wires across the state. The state, the federal government, and Clemson engineers began building the vast Santee-Cooper electric power generating plant, under the direction of a U.S.C.-educated Clemson trustee. Moreover, Clemson extension agents were the key to fighting the dislocation and hunger that accompanied the terrible drought period from 1930 to 1936.

Soon war clouds began gathering in Asia in the early 1930s and in Europe in the later 1930s. Although American eyes were more fixed on the European dangers, the United States' greater territorial interest lay with the Hawaiian territory and the Philippine protectorate in Asia. By the time the United States entered World War II in 1941, Clemson men were already on the Asian front.[56]

In December 1941, Clemson's student body numbered 2,381, still overwhelmingly South Carolinians, but also with students from twenty-three other states, the District of Columbia, Hawaii, Puerto Rico, and several Latin American countries. About half of Clemson's 5,177 living graduates resided in South Carolina, but another 2,379 lived in

**This bronze sculpture, sculpted by T. J. Dixon and James Nelson in 1993, was commissioned by the Class of 1944 in memory of classmates who died and in honor of those who survived World War II. Located in front of Mell Hall, the sculpture's back-to-back figures depict a carefree college student and a combat-worn veteran. Clemson University Department of Creative Services.**

forty-four other states and the District of Columbia, while around twenty lived in other countries. In addition to the 5,177 graduates, approximately 23,000 students had matriculated through Clemson. Of all those, over 6,000 Clemson men—of whom 5,000 were officers—would serve in the armed forces. Some fought to hold the Philippines and were imprisoned by the Japanese. Some—including a Clemson man who received a Congressional Medal of Honor for extreme heroism—fought in other Pacific sites. Some were in China, while others landed in North Africa in Operation Torch, or in Sicily, or in the Normandy invasion in 1944. During that bloody world war, 385 Clemson men gave their lives. Shortly afterward, another Clemson trustee, serving as the principal United States delegate, helped create the United Nations.[57]

In the early postwar period, the Clemson Agricultural College continued to flourish. Having already granted a few master's degrees in vocational agriculture or industrial education, Clemson now added, despite some hesitancy, two new graduate degree programs: education and professional engineering. For the undergraduate level, it hired a professor of forestry and a professor of ceramic engineering to create new programs in their respective fields. By the first year after the war (1946–1947), with the arrival of veterans sent to college by the G. I. Bill, the enrollment rose to 3,550, 80% of whom were from South Carolina and the other 20% from twenty-four states and the District of Columbia, Puerto Rico, Cuba, and Costa Rico.[58]

The next two decades (1945–1965) were critical. Unlike most higher education institutions, Clemson remained an all-male, military college. The enrollment, artificially bolstered by the veterans, rose until 1949, after which it turned downward. The trend could not be changed by Clemson's new buildings and new dormitories. After a study conducted by the registrar, the trustees replaced the mandatory, four-year military regimen with R.O.T.C. and, a few months later, opened Clemson College to women. The highly regimented life of the Clemson man gave way through a series of careful decisions, not by courts or by legislature, but by the genius of Thomas Green Clemson's will.

All forces in South Carolina were not happy. A legislator introduced a bill to close women out of the all-male Citadel; the University of South Carolina, which had long admitted women and men; and Clemson. The bill would also require women to attend Winthrop College for the first two years, at which time they might transfer to Clemson or U.S.C. The Clemson student newspaper reminded its reading public that the more scientific nature of the Clemson education required a very different base level of mathematics and chemistry, accompanied by heavier doses of other science, grammar, communications, and literature than was usual. Therefore, the legislator's plan would condemn women who wished to study such fields as plant pathology or textile science to spend at least one and sometimes two extra years in college at a tremendous cost to their parents. The bill

**In January 1955, Clemson College's men welcomed women students to campus with a huge "WELCOME COEDS" sign on Bowman Field.
The *Anderson Independent-Mail*.**

did not make it out of committee. However, it would take the legislature over five years to allow Clemson to issue state-guaranteed secured bonds to build a women's dormitory. On the issue of women's enrollment, Clemson alumni were split. The Clemson faculty, although nervous, were in favor, and the students gleeful.[59]

A second challenge to state law, policy, and custom was the effort of African Americans to enroll in the three, all-white public colleges in South Carolina. The issue was playing out in world newspapers and in state and federal courts. Re-

**On January 28, 1963, Charleston-born Harvey Bernard Gantt became the first African American to be enrolled at Clemson College; he is shown speaking to a large crowd of national, state, local, and college reporters, photographers, and television cameramen. Clemson University Photographs, Special Collections, Clemson University Libraries.**

quired by state law and custom and perhaps by the wishes of some of Clemson's leadership, all legal avenues were explored until, as the governor stated to the legislature, "We have run out of courts." But Mr. Clemson's will did not mention any racial barriers. Against the background of riots, deaths, and destruction in other southern states and with the resolve of most Clemson students, faculty, staff, and alumni, the first African American quietly joined the student body.[60]

In the midst of these changes, Clemson granted its first Ph.D. degree and the first of its Bachelor and Master of Arts degrees and added a program in nursing to meet a growing regional need. Of course, this amount of change required a reorganization of the entire institution. A management consulting firm made a lengthy study and proposed a solution that grouped all the disparate parts of the institution into four major categories and counseled the president to give the category heads the authority to manage their own demesnes. It worked. Soon, with multiple types and levels of degrees, with agenda of research and service in all areas, and not without some misgivings, the Clemson Agricultural College of South Carolina was renamed Clemson University in 1964 by an act of the legislature, an opinion of the attorney general, a court ruling, and the signature of the governor.[61]

In March 1964, Governor Donald Russell signed the bill which changed the name of The Clemson Agricultural College of South Carolina to Clemson University. Standing left and right of the governor are Senator Edgar Brown, who sponsored the bill, and Clemson President R. C. Edwards. Clemson University Photographs, Special Collections, Clemson University Libraries.

Meanwhile, the United States had become deeply embroiled in the second Asian war since the end of World War II. In the earlier Korean War, seventeen Clemson men had been killed. Then came the Vietnam War which affected Clemson students, especially those whose less-than-stellar academic work increased the likelihood of their serving in the increasingly unpopular war. Campus after campus was struck first by protests and then by violence and burning. On the Clemson campus, there were orderly protests, but, other than occasional articles in the student newspaper and a few minor scuffles, the era passed fairly quietly for the students, even though a significant number of Clemson students and graduates either volunteered for or were drafted into the war. Of those, twenty-five Clemson men lost their lives.

Back on the Clemson campus, new buildings had sprung up all over the Fort Hill area. A crucial addition was the main library, built to be expanded internally. At the time it easily accommodated about 250,000 volumes and now is filled with 1.5 million. A sports and large concert facility, built to hold 10,000, became the site of graduations, commencements, and other events that required a large arena. While the undergraduate body increased to 8,797 students, the graduate program grew at an even greater rate, with the enrollment of 201 doctoral and 1,345 master's students. Part of what drew applicants was the University's 1,077 faculty members and its wide-ranging curricula: by 1979–1980 Clemson was offering 130 bachelor's degrees, sixteen master's degrees, and seventeen Ph.D. degrees, which attracted some 8,000 South Carolinians as well as students from forty-two other states, three American territories, and thirty-nine other countries.[62]

At that point in July of 1979, Clemson was obviously a mature teaching and public service land-grant university. Its major research was in various agricultural sciences. The next thirty years, however, reflect growing strengths in the students, the faculty and staff, and in every field of study. For instance, the size of the student body grew as Clemson pushed ahead with new curricula designed to stimulate and enrich the economy. At the undergraduate level, following the long pattern that can be traced back to 1897, the admissions rigor has gradually been increased.

The raised bar for admission has generated remarkable innovations. First, and most desirably, educators' focus has shifted more and more toward pre-college preparedness. To help mitigate the negative in-state effects, for instance, regular summer programming at Clemson was expanded quickly to include multiple courses designed to train high school students in critical and analytical approaches to learning and test-taking. For high school students who were advancing more rapidly than their peers, Clemson has long been offering more advanced summer courses than could be offered by public schools. A second effect is seen in the Clemson honors program. Founded in the early 1960s, the Calhoun Honors College has blossomed into a national leader. Moreover, Clemson University now offers permanent overseas study centers, as well as a wide range of semester-long and summer study programs in languages, business, art, architecture, interdisciplinary humanities, the sciences, history, music, and education.

All these special opportunities have had the effect of encouraging bright young people to stay in South Carolina for their education, while attracting excellent out-of-state students to Clemson. At the same time, the raised admissions standards, stronger pre-college preparation, and special opportunities have created a very promising effect: the actual percentage of individuals who have entered Clemson as freshmen and persisted to graduation has continued to rise from about 20% in 1896 to 34% in 1941 and to 78.3% in 2007.

Although in 2008 the applications to Clemson far exceed the number of students who can be accepted, the diversity of the student body has improved in significant ways. For example, the gender make-up of students is now almost balanced, while ethnic diversity has risen from 1.5% in 1979 to 9.8% in 2008. While the latter fails to achieve the University's goal, it is similar, unfortunately, to that of other institutions with similar course offerings.

Clemson University now offers a dazzling array of course work in 300 different subject fields within seventy-seven curricula, many with concentrations in a number of fields, majors, double majors, and minors. These combinations offer Clemson's undergraduate students some 274 curricular tracks and its graduate students thirty-eight doctoral and seventy-eight master's programs. To lead and sustain those fields and degree programs, Clemson University employs 1,596 faculty members who hold degrees from slightly over a thousand Ph.D.-granting universities. The faculty and programs are supported by a large, highly skilled, on- and off-campus staff. In addition, many of Clemson's 721 faculty emeriti regularly sit on graduate committees and juries and teach upon request.[63]

This brief review of Clemson University's history brings the reader back to the question which has driven every chapter of this biography: how can one best assess and summarize Thomas Green Clemson's life and legacy? The most obvious answer is statistical. From its first graduation in December 1896 through the May 2008 graduation, Clemson Agricultural College and Clemson University have awarded 137,959 degrees: 426 associate degrees in nursing; 105,241 undergraduate degrees; 28,814 master's degrees; 363 education specialist levels; and 3,115 doctoral degrees. Other crucial answers to this question can be discovered in Clemson's 17,585 current students and in the lives and careers of Clemson College and Clemson University's graduates who now live in all fifty states, all American districts and territories, and in ninety countries on all habitable continents. Equally important answers can be found in the remarkable expertise, achievements, and service of Clemson's administration, faculty, and staff, past and present.[64]

The combined answers would affirm the extraordinary ways in which Thomas Clemson's *high seminary of learning* continues to shape professional and personal lives. These lives, in turn, shape millions of lives in South Carolina, across the United States, and around the globe. Here is the living legacy of Thomas Green Clemson. He had a vision for this school—which he described as "the one great desire of my life"—and for what its graduates might contribute and achieve. His immovable vision was, to borrow from poet Robert Frost, "the gift outright."

### Notes

1.   Alester G. Holmes and George R. Sherrill, *Thomas Green Clemson: His Life and Work* (Richmond, VA: Garrett & Massie, 1937), 1–3; Ernest McPherson Lander Jr., *The Calhoun Family and Thomas Green Clemson: The Decline of a Southern Patriarchy* (Columbia, SC: University of South Carolina Press, 1983), 1–2.
2.   Alfred C. True, *History of Agricultural Education in the United States* (Washington, DC: U.S. Government Printing Office, 1929), 82.
3.   Ibid., 82–83.
4.   Ernest McPherson Lander Jr., "The Founder, Thomas Green Clemson, 1807–1888," in *Tradition: A History of the Presidency of Clemson University*, eds. Donald M. McKale and Jerome V. Reel Jr. (Macon, GA: Mercer University Press, 1998), 4; Holmes and Sherrill, *Thomas Green Clemson*, 4–11.
5.   Lefte Neal to Thomas Green Clemson, 17 July 1831, Clemson Papers, Special Collections, Clemson University Libraries, Clemson, SC (hereafter cited as SCCUL).
6.   Thomas G. Clemson, "Agricultural College in Maryland," *American Farmer* 12, no. 6 (1856): 161–163.
7.   Holmes and Sherrill, *Thomas Green Clemson*, 11–14; Lander, "The Founder, Thomas Green Clemson," in *Tradition*, 3–5.
8.   Holmes and Sherrill, *Thomas Green Clemson*, 14–16, 38; Lander, "The Founder, Thomas Green Clemson," in *Tradition*, 4–7.
9.   Holmes and Sherrill, *Thomas Green Clemson*, 16; Lander, *The Calhoun Family and Thomas Green Clemson*, 19; Nancy Ann Russell, "Legacy of a Southern Lady, Anna Calhoun Clemson, 1817–1875" (PhD diss., University of South Carolina, 2003), 28–29.
10.  Holmes and Sherrill, *Thomas Green Clemson*, 17–18, 92–93; Lander, "The Founder, Thomas Green Clemson," in *Tradition*, 6–7.
11.  Holmes and Sherrill, *Thomas Green Clemson*, 17.
12.  True, *History of Agricultural Education*, 2–6.
13.  Thomas G. Clemson, "Maryland Agricultural College," *American Farmer* 12, no. 3 (1856): 69.
14.  Lander, "The Founder, Thomas Green Clemson," in *Tradition*, 8–9; Holmes and Sherrill, *Thomas Green Clemson*, 88-91, 95.
15.  Lander, *The Calhoun Family and Thomas Green Clemson*, 179–182.
16.  Lander, "The Founder, Thomas Green Clemson," in *Tradition*, 9.
17.  True, *History of Agricultural Education*, 65–66.
18.  Thomas G. Clemson, "Maryland Agricultural College," *American Farmer* 12, no. 3 (1856): 69.

19. True, *History of Agricultural Education*, 65–66, 99.
20. Thomas G. Clemson, "The Necessity and Value of Scientific Instruction," *American Farmer* 14 (1859): 275, cited in Holmes and Sherrill, *Thomas Green Clemson*, 129–130.
21. True, *History of Agricultural Education*, 99–104.
22. Holmes and Sherrill, *Thomas Green Clemson*, 131–135.
23. Lander, "The Founder, Thomas Green Clemson," in *Tradition*, 11–12; Lander, *The Calhoun Family and Thomas Green Clemson*, 207; Holmes and Sherrill, *Thomas Green Clemson*, 21–26.
24. Lander, *The Calhoun Family and Thomas Green Clemson*, 220–222, 227.
25. Ibid., 228; Lander, "The Founder, Thomas Green Clemson," in *Tradition*, 13.
26. Lander, "The Founder, Thomas Green Clemson," in *Tradition*, 14.
27. Holmes and Sherrill, *Thomas Green Clemson*, 140.
28. Ibid., 145; Lander, "The Founder, Thomas Green Clemson," in *Tradition*, 14.
29. Holmes and Sherrill, *Thomas Green Clemson*, 145–146; Lander, "The Founder, Thomas Green Clemson," in *Tradition*, 14.
30. Thomas Green Clemson, "The Principles of Agriculture," in *The Land We Love*, vol. 11, 245, cited in Holmes and Sherrill, *Thomas Green Clemson*, 147–148.
31. Holmes and Sherrill, *Thomas Green Clemson*, 148; Lander, "The Founder, Thomas Green Clemson," in *Tradition*, 14. At several points in his life, James Edward Calhoun changed his surname to "Colhoun." To avoid confusion, we are using the James Edward Calhoun form throughout the biography.
32. Thomas Green Clemson to James Edward Calhoun (13 September 1870), quoted in Lander, "The Founder, Thomas Green Clemson," in *Tradition*, 14.
33. Holmes and Sherrill, *Thomas Green Clemson*, 150; Lander, *The Calhoun Family and Thomas Green Clemson*, 237; Lander, "The Founder, Thomas Green Clemson," in *Tradition*, 15.
34. Lander, *The Calhoun Family and Thomas Green Clemson*, 232–233, 239; Lander, "The Founder, Thomas Green Clemson," in *Tradition*, 15–16.
35. Will of Anna C. Clemson, in Julia W. Sublette, "The Letters of Anna Calhoun Clemson, 1833–1873" (PhD diss., Florida State University, 1993), 896; Ann Russell, "Anna Calhoun and the Origins of Clemson University," *The United Daughters of the Confederacy Magazine* (June 1990): 15; Lander, "The Founder, Thomas Green Clemson," in *Tradition*, 14–15; Holmes and Sherrill, *Thomas Green Clemson*, 32, 150, 173.
36. Holmes and Sherrill, *Thomas Green Clemson*, 150–153; Russell, "Anna Calhoun and the Origins of Clemson University," 15.
37. Lander, *The Calhoun Family and Thomas Green Clemson*, 241–242; Lander, "The Founder, Thomas Green Clemson," in *Tradition*, 15; Holmes and Sherrill, *Thomas Green Clemson*, 32, 152.
38. Thomas G. Clemson to Henry Gourdin (11 October 1875), quoted in Lander, *The Calhoun Family and Thomas Green Clemson*, 242.
39. Will of Anna C. Clemson, in Sublette, "The Letters of Anna Calhoun Clemson," 896; Lander, *The Calhoun Family and Thomas Green Clemson*, 245–252.
40. Thomas G. Clemson to W. W. Corcoran in Holmes and Sherrill, cited in *Thomas Green Clemson*, 152–154.
41. Holmes and Sherrill, *Thomas Green Clemson*, 154; R. W. Simpson to Thomas Green Clemson (11 January 1882) in Clemson Papers, SCCUL; Lander, *The Calhoun Family and Thomas Green Clemson*, 250–251.
42. Holmes and Sherrill, *Thomas Green Clemson*, 156–157; Lander, "The Founder, Thomas Green Clemson," in *Tradition*, 17.
43. Will of Thomas Green Clemson, quoted in Holmes and Sherrill, *Thomas Green Clemson*, 199; Holmes and Sherrill, *Thomas Green Clemson*, 157–159, 162; Lander, "The Founder, Thomas Green Clemson," in *Tradition*, 17–18; Lander, *The Calhoun Family and Thomas Green Clemson*, 259.
44. Ibid., 193.
45. Ibid., 194–195.
46. Ibid., 193–194.
47. Ibid., 195–196.

48. Holmes and Sherrill, *Thomas Green Clemson*, 162; Lander, "The Founder, Thomas Green Clemson," in *Tradition*, 18; Lander, *The Calhoun Family and Thomas Green Clemson*, 257.

49. Holmes and Sherrill, *Thomas Green Clemson*, 170–176, 179–188.

50. Holmes and Sherrill, *Thomas Green Clemson*, 187–189.

51. Robert S. Lambert, "The Builder of a College: Henry Aubrey Strode, 1890–1893," in *Tradition*, 24–25.

52. John L. Idol Jr., "The Controversial Humanities Professor: Edwin Boone Craighead, 1893–1897," in *Tradition*, 37–39.

53. *The Clemson Agricultural and Mechanical College of South Carolina: Annual Catalogue, 1897–1898* (Fort Hill: Clemson Agricultural College of South Carolina, 1898), 6–8.

54. *Catalog of the Clemson Agricultural College of South Carolina, 1910–1911* (Fort Hill: Clemson Agricultural College of South Carolina, 1911), 6–13, 160–162.

55. D. L. Folger, ed. *The Clemson Alumnus* (Fort Hill: Clemson Agricultural College of South Carolina, 1921), vol. 1, no. 2: 24–27; vol. 1, no. 3: 20–22; vol. 1, no. 4: 17–20; vol. 2, no. 1: 24–27; vol. 2, no. 2: 23–25; vol. 2, no. 3: 19–21. Also see *Clemson Agricultural College of South Carolina, 1922–1923*, 194–208, and *The Tiger*, 9 March 1921.

56. *The Clemson Agricultural College Record, 1940* (Fort Hill: Clemson Agricultural College of South Carolina, 1941); *Clemson Agricultural College Record, 1941–1942* (Fort Hill: Clemson Agricultural College of South Carolina, 1942), 7–32, 239–265.

57. James F. Byrnes, *All in One Lifetime* (New York: Harper, 1958). Although this autobiography mentions little about Clemson Agricultural College of South Carolina, it is an interesting personal account by an extraordinary man who made time for the College throughout his career.

58. *The Clemson Agricultural College Record, 1942–1945*, 9–20; *1945–1946*, 9–20, 175–176, 180–181, 199–200, 213, 225–226; *1946–1947*, 230–231, 287–288 (Fort Hill: Clemson Agricultural College of South Carolina, 1945, 1946, 1947).

59. Jerome V. Reel Jr., *Women and Clemson University: Excellence—Yesterday and Today*, Alma Bennett, ed. (Clemson, SC: Clemson University Digital Press, 2006). This study includes attention to the efforts of highly qualified women and women students to gain, respectively, faculty and staff positions and student leadership positions in this predominately male institution and student body.

60. Sterling Eisiminger, *Integration with Dignity: A Celebration of Harvey Gantt's Admission to Clemson* (Clemson, SC: Clemson University Digital Press, 2003). This is an important multifaceted exploration of the desegregation episode.

61. *Clemson College Record, 1960–1961* (Clemson: Clemson Agricultural College of South Carolina, 1961), 9–16, 17–34, 271–173, 308, 313.

62. *Clemson University Record, 1979–1980* (Clemson, SC: Clemson University, 1980), 4–11, 383–429, 488–497.

63. *Clemson University Undergraduate Announcements, 2007–2008* (Clemson, SC: Clemson University, 2008), 4–6, 220–243.

64. Clemson University Office of Institutional Research, *Factbook 2008* (www.clemson.edu/oir/factbook.htm).

# BIBLIOGRAPHY

## PRIMARY SOURCES

### *Manuscript Collections*

American Philosophical Society, Philadelphia, PA.
    Clemson Papers in Smith Family Papers.

Clemson University, Clemson, SC.
    Department of Creative Services.
    Fort Hill Collection.
    President's Office.

Clemson University, Special Collections, Clemson University Libraries, Clemson, SC.
    John C. Calhoun Papers.
    Thomas Green Clemson Papers.
    Alester G. Holmes Papers.
    James C. Littlejohn Papers.
    Walter M. Riggs Papers.
    Richard W. Simpson Papers.
    Mary Pasco Conrad Stevenson Papers.

Corcoran Gallery of Art, Washington, DC.
    Curator William MacLeod (1811–1892) Journals.

Historical Society of Pennsylvania, Philadelphia.
    Bausmann Collection.
    Elias Baker File.
    Elizabeth Clemson, "Autograph Album."
    Clementson Papers.

Library of Congress, Manuscript Division, Washington, DC.
    William W. Corcoran Papers.

Pennsylvania Archives, Philadelphia.
    Bureau of Land Records: *Index to Patents*, 1701–1715; 1715–1737; 1737–1743; 1743–1750; 1750–1753; 1753–1756; 1756–1762; 1762–1764; 1764–1767; 1767–1771; 1771–1774; 1774–1787. Microfilms, Vols. 1–7, also in Historical Society of Pennsylvania.
    Index of Wills and Administrative Records.
    Letters of Wills and Administration of Estates.

Philadelphia, City of: Record Office.
  Abstracts of Wills, 1682–1726, Philadelphia. MS. Microfilm.
  Index of Wills and Execution of Estates, Philadelphia. MS. Microfilm.

University of Maryland, Archives, College Park.
  Charles Benedict Calvert Papers.

University of South Carolina, The South Caroliniana Library, Columbia.
  John C. Calhoun Papers.

## Government Documents

### Kingdom of Belgium

Extrait du rapport décennal sur la situation administrative de la Belgique (1841–1850), Analyse du commerce belge. Antwerp, Belgium: Standaard Wetenschappelijke Uitgevri, n.d.

Ministry of Foreign Affairs, Archives, Brussels, Belgium. Dossier 10 377, personnel de la Légation US à Bruxelles: Correspondance politique entre la Légation belge à Washington et le Ministre des Affaires Etrangères 1841–1846, 1847–1850, 1851–1855.

Ministry of Foreign Affairs, Archives, Brussels, Belgium. Dossier 2062: Negociations commerciales—Traités de commerce Belgique/Etats-Unis—Négociations 1842 à 1852, Traité du 10 novembre 1845.

### State of South Carolina

*Constitution of the Commonwealth of South Carolina, Ratified April 16, 1868. Together with the Constitution of the United States of America.* Columbia, SC: Senate of South Carolina, 1883.

*Constitution of the State of South Carolina with the Ordinances Thereunto Appended, Adopted by the Constitutional Convention, Which Was Held at Charleston, and Adjourned on the 17th March 1868.* Charleston, SC: Denny and Perry, Book and Job Printers, 1868.

Floride Isabella Lee by her Next Friend, Gideon Lee, Complainant against Richard W. Simpson, Defendant in the Circuit Court of the U.S., for the Fourth Circuit District of South Carolina, 26 November 1888: Documents 1856–1894: MSS 256.

*Journal of the House of Representatives of the General Assembly of the State of South Carolina, Being the Regular Session Commencing November 17,*

*1888.* Columbia, SC: James H. Woodrow, State Printer, 1888. Includes order to print executor R. W. Simpson's communication of 4 December 1888, along with will of Thomas G. Clemson: 102.

Last Will and Testament of Anna Calhoun Clemson. Dated 29 September 1871. Recorded in Probate Court Records of Oconee County, Walhalla, SC. Will Book: 123–124.

Last Will and Testament of Thomas Green Clemson. Dated 6 November 1886. Codicil dated 26 March 1887. Recorded on 20 April 1888 in Probate Court Records of Oconee County, Walhalla, SC. Will Book: 234–244.

Lee v. Simpson, Circuit Court, District of South Carolina, in *Federal Register* 39: 235. 1889 U.S. App. LEXIS 2278.

**United States of America**

Clemson, Thomas Green. *Report of the Commissioner of Patents for the Year 1860.* Washington, DC: Government Printing Office, 1861.

"Commerce of the United States with European Countries, 1790–1896." In *Summary of Finance and Commerce.* Washington, DC: Government Printing Office, 1896.

Dispatches from the United States Ministers to Belgium, 1832–1906. MSS in National Archives, Washington, DC, Microfilm roll 4, vol. 3: 17 October 1844–8 January 1851.

Pardon of Thomas G. Clemson, 18 May 1866 [signed by President Andrew Johnson]. In Richard W. Simpson Papers, Special Collections, Clemson University Libraries, Clemson, SC: oversize folder 2, MSS 96.

Parole of Thomas G. Clemson, 9 June 1865 [several signatures]. In Thomas Green Clemson Papers, Special Collections, Clemson University Libraries, Clemson, SC: box 5, folder 2, MSS 2.

U.S. Census Bureau (www.census.gov/population).

U.S. Department of Health and Human Services. National Institutes of Health. *Depression: Effective Treatments Are Available.* NIH Publication No. 96–3590. Rockville, MD: National Institutes of Health, 1996.

## Printed Primary Sources

Boyd, George. *A Discourse delivered March 4, 1838, in the Church of the Ascension…on the occasion of the death of Mrs. Margaretta Jacobs Clemson.* Philadelphia: William Stavely, 1838.

*Catalogue of the Fourth Annual Exhibition of the Washington Art Association. 1860.* Washington, DC: Henry Polkinhorn, Printer, 1860.

Chadwick, Henry. "Old Uncle Ned." *Black Quadrille.* New York: Paul K. Weizel, 1854.

Clemson, Thomas G. "Agricultural College in Maryland." *American Farmer* 12, no. 6 (1856): 161–163.

———. "Analysis and Observations on Diverse Mineral Substances." *Journal of Franklin Institute* 13 (1834): 78–79. Originally presented as a paper to the Geological Society of Pennsylvania.

———. "Analysis of American Spathic Iron and Bronzite." *American Journal of Science and Arts* [aka *Silliman's Journal*; since 1880, entitled *American Journal of Science*] 24 (July 1833): 170–171.

———. "Analysis of Some of the Coal from the Richmond Mines." *Transactions of the Geological Society of Pennsylvania* 1 (1835): 295–297.

———. "Analysis of the Copper Ore of Hunterdon County, New Jersey." *Transactions of the Geological Society of Pennsylvania* 1 (1835): 167.

———. "Analysis of the Minerals Accompanying Mr. E. Miller's Donation." *Transactions of the Geological Society of Pennsylvania* 1 (1835): 271–274.

———. "Analysis of Two Varieties of Hydraulic Limestone from Virginia." *Journal of the Franklin Institute* 13 (1834): 80. Originally presented as a paper to the Geological Society of Pennsylvania.

———. "Assay and Analysis of an Iron Ore (fer titanne), from the Environs of Baltimore, (land of Mr. Patterson), received through Mr. Warden." *American Journal of Science and Arts* [aka *Silliman's Journal*; since 1880, entitled *American Journal of Science*] 17 (January 1830): 42–43. Reprinted in *Journal für Chemie und Physik* 64 (1832).

———. "Assay of an Iron Ore from Franklin County, New York." *Journal of the Franklin Institute* 13 (1834): 79–80.

———. "Description et analyse de la Seybertite, nouvelle espèce minérale." *Annal. des Mines* 2 (1832).

———. "Examination and Analysis of Several Coals and Iron Ores Accompanying Mr. R. C. Taylor's Account of the Coal-field of Blossburg." *Transactions of the Geological Society of Pennsylvania* 1 (1835): 220–223.

———. "Gold and the Gold Region," *The Orion* 4, no. 2 (April 1844): 57–66.

———. "The Hartz—Its Physical Geography, State of Industry, Etc.," *American Journal of Science and Arts* [aka *Silliman's Journal*; since 1880, entitled *American Journal of Science*] 19 (January 1831): 105–130. Reprinted in *Journal für Chemie und Physik* 64 (1834): 63–65.

———. "The Importance and Advantage of a Scientific Institution for the Advancement of Agriculture." (Letter to J.T. Earl, Esq., President of Maryland State Agricultural Society, 4 October 1856), *American Farmer* 12, no. 6 (1856–57): 161.

———. "Infusorial Organisms." *American Farmer* 13 (1858): 5.

———. "The Marl Formations: Their Composition and Value." *American Farmer* 13 (1858): 5.

———. "Maryland Agricultural College." *American Farmer* 12, no. 3 (1856): 69.

———. "Microscopic Organisms, Etc." *American Farmer* 12 (1857): 114.

———. "The Necessity and Value of Scientific Instruction." *American Farmer* 14 (1859): 275–277.

———. "Notice of a Geological Examination of the Country Between Fredericksburg and Winchester, in Virginia, Including the Gold Region." *Transactions of the Geological Society of Pennsylvania* 1 (1835): 298–313.

———. "Notice of Native Iron from Pen Yan, Yates County, New York." *Transactions of the Geological Society of Pennsylvania* 1 (1835): 358–359.

———. "Notice of Piperin." *American Journal of Science and Arts* [aka *Silliman's Journal*; since 1880, entitled *American Journal of Science*] 17 (1830): 325–356.

———. "Notice of the Method of Manufacturing the Smoking Sulphuric Acid, as Practiced at Nordhausen, Braunlage, and Tanne in Germany." *American*

*Journal of Science and Arts* [aka *Silliman's Journal*; since 1880, entitled *American Journal of Science*] 20 (1831): 347–350.

———. *Observations of the La Motte mines and domain in the State of Missouri,* (Washington, DC: Blair and Rives, 1839), 1–16.

———. "Sources of Ammonia." *American Farmer* 11 (1856): 339.

———. "Thomas Green Clemson letter to Jacob Green, 18 September 1828." *Journal of the Franklin Institute* 8 (1829): 356.

Clemson, T. G., and R. C. Taylor. "Notice of a Vein of Bituminous Coal, Recently Explored in the Vicinity of Havana, in the Island of Cuba" (1836). *American Philosophical Society Transactions* 10 (1839): 191–196. Prev. pub. in *Philadelphia Magazine* (1837): 161–167.

Colhoun, Martha (attr.). *Keowee Waltzes.* Charleston, SC: George Oates, 1847.

*Constitution of the Philadelphia Society for the Establishment and Support of Charity Schools: Incorporated the eighth day of September, 1810.* Philadelphia: privately published, 1840.

Dodworth, [Allen]. "Old Uncle Ned." *Dodworth's Dark Sett Quadrilles.* New York: William Hall and Son, and Philadelphia: E. L. Walker, 1850.

Dressler, William, arr., *Comin' Thro' the Rye: Scotch Ballad, as sung by Madlle. Jenny Lind.* New York: William Hall and Son, 1851.

*Ethiopian Melodies No. 5: Jim along Josey, Old Rosin the bow, The Log Hut, Arranged for the Piano Forte.* Baltimore: F. D. Benteen, and New Orleans: W. T. Mayo, 1852.

Farish, Hunter Dickinson, ed. *Journal and Letters of Philip Vickers Fithian, 1773–1774: A Plantation Tutor of the Old Dominion.* Williamsburg, VA: Colonial Williamsburg, 1943.

Featherstonhaugh, George W. *A Canoe Voyage up the Minnay Sotor: with an Account of the Lead and Copper Deposits in Wisconsin; of the Gold Region in the Cherokee Country; and Sketches of Popular Manners.* Vol. 2. St. Paul, MN: Minnesota Historical Society, 1970. First published 1847 by Richard Bentley of London, England.

Foster, Stephen C. *Old Uncle Ned: An Ethiopian Melody, Arranged with Symphonies and Accompaniments for the Voice and Piano.* Arr. R. O. Wilson. Baltimore: F. D. Benteen; New Orleans: W. T. Mayo, 1848.

Hewitt, John Hill. *All Quiet Along the Potomac Tonight.* Lyrics by Ethel Lynn Beers. Baltimore, MD: Miller & Beacham, 1863.

Holman, Harriet R., ed. *The Verse of Floride Clemson.* Columbia: University of South Carolina Press, 1965.

Jameson, J. Franklin, ed. *Correspondence of John C. Calhoun.* Fourth Annual Report for 1899 of the Historical Manuscripts Commission of the American Historical Association, Washington, DC: Government Printing Office, 1900.

Lady of South Carolina. *Jasper Guards' March, composed and dedicated to the Officers & Members of the Jasper Guards of Charleston, S.C.* Charleston, SC: George Oates, 1848.

———. *The Volunteer March, composed & respectfully dedicated to the Palmetto Regiment.* New York: Firth Hall and Pond, 1847.

Lancaster County: *Deeds of Lancaster Cty. 1797–1800.* Lancaster, PA: Record Office, 1987.

Lander, Ernest M. Jr., and Charles M. McGee Jr., eds. *A Rebel Came Home: The Diary and Letters of Floride Clemson 1863–1866.* Columbia: University of South Carolina Press, 1961.

Martin, Jacob, and Gilbert Cope. *Abstract of Wills of Chester County, Pennsylvania.* Philadelphia: Genealogical Society of Pennsylvania, 1999.

McGee, Charles M. Jr., and Ernest M. Lander Jr., eds. *A Rebel Came Home: The Diary and Letters of Floride Clemson 1863–1866.* Revised Edition. Columbia: University of South Carolina Press, 1989.

Oliver, Robert T., ed. *A Faithful Heart: The Journals of Emmala Reed, 1865 and 1866.* Columbia, SC: University of South Carolina Press, 2004.

Parrága, Manuel M. *Barhamville, Valse Brillante pour le Piano.* New York: William Hall & Son, 1854.

*Register of Deaths: Cemetery Returns.* Philadelphia: Historical Society of Pennsylvania, 1922.

Reingold, Nathan, ed. *The Papers of Joseph Henry.* Vols. 1 and 2. Washington, DC: Smithsonian Institution Press, 1972, 1975.

Rogers, Emma, ed. *Life and Letters of William Barton Rogers.* Vol. 1. New York: Houghton, Mifflin and Company, 1896.

Stevenson, Mary Pasco Conrad, ed. *The Diary of Clarissa Adger Bowen, Ashtabula Plantation, 1865, with Excerpts from Other Family Diaries and Comments by Her Granddaughter, Clarissa Walton Taylor, and Many Other Accounts of The Pendleton Clemson Area, South Carolina, 1776–1889.* Pendleton, SC: Research and Publication Committee Foundation for Historic Restoration in Pendleton Area, 1973.

Vedder, Edwin H., comp. *Records of St. Paul's Episcopal Church of Pendleton, South Carolina.* Greenville, SC: A Press, 1982.

Wilson, Clyde N., ed. *The Papers of John C. Calhoun.* Vols. 14–15. Columbia: University of South Carolina Press for the South Carolina Department of Archives and History and the South Caroliniana Society, 1981, 1983.

————. *The Papers of John C. Calhoun,* Vols. 16–21. Columbia: University of South Carolina Press, 1984–1993.

Wilson, Clyde N., and Shirley Bright Cox, eds. *The Papers of John C. Calhoun.* Vol. 24. Columbia: University of South Carolina Press, 1998.

### Newspapers

*Anderson Independent-Mail,* Anderson, SC.
*Arc American Republican,* West Chester, PA.
*Greenville News,* Greenville, SC.
*The Pendleton Messenger,* Pendleton, SC.
*National Intelligencer,* Washington, DC.
*News and Courier,* Charleston, SC.
*News and Herald,* Winnsboro, SC.
*The State,* Columbia, SC.
*The Tiger,* Clemson University, Clemson, SC.
*Washington Post,* Washington, DC.

# Secondary Sources

### Books and Articles (including reference books)

Agricola, Georgius. *De Re Metallica,* Trans. from 1st Latin ed. of 1556 by H. B. Hoover and L. H. Hoover, 1912. Reprint, New York: Dover, 1950.

"All is Quiet Along the Potomac Tonight." *Wikipedia, The Free Encyclopedia.* http://en.wikipedia.org/wiki/All_Quiet_Along_the_Potomac_Tonight.

American Psychiatric Association. *Diagnostic and Statistical Manual of Mental Disorders*, 4th ed. Washington, DC: American Psychiatric Association, 2000.

Appleby, Arnold P., comp. "Milestones in the Legislative History of U.S. Land-Grant Universities." http://cropandsoil.oregonstate.edu/.../details/applebyarnold/...Milestones%20in%20the%20History).

Arnebeck, Bob. "Insecurity and Grandeur: 1841 to 1861." In *The Seat of Empire. A History of Washington, D.C., 1790–1861.* http://geocitiescom/bobarnebeck/finalfour.htm.

*Atlas of Fifteen Miles around Washington, including the County of Prince George, Maryland.* Philadelphia, PA: Hopkins, 1878.

*Atlas of Prince George's County, Maryland, 1861.* Adapted from Martenet's Map of Prince George's County, Bladensburg District 2. Baltimore, MD: Simon J. Martenet, 1861.

Bairoch, P. "Histoire économique et sociale du monde du XVIe siècle à nos jours." In *Victoires et déboires.* Vol. 2. Brussels, Belgium: Gallimard Folio histoire, 1997.

Bartlett, Irving H. *John C. Calhoun: A Biography.* New York: Norton, 1993.

Basyn, Th. "Karl Marx à Bruxelles (1845–1848)." *Revue Générale* (15 Nov. 1927).

———. L'Arrestation de Karl Marx à Bruxelles le 4 mars 1848." *Revue Générale* (September 1828).

*Belgium, a Historical View.* Brussels, Belgium: Belvue Museum, 2005.

Bell, Raymond M., Frank Baird, and Margaret Ward. *The Clemson Family of Pennsylvania.* Washington, PA: Washington and Jefferson College, 1971.

Biesboer, Pieter et al. *Pieter Claesz: Master of Haarlem Still Life.* Washington, DC: National Gallery of Art; Zwolle, Netherlands: Waanders Publishers, 2005.

Birdsall, Clair M. *The United States Branch Mint at Dahlonega, Georgia: Its History and Coinage.* Easley, SC: Southern Historical Press, 1984.

Boatright, Sherry L., *The John C. Calhoun Gold Mine: An Introductory Report on its Historical Significance.* Report to State of Georgia, Department of Natural Resources, Historic Preservation Section. Photocopy, dated 15 June 1974, in Clemson Papers, Clemson University Libraries, Special Collections, Clemson, SC.

Bockelman, Wayne L. "Local Politics in Lancaster County." *Pennsylvania Magazine of History and Biography* 97 (1973): 97.

Brackett, R. N. "Thomas Green Clemson, LL.D., the Chemist, Part I." *Journal of Chemical Education* 5, no. 4 (April 1928): 433–444.

———. "Thomas Green Clemson, LL.D., the Chemist, Part II." *Journal of Chemical Education* 5, no. 5 (May 1928): 576–585.

Brewster, Lawrence Fay. *Summer Migrations and Resorts of South Carolina Low-Country Planters.* Historical Papers of the Trinity College Historical Society XXVI. Durham, NC: Duke University Press, 1947.

Brigstocke, Hugh. "Poussin, Nicolas." *Grove Art Online*, Oxford University Press, 2006.

Brown, Jonathan. *Velasquez: Painter and Courtier.* New Haven, CT: Yale University Press, 1986.

Bryan, Wright. *Clemson: An Informal History of the University, 1889–1979.* Columbia, SC: R. L. Bryan Company, 1979.

Byrnes, James F. *All in One Lifetime.* New York: Harper, 1958.

Callcott, George H. *A History of the University of Maryland.* Baltimore: Maryland Historical Society, 1966.

———. *The University of Maryland at College Park, A History.* Baltimore: Noble House, 2005.

Campbell, John R. *Reclaiming a Lost Heritage: Land-Grant and Other Higher Education Initiatives for the Twenty-first Century.* Ames: Iowa State University Press, 1995.

Carmichael, Leonard. *Joseph Henry and His Smithsonian Institution.* New York: Newcomen Society in North America, 1956.

*Catalog of the Clemson Agricultural College of South Carolina: 1910–1911.* Fort Hill: Clemson Agricultural College of South Carolina, 1911.

Charlton, David, John Trevitt, and Guy Gosselin. "Paris." *Grove Music Online.* http://sys.lib.clemson.edu:2286/shared/views/article.html?section=music.40089#music.40089.

Chudacoff, Howard, and Judith Smith. *The Evolution of American Urban Society.* 6th ed. Upper Saddle River, NJ: Pearson Prentice Hall, 2005.

Cicero, Marcus Tullius. *De Officiis* I: XLIII, cited by Vaclav Smil, Preface to *Enriching the Earth: Fritz Haber, Carl Bosch, and the Transformation of World Food Production*, v.

*The Clemson Agricultural and Mechanical College of South Carolina: Annual Catalogue, 1897–1898*. Fort Hill, SC: Clemson Agricultural College of South Carolina, 1898.

*The Clemson Agricultural College Record*. Clemson, SC: Clemson Agricultural College of South Carolina, 1940, 1941–1942, 1942–1943, 1943–1944, 1944–1945, 1945–1946, 1946–1947.

Clemson, Charles. *Clemson Family Genealogical Data*. West Chester, PA: West Chester Historical Society, 1920.

*Clemson College Record: 1960–1961*. Clemson, SC: Clemson Agricultural College of South Carolina, 1961.

*Clemson's Answer to her Country's Call*. Fort Hill, SC: Clemson Agricultural College of South Carolina, 1917.

Clemson University Office of Institutional Research. *Factbook 2008*. www.clemson.edu/Oir/factsBook.htm.

*Clemson University Record: 1979–1980*. Clemson, SC: Clemson University, 1980.

*Clemson University Undergraduate Announcements, 2007–2008*. Clemson, SC: Clemson University, 2008.

Clinton, Catherine. *The Plantation Mistress: Woman's World in the Old South*. New York: Pantheon, 1982.

Cohen, Henry. *Business and Politics in America from the Age of Jackson to The Civil War: The Career Biography of W. W. Corcoran*. Westport, CT: Greenwood Publishing, 1971.

Coit, Margaret. *John C. Calhoun: An American Portrait*. 1950. Columbia: mn Press, 1989.

Conner-Greene, Patricia (Alumni Professor of Psychology, Clemson University), in discussion with Ann Ratliff Russell, 21 May 2003.

Cook, Harriet Hefner. *John C. Calhoun: The Man*. Columbia, SC: R. L. Bryan Company, 1965.

Coolsaet, R. *Histoire de la politique étrangère belge*. Brussels: Belgium: Vie ouvr-ière, 1988.

Cotte, Sabine. *Claude Lorrain*. New York: Barons, 1970.

Davis, Christina, ed. *The Riverdale Story: Mansion to Municipality*. Riverdale, MD: Town of Riverdale, 1996.

Davis, John, and James Maas, eds. *The Affective Disorders*. Washington, DC: American Psychiatric Press, 1983.

Denny, George D. Jr. *Proud Past, Promising Future: Cities and Towns in Prince George's County, Maryland*. Brentwood, MD: Dilden Company, n.d.

*Diagnostic and Statistical Manual of Mental Disorders*. Fourth Edition. Washington, DC: American Psychiatric Association, 2000.

Dickson, Frank A. *Journeys into the Past: The Anderson Region's Heritage*. N.p.: Frank A. Dickson, 1975.

"Digest of Court Opinions." *Clemson Agricultural College Bulletin* 21 (January 1925): 17–29.

Dodge, Grenville M., and William Arba Ellis. *History of Norwich University 1819–1911: Her History, Her Graduates, Her Roll of Honor*. 3 vols. Montpe-lier, VT: Capital City Press, 1911.

Doerflinger, Thomas M. *Merchants and Economic Development in Revolutionary Philadelphia*. Chapel Hill: University of North Carolina Press for the Insti-tute of Early American History and Culture, Williamsburg, VA, 1986.

Donnelly, John V. "Genesis: The Birth of the FDA in the Patent Office." http://leda.law.harvard.edu/leda/search/loc.php3?handle+HLS.Library.Leda/donnelly/v-genesis_birth_fda.4k.

Edgar, Walter. *South Carolina: A History*. Columbia: University of South Carolina Press, 1998.

———, ed. *The South Carolina Encyclopedia*. Columbia: University of South Carolina Press, 2006.

Eisiminger, Sterling. *Integration with Dignity: A Celebration of Harvey Gantt's Ad-mission to Clemson*. Clemson, SC: Clemson University Digital Press, 2003.

Ellers, Joseph C. *Getting to Know Clemson University Is Quite an Education*. Co-lumbia, SC: R. L. Bryan Company, 1987.

Elliott, Clark A. *Biographical Dictionary of American Science: The Seventeenth Through the Nineteenth Centuries*. Westport, CT: Greenwood Press, 1979.

Federal Writers' Program, Work Projects Administration. *South Carolina: A Guide to the Palmetto State*. New York: Oxford University Press, 1941.

Federal Writers' Project, Work Projects Administration. *Thomas Green Clemson, Farsighted Farmer: An Adopted South Carolinian Who Served the Palmetto State*. Columbia, SC: State Department of Education, n.d. [ca. 1935–1937].

Ferleger, Lou, ed. *Agriculture and National Development: Views on the Nineteenth Century*. Ames: Iowa State University, 1990.

Finkleman, Paul. *Defending Slavery: Proslavery Thought in the Old South: A History with Documents*. New York: Bedford/St Martin's Press, 2003.

Folger, D. L., ed. *The Clemson Alumnus*. Fort Hill: Clemson Agricultural College of South Carolina, 1921.

Foner, Eric. *Reconstruction: America's Unfinished Revolution 1863–1877*. New York: Harper and Row, 1988.

"Francken; Frans Francken II." *Grove Art Online*, Oxford University Press, 2006.

Franklin, John Hope, and Alfred Moss. *From Slavery to Freedom: A History of African Americans*. New York: McGraw-Hill, 1994.

Furer, Howard B. *Washington: A Chronological and Documentary History*. Dobbs Ferry, NY: Oceana Publications, 1975.

Gates, Paul W. *The Farmer's Age: Agriculture, 1815–1860*. New York: Holt, Rinehart and Winston, 1960.

Gerstner, Patsy. *Henry Darwin Rogers, 1808–1866, American Geologist*. Tuscaloosa: University of Alabama Press, 1994.

Gillispie, Charles Coulston, et alia, eds. *Dictionary of Scientific Biography*, 16 vols. New York: Charles Scribner's and Sons, 1970–1980.

Goodloe, Daniel R. *Inquiry into the Causes Which Have Retarded the Accumulation of Wealth and Increase of Population in the Southern States: in Which the Question of Slavery is Considered in a Politico-Economical Point of View*. Washington, DC: W. Blanchard, 1846. http://docsouth.unc.edu/nc/goodloe/menu.html.

Gray, Lewis Cecil. *History of Agriculture in the Southern United States to 1860*. Vol. 2. Gloucester, MA: Peter Smith, 1958.

"Greuze, Jean-Baptiste." *Grove Art Online*, Oxford University Press, 2006.

Gubin, E. "La crise linière à domicile dans les Flandres, 1840–1850." In *Revue belge d'histoire contemporaine*. XIV: 3–4 (1983): 369–402.

Gudger, William D. "Charleston." *The New Grove Dictionary of Opera*. http://sys.lib. clemson.edu:2286/shared/views/article.html?section=opera.900945#opera. 900945.

Haberland, Irene. "Seghers, Daniel." *Grove Art Online*, Oxford University Press, 2006.

Haden, Bob (Director of the Haden Institute in Charlotte, N.C., Episcopal priest, and diplomate of the American Psychotherapy Association), 2007 Analysis, requested by Ann Ratliff Russell, of "Anna C. Clemson's Vision of Her Father, John C. Calhoun, Ten Years After His Death."

Hamm, Charles. *Music in the New World*. New York, New York: Norton, 1983.

Hazard, Willis P. *A Continuation of "Watson's Annals."* Philadelphia: privately published, 1830.

Heartny, Eleanor. *A Capital Collection: Masterworks from the Corcoran Gallery of Art*. Washington, DC: Corcoran Gallery of Art; London: Third Millennium Publishing, 2002.

"Heem, de: (1) Jan Davidsz. De Heem." *Grove Art Online,* Oxford University Press, 2006.

"Hewitt, John Hill." *Wikipedia, The Free Encyclopedia*, http://en.wikipedia.org/ Wiki/John_Hill_Hewitt.

Hindman, John Joseph, and Douglas Ashley. "Charleston." *Grove Music Online*. http://sys.lib.clemson.edu:2286/shared/views/article.html?section=music.05 462#music.05462.

Hines, Darlene Clark, et al. *African American Odyssey*. Upper Saddle River, NJ: Pearson Prentice Hall, 2006.

Hiott, Susan Giaimo. "Thomas Green Clemson, IV." In *The South Carolina Encyclopedia*, edited by Walter Edgar. Columbia, SC: University of South Carolina Press, 2006, 188–189.

Hiott, William D. *African-Americans at Fort Hill*. Pamphlet. Clemson, SC: Clemson University Publications and Graphics, 1991.

————. *Calhoun, Fort Hill and States' Rights: The Political Career of John Caldwell Calhoun*. Pamphlet. Clemson, SC: Clemson University Publications and Graphics, 1993.

————. *Five Generations of Calhoun and Clemson Women: Their Legacy to Fort Hill*. Pamphlet. Clemson, SC: Clemson University Publications and Graphics, 1992.

————. "Fort Hill." In *The South Carolina Encyclopedia*, edited by Walter Edgar, Columbia, SC: University of South Carolina Press, 2006, 334.

————. *Fort Hill: Home of John C. Calhoun and Thomas G. Clemson*. Historic American Buildings Survey (HABS), Report no. SC-344, United States Park Service, Department of the Interior, 1997.

————. "Fort Hill Plantation at Clemson University." *Sandlapper Magazine* (Autumn 2004): 72–73.

Hiott, William D., Robert W. Bainbridge, and Monique Swinger Mattison. "Physical History of the Clemson Campus." In *Campus Preservation and Clemson Historic Resources Seminar Proceedings*. Clemson, SC: Clemson University College of Architecture, Arts and Humanities, Department of Planning and Landscape Architecture, 1995.

Holmes, Alester G., and George R. Sherrill. *Thomas Green Clemson: His Life and Work*. Richmond, VA: Garrett and Massie, 1937.

Howe, Elias. *Complete Ball-Room Hand Book*. Boston, MA: Oliver Ditson, 1858.

"Hunter, Robert Mercer Taliaferro." *Biographical Directory of the United States Congress Online*. http://bioguide.congress.gov/biosearch.asp.

Hutchkin, S. F. *Memoir of the Rev. John Baker, D.D.* Philadelphia: George W. Jacobs, 1896.

Ingersoll, Ernest. "The Calhoun Summer Home." *Scribner's Monthly* (Century) 21 (1881): 893–895.

Jack, Belinda. *Beatrice's Spell: The Enduring Legend of Beatrice Cenci*. New York: Other Press, 2005.

Jackson, Luther P. "The Educational Efforts of the Freedmen's Bureau and Freedmen's Aid Societies in South Carolina." *Journal of Negro History*. Vol. 8, no. 1 (January 1923): 14.

Jacquemijns, G. *Histoire de la crise économique des Flandres, 1845–1850*. Brussels, Belgium: Maurice Lamertin, 1928.

Jaffe, Bernard, *Men of Science in America,* revised ed., New York: Simon and Schuster, 1958.

———. *Crucibles: The Story of Chemistry*, 4th ed., revised. New York: Dover Publications, 1976.

Jamison, Kay Redfield. *Touched with Fire: Manic-Depressive Illness and the Artistic Temperament*. New York: Simon and Schuster, 1993.

Johnson, Curtiss S. *Politics and a Belly-full: The Journalistic Career of William Cullen Bryant, Civil War Editor of the* New York Evening Post. New York: Vantage Press, 1962.

Johnson, Walter. *Soul to Soul: Life Inside the Antebellum Slave Market*. Cambridge, MA: Harvard University Press, 2001.

Jones, Lewis P. "History of Public Education in South Carolina," In *Public Education in South Carolina: Historical, Political, and Legal Perspectives*. Ed. Thomas McDaniel. Spartanburg, SC: Converse College, 1984.

Klosky, Beth Ann. *The Pendleton Legacy*. Columbia, SC: Sandlapper Press, 1971.

Lamb, Andrew, and Helen Thomas. "Dance." *Grove Music Online*. http://sys.lib.clemson.edu:2286/shared/views/article.html?section=music.45795#music.45795.

Lander, Ernest McPherson Jr., *The Calhoun Family and Thomas Green Clemson: The Decline of a Southern Patriarchy*. Columbia: University of South Carolina Press, 1983.

———. "The Founder, Thomas Green Clemson, 1807–1888." In *Tradition: A History of the Presidency of Clemson University*. 2nd ed. Eds. Donald M. McKale and Jerome V. Reel. Macon, GA: Mercer University Press, 1998.

———. *The Life And Times Of Ella Lorton, A Pendleton SC Confederate*. Clemson, SC: Clemson Printers, 1996.

Learned, Henry Barrett. *The President's Cabinet: Studies in the Origin, Formation and Structure of an American Institution*. New York: Burt Franklin, 1972. First published 1912 by Yale University Press.

Lewis, Robert S. *Elements of Mining*. New York: John Wiley and Sons, 1945.

Litwack, Leon. *North of Slavery: The Negro in the Free States 1790–1860*. 7th ed. Chicago, IL: University of Chicago Press, 1961.

Loos, Wiepke F. "Schendel, Petrus van." *Grove Art Online*, Oxford University Press, 2006.

Magi, William Francis, *A Source Book of Physics,* New York: McGraw-Hill, 1935.

Mathias, Deborah. *Tabernacle Church (Presbyterian and United Church of Christ), A History*. Philadelphia, PA: privately published, 1974.

Matthews, Glenna. *Just a Housewife: The Rise and Fall of Domesticity in America*. New York: Oxford University Press, 1987.

Maxwell, Carl. *The History and Genealogy of Frederick Baker, Jr., of 1775–1862, together with a brief history of his father, Frederick Baker, Sr., and his uncle, John Samuel Baker, Sr.* Farmville, VA: Farmville Herald, 1965.

Mazo, Earle. "Clemson Praised by Housekeeper." *Greenville News* (Greenville, SC), 1938.

———. "Former Fort Hill Housekeeper Cherished Relics Left Her by Thomas G. Clemson." *The Tiger* (Clemson University), 1938.

McDaniel, Thomas, ed. *Public Education in South Carolina: Historical, Political, and Legal Perspectives*. Spartanburg, SC: Converse College, 1984.

McKale, Donald M., and Jerome V. Reel, eds. *Tradition: A History of the Presidency of Clemson University*. 2nd ed. Macon, GA: Mercer University Press, 1998.

McPherson, James. *Ordeal By Fire: The Civil War and Reconstruction*. 2nd ed. New York: McGraw-Hill, 1992.

Megginson, William J. *African American Life in South Carolina's Upper Piedmont 1780–1900*. Columbia: University of South Carolina Press, 2006.

Merrill, George P. *The First One Hundred Years of American Geology*. New Haven, CT: Yale University Press, 1924.

Mish, F. C., ed. *Webster's Ninth New Collegiate Dictionary.* Springfield, MA: Merriam Webster, 1983.

Moore, Forrist Jewett. *A History of Chemistry.* 1918. 3rd ed., revised by William T. Hall. New York: McGraw-Hill, 1939.

Mortimer, Favell Lee. *Far Off, Part II: Africa and Asia Described, 1854, in The Clumsiest People in Europe; Or, Mrs. Mortimer's Bad-Tempered Guide to the Victorian World.* Edited by Todd Pruzan. New York: Bloomsbury, 2005.

Newmann, C. L., and J. C. Stribling, *Pendleton Farmers' Society* (Atlanta, GA: Foote & Dawes,1908).

Numbers, Ronald L., and Janet S. Numbers. "Science in the Old South: A Reappraisal." *Journal of Southern History* 48, no. 2 (May 1982):163–184. http://www.jstor.org/ view/00224642/di982364/98p11047/0.

Otto, John Solomon. *Southern Agriculture during the Civil War Era, 1860–1880.* Westport, CT: Greenwood Press, 1994.

Parker, Franklin. "Goerge Peabody, 1795–1869: His Influence on Educational Philanthropy." *Peabody Journal of Education* 49, no. 2 (January 1972): 139.

Parsons, William Barclay*, Engineers and Engineering in the Renaissance.* Baltimore, MD: Williams and Wilkins, 1939.

Pike, James Shepherd. *The Prostrate State: South Carolina under Negro Government.* New York: n.p., 1874.

Pirenne, H. "De la revolution de 1830 à la guerre de 1914." In *Histoire de Belgique.* Vol. 12. Brussels, Belgium: Lamertin, 1932.

Pitt, Charles. "Brussels." *The New Grove Dictionary of Opera.* http://sys.clemson.edu:2286/shared/views/article.html?section=opera.900679#opera.900679.

———. "Paris." *The New Grove Dictionary of Opera.* http://sys.lib.clemson.edu:2286/shared/views/article.html?section=opera.005519#opera.005519.

Poole, Robert F. *Thomas G. Clemson (1807–1888): His Influence in Developing Land-Grant Colleges.* New York: Newcomen Society in North America, 1957.

Preston, Katherin K. "Washington, D.C." *Grove Music Online.* http://sys.lib.clemson.edu:2286/shared/views/article.html?section=music.29935#music.29935.

*Prince George's County: Over 300 Years of History.* http://www.pghistory.org/PG/PG300.

Purrington, Robert D. *Physics in the Nineteenth Century.* New Brunswick, NJ: Rutgers University Press, 1997.

Rasmussen, Wayne David, ed. *Readings in the History of American Agriculture.* Urbana: University of Illinois Press, 1960.

Rasmussen, Wayne D., and Gladys L. Baker. *The Department of Agriculture.* New York: Praeger Publishers, 1972.

Reel, Jerome V. *Women and Clemson University: Excellence—Yesterday and Today.* Ed. Alma Bennett. Clemson, SC: Clemson University Digital Press, 2006.

Rembert, Sarah H. "Barhamville, A Columbia Antebellum Girls' School." *South Carolina History Illustrated* 1, no. 1 (February 1970): 44–48.

Reps, John W. *Washington on View: The Nation's Capital Since 1790.* Chapel Hill: University of North Carolina Press, 1991.

Roark, James L. *Masters Without Slaves: Southern Planters in the Civil War and Reconstruction.* New York: Norton, 1977.

Rooney, J. W. *Belgian Diplomatic and Consular Relations, 1830–1850: A Mid-Nineteenth-Century Study.* Louvain, Belgium: Universitè de Louvain, Recueil des travaux d'histoire et de philology, série 441, 1969.

———. *A Study in American Foreign Policy in Mid-Nineteenth Century: Belgian-American Diplomatic and Consular Relations, 1830–1850.* Louvain, Belgium: Universitè de Louvain, 1967.

Ross, Earle D. *Democracy's College: The Land-Grant Movement in the Formative Stage.* Ames: Iowa State College Press, 1942.

Rothenberg, Marc, ed. *The History of Science in the United States: An Encyclopedia.* New York: Garland, 2001.

*Rural Carolinian.* Charleston, SC: Walker, Evans, & Cogswell, 1870.

Russell, Ann. "Anna Calhoun Clemson and the Origins of Clemson University." *United Daughters of the Confederacy Magazine* (June 1990): 13–15.

———. "Her Father's Daughter, Anna Calhoun Clemson." *Carologue* (Autumn 1996): 14.

———. "'Holding Court' at a Yankee Prison: Anna Calhoun Clemson Behind Enemy Lines." *Carologue* (Spring 1990): 4.

———. *Legacy of a Southern Lady: Anna Calhoun Clemson, 1817–1875*. Clemson, SC: Clemson University Digital Press, 2007.

Schaffer, Alan. *Visions: Clemson's Yesteryears, 1880s–1960s*. Louisville, KY: Harmony House, 1989.

Simpson, Richard Wright. *History of Old Pendleton District, with a Genealogy of the Leading Families of the District*. Anderson, SC: Oulla Printing & Binding Company, 1913.

Sloan, Dave U. *Fogy Days, and How; or, The World has Changed*. Atlanta, GA: n.p., 1891.

Smil, Vaclav. *Enriching the Earth: Fritz Haber, Carl Bosch, and the Transformation of World Food Production*. Cambridge: MIT Press, 2001.

Smith, Edgar F. *Chemistry in America: Chapters From the History of the Science in the United States*. New York: D. Appleton, 1914.

Smith, John J. *Celebrated Trials of All Countries*. Philadelphia: Jesper Harding, 1846.

Soderlund, Jean. *Quakers and Slavery: A Divided Spirit*. Princeton, NJ: Princeton University Press, 1985.

Steed, James A. (associate archivist, Smithsonian Institution Archives), email communication with Chalmers M. Butler, 17 January 2007.

"Stuart, Julia Calvert, Cleydael's History: Calverts and Stiers." http://www.cleydael.org/Calverts.shtml.

Suetens, Max. *Histoire de la politique commercial de la Belgique depuis 1830 jusqu'à nos jours*. Brussels, Belgium: Editions de la Librairie encyclopédique, 1955.

*The Symbol and the Sword: Washington, D.C., 1860–1865*. Washington, DC: District of Columbia Civil War Centennial Commission, 1962.

Taylor, Alrutheus A. *The Negro in the Reconstruction of South Carolina*. New York: AMS Press, 1924.

Taylor, Rosser H. *Ante-Bellum South Carolina: A Social and Cultural History*. New York: Da Capo Press, 1970. First published 1942 by University of North Carolina Press.

Thompson, Henry T. *The Establishment of the Public School System of South Carolina*, Columbia, SC: R. L. Bryan Company, 1927.

Tindall, George. *South Carolina Negroes 1877–1900*. Baton Rouge: Louisiana State University Press, 1952.

Tolles, Frederick B. *Meeting House and Counting House: The Quaker Merchants of Colonial Philadelphia*. Chapel Hill: University of North Carolina Press for the Institute of Early American History and Culture (Williamsburg, VA), 1948.

"Town History, 1800–1899." http://ci.riverdale-park.md.us/History/Nineteenth.html.

True, Alfred Charles. *A History of Agricultural Education in the United States, 1785–1925*. U.S. Department of Agriculture Miscellaneous Publication, No. 36. Washington, DC: Government Printing Office, 1929.

———. *A History of Agricultural Experimentation and Research in the United States, 1607–1925*. U.S. Department of Agriculture Miscellaneous Publication, No. 251. Washington, DC: Government Printing Office, 1937.

"Veen, Otto van." *Grove Art Online*, Oxford University Press, 2006.

Vlieghe, Hans. "Schut, Cornelis, I." *Grove Art Online*, Oxford University Press 2006.

———. "Teniers: David Teniers II." *Grove Art Online*, Oxford University Press, 2006.

Von Meyer, Ernst. *A History of Chemistry*. Trans. from German. London: Macmillan, 1891.

Wangermée, Robert and Henri Vanhulst. "Brussels." *Grove Music Online.* http://sys.lib.clemson.edu:2286/shared/views/article.html?section=music.04203#music.04203.

Ward, William R., ed. *The American Bicentennial Songbook, Volume 1: 1770–1870s*. New York: Charles Hanson Music and Books, 1975.

Weigley, Russell R., Nicholas B. Wainwright, Edwin Wolf, Mary Maples Dunn, et al. *Philadelphia: A 300-Year History*. New York: Norton, 1982.

Wemhoff, Rich. ed. *Anxiety and Depression: The Best Resources to Help You Cope*. Seattle, WA: Resource Pathways, 1999.

Wick, Mildred Calhoun. *Living With Love*. Newport, DE: Serendipity Press, 1986.

Witte, E., E. Gubin, J. P. Nandrin, and G. Deneckere. *Nouvelle Histoire de Belgique*. Vol. 1: 1830–1905. Brussels, Belgium: Editions Complexes, 2005.

Woodson, Carter G. *The Negro in Our Times*. Washington, DC: Associated Publishers, 1922.

Yarnell, Susan L. *The Southern Appalachians: A History of the Landscape*. Report SRS-18. Asheville, NC: Southern Research Station (USDA), 1998.

Young, James Sterling. *The Washington Community, 1800–1828*. New York: Columbia University Press, 1966.

### *Theses and Dissertations*

Beacham, N. R. "Thomas Green Clemson, a Minor Diplomat of the Old South." MA thesis, Duke University, 1933.

Fravel, Philip M. "A History of Agricultural Education in South Carolina with an Emphasis on the Public School Program." PhD diss., Virginia Polytechnic Institute and State University, 2004. http://scholar.lib.vt.edu/theses/available/etd-04242004-202220/.

Laurent, P. H. "Conflict and Accommodation in Belgian-American Diplomatic and Commercial Relations, 1830–1846." PhD diss., Boston University, 1964.

Russell, Nancy Ann. "Legacy of a Southern Lady, Anna Calhoun Clemson, 1817–1875." PhD diss., University of South Carolina, 2003.

Sublette, Julia Wright. "The Letters of Anna Calhoun Clemson, 1833–1873." PhD diss., 2 vols. Florida State University, 1993.

# Notes on Contributors

## Abel A. Bartley

*Chapter 8: "Race, Reconstruction, and Post-bellum Education
in Thomas Green Clemson's Life and World"*

Abel Bartley is an associate professor of African American and urban history and the director of the Pan African Studies Program at Clemson University. He received his Ph.D. degree in African American and urban history from Florida State University. Before coming to Clemson, he spent ten years at the University of Akron where he directed their Pan African Studies Program and taught history. Bartley, who has published several articles on race, politics, and education, is the author of two books: *Keeping the Faith: Race, Politics, and Social Development in Jacksonville, Florida: 1940-1970* and *Akron's Black Heritage*.

## Alma Bennett *(Editor)*

*Introduction & Acknowledgments*

Alma Bennett, a professor of humanities and English, also directs the M.A. in English Program at Clemson University. She joined the Clemson faculty in 1991, after receiving her Ph.D. in humanities degree in literary and aesthetic studies from the University of Texas at Dallas. Her publications include two books on American novelist Mary Gordon and essays that range from interdisciplinary pedagogy to Dante and Cindy Sherman. A contributing poetry editor for *The South Carolina Review*, Bennett also edited Jerome V. Reel's *Women and Clemson University: Excellence—Yesterday and Today*.

## Chalmers M. Butler

*Chapter 6: "Thomas Green Clemson: Scientist and Engineer"*

Chalmers Butler received his B.S. and M.S. degrees from Clemson University and his Ph.D. degree from the University of Wisconsin, Madison, all in electrical engineering. He joined the Clemson University faculty in 1985 and is presently Alumni Distinguished Professor and the Warren H. Owen Professor of Electrical and Computer Engineering. His publications on applied electromagnetic theory include a hundred papers in refereed journals and seven chapters in monographs. He also has served as associate and guest editor of several journals and as chair of the U.S. National Committee for the International Union of Radio Science.

## James P. Cross

*Chapter 4 (co-author): "The European Years:
Thomas Green Clemson as Student, Activist, and Diplomat"*

James Cross is the vice provost of international affairs and a professor of political science at Clemson University. He earned his Ph.D. degree in political science (international relations) from the Graduate Institute for International Studies at the University of Geneva, Switzerland. He has over twenty-five years of experience in international diplomacy, negotiations, corporate relations, research, and education in both academic and applied settings.

### Deborah G. Dunning *(Managing Producer)*

Deborah Dunning is the manager of editorial services in Clemson University's Department of Creative Services. She holds a bachelor's degree in English from Clemson. She has written and edited University publications for more than 34 years, serving all departments across campus, and has coordinated publications support for Clemson milestones such as the Centennial Celebration in 1989 and the Bicentennial Celebration of Thomas Green Clemson's birth in 2007.

### Sabine Godts-Péters
*Chapter 4 (co-author): "The European Years: Thomas Green Clemson as Student, Activist, and Diplomat"*

Sabine Godts-Péters is a professor of economic history and the history of Europe at the ICHEC Business School in Brussels, Belgium. She received her B.A. degree in history from the Catholic University of Louvain in Belgium and her Ph.D. degree in history and civilization from the European University Institute of Florence in Italy. Her research areas include twentieth-century Belgian foreign policy and the history of European integration, and her publications focus on monetary integration after World War II.

### Alan Grubb
*Chapter 5: "The Washington Years"*

Alan Grubb is an associate professor of history at Clemson University. He received his Ph.D. in French history from Columbia University and is the author of *The Politics of Pessimism: Albert de Broglie and the Conservative Party in the Early Third French Republic* and several works in southern history. Grubb teaches courses in French history and food history.

### William David Hiott
*Chapter 9: "Thomas Green Clemson: Art Collector and Artist"*
*Chapter 11: "The Fort Hill Years"*

William Hiott, director of historic properties, curator of Fort Hill, and adjunct instructor of history, has served as the curator of Fort Hill for almost twenty years and has done extensive research on the Calhoun and Clemson families, including a comprehensive Historical Report on Fort Hill for the Historic American Buildings Survey (HABS) in 1997. Hiott received a master's degree in public history from the University of South Carolina. He has also done postgraduate study in parks, recreation and tourism management; higher education leadership; and public policy at Clemson University.

## Verna Gardner Howell
*Chapter 13 (co-author): "Passing in Review: Thomas Green Clemson's Life and Legacy"*

Verna Gardner Howell is an associate vice president for student affairs at Clemson University. She holds an M.Ed. degree in counselor education from Wake Forest University and a B.A. in English degree from Clemson University. Howell has been employed in Clemson's Division of Student Affairs since 1980. For sixteen years, she served as executive director of university housing; now she oversees several student affairs departments and helps plan and coordinate campus-wide student engagement and success initiatives.

## John W. Kelly
*Chapter 7: "The Scientist as Farmer"*

John Kelly has served as the vice president for public service and agriculture at Clemson University since 1996. As such, he directs the S.C. Experiment Station, the Clemson University Extension Service, the McIntire-Stennis Forestry Program, and the S.C. Botanical Garden. He is also the executive director of the Clemson University Restoration Institute. Kelly earned his B.S. degree in horticulture from Clemson University and his M.S. and Ph.D. degrees from Ohio State University.

## Andrew Levin
*Chapter 10: "Music in the Life and World of Thomas Green Clemson"*

Andrew Levin, an associate professor of music at Clemson University, conducts the Clemson University Symphony Orchestra and teaches a variety of music courses. He also is a violist, pianist, arranger, and composer. His compositions include works for orchestra, chamber groups, choir, the theatre, and traditional dance ensembles. He earned a double Master of Music degree in conducting and piano performance from Rice University and his Doctor of Arts degree in orchestral conducting from Ball State University.

## Jerome V. Reel
*Chapter 1: "The Family of Thomas Green Clemson"*
*Chapter 2: "The 1807-1838 Life and Education of Thomas Green Clemson"*
*Chapter 13 (co-author): "Passing in Review: Thomas Green Clemson's Life and Legacy"*
*Genealogies*

Jerome Reel, University historian and professor of history at Clemson University, was educated at Tulane University, the University of Southern Mississippi, and Emory University, from which he received his Ph.D. in British medieval history. He joined the Clemson faculty in 1963 and in 1979 became the dean of undergraduate studies. In 1992 he was named senior vice provost and in 2003 University historian. In addition to his recent *Women and Clemson University: Excellence—Yesterday and Today* book, Reel's publications and research emphases include fourteenth-century English parliamentary history, Arthurian legends, and the history of Clemson University.

### Ann Ratliff Russell
*Chapter 3: "Anna Maria Calhoun Clemson: 'a wife worthy of any man that ever lived'"*

Ann Russell received her Ph.D. in American history from the University of South Carolina in 2003. She taught modern western civilization at Clemson University from 1967 to 1971 and worked as a public information specialist at the University's historic houses, Fort Hill and Hanover, from 1984 to 1989. In addition to a number of articles, she is the author of *Legacy of a Southern Lady, Anna Calhoun Clemson, 1817-1875*, published by the Clemson University Digital Press in 2007.

### Clayton D. Steadman
*Chapter 12: "Clemson's Last Will and Testament"*

Clayton Steadman is Clemson University's general counsel and, in that role, coordinates all University legal matters. He earned his B.A. degree in history from Clemson University and his law degree from Emory University. He has practiced higher education law for over twenty years and previously served as vice president for legal affairs at the Medical College of Georgia.

### Allen P. Wood
*Foreword*

Trustee Emeritus Allen Wood, AIA, has served on the Clemson University Board of Trustees since 1988. He holds a B.S. degree in architecture from Clemson and has had extensive design experience in public school and higher education facilities. He retired as president emeritus and chair of the board of Wilkins Wood Mace and Associates Architects, the oldest continuously operating architectural firm in South Carolina.

# INDEX